THE GRACCHI

THE GRACCHI

DAVID STOCKTON

Fellow and Tutor of Brasenose College
Oxford

CLARENDON PRESS · OXFORD
1979

Oxford University Press, Walton Street, Oxford OX2 6DP

OXFORD LONDON GLASGOW
NEW YORK TORONTO MELBOURNE WELLINGTON
KUALA LUMPUR SINGAPORE JAKARTA HONG KONG TOKYO
DELHI BOMBAY CALCUTTA MADRAS KARACHI
NAIROBI DAR ES SALAAM CAPE TOWN

British Library Cataloguing in Publication Data

Stockton, David
   The Gracchi.
   1. Gracchus, Tiberius   2. Gracchus, Gaius
   3. Rome – Politics and government – 265–30 B.C.
   I. Title
   937'.05'0922   DG254.5   78-41143

   ISBN 0 19 872104 8
   ISBN 0 19 872105 6 Pbk

Set by Hope Services, Abingdon
Printed and bound in Great Britain by
Morrison & Gibb Ltd, London and Edinburgh

FOREWORD

For any reader who is not familiar, or not yet familiar, with the details of the Roman constitution in the second century B.C. a few guidelines are set out here.

The formal designation of the Roman state was 'The Senate and People of Rome': *Senatus Populusque Romanus*.

The Senate was the great council of state, *consilium rei publicae*, to which the 'magistrates' (as Rome termed her officers of state) turned for advice on any controversial matter. It was itself essentially composed of magistrates and former magistrates. Once a member of the Senate, a man remained a senator for the rest of his life, unless his name was struck off the senate-roll in consequence of conviction for a serious crime or gross delinquency in the conduct of his private life. Every five years it fell to the censors to 'adlect' sufficient new members to make good the vacancies which had arisen since the last revision of the roll. This they did by admitting to membership anyone who had held a junior magistracy but was not yet a senator, along with others who by one criterion or another were judged fitted and qualified for membership. Generally, a man would not become a senator until he was in his late twenties, at the earliest.

The two censors were always former consuls, and were elected by the Roman People every five years to hold office for eighteen months. Apart from revising the senate-roll, they conducted the quinquennial census of the population, assigned citizens to their tribes and centuries and census-classes, and were responsible for letting a wide range of state contracts for public works, leases of state lands and quarries and mines and so on, and the collection of moneys due to the state in taxes and customs-dues. The men who took these on were called 'publicans' (*publicani*); members of the Senate were themselves debarred from undertaking such contracts.

The chief officers of the Roman state were the consuls, two in number, elected annually to hold office for twelve months beginning on 1 January each year (until 153 B.C. their year of office had begun on 15 March). They were the presidents of the Senate, and they had the right to summon and preside over the centuriate and tribal assemblies of the Roman People at elections and for legislation. They enjoyed judicial powers, and in the last resort they were responsible for the maintenance of public order and security. They possessed *imperium*, the authority to exercise supreme military command and to enforce and execute the law. In the post-Sullan period it came to be normal for consuls to go out to govern a province only after the completion of at least the bulk of their year of office at Rome; but, in the time of the Gracchi, a consul would regularly leave to govern a province during most or all of his consular year. His command might be 'prorogued', that is extended, so that he could continue to govern his province or fight his war as a 'proconsul', *pro consule*. If both consuls should happen to be away at the same time, the urban praetor could act as *locum tenens*; but generally at least one of the two consuls would be assigned Italy as his 'province', so that he would remain in or near Rome all year. Provinces were allocated by the Senate, but the consuls drew lots to determine which of the two consular provinces each should have—although sometimes this was settled by mutual agreement or exchange between the two men themselves. In theory the Roman People had a superior power to assign such tasks, but it was very rarely used; although in the later Republic it came to be used more often, especially in conferring the so-called 'long-term commands' enjoyed by men like Pompey and Julius Caesar. A man generally held the consulship in his late thirties or early forties, though some came to the office older than that. At this period a second consulship was almost unheard of. The ex-consuls, *viri consulares* or 'consulars', constituted the most influential bloc of men within the Senate, and the consulship itself was the patent of 'nobility': any man who could count a consul among his direct male forebears was a *'nobilis'* (a syncopated form of *'notabilis'*).

The next senior magistracy was the praetorship, also tenable for one year beginning on 1 January. In the Gracchan period six praetors were elected every year: two, the *praetor urbanus* and the *praetor peregrinus*, were the chief officers of the civil law, and the other four were available as governors of provinces or for other tasks like the presidency of special courts or even special duties within Italy—it was the praetor Opimius who was charged with the suppression of the revolt of Fregellae in 124 B.C. The praetors also had *imperium*, like the consuls, but it was subordinate to that of the consuls in the rare event of any clash of authority or overlap of function. They also had the right to introduce legislation, but in practice they very rarely did so.

The junior magistracies, the aedileship and the quaestorship, lacked *imperium*. The aediles' chief tasks were to look after the streets and markets of Rome and its water-supply, to maintain public order in religious and cult matters, and to organize and supervise the public games and shows. Of the quaestors, two (the *quaestores aerarii*) had executive charge of the state treasury (the *aerarium Saturni*) and coinage, while the others acted as assistants to consuls or provincial governors and so on. All held office for one year, the quaestors from 5 December in each year.

The tribunes of the plebs, *tribuni plebis*, frequently referred to simply as 'tribunes', were ten in number, and held office for twelve months beginning on 10 December. They were elected by the Plebs and not by the People (the distinction will be explained in due course), and they had originally been summoned into existence to champion the rights and grievances and demands of the plebeians or 'commons' against a narrow and exclusive patrician ruling aristocracy. But, as time passed, the tribunate came to be assimilated to the regular magistracies, and indeed the tribunes had often been employed by the ruling nobility as their instruments. Only those of plebeian birth could hold the office—when in 58 B.C. Publius Clodius of the great patrician house of the Claudii Pulchri became a tribune, he had had first to go through the formality of being adopted into a plebeian family—but by the Gracchan period the ruling nobility had for more than two hundred years ceased to be exclusively patrician, and in fact the patricians were only a minority in what had by now become a mixed patricio-plebeian ruling class. To take just one example, Tiberius and Gaius Gracchus had a patrician mother and a plebeian father, and they belonged to the highest aristocracy of Rome, with three generations of consuls behind them in the direct male line.

Apart from their power to introduce legislation in the plebeian assemblies, the tribunes enjoyed a power of veto (*ius intercessionis*) over all legislative and most executive acts of state, and of rendering assistance or protection (*ius auxilii*) to individuals who were threatened by the executive action of a magistrate. This power of veto had often in the past been useful in checking the activity of independent-minded magistrates.

There were a number of minor magistracies which were held by young men below quaestorian rank, but they need not be enumerated here.

A Roman who aspired to a political career had first to serve a stipulated number of *stipendia*, years of service with the Roman army often (though not always) as an officer or staff-officer, or executing the duties of one of the minor magistracies. In effect, election to the quaestorship was the vital first step on the ladder of office, *cursus honorum*, which stretched upwards to consulship and censorship. The next steps were the tribunate and the aedileship—one or both or which might be omitted—and then praetorship and finally consulship. Competition stiffened as a man sought to climb higher: some ten to fifteen new senators were on average needed annually to maintain the total membership of the Senate at around its full complement of three hundred, but each year there were only six praetorships and two consulships to contend for, so that only something like one in three even of the praetors could hope to reach the consulship. Not surprisingly, then, while it was not too difficult for new blood to infuse into the lower reaches of the senatorial order, the highest offices of state, and especially consulship and censorship, were very much the preserve of a small circle of established noble families. 'New men' did from time to time reach the heights, but it was a very stiff climb even as a protégé of one of the great houses, and called for outstanding ability and determination. There was nothing especially surprising if a man whose father and grandfather had reached the praetorship should himself at last attain a consulship; the really remarkable 'new men' were those like Cato the Elder and Gaius Marius who achieved a consulship 'from scratch'.

The two principles of limitation of tenure and collegiality made it impossible for any politician to make tenure of a magistracy a lasting basis for power, and any magistrate who set himself against the will and wishes of the ruling class as a whole was giving many hostages to fortune. He did well to remember that the power and immunity which his office gave him would last for only twelve months, after which he would revert to private status.

Apart from the magistracies, the great priesthoods were of enormous prestige and influence. They were tenable for life, and were held by members of the political ruling class, and indeed were often virtually hereditary in certain families. The two greatest 'colleges' of priests were the *pontifices* and the *augures*, and the Chief Pontiff, *pontifex maximus*, was effectively the head of the state religion, in many respects intertwined with politics. Another very important non-magisterial position of great prestige and influence was that of *princeps senatus*, the man whose name stood at the head of the roll of the Senate; he was by custom the first to be invited to speak in any senatorial debate or discussion.

The citizenry of Rome were enrolled both in 'classes' and in 'tribes'. There were five classes, based on personal wealth, ranging from the first and wealthiest to the fifth and least wealthy; there was also a very numerous category of citizens who were *'infra classem'*, too poor to be registered in any of the five—these poorest citizens were also referred to as *'proletarii'* or *'capite censi'*. Naturally, the number of citizens in each class increased as the property qualification diminished. The tribes, on the other hand, had no property criterion of this nature, and were effectively electoral divisions of the citizen population, a man's tribe being determined by his domicile. There were thirty-five tribes in all, four 'urban' covering the city of Rome itself, and thirty one 'rural' tribes comprising the territory of the Roman state in Italy outside the city—the rural tribes were not necessarily single blocs of territory, and one tribe might be made up of a number of scattered areas.

The three chief assemblies of the Roman state were the centuriate assembly (*comitia centuriata*) and the tribal assemblies (*comitia tributa*) of the People and of the Plebs. The first was organized in 'centuries', so many centuries being allocated to each of the property classes. The centuries registered bloc votes, the vote of the majority in each century determining the vote of the century as a unit. The allocation was uneven, the higher classes having fewer members per century than the lower; indeed, the first class comprised seventy centuries, and the equestrian centuries—also the richest—numbered eighteen, while the overall total of all the centuries was one hundred and ninety three. Hence, the wealthier a citizen was, the weightier was his vote. But in the tribal assembly each 'tribesman's' vote was as good as his neighbour's. Inevitably, the 'out-of-town' tribes were represented at the meetings at Rome by fewer members than the urban tribes, since only the relatively well-to-do could afford the time and cost of travelling to the capital to cast a vote; hence quite large turnouts from the urban tribes could be outvoted by smaller numbers turning up to represent the generally more conservative country vote.

The centuriate assembly elected consuls, censors, and praetors. It was occasionally used for legislation, but not often. Legislation tended to be the province of the two tribal assemblies. These were as good as identical, the only difference being that the tribal assembly of the Plebs excluded patricians from membership; but by now the patricians were so very few in number that to all intents and purposes the two assemblies of People and Plebs were the same body, and the vital difference between them lay not in their composition but in their presiding officers: the consuls and praetors, senior magistrates elected by the property-biassed centuriate assembly, presided over the tribal assembly of the People, junior and relatively young tribunes over that of the Plebs. Strictly, the assemblies of the People alone could pass laws (*leges*), while what the Plebeian assembly (often called the *concilium plebis*) passed were 'plebiscites' (*plebiscita*). But ever since 287 B.C. a *plebiscitum* had had validity and force equal to a *lex*, and the distinction became blurred, so much so that even official state documents could refer to a *plebiscitum* as a *lex*.

Only a magistrate or a tribune could convene an assembly and put business before it; the members of the assembly could only vote 'yes' or 'no' to proposals put to them, and they enjoyed no right themselves to initiate or amend proposals. However, the actual legislative and electoral meetings of the assemblies were preceded by a number of less formal public meetings called *contiones* at which the merits and demerits of proposals or candidates could be aired by magistrates and also by any others who were invited to speak by the magistrate(s) who had convened the *contio*; such occasions could be very noisy and boisterous.

By the middle of the second century B.C. the physical extent of the Roman state had spread far beyond its original narrow confines to cover something approaching half the territory and population of Italy south of the valley of the Po, with the consequence that very large numbers of Rome's citizens were living at considerable distances from the capital, which still remained the venue for all elections and legislative assemblies. (The remainder of the peninsula consisted of communities of 'Latins' and 'Italian allies', whose position is examined in some detail in Chapter V of this book.) The financial resources and political self-consciousness of the citizen body as a whole varied very much. The terms '*equites*' and 'equestrian' are and were often employed to designate the richest stratum of citizens outside the members of the senatorial class; these terms also are examined fully in Chapter V.

By now pretty well all the Mediterranean and its immediate hinterland was subject to Roman control or influence. The areas under direct control, the *provinciae*, were governed by Roman consuls or praetors; but the shortness of a governor's tenure and the smallness of his staff, the considerable size of the provinces and the absence of any permanent equivalent of a 'colonial civil service', meant that a large measure of autonomy had to be devolved onto the constituent cities and peoples of the province, especially in the more advanced regions. Other areas constituted what were in effect 'protectorates', which on the whole danced to the tunes which Rome called.

Finally, it should be noted that the Roman courts, outside the realm of what we may crudely term private civil law, could be very 'political' in character, composition and operation, and were only too often concerned (to use the useful dichotomy employed by Professor Dworkin in his writings on modern jurisprudence) with questions or decisions of 'policy' rather than with those of 'principle'. But this is a theme which is developed further in this book in its own right.

ACKNOWLEDGEMENTS

The footnotes and the bibliography will reveal, albeit inadequately, how much the author of this book has stood on the shoulders of many scholars who have patiently teased out the detail of the Gracchan period and its background. There is, some might say, little to write about the Gracchi that is 'both new and true'. But I hope that this attempt to synthesize and set out within a single pair of covers a self-consistent and comprehensive account of 'the present state of play' will be found to be instructive and interesting and at least in some respects novel.

I have debts to pay, and I acknowledge them gladly. My old tutor, the late C.E. Stevens, first fired my interest in the subject with his ingenious and infectious enthusiasm: the authentic 'Stevens version' of the history of the late Roman Republic is the saddest loss among all the hoped-for but unwritten works of that remarkable man. I owe much to the lectures of A.N. Sherwin-White, although it is thirty years since I sat in the Hall of St. John's and there heard stated or suggested many ideas and interpretations which I have since seen published in the books and articles of others; he has also read my appendix on chronology, made helpful comments, and reassured me that my approach is sound. Others have been generous with advice and comment on particular points, or with loans of books and offprints, among them Peter Cuff, Martin Frederiksen, and Barry Nicholas; and for this book I can record thanks for helpful criticism from all three of my daughters, Sally, Deborah, and Candida—the youngest especially, since as herself an undergraduate reading Greats she knows what it is like to be 'at the receiving end'.

Above all others, however, Peter Brunt, Camden Professor of Ancient History and my colleague as a Fellow of Brasenose, has been a rich and never-failing source of assistance, sharp criticism, and encouragement; frequent conversations and his searching written comments on my first draft have done much to improve my thinking and my exposition. It is customary and proper to warn the reader that help thus generously given should not be taken to involve the helper in a share of the blame for any shortcomings which remain in the finished product.

Finally, I must record my warm thanks to Brasenose College and to the University of Oxford for granting me leave from my statutory duties, thereby enabling me to complete this book far more quickly than would otherwise have been possible.

David Stockton

Brasenose College, Oxford
May 1978

MAGISTRIS MEIS
DISCIPVLISQVE

CONTENTS

INTRODUCTION

The Nature of the Evidence

'There are in history no beginnings and no endings. History books begin and end, but the events they describe do not.' That may sound self-evidently, even tritely, obvious—although Collingwood had of course a subtler and deeper truth in his mind when he wrote those words. Yet, for all that related events certainly did both precede and follow the period during which Tiberius and Gaius Gracchus were politically active, those events are largely irrecoverable, and the history of the Gracchi is enisled in a sea of obscurity and doubt which laps against both its nearer and its further shore in time. The loss of Livy's continuous history for the years after 167, and the large absence of other material which could counterbalance that loss, make it impossible to try to interweave an account of the Gracchi with the events which came immediately before and afterwards in anything but broad outline. Thus, for example, we know neither the date nor the circumstances nor the nature of Gaius Laelius' reported move to introduce a land bill, nor how far—if at all—it shared any common ground with the *lex Sempronia agraria* which Tiberius Gracchus carried some years later; our information about judicial legislation and actual court-trials during the forty or so years which followed Gaius Gracchus' death in 121 is so thin and unreliable that it has always left wide room for scholarly debate about the nature and scope of Gaius' own changes and advances in this field; indeed, even the events of the nine years which separated the death of the elder brother from the first tribunate of the younger have been sadly stricken by the same wasting disease.

It was not always so. Livy needed six books (LII-LVII) to cover the history of the years 145-134, three (LVIII-LX) that of 133-123, and nine (LXI-LXIX) that of 122-100. (By contrast, he found a single book—LXX —sufficient to deal with the events of 99-92). Those eighteen books, LII-LXIX, have disappeared, leaving us with fewer than seventeen small pages in the modern Teubner text of the inept and drastically reduced abbreviation of these books by Livy's careless and obtuse Epitomator. Similarly, the continuous accounts of Diodorus Siculus and Cassius Dio have disintegrated into patchy *excerpta*.

For anything approaching a continuous narrative account we have to fall back on Plutarch and Appian. That both in their different ways are unsatisfactory is by no means altogether their fault. Plutarch was a biographer and not an annalistic historian: histories of Rome his readers could find elsewhere, if they wanted them and did not already know them. Plutarch's own interest lay chiefly in the characters of his subjects and in the development of their personalities and their interplay with events. Often he includes detail of at best peripheral interest to the narrative historian and omits detail which the latter would be anxious to include. He will bring together different actions if they serve to illustrate or evince a particular facet of his subject's character or policy without troubling to make clear their precise temporal sequence or relationship. The early chapters of the first book of Appian are a sort of prolegomena to his main subject, the civil wars of Rome; and he is here concerned above all to review those points in the recent history of Rome where violence broke surface and where at least some of the issues involved presaged the future conflicts which were his chosen theme. Both 133 and 121 saw violence and slaughter in the streets of Rome, a foretaste of what was to happen on a far more massive scale and a far wider stage in the days of Cinna and Sulla, Julius Caesar and Pompey, Antony and Octavian; the thrust of tribunician methods, issues like land reform and Rome's relations with the non-Roman communities and peoples of Italy, cast a long shadow before them. Like Plutarch, Appian is deliberately and not accidentally eclectic: thus he moves on from 133 to 123 with barely a glance at what happened in between; he preserves priceless material on the background to Tiberius Gracchus' agrarian law, but elsewhere is miserly of detail about Gracchan legislation and the development of Gracchan programmes, even more so than Plutarch—the speed with which he hurries forward from Gaius Gracchus' first tribunate in 123 to the street-fighting in which Gaius met his death in 121 is casually and carelessly breathtaking. If we had no evidence save that of Plutarch and Appian, we should have no inkling, to take one or two instances, that Gaius Gracchus passed a *lex de provinciis consularibus* or a *lex ne quis iudicio circumveniatur*, and be left very much more up in the air concerning his *lex de capite civis*. Taken separately, Plutarch would bequeath us confusion and puzzlement about Gaius' enfranchisement policy, Appian silence about his attack on Popillius Laenas and about his *lex agraria*. That is far from the full tale of their shortcomings, and merely indicates the importance of their joint or individual omissions or obfuscations. Luckily, there is a good deal of additional information at our disposal; but it has to be garnered from detached comments and brief asides, casual references and stray snippets, scraps of speeches and fragmentary inscriptions, which we must endeavour to fit into the framework which Plutarch and Appian provide. So, given our even greater ignorance of the detailed history of events before 133 and after 121, and of what was happening between 133 and 123, it is not surprising that there should long have existed a very wide arena for scholarly controversy, and that any new attempt at a continuous account of the Gracchi must cover an unusually large proportion of ground which cannot be treated as common to all earlier expositors, and must perforce devote a lot of space to detailed argumentation and controversial justification of what might be expected to be basic and accepted facts. I have tried to keep that element within reasonable bounds; but to pen it too narrowly would be deceptive and arrogant. I can only ask for, even require, the reader's tolerance.

Plutarch, Appian, Livy, Diodorus, and Cassius Dio were themselves only secondary sources. We cannot begin to assert what or which earlier sources they themselves drew on either at first hand or through some intermediary channel. Diodorus is an exception, for I have no wish to quarrel with the consensus of scholarly opinion that Diodorus largely used Posidonius, who lived from about 135 to 50 B.C., first arrived in Rome in 87, and later wrote a history in fifty-two books starting from the point where Polybius left off and carrying on down to Sulla; but, though Posidonius may have picked up something from a living oral tradition, even he must have relied heavily on earlier written accounts. We cannot even be confident that we know even the names of all the contemporary and nearly contemporary writers who covered the history of the years from 133 to 121 in whole or in part, comprehensively or selectively; a fairly cursory glance at Peter's *Historicorum Romanorum Reliquiae* will reveal how accidental and shallow is our knowledge of such writers and of the scope and completeness and detail of what they wrote. To try to determine which of them may lie in whole or in part behind the surviving accounts is largely wasted labour.

However, it is important to stress that detailed accounts by contemporary or nearly contemporary writers did once exist, and that official records could be consulted. Cicero's frequent references to what the Gracchi did presuppose that his audience or his readers shared with him a common knowledge of the facts; and his request to Atticus to 'dig out somewhere' the names of the ten men who served as *legati* to Lucius

Mummius in the year 146 received a prompt answer (*ad Atticum* 13.20.2; 13.32.3). However partisan the original accounts were, it is implausible to suppose that they were widely aberrant or mutually contradictory so far as concerned the public events of the Gracchan period—although on occasion even a contemporary's memory can innocently betray him in matters of detail and the exact temporal sequence of what happened. It is overwhelmingly probable, then, that what we read in the works now available to us about the overt events of the Gracchan period had a basis in truth, in contemporary factual report or record. But we still have to allow for occasional later careless misplacement in time, or serious distortion of original material in the process of inaccurate abbreviation or borrowing. Facts may be, to some extent have to be, selected; such selection may be unsophisticated or due to the accident of interest, or it may be slanted and reflect partisan bias, especially where motives and intentions are implied or assigned or insinuated, or where rumours and anecdotes and bon mots are reported—or perhaps subsequently invented. There is small doubt that the original accounts, and at least some of those which depended on them, were biassed, often markedly so: the nature of the activities of the Gracchi guaranteed that. Such bias was generally, though not always, anti-Gracchan. We have to bear all these factors in mind, and do what we can to assign to them their due weight.

The tribunates of Tiberius and Gaius Gracchus mark a watershed in the history of the later Roman Republic. Behind them we can discern pent-up forces waiting irresistibly to break through a barrier of unimaginative conservatism and entrenched interest. The chief themes of these years are like the leading motifs in the first movement of a Sibelius symphony, stated there only to be worked out fully in those that follow. The Rome and Italy of the Gracchan period had reached a stage where it is possible to perceive in the light of hindsight that there had to be large changes, and that some of those changes were in broadest outline predictable. More than usually, these years were, in Leibniz's words, 'chargés du passé et gros de l'avenir'. Some men living at the time grasped that fact, however inchoately; others were blind to it; and some saw it, but refused to accept it, or hoped that some other way out might be found, or simply determined to resist change for as long as possible. In studying the Gracchi, we are witnessing the beginnings of the 'Roman revolution'; afterwards, Roman politics were never the same again. Appian was right to set the Gracchi at the outset of his account of the civil wars that were to destroy the Republic in the course of the next hundred years; they failed to breach and storm the citadel of the ruling nobility, but they pointed the way for others to follow. They revealed one of the *arcana imperii*: the potential power of the popular assemblies and how it could be used to sap or circumvent the power of the nobility. But their failure showed that those assemblies needed further education, and that civil power was not in itself enough, or secure enough. The assemblies could be fickle, gullible, and short-sighted. And the ruling nobility was not prepared to sit quietly by and watch while its power was being eroded by what it saw as demagoguery. The nobles were ready to fight for their interests *vi et armis*. It was that which made it certain that in the end a successful assault could not be mounted by tribunes but only by men who championed 'Gracchan' causes and employed 'Gracchan' methods to secure *imperium*, and with it *clientelae*, patronage, loyal veteran armies, and immense disposable wealth with which to challenge the resources of 'the establishment'. It was Pompey who first grasped this truth fully, and who had the ability and energy and courage and ambition to exploit it. And it was Julius Caesar's army which decided the issue. Without that army at his back, Caesar would have joined Milo in exile at Marseilles, or his corpse would have followed that of Tiberius Gracchus into the Tiber.

I

POLITICS AND THE LAND

A marked decline in the numbers of free men on the land, which went hand in hand with an increase in the slave population of Italy, engaged the attention of Tiberius Gracchus and provided the *leitmotif* of his activity as tribune in 133.[1] That much, leaving aside for the moment questions about motives and intentions, is beyond dispute. His younger brother Gaius told how Tiberius' eyes had first been opened when he had passed through Etruria a few years earlier on his way to Spain and was struck by the 'emptiness' of the countryside and by the observation that the field-workers and herdsmen were all foreign slaves. Although that story has been impugned as an interested invention on Gaius' part, the mere fact that it was he who reported it cannot in itself constitute disproof; and, in any case, the story must at least have been plausible, and it would have made no sense had it not reflected a general truth about contemporary conditions in at least some parts of Italy.[2]

Wars, especially if they are successful, breed war-profiteers; and the victorious wars Rome fought in the second century had proved no exception to the rule. The profits and the pickings were abundant, and (like the booty and prize-moneys of later ages) they found their way more readily into the coffers of the generals and their staffs than into the purse of the common soldier.[3] Large fortunes, or generous competences, were also made out of state contracts for provisioning of armies and fleets, for manufacture and supply of arms and equipment, for public works (build-

[1] All dates are B.C., unless otherwise indicated.

[2] Plutarch (*TG* 8.4) records Gaius' publication—discounted by Badian (*FC* 172), but contrast the scepticism of Sherwin-White (*RC²* 218) about over-ready recourse to Badian's sort of explanation. Ignorance of conditions in Italy by the Roman ruling-class can be seen in the story (Livy 39.23.3) of how in 186 only a chance visit by a consul revealed that the colonies of Sipontum and Buxentum had been abandoned. On the 'emptiness' of much of Italy ('Italiae Solitudo') see Brunt, *IM* 345 ff. For a demonstration that on such a trip Tiberius would have traversed *ager publicus*, see Harris, *Rome in Etruria and Umbria*, 203–4.

[3] Data in Tenney Frank, *ESAR* 1.126 ff; Vogel, *Zschr. Sav. Stift.* 66.2 (1948), 394–423; Brunt, *IM* 393–6, 401; Shatzman, *Historia* 21 (1972), 177–205, and *Senatorial Wealth and Roman Politics*, 63 ff. The elder Cato made a speech (*de praeda milititbus danda*: Malcovati, *ORF²*, p.91) in which he attacked the selfish rapacity of commanders.

ings, roads, sewers, aqueducts, and suchlike), for leasing state-owned mines and quarries and woodland, and for farming taxes and customs-dues. Roman and Italian alike, the entrepreneurs spilled out over the Mediterranean world to take advantage of the multifarious opportunities that conquest and influence opened up to them.[4] At home, this new wealth induced its possessors to build fine houses and to furnish and decorate them lavishly, to improve and extend their estates, to purchase slaves (in plentiful supply thanks to war—they formed part of the booty—and also to access to the slave-trade of the Levant), or simply to engage in 'conspicuous consumption'. The gulf dividing rich and poor widened as the century grew older, persisting as a chronic source of bitterness and political conflict down to the end of the Republic a century later. Some thirty years after Tiberius' death, another tribune was to declare that among the Roman citizen body there were fewer than 2,000 men of real wealth. It is instructive to contrast the second-century legionary's pay of 450 or 480 HS a year with the 1,500,000 HS which L. Aemilius Paullus (consul 182 and 168, censor 164) left when he died in 160, especially since the latter figure was noted as a very modest sum for a leading senator.[5]

This new wealth sought investment as well as immediate expenditure; and the readiest and safest and, for a gentleman, the only gentlemanly investment was real property, and especially land.[6] At the same time the small farmers of Italy both Roman and non-Roman were being called on to serve in a succession of distant and protracted military operations; and the absence of their adult males, who were liable to conscription up to the age of forty-six, made it difficult for peasant families to carry on working their land. Apart from the obvious hardships involved, it is easy to picture the pressures brought to bear on these 'little people' by powerful, ambitious,

---

[4] Polybius 6.17, with Walbank ad loc.; Brunt, *Second Int. Confr. of Econ. Hist.* (Aix-en-Provence, 1962) 1.129ff.; Badian, *Publicans and Sinners*, ch. 2.

[5] Marcius Philippus declared in 104 'non esse in civitate duo milia hominum qui rem haberent' (Cicero, *de off.* 2.73). See Shatzman, *Senatorial Wealth*, 18ff. For legionary pay, see Brunt, *IM* 411; for Paullus, see Polybius 31.28, Plutarch, *Paullus* 39. Cicero's observation that the number of citizens in the single century of *proletarii* nearly exceeded the number in all seventy centuries of the first class put together (*de rep.* 2.40) probably reflects the situation in Gracchan times. (But it is perhaps worth observing that even after the Reform Act of 1832 less than one-fifth of all adult male Englishmen had the vote, and that even after the Act of 1867 fewer than two in every five had it.)

[6] Cato, *praef.* to *de agri cultura*. Cf. Cicero, *de off.* 1.151: 'nihil est agri cultura homine libero dignius'. Sallust's sneer at agriculture as 'servile officium' (*Cat.* 4.1) was *avant-garde* and provocative.

and greedy men who were eager to invest and deploy their new wealth. As Appian has it (with particular reference to public land, but similar conditions must have obtained elsewhere), 'the rich got possession of the great part of this undistributed land, and as the passage of time emboldened them to believe that nobody would ever take it away from them they went on to acquire adjoining areas and the small-holdings of the poor, partly by persuasion and partly by force, turning their farms into vast estates worked by slave labourers and herdsmen instead of free.'[7] All this came on top of the Hannibalic War at the very end of the third century, with its destruction of crops and buildings and its requisitions of produce and livestock. It has been contended that the modern world has seen remarkably swift recoveries from far worse ravages;[8] but the peasant farmers of ancient Italy exercised far less influence over their government than the farmers of modern Champagne and Picardy have over theirs, and Rome had no war damage commissions to pay compensation or help spread the losses caused by war equitably. The land itself may well have recovered quickly, but not necessarily under its previous owners. It is true that the old *ager Romanus* had hardly been devastated at all, but Tibiletti has emphasized the depopulation of the area around Rome at this time;[9] and former allied land sequestrated after the Hannibalic War and made *ager publicus populi Romani* had been devastated (and perhaps had lost cultivators too).[10] Moreover, it is far from certain that Tiberius was not concerned with the condition of the non-Roman peasantry of Italy as well as with the Roman.[11]

The system of compulsory citizen service as opposed to the maintenance of a regular professional army was common in the ancient world. In Rome's earlier days it had worked well, since campaigns were usually local and brief, and the prize of victory was confiscated enemy land to settle. But after 218 Rome's wars involved protracted extra-Italian operations, some of them (especially in Spain) very unrewarding to the common soldier. The career of a certain Spurius Ligustinus, although not

---

[7] Appian, *BC* 1.7.5. Significantly, Cassius Hemina, writing in or about the mid-second century, refers to men 'qui propter plevitatem [= 'poverty'] agro publico eiecti sunt' (frag. 17 Peter).

[8] Last, *CAH* ix.4.

[9] Athenaeum, N.S. 28, 188–91.

[10] On confiscations around 200–199, and on the devastation, Brunt, *IM*, chs. 16 and 17.

[11] See below, p. 42.

typical, is illuminating. He was born on a small Sabine peasant holding just before the outbreak of the Hannibalic War, and was called up in 200; by 171, having passed his fiftieth birthday, he had seen twenty-two years of active service all over the Mediterranean and was about to leave for his third tour of service in Spain. He had done very well, for he had been promoted to the centurionate early, and now in 171 he was Senior Centurion of the First Legion; but very few peasant conscripts could have aspired so high, or survived so long.[12] Just how many years a conscript might be called on to serve before he was forty-six is disputed, and the commonly accepted figure of sixteen years is probably too high; but a six-year tour of service seems to have been standard in the Spanish wars of the second century (experienced, long-serving troops were obviously preferable to successive new drafts, for several reasons), and six years is a very long time for a peasant to spend away from his land.[13] Small wonder, then, that protests against the draft were frequent and vigorous. Moreover, the incidence of conscription did not fall evenly on all citizens alike, but only on those registered as possessing a stated minimum property qualification; accordingly, as the numbers of the free property-owning peasantry declined, so the burden fell on a diminishing proportion of the whole citizen body.[14]

The growth of large estates at the expense of the free peasantry is remarked by Appian and Plutarch in their accounts of Tiberius Gracchus. They seem to have been thinking chiefly of developments on the *ager publicus*, those areas of Italy that is which were the property of the Roman state, and especially marginal land or those areas where the practice of transhumance encouraged the growth of ranching as against arable farming.[15] The *ager publicus* was overwhelmingly land which Rome had acquired by confiscation from defeated enemies and rebels in Italy in the

[12] Livy 42.34 — believable enough, despite the rhetorical colouring.

[13] For a full discussion, see Brunt, *IM* 399 ff.

[14] On the burden and unpopularity of conscription, see Taylor, *JRS* 52 (1962), 19–27; Astin, *Scipio Aem.* 167–72; Earl, *Ti. Gracchus,* 33–4; Brunt, *JRS* 52 (1962), 75, and *IM*, ch. 22. Progressive and very large reductions in the minimum property qualification required for legionary service from the late third century onwards explain why it was thought necessary by Gaius Gracchus in 123 to enact that the state should supply a legionary's equipment and clothing free of charge, since the level was now so low that it was unrealistic to expect an *adsiduus* to provide them himself. See below, p. 137, and in general Gabba's *Esercito e società*, 47–174. Tiberius Gracchus very likely mooted a similar proposal (below, p. 73).

[15] Appian, *BC* 1.7–10; Plutarch, *TG* 8; cf. Livy 35.10.1–2, 42.1.6. On transhumance, see the excellent account in Toynbee, *HL* ii.286–95.

period extending down to about 200. It had been regular practice to distribute large amounts of it among Roman citizens and Latins and even Italians, either by planting colonies or in individual allotments.[16] Land assigned to individuals by such acts ceased thereby to be *ager publicus populi Romani* and became the private property of the grantees; and by 133 much of the better land had been disposed of in these ways with the exception of some notably fertile land like the *ager Campanus* around Capua which was retained by the state and let out on lease at regular intervals by the censors. Even so, large amounts of the land assigned to colonies were not distributed to individuals but remained in some sense common land at the disposal of the colonies, or were left in the occupation of the former inhabitants: at Bononia in 189 only one-third of the total territory of the colony was distributed (some 400 out of a total 1,200 square kilometres), and at Mutina in 183 not much more than one-eightieth (25·2 out of 2,000).[17] As to the state-owned land which was not assigned or distributed thus nor reserved to be specially leased to increase the public revenues, it was thrown open to cultivation and grazing, subject to certain conditions which no doubt varied in the course of Roman history, but always with only precarious tenure in law, and subject (in at any rate the case of the better land) to a rent or *vectigal*. In its latest form in the period just before the Gracchi, the law *de modo agrorum* forbade any individual to occupy more than 500 *iugera* of public land (one *iugerum* was equal to about five-eighths of a modern English acre) and in addition pasture more than 500 small beasts and 100 large beasts. However, the rents had come to be disregarded and the limits on holdings and pasturage ignored or evaded, and the occupiers to look on such land as virtually their private property; the fact that by 129 it had often become difficult to determine what was public land and what private shows that rents and grazing-fees must have ceased to be exacted scrupulously for some long time past. Nor surprisingly, therefore, when in 133 Tiberius Gracchus published his proposal to reclaim illegal excess holdings of public land in order to distribute these lands among needy individuals, the larger and wealthier occupiers protested vehemently that they were being robbed: they had over a long period put a lot of good money and hard work into improving the land with buildings and plantations: some had paid fair prices for it, had family graves on it, had accepted it as their share of an inheritance

[16] See Appendix 1, *Ager Publicus Populi Romani*, below pp. 206 ff.
[17] Ibid. p. 212.

or as a wife's dowry, or spent dowries on its purchase, or borrowed money on its security, as equivalent to private property to all intents and purposes. No doubt some of these complaints were false and exaggerated, and Appian also reports that an earlier attempt to enforce the legal restrictions had led many large occupiers and graziers either to ignore the regulations altogether or to make 'paper transfers' to kinsmen who were simply men of straw so as to give the appearance of complying. All the same, there was surely a lot of real substance in the complaints, and one must not minimize the serious upsets that were caused, and could at the time have been expected to be caused, by a move to recover such land for redistribution, especially in the areas nearer Rome.[18]

It is a reasonable assumption that a good deal of this unassigned *ager publicus* was in the possession of non-Romans. The land had originally been confiscated from Italian peoples, and the old occupants were unlikely to move off their land unless or until they were forcibly ejected, or at any rate they would soon have drifted back, increasingly confident that they would be left alone. As time passed and Rome's former Italian enemies made their contribution to the extension of her dominion, the unfairness of enforcing an old and (it might be averred) long-discharged penalty would become all the more evident. Certainly, we know that by 129, some three years or so after Tiberius Gracchus' land commission had begun its work of recovery and allocation, serious disputes had arisen between the commissioners and allied Italian and Latin communities over the precise determination of what was *ager publicus* and what was not—and perhaps too over the destination of large areas of colonial land which had been assigned to colonies in Italy but not to individual colonists.[19]

It has been common to write of the growth of extensive continuous estates (the so-called *latifundia*) at this time and in this context. For all that the word *latifundia* does not occur in surviving Latin literature before early imperial times, that is not in itself a compelling reason to conclude that the phenomenon which it describes was not already present in second century Italy. As it happens, we have a lively description of what some of

[18] Ibid. p. 213

[19] On the disputes of 129, see below, pp. 92 and 213. In the year 91 Appian (*BC* 1.36) attests widespread allied cultivation of *ager publicus* by the Italians: τῆς δημοσίας Ῥωμαίων γῆς, ἣν ἀνέμητον οὖσαν ἔτι οἳ μὲν ἐκ βίας οἳ δὲ λανθάνοντες ἐγεώργουν. On Laelius' allegation of invasion of Latin and allied rights by the agrarian commissioners, see below, p.43.

these great ranches were like in a speech which Cicero delivered in 71, over a century before the first surviving occurrence of the word itself. The conditions which Cicero describes and implies in the *pro Tullio* as existing in the Lucanian hill-country in southern Italy remind the reader of the old Wild West, with cattle-barons and their armed slave-hands raiding herds and homesteads in the true spirit of Texas and Colorado. It is probable that such activities were a particular feature of the south, where there was much marginal land suitable for ranching, which needed to be on a large scale given the need for separate winter and summer pasturage on low and high ground. Although in such areas ranching may have been a more efficient system of land use, it called for a less intensive use of labour than arable farming, and most of the labour employed was slave-labour. Dispossessed peasants thus had little or no chance of earning a living by hiring themselves out.[20]

The practice of transhumance meant that there had to be freedom to move flocks and herds, twice in each year, between highland summer pastures and lowland winter pastures. Often great distances had to be travelled, and the cattlemen needed capital to buy stock and the slave-herdsmen required to handle the stock. The upland pastures probably belonged to the state or to allied communities (which had their own *ager publicus*); but at least on occasion the cattlemen would need to lease lowland pastureland from private owners for the winter season—Cato gives the terms for the lease of such winter pasturage (*pabulum hibernum*) in chapter 149 of his *de agri cultura*. Thus ranching did not require extensive areas in the exclusive private ownership or occupation of particular individuals, but rather access to and exploitation of extensive areas of *ager publicus* or *ager compascuus*, often in diverse regions.[21]

Latifundia were, however, not by any means the whole story, and their importance must not be exaggerated at the expense of other forms of land-use. Cato the Elder, so the story goes, was once asked what was the most profitable way to lay out one's capital, and replied: 'On good pasturage' ('bene pascere'). And what was next best?: 'Fair pasturage' ('Satis

---

[20] Brunt, *IM* 370–5; Toynbee, *HL* ii.286ff.; Kahrsted, *Historia Einzelschr.* 4 (1960); White, *BICS* 14 (1967), 62–79. As Frederiksen wisely notes (*Dial. di arch.* 4–5 (1970–1), 331 n.3), 'the word *latifundia* is treacherously vague in its meaning'. Cicero in the year 63 (*de lege agr.* ii.70) could talk of 'agrorum vastitatem' and 'ager a certis hominibus latissime continuatus'.

[21] Toynbee, l.c.

bene pascere'). And next?: 'Poor pasturage' ('male pascere'). And fourth best?: 'Arable farming' ('arare').[22] But we must not elevate illuminating witticisms to the status of revealed truths. No doubt Cato's wry humour reflects the fact that in his own day—the early to middle second century— the most startlingly obvious profits in agriculture were being made by the big ranchers; but ranching, no more than speculative office building in England in the 1960s, was not the only remunerative branch of real estate. Cato, an acknowledged expert, himself wrote a treatise on farming, and nothing in his *de agri cultura* suggests that he thought that decent arable land should be turned over to cattle-raising—though it seems that some may have been, if we may judge from a chance epigraphic survival from the fertile Val di Diano.[23] In any case, it does not so much matter whether there were many large continuous estates as whether in general there was a concentration of landholdings in relatively few hands.

Cato, like Varro who *Res Rusticae* was written just over a century later at the very end of the Republican period, had much to say about the culti- vation of vines and olives. Both were very much business undertakings, cash crops which involved considerable outlay on stocks and props and presses and storage, with olives in particular needing many years before they came into production. The poor subsistence farmer might manage to plant a few vines or olives, but could not spare much land if he was aiming at family subsistence. The richer man, who was in farming not for mere subsistence but for profit, could afford to lay out the capital and wait for the excellent return these crops promised; and 'only a grower with some capital could bear the loss of a poor season, or even the unprofitability of a bumper vintage. Only he could afford to wait for the best prices.'[24] Markets expanded as Rome's influence extended to include areas north of the Alps where the vine and the olive were not native. Pliny the Elder re- corded that Italian wines began to acquire an international reputation about the middle of the second century, and that by 121 at the very latest vintage wines were being specially casked and dated and laid down.[25]

None of this necessarily implied a serious crisis in cereal production, though there was a change from arable farming to ranching in some areas.[26] South of the Po valley the peninsula was not, with some exceptions, notably good cornland. Cato, when discussing what was the best kind of

---

[22] Cicero, *de off.* 2.89.
[23] See below, p. 55.
[24] Brunt, *IM* 709.
[25] Pliny, *NH* 14.87; 14.94.
[26] See above, p. 12, n.20.

farm, puts cereal cultivation only sixth in order of desirability: his list begins with viticulture, followed by market-gardening, osier plantations, olives, and meadowland, before we reach grain.[27] It is true that over a century after the Gracchan period, in the late Republic and early Principate, large amounts of grain were regularly shipped into Italy from abroad, from Sardinia and Sicily and Egypt especially, and that the city of Rome itself had come to depend for its survival on these imports—Tacitus gives as a major reason for the special arrangements which Augustus made for the government of Egypt his apprehension lest a disaffected vice-gerent might starve Italy into surrender.[28] But this is to look a long way into the future, and our evidence (such as it is) certainly does not suggest that for most of the second century imported corn had any noteworthy effects on Italian production.[29] In the Greco-Roman world the cost of overland transport of bulk commodities like grain was prohibitive if anything but short local haulage was involved. While the transport of corn by sea or navigable waterways made economic sense, inland regions cannot have been much affected since carrying costs would have been so heavy that the growing of cereals even on land not particularly suited to such crops must have continued to be both necessary and worthwhile in order to meet local needs. Some foreign corn was coming in and affecting the market, but the consequences were confined to Rome and its immediate surroundings; and farms in this area were now free to switch to more profitable cash-crops like fruit and vegetables to sell in the big local market which Rome provided.[30]

Latifundia, as already observed, in the sense of huge continuous tracts of land in individual ownership, were far from being the whole tally of the landed property of the rich. On the contrary, our evidence from the late Republic and the early Principate indicates that the big proprietors usually owned a number of moderately sized estates which might be widely scattered over Italy.[31] Outside ranching, the technology of the ancient

---

[27] Cato, *de agri cult.* 1.7. Professor Brunt has told me that he is not convinced that Cato 'is not here listing crops in order of profitability on a single mixed farm'. That could be true, but the comparative profitability still holds good. On the likelihood that most small farmers went in for mixed farming, see Frederiksen, o.c. 354-5.

[28] Tacitus, *Annals* 2.59.

[29] Tenney Frank, *ESAR* i. 158-60; Brunt, *IM* 273-5.

[30] Brunt, *IM* 703-6.

[31] Ibid. 331, 352, 365, and the works there cited, especially Yeo in *Finanzarchiv* 13 (1952), 495ff. See too Frederiksen *JRS* 65 (1975), 168, and Shatzman, *Senatorial Wealth*, 18ff., 241ff.

world was such that a limit was quickly reached to economies of scale in farming as in other activities. Both Cato and Varro in writing their treatises had in mind the better-off men who farmed for profit and not for mere subsistence. Thus Cato, in the passage already referred to where he sets out his order of preference for different types of farms, assumes an estate of 100 *iugera*, or over 60 acres; his olive plantation is 240 *iugera*, his vineyard again 100 *iugera*; and his typical farmhouse is a substantial affair solidly built of concrete and squared stone and timber, with stalls for cattle, a stable, accommodation for slave-hands etc. All this was of course a very far cry from the condition of the small peasant proprietors.[32]

Not all peasants owned the land which they worked. Cato refers to share-cropping as a regular practice in his day, and share-cropping is in essence simply a form of tenant-farming where the rent is in kind rather than in money.[33] Our evidence for tenant-farming in general comes from the post-Gracchan period. Cicero implies in a speech delivered in 63 that most of the work on the public land in the *ager Campanus* was done by small tenant-farmers: 'Totus enim ager Campanus colitur a plebe, et a plebe optima et modestissima'; and, while in this particular speech we must be wary of distortion and exaggeration, he can hardly have been guilty of a blatant and immediately obvious lie. In 49, the great noble Ahenobarbus could fill seven transports with men from his estates who included his tenants: 'navibus actuariis vii, quas . . . servis libertis colonis suis compleverat'.[34] The silence of our sources for the earlier period (and it must be remembered that our evidence on this sort of subject is scanty in the extreme) cannot be taken as decisive, and it is reasonable to put it down to accident of interest or survival, or both, and allow that tenant-

---

[32] Cato, *de agri cult.* 1.7–14. Incidentally, as Frederiksen has observed (*Dial. di arch.* (1970–1), 337–8), 'there is . . . no reason in the economic assumptions that make Cato's farm either optimum in theory or inevitable in fact.'

[33] Cato, *de agri cult.* 136 for share-tenants. Tenney Frank calculated (*ESAR* i. 168) that on Cato's figures the tenant paid 50 per cent to the owner and retained 50 per cent for himself.

[34] Cicero, *de lege agr.* ii.84. For Ahenobarbus, see Caesar, *BC* 1.34. Tenant-farmers were termed *coloni*, and 'for *coloni* it must be remembered that Roman law did not distinguish sharply between lease and hire, and there is a real sense in which the *coloni* were considered as employees' (Frederiksen, *JRS* (1975), 169). This was especially true since there was a fair amount of tenancy at will (*precario*): see Jolowicz, *Hist. Intr. to the Study of Roman Law*[3], 226, 230–1; Lintott, *Violence in Rep. Rome*, 27 ff.

farming was probably an established feature of the Italian scene in the second century.[35]

It cannot be contested that agrarian discontent was a persistent factor in the turbulent politics of the last century of the Republic. Measures for agrarian reform bulked large in the programmes of the brothers Gracchi, and called forth generous counter-proposals and promises from the elder Livius Drusus. Marcius Philippus in 104, Saturninus in 100, the younger Livius Drusus in 91, all advanced contentious and explosive proposals in this field. The possessing classes felt threatened. Marcius Philippus' claim that there were fewer than 2,000 Romans of substance drew from Cicero years later the criticism, not that his figures were wrong, but that such words were pernicious as tending towards equalization of property—yet what was a state constituted for if not above all else for the protection of the rights of property?[36] In the late eighties Sulla was to settle many thousands of veteran soldiers on the land, and Catiline in 63 looked for his staunchest support from a distressed and desperate peasantry. The agrarian bills of Rullus and Flavius in 63 and 60, Caesar's legislation as consul in 59, and the allotments and colonies of his dictatorship and of the triumviral and early Augustan periods continue the series to the end of the Republic and beyond.

The evidence we have does not permit us to produce the close columns of statistics which can be paraded by economic historians of more recent times; but it does allow us to discern in outline the general factors which combined to generate and exacerbate the situation, even if we cannot ascribe to each its precise proportionate weight.[37] The root of the matter is so obvious as to be a truism: it was Rome's very success as an imperial power and the consequences of the empire which she won that created the strains and the problems which expansion brought in its train.

At the very end of the third century, the war with Hannibal not only spread destruction and disarray over wide areas of Italy but also compelled

[35] Brunt, *JRS* (1962), 71.

[36] *de off.* 2.73. In the same spirit John Locke could write (*Essay concerning Civil Government*, ch.9): 'The great and chief end of men uniting into commonwealths is the preservation of their property.' And even the reformer Bentham insisted (*Principles of Legislation* (1876), 119-20) that 'when security of property and equality are in conflict, it will not do to hesitate a moment. Equality must yield.'

[37] Brunt's *Italian Manpower*, with its excellent indices, assembles and discusses the available data comprehensively. And see in general the works cited in n.59, p. 22 below.

Rome and her Italian allies to raise large armies and to keep them in the field for years. Out of a total of perhaps 300,000 adult male Romans an average of some 60,000 were under arms each year from 217 to 201. In the decades that followed, the best recent estimate suggests that of all free adult male Italians some 10 per cent served with the forces year by year down to 167 (when unhappily Livy's text and with it his figures cease to be extant).

This diversion of so much free labour from essential production was only possible because the profits of war enabled Italy to import supplies from abroad and above all slaves who could replace free men in agriculture, trade, and industry. The military power of Rome was now based on abundant slave labour. . . . But the burden of conscription and the economic effects of Rome's conquests combined to bring about . . . the deracination of the Italian peasantry.[38]

Thus the peasant soldiery of Italy was being subjected to crushing difficulties while at the same time the second century was witnessing the emergence of a class of immensely rich men, above all among the ruling aristocracy itself, which was in the best position to profit from the empire and garner the fruits of office. The development of large-scale ranching, the growth of individual agglomerations of estates, and the spread of farming for profit were all nurtured by this new wealth which sought investment and deployment in a world with few other safe homes for capital outside real property. Superior agricultural techniques were introduced from Carthage and the Greek east.[39] Warfare, assisted by the piracy that became endemic in an unsettled Mediterranean, produced a multitude of cheap slaves to work the lands of the wealthy and thereby severely limited the opportunities for free peasants to take up tenancies or hire themselves out as day-labourers. Cato and Varro are alike in assuming slaves as the normal workforce on the farms about which they write;[40] and Caesar as dictator

---

[38] Brunt, *IM* 426. On population and men under arms, see 61ff. and 416–34. In 1914–18 Germany mobilized 10 per cent of her total population; though modern *per capita* production is immeasurably greater than that of ancient Italy, nevertheless the terrible effects of the four years of the Great War on all the belligerents are notorious.

[39] Varro, *RR* 1.8ff. See Frederiksen, *PBSR* (1959), 108ff. The agricultural treatise of the Carthaginian Mago (in 28 books) was translated into Latin by order of the Senate after the fall of Carthage in 146 (Pliny, *NH* 18.5.22).

[40] Cato and Varro, *passim*. Cato says (*de agri cult*. 10–11) that a typical olive plantation of 240 *iugera*—say, 150 acres—needed thirteen slaves, a vineyard of 100 *iugera*—say, 60 acres—sixteen slaves.

was to require ranchers to employ free labour for at least one-third of their workforce, a directive that indicates that normally they employed far fewer and implies that the free labour was there if needed.[41]

What happened to the dispossessed peasants? Rome was the magnet that drew some of them. For much of the second century it was a busy place with a good deal of construction both private and public in progress, funded by the profits of conquest. There were armies to be supplied, ships to be built, and so on.[42] In the early part of the century there were extensive colonization projects in Italy and in Cisalpine Gaul; yet the mid-century saw a cessation of this activity, the reasons for which are obscure— it may be that many people were being absorbed in a prosperous and expanding economy in Rome and other towns, although other and more self-interested explanations are available. But our evidence may point to a falling off in private and public spending in the late '40s, and if this be so it may be that diminishing opportunities for urban employment constituted a contributory factor to the situation which the Gracchi sought to remedy.[43]

All the same, it remains true that, whatever we make of this factor, Rome and the other towns of Italy had no large industries or manufactories to employ and absorb rural immigrants in any quantity, and that such skilled or semi-skilled work as was available was usually best performed by slave and freedmen craftsmen from the more advanced societies of the eastern Mediterranean, while unskilled work was often in the hands of slaves who needed food and clothing only for themselves and had no families to support.[44] Such scraps of casual labour as were available

---

[41] Suetonius, *DJ* 42; cf. Earl, *Tiberius Gracchus,* 28.

[42] See (e.g.) Polybius 6.17, with Walbank ad loc.

[43] Boren, *AHR* 63 (1957–8), 890–902. On Boren's calculations from coinage issues, see now Crawford, *RRC* ii.633ff. Personally, I have grave doubts about the basic soundness of the sort of statistical calculations involved in trying to compute total annual issues of coins from surviving examples. (On colonization, see Appendix 1 below, p. 214. For possible reasons for its cessation, see below, p. 135.)

[44] I assume that most slaves were imported and not home-bred, but that makes little difference. Whether slaves were in fact cheaper than free labourers we lack the figures to determine: cf. Yeo, *Finanzarchiv* (1952), 442–85. There is controversy enough even about the economics of negro slavery in the U.S.A. in the ante-bellum period, for all its far richer sources of material evidence: see the excellent chapter 'Profit and Loss' in Stampp, *The Peculiar Institution,* 363–95. As Stampp puts it succinctly, the capital invested in a slave 'was merely the payment in a lump sum of a portion of what the employer of free labour pays over a period of years. The price of a slave, together with maintenance, was the cost of a lifetime claim to his labour;

probably satisfied far fewer than might seek it. Many—I suspect most—of the dispossessed peasantry must have stayed on in the country, relying for a bare and meagre existence on the produce of tiny plots and on such seasonal work—at harvest-times, for instance—as required temporary extra hands, or on other casual work, especially unhealthy or dangerous work that could prove expensive in slave losses. Certainly Cato shows that in his day there was a reservoir of free labour that could be reckoned to be available for seasonal work on the larger farms in districts not too far from Rome.[45] When in 107 Marius began recruiting for the legions from all citizens without any regard to their property qualification, an example regularly followed for the rest of the life of the Republic, men came forward in large numbers from the rural regions of Italy for the harsh, ill-paid, and often short life of a soldier which at least promised them regular meals and clothes for their backs.[46]

Gaius Gracchus was to introduce arrangements for distributions of corn at reasonable and stable prices; but only the population of Rome itself benefited, and between 123 and 58 (when Clodius made them free) the distributions were neither regular nor widespread, and there were still scarcities from time to time.[47] The bulk of Tiberius Gracchus' supporters, Appian says, were drawn from the countryside rather than from the capital itself. After he had carried his agrarian bill, his victorious supporters 'returned to the country districts whence they had come'; and when not

it was part of the wage an employer could have paid a free labourer. The price was what a master was willing to give for the right to maintain his workers at a subsistence level, and to gain full control over their time and movements' (p.382). Stampp reckons (ibid.) that there is 'ample evidence that the average [American] slaveholder earned a reasonably satisfactory return upon his investment in slaves.' It is clear that the average Roman slaveholder must have believed the same to be true; and it is not easy to suppose that such a belief would have survived as long as it did, custom and habit and lethargy and social prestige and inadequate accounting procedures notwithstanding, if it had been without foundation in fact.

It should be emphasized that the prudent slaveholder knew that he had to keep his slaves continuously employed if they were to be properly profitable, and that accordingly he preferred free labour or subcontracted slave-labour for seasonal and occasional work (e.g. harvesting). This consideration is also relevent to non-agricultural work like dockwork and porterage and building; on which see Brunt, *Social Conflicts* (s.v. 'public works') and 'The Roman Mob', 3–27.

[45] *de agri cult.* 144–5. In general, see Frayn, *JRS* (1975), 32–9.

[46] Brunt, *JRS* (1962), 69–80; Badian, *Aufst. u. Niederg.* I.i.671, and the works there cited.

[47] Brunt, *IM*, ch. 21. (Brunt's chronology of the *leges frumentariae* is criticized and corrected by Schneider, *Wirtsch. u. Politik*, 362 ff.). See further, below p. 126.

long afterwards he sought re-election as tribune 'he began calling in the
people from the country to come to the voting, but they could not spare
the time, as was natural in summer', and he was driven back onto the
urban commons and to failure and death.[48] A few years later it was in the
small towns and villages of central Italy that Gaius appealed for support
against Popillius Laenas, the scourge of his brother's adherents.[49] There is
also the story in Plutarch of how Gaius' mother Cornelia hired men to
help her son and sent them into Rome disguised as harvesters: it may be
apocryphal, but behind it lies the assumption that such men were the
natural supporters of a Gracchus.[50] Diodorus Siculus writes that enthusiastic countrymen poured into Rome to vote for Tiberius' bill like so
many rivers into the all-receiving sea.[51] It has been contended that such
categorization is too simple;[52] and we must certainly not discount the
existence of citizens living in or near the capital and doing seasonal and
casual work in the country, nor of recent immigrants into Rome who still
thought of themselves as countrymen and were eager to return to the land.
Appian, Plutarch, and Diodorus may be the vehicles of rhetorical exaggeration or anachronism. But their evidence is not to be brushed aside cava-
lierly, and it is more prudent in my opinion to follow those scholars who
accept the broad picture it presents.[53] It is not to be doubted that the
population of Rome in the Gracchan period included large numbers of
slaves and ex-slaves, and that the latter, although as *libertini* they were
now citizens and voters, had a tradition of crafts rather than of hus-
bandry.[54] Further, of the thirty-five electoral groupings whose block votes
determined the decisions of the tribal assemblies, only four lay within the
old city boundary of the *pomerium*, and only some seven or eight of the
remaining thirty-one were represented within the area we might term

---

[48] Appian, *BC* 1.13–14.

[49] Aulus Gellius, *NA* 1.7.7. The speech was referred to as 'de P. Popillio circum
conciliabula' (cf. Appendix 2 below, p. 220). Since tribunes were not normally
allowed to be absent for more than 24 hours from Rome (below, p. 172) the places
concerned were probably within a day's journey from the capital.

[50] Plutarch, *CG* 13.

[51] Diodorus Siculus 34/5. 6.1.

[52] Astin, *Scipio Aemilianus*, 345–6. Badian, *Aufst. u. Niederg.* I.i.717ff.

[53] Gabba, *Appiani B.C. Liber Primus*, 41. Brunt, *JRS* (1962), 72. Sherwin-White,
RC[2] 218.

[54] The evidence for Rome's urban population is assembled and discussed in
Brunt, *IM*, ch. 21. See Treggiari, *Roman Freedmen*, 87–161 for careers of *libertini*.

'greater Rome'.[55] Hence, even if we allow for voters who had recently drifted into Rome and had not yet been re-registered in urban tribes, the need for the support of considerable numbers of rural voters to secure the passage of an agrarian bill faced with vehement opposition from wealthy and influential interests is obvious.

Inevitably, Rome's metamorphosis into a Mediterranean power had momentous consequences in the field of her domestic politics. In particular, the extension of the territory of the Roman state even before the second century had begun had brought it about that more and more of the citizens had ceased to be domiciled within reasonable distance of the capital. Yet all electoral and legislative assemblies and the discussion meetings or *contiones* which preceded them continued to be held within or just outside the old city-limits, and a citizen could exercise his public rights only by attending these meetings in person. Thus distance led to the effective disfranchisement of those poorer country voters who could afford neither the time nor the money for the journey—and such people would normally either lack any interest in what was going on at Rome, or feel powerless to influence affairs; and they were at best ill-informed and at worst totally ignorant about the content and timing and implications of assembly agenda. At the same time the capital came to house an increasing proportion of slaves and ex-slaves, as is witnessed by the sharp retort allegedly delivered to a hostile assembly by Scipio Aemilianus, who refused to be moved by the clamour of a crowd of men 'to whom Italy was but a stepmother' ('quorum noverca est Italia').[56] Hence, even if the second century had not seen, as it in fact did see, a continuing tendency towards the arrogation of power by the Senate as a body and the hardening within the senatorial class itself of a core of ruling families who virtually monopolized the highest magistracies and the immense patronage and influence and opportunities that went with them, the customary attendance at assemblies and *contiones* would still have failed faithfully to reflect the true interests of the bulk of a citizen body whose city had ceased to be a *polis* and was well on the way to attaining the physical dimensions of a modern nation state.[57]

However much some modern scholars have sought to minimize it, it seems an inescapable conclusion that there were agrarian problems of great

[55] See the map printed in Taylor, *Voting Districts* (opp. p. 35).

[56] Vell. Pat. 2.4.4.

[57] I have gone into this more fully in my *Cicero*, ch. II.

seriousness in the Italy of the Gracchan period. There were men living in or near Rome who were anxious to return to the country from a city which could not offer them regular employment. There were many more in the country districts who scratched a bare living in the mysterious way that even nowadays poor peasants contrive to do in the less prosperous parts of our own world. The exigencies and devastation and disruption of the Hannibalic War; the long and distant campaigns that marched relentlessly along in the next half-century or so, with their heavy demands on peasant manpower; an outdated system of militia service persisted in in circumstances alien to its origins; harsh laws of debt;[58] formidable difficulties in the way of securing legal redress against oppression and expropriation by the possessing classes; a massive influx of cheap slaves and huge fortunes; a growth in the non-free and non-native elements in the population of the capital; the dissemination of new techniques and practices in agriculture; the scarcity of investment and employment opportunities outside the land; a political system which had been devised for a *polis* and not for a nation state, and which was heavily weighted in favour of the rich, while still offering formal opportunities for citizen control; the continuing reluctance of the ruling class to tackle or even to recognize the problems—all these elements combined to generate an explosive situation which engaged the attention and the energies of Tiberius and Gaius Gracchus and their collaborators and spurred them into actions which were to provide the central themes of Roman political issues for the next century.[59]

[58] The burden of debt is easier to recognize than to quantify: in general see Brunt, *Social Conflicts* (s.v. 'debt problem'). It is only too likely that many conscripts or their families fell into debt and were forced to sell or give up. The small size of the typical peasant holding made it necessary for a peasant to supplement its return by exploiting common land for firewood or casual pasturing of a few cattle or pigs, by share-cropping, by occasional day-labouring, or some combination of any or all of these. But enclosure of common land by the wealthy, and the ready availability of cheap slave-labour, reduced or removed such opportunities, and must often have pressed the peasant into debt and loss of his holding by seizure for non-payment.

[59] In general for the topics discussed in this chapter see the following detailed treatments: Toynbee, *Hannibal's Legacy*; Brunt, *Italian Manpower*; Tenney Frank, *Economic Survey of Ancient Rome* i; Schneider, *Wirtschaft u. Politik*; Shatzman, *Senatorial Wealth*; Badian, *Aufstieg u. Niedergang* I.i.668–731. Tibiletti's work on the *ager publicus* is fully discussed in Appendix 1 (below, pp. 206 ff.) Brunt's article in *JRS* (1962), 69–86 ('The Army and the Land in the Roman Revolution') is also particularly noteworthy. For the archaeological evidence, see the cautious survey by Frederiksen in *Dialoghi di archeologia* (1970–1), 330–57 ('The Contribution of Archaeology to the Agrarian Problem in the Gracchan Period').

II
TIBERIUS GRACCHUS

The Sempronii Gracchi were a plebeian family, but they belonged to the nobility of Rome, the aristocracy of office.[1] Their branch of the *gens Sempronia* had first come to prominence in 238, when the great-grand-father of the tribune of 133 became consul and won fame as the conqueror of Sardinia. In the next generation their position was consolidated and advanced, aided perhaps by the wider opportunities which were opened up to those noble houses whose adult members had escaped the broad swathe scythed through the ranks of the Roman aristocracy by Hannibal's troops at Cannae in 216. In the crisis which followed the news of that disaster a dictator was appointed who chose as his deputy or *magister equitum* the son of the consul of 238, who went on to be consul in 215 and again in 213. This man's nephew Tiberius Sempronius Gracchus, the father of Tiberius and Gaius, climbed still higher: like his uncle before him, he secured the rare prize of two consulships (in 177 and 163); he celebrated two triumphs (from Hither Spain and Sardinia); and set the seal on his family's greatness by his election to the coveted office of censor in 169. He was also a member of the great priestly college of Augurs, to which his elder son too was to be appointed as a very young man.[2]

But, brilliant as his achievements were in the public field, to many people at the time it appeared that the greatest honour which the father of the two Gracchi won was the hand in marriage of their remarkable mother. Cornelia was the younger daughter of the incomparable Scipio Africanus the Elder by his wife Aemilia—herself sprung from the great patrician noble family of the Aemilii Paulli: her father had fallen as consul at the head of the Roman army at Cannae. Romance painted a colourful picture of the match: of virtue triumphant over political differences; of an honourable and patriotic Gracchus who as tribune in 184 twice interposed his veto during the trials of the Scipio brothers and who, despite personal differences, would not stand by and watch a man who had led Rome's

---

[1] On *nobilitas*, see Gelzer, *The Roman Nobility*, 27–40.
[2] See Broughton, *MRR* i *sub annis*. The younger Tiberius' augurship at an early age is attested by Plutarch, *TG* 4.1.

enemies through her streets in triumph be himself haled off to that same prison where he had lodged them; of an Africanus who had long admired the sterling qualities of his destined son-in-law even in opposition; of a dramatic public reconciliation, and the spontaneous offer of a daughter's hand; of a mother whose initial pique at not having been consulted beforehand changed to delight once she learned the name of her daughter's husband-to-be.[3] Sadly, the truth seems to have been different.[4] Polybius attests that the betrothal of the younger Cornelia to Tiberius Gracchus (the elder Cornelia married Scipio Nasica, the son of Africanus' cousin) occurred some time after Africanus' death in 183,[5] and was arranged by her close relatives.[6] Since Polybius was the friend and confidant of Scipio Aemilianus, husband of Cornelia's daughter by Gracchus and adoptive grandson of Africanus, his testimony must command our confidence.

The date of the marriage is uncertain: it could have been as early as 175 or anything up to ten years later. All we know for certain is that our Tiberius Gracchus, who was the eldest surviving son of the marriage, was born in 163, and that his father was a fair bit older than his mother.[7] In all, twelve children were born of the marriage, but only three survived to reach adulthood: Tiberius, Gaius, and their sister Sempronia.[8] We know that Gaius was nine years younger than Tiberius.[9] Sempronia was probably older than both of them, since she was already the wife of Scipio Aemilianus,

[3] Cicero, de prov. cons. 18; Livy 38. 52 and 57; Aulus Gellius, NA 6.19. 6-7, 12.8.3-4; Val. Max. 4.1.8, 4.2.3; etc.

[4] Livy (38.57.8) did not claim truth for the story, only that it was too good to omit. Plutarch (TG 4.3) says that most writers rejected it. A similar story was told of the younger Tiberius' marriage to Claudia!

[5] For this date see Scullard, Roman Politics 220-150 B.C.[2], 152.

[6] Polybius as cited by Plutarch, TG 4.3. Polybius (31.27) also shows that the first instalment of Cornelia's dowry was paid over by her widowed mother.

[7] Plutarch, CG 1.2, TG 1.2. Cicero, de div. 1.18.36. The dates of the marriage of Tiberius senior and Cornelia, and of their respective births and those of their children, are exhaustively discussed by Carcopino, Autour des Gracques, ch. 2. That the tribune of 133 was the eldest son to survive is shown by his possession of his father's praenomen Tiberius; although in theory an older brother or brothers could have died before he was born, Plutarch says that all Tiberius senior's children were still alive when their father died. For interpretations of the father's political position, see Carcopino, loc. cit., and Earl, Tiberius Gracchus, 49-66. Earl is to my mind rather too schematic, and makes too little allowance for the flexibility and fragmentation of the Roman ruling nobility.

[8] Plutarch, TG 1.2. Pliny, NH 7.57. Cf. Carcopino, 71-5.

[9] Plutarch, CG 1.2, TG 3.

her mother's cousin and subsequently nephew by adoption, when the seventeen-year-old Tiberius was serving under Aemilianus' command in North Africa;[10] she was still alive in 101, for in that year she made a vigorous public denial of the claim of a certain Equitius to be her dead brother's son.[11] Tiberius *père* probably died about 154, leaving his widow to bring up her two 'jewels' herself, the one from the age of nine or ten, the other from the cradle.[12]

Cornelia was by any account a remarkable woman. After her husband's death she was sought in marriage by a king (probably Ptolemy VIII Physcon), perhaps not entirely because of the importance of her family connections to a man anxious to enlist Roman support in his dispute with his brother for a throne. She took the greatest pains over the education of her two sons. Plutarch says that their later pre-eminence among their contemporaries owed even more to her care for their upbringing than to their considerable natural talents. Cicero speaks of her *diligentia* in this matter and specifies her careful seeking out of the finest Greek tutors. Apart from the famous rhetorician Diophanes of Mitylene, named by Cicero as Tiberius' especial teacher in the art of public speaking, the Stoic Blossius of Cumae stands out as a devoted guide, philosopher, and friend, loyal to death and even beyond.[13]

Precisely how intimate and pervasive Cornelia's influence was we cannot be sure. Some went so far as to make her an active partisan of her younger son Gaius in 121, something allegedly disclosed in her letters in a disguised fashion; but the mention of some sort of riddling cipher shows that there was no clear evidence, and others claimed that she was actually opposed to his activity.[14] As to these letters, there was a collection of them which was known to Cicero, who found them impressive: 'We read

[10] Id. *TG* 4.4.

[11] Val. Max. 3.8.6.

[12] Carcopino argues persuasively (*Gracques*, 77ff.) for 154, and this seems the likeliest date; but one a few years later is possible (Astin, *Scipio Aemilianus*, 36). The story of Cornelia and her 'jewels'—'Haec ornamenta sunt mea'—is told by Val. Max. 4.4.

[13] Plutarch, *TG* 1.3 (cf. Carcopino, 77–9), 8.3, 17.3, 20.3. Cicero, *Brutus* 104. Tacitus, *Dialogus* 28. Quintilian 1.1.6. Strabo 18.617. See too Rawson (*JRS* 55 (1975), 154) for how the great Roman nobles treated on terms of equality or superiority with kings, holding themselves to be their peers or even their betters.

[14] Plutarch, *CG* 13.1. But Cornelia certainly seems to have been publicly attacked by Gaius' opponents, to judge by references to public rejoinders to such attacks by Gaius (*CG* 4; cf. Seneca, *cons. ad Helv.* 16.6): Appendix 3, p. 224 below.

the letters of Cornelia the mother of the Gracchi, from which it appears
that they were reared rather on their mother's discourse than on their
mother's milk.'[15] The critic Quintilian knew and admired their writer's
'doctissimus sermo'.[16] A couple of fragments totalling some three dozen
lines are preserved by Cornelius Nepos: their genuineness has inevitably
been questioned, but sound modern judges have accepted them.[17] Some
people are said to have upbraided Cornelia for firing her sons with ambition, taking them to task for allowing her to be famous as the mother-
in-law of Scipio Aemilianus rather than as the mother of the Gracchi:[18]
not a very plausible anecdote, given the nine years' difference between the
ages of the boys, the fact that neither showed any hesitation in plunging
early into politics, and the considerable seniority of Aemilianus who was
already consul and in command of the war against Carthage when Tiberius
was only seventeen and just beginning the military service that was then a
required preliminary to public office. Others had it that she intervened in
123 to induce Gaius to spare Tiberius' old enemy Octavius,[19] and that
Tiberius used her along with his own children to make his emotional
appeal to the Roman commons in his hour of peril in 133.[20] There was
even a story that the death of Aemilianus in 129 at the height of his
opposition to Tiberius' land commissioners was the work of Cornelia and
her daughter Sempronia, Aemilianus' barren, unloved, and unloving wife.[21]
Evidently a good deal of invention was at work. But there is no smoke,
however much it may blur the view, without some fire; whatever we make of
the details, a picture emerges of a woman of exceptional character, intelligence, culture, and energy, who exerted a powerful formative influence over
two remarkable sons left in her sole care from their early childhood.

It was with Aemilianus, his sister's husband and his mother's cousin,
that Tiberius Gracchus began his military service as a member of the
commander's staff in North Africa during the Third Punic War. He quickly

---

[15] *Brutus* 211: 'Legimus epistulas Corneliae matris Gracchorum; apparet filios
non tam in gremio educatos quam in sermone matris.'

[16] Quintilian 1.1.6.

[17] They can be found printed at the end of the Oxford text of Nepos, *Vitae* (ed.
Winstedt), and are accepted as genuine by Leo, *Roem. Lit.* i.304ff., and Bardon,
La Lit. latine inconnue i.88ff. For full references to modern discussions, see
Schanz–Hosius, 219.

[18] Plutarch, *TG* 8.4.

[19] Id. *CG* 4.1; Diodorus 34/5 25.2. See below, p. 116.

[20] Dio Cassius fr. 82.8.

[21] Appian, *BC* 1.20 (his only mention of Cornelia).

won a reputation for sound sense and for courage, on one occasion sharing a high award for bravery, the *corona muralis*, with Gaius Fannius for being first over the wall of an enemy town.[22] Gaius Gracchus was likewise to serve on Aemilianus' staff not many years later in Spain, along with two other young men destined to win a large place in Roman history, Gaius Marius and the Numidian prince Jugurtha.

Aemilianus, sometimes known as Scipio Africanus Minor in recognition of his victory over Carthage in 146, was the outstanding political figure of his day. He was the son of L. Aemilius Paullus, consul in 182 and 168 and censor in 164, and was adopted as his son by his childless cousin Publius Scipio, only son of Africanus Major, to save his line from extinction. He enjoyed considerable support in the Senate and also a broadly based popular following.[23] Not that he was unchallenged. Cicero cast his dialogue *de re publica* in the form of a conversation between Aemilianus and his closest friend Gaius Laelius and some other companions in the garden of his house a few weeks before his sudden death in 129. One of the speakers refers to the 'jealous disparagers' of Aemilianus, who lead the rival group in the Senate, at variance with his own. Until their deaths a year or two earlier, this opposition had been led by P. Licinius Crassus Mucianus (*pontifex maximus*, consul 131) and his brother-in-law Appius Claudius Pulcher (consul 143, censor 136); by 129 they had been succeeded by Crassus' natural brother P. Mucius Scaevola (consul 133, *pontifex maximux* after his brother's death in 130) and Q. Caecilius Metellus Macedonicus (consul 143, censor 131).[24] Crassus, Claudius, and Scaevola are attested as backers of Tiberius Gracchus. Tiberius himself married a daughter of Claudius, his brother Gaius a daughter of Crassus (a niece of Scaevola). Both Claudius and Crassus became members of the land commission created by Tiberius' bill; and Cicero records a tradition that the brothers Crassus and Scaevola were very much behind his actual legislation: 'Crassum et P. Scaevolam aiunt Ti. Graccho auctores legum fuisse';[25] although he goes on to add that Scaevola's assistance was less open

---

[22] Plutarch, *TG* 4.

[23] For a full treatment, see Astin's excellent *Scipio Aemilianus.*

[24] *de re pub.* 1.31: 'obtrectatores et invidi Scipionis, initiis factis a P. Crasso et Appio Claudio, tenent nihilominus illis mortuis senatus alteram partem, dissidentem a vobis, auctore Metello et P. Mucio' (Claudius' hostility to Scipio was of very long standing).

[25] *Ac. Pr.* 2.13.

('obscurius') than his brother's. To these names we may add those of a Fulvius Flaccus (probably either Gaius, consul 134, or Servius, consul 135) and a Manilius or Manlius mentioned by Plutarch in a context which suggests a friendly association with Tiberius.[26] However, the backing and co-operation of the powerful men already mentioned is sufficient assurance that Tiberius began with considerable influential support in the Senate.

The pattern of Tiberius' connections is not a simple one. He had close ties with both the leading groups in the ruling oligarchy of the time. That ought not to be surprising. The much fuller evidence of the Ciceronian period shows similar complexities, and warns against the unsubtle abuse of prosopography. And Tiberius was not unique in his own day: Q. Mucius Scaevola the Augur and possibly Gaius Fannius were both married to daughters of Laelius, Aemilianus' closest friend; yet the former was a cousin of Crassus and Scaevola, the latter a leading supporter of Gaius Gracchus until his late defection in 122; Q. Aelius Tubero and Gaius Cato were both nephews of Aemilianus; while Tubero broke with Tiberius over his activity ('rei publicae causa'), Cato was a supporter. The dividing lines in a tight aristocracy were not rigid, and individuals might shift allegiance as circumstances changed, answering the demands of ambition or loyalty, affection or antipathy, favour or obligation, fear or calculation, or even genuine disagreement over what was the right policy to pursue at any particular moment. It is usually impossible for us at this great distance to penetrate behind a bare record of names to the reasons which led this man or that to co-operate with this or that group over a given issue. And it would certainly be extremely rash to follow some scholars in picturing the ruling oligarchy as neatly divided into clearly defined factions under a recognized and continuing leadership. Even to talk of 'groups'—although it is hard to eschew the word altogether—may mislead. Although from time to time a specific issue could produce polarization, in general the ruling oligarchy was surely more fragmented.[27]

Still, we have to face up to the question (even if we finish up by having

---

[26] If Plutarch is accurate in calling this man a consular at the time, he cannot have been the M. Fulvius Flaccus who was not consul till 125. His Μάλλιος could be T. Manlius Torquatus (*cos.* 165), A. Manlius Torquatus (*cos.* 164), or perhaps M'. Manilius (*cos.* 149).

[27] The identity of the C. Fannius who was son-in-law to Laelius is debatable: see Fraccaro, *Opusc.* ii. 103ff., 119ff. For Tubero and Cato, Cicero, *de amic.* 37–9. On the general point, see Last, *Gnomon* 22 (1950), 361–2; Sherwin-White, *JRS* 46 (1956), 1–2; Brunt, *Gnomon* 37 (1965), 190–2.

to admit that we cannot be sure of the answer) of what led Tiberius Gracchus into association with men like Claudius and Crassus and Scaevola rather than with Aemilianus and his friends.

It is highly probable that there was a personal quarrel with Aemilianus. As quaestor in 137 Tiberius had had to draw heavily on his father's fine reputation and *clientela* in Spain to negotiate on behalf of his commander, the consul C. Hostilius Mancinus, favourable terms for the capitulation of a Roman army which was in a hopeless position. Subsequently, this agreement was disavowed by the Senate.[28] Cicero and Velleius Paterculus stress the anger Tiberius felt at this decision, which was a brutal blow to his own prestige and standing.[29] The influence of Aemilianus' friends behind the disavowal is revealed by the fact that the man behind it in 136 was the consul L. Furius Philus, one of the speakers in the dialogue *de re publica*, where Cicero makes it plain that the others approved his action and indeed shared responsibility for it.[30] Since the very next year saw Aemilianus elected to a second consulship for 134, and as consul taking command in Spain against the Numantines, it is not far-fetched to allow that his personal ambition could have been a factor in the move to disavow the Numantine peace treaty which Mancinus and Tiberius had negotiated.

Even if some may find such a motive trivial (although slights far more trivial can still be seen to occasion or sharpen political bitternesses today), it certainly did not seem so to a Roman noble, who placed the highest value on his personal prestige, especially if his *clientes* were involved.[31] The repudiation of the Numantine treaty, regardless of the good sense or propriety of Tiberius' handling of the business, was a severe blow to his

---

[28] Reff. in *MRR* i. 484-5. Cf. Scullard, *JRS* 50 (1960), 71-3.

[29] Cicero, *Brutus* 103: 'ex invidia foederis Numantini bonis iratus'; cf. *de har. resp.* 43: 'senatus severitas dolori et timori fuit, eaque res illum fortem et clarum virum a gravitate patrum desciscere coegit.' Velleius 2.2: 'graviter ferens aliquid a se pactum infirmari'.

[30] Cicero, *de re pub.* 3.28 (Philus is the speaker): 'consul ego quaesivi cum vos mihi essetis in consilio de Numantino foedere . . . me ex senatus consulto [rogationem] ferente.' Cf. Plutarch, *TG* 7.3: ἀλλ' οὐδὲν ἧττον ἐν αἰτίαις ἦν [Σκηπίων] ὅτι . . . οὐδὲ τὰς σπονδὰς ἐμπεδωθῆναι τοῖς Νομαντίνοις δι' ἀνδρὸς οἰκείου καὶ φίλου τοῦ Τιβερίου γενομένας. The fact that Aemilianus may (δοκεῖ, says Plutarch) have supported the move to see that Tiberius was spared from any personal harm will have weighed little against his failure to back him on the issue of the Numantine treaty itself.

[31] Note, for instance, Julius Caesar's proud claim that 'sibi semper primam fuisse dignitatem vitaque potiorem' (Caesar, *BC* 1.9). On the central importance in Roman political life of *clientela*, see Gelzer, *Roman Nobility*, 62-70; Badian, *FC* 1-14.

dignity and patronage, and those responsible were guilty of a hostile political act to which he could be expected to take forceful exception. It is annoying that we do not know the date when Tiberius married Claudia, the daughter of Aemilianus' chief rival in the Senate. If it was in 143, as is commonly accepted, it need not have had much significance. But it could have been as late as 136 or even 135; and if so it could mark the occasion of the deliberate alignment of a Tiberius by now in his middle or late twenties with Aemilianus' antagonist, either producing a hostile response from Aemilianus and his friends over the treaty or representing Tiberius' prompt reaction to the slight he had received.[32]

What is certainly evident, from the event, is that in the Claudio-Crassan circle Tiberius found very influential and established men who were disposed to assist him in his programme and perhaps even in some measure provide its inspiration.[33] Given the political association between Tiberius'

[32] Earl (*Tiberius Gracchus,* 67–9; cf. Briscoe, *JRS* (1974), 126–7) rightly pointed out that Münzer's date of 143 is far from secure. In his speech *de legibus promulgatis* (see Appendix 2 below, p.221), Gaius Gracchus declared that there remained no (he must mean male) descendants of Scipio Africanus Major and Tiberius Gracchus senior except himself and 'a boy': 'nec quisquam de P. Africani et Tiberi Gracchi familia nisi ego et puer restaremus.' The speech was delivered in 123 or 122. Valerius Maximus 9.7.2. asserts that Gaius' brother Tiberius 'had only three sons, one of whom died while on military service in Sardinia, one in infancy at Praeneste, and one who was born posthumously and who died at Rome.' Who then was the 'puer' of Gaius' speech? Not a son of Scipio Aemilianus and Gaius' sister Sempronia, for their marriage was childless (Appian, *BC* 1.20). Possibly a son of Gaius himself, but that is unlikely since he probably had only a daughter, and we hear of no sons of his (Münzer, *Roem. Adelspart.* 273). Hence most probably one of the three sons of the tribune of 133— but which? Scarcely the son who died in infancy, since in a speech delivered ten years or so after the father's death we are dealing with a boy of at least ten or eleven, who could not be described as 'infans'. Perhaps the posthumous son, though Valerius' notice perhaps implies that this child did not long survive. The likeliest answer is the son who subsequently died in Sardinia. Münzer assumed that he is to be ruled out since he will have died while serving with his uncle Gaius in Sardinia in 126 (and hence must have been born about 143 or 142 at latest); but nobody says he did, and he could well have died some years later, perhaps (as Earl suggests) in the Sardinian campaigns of 115–111. Hence we cannot follow Münzer in asserting that he must have been born by 143/142 at latest. The truth is that we do not know when Tiberius' two elder sons were born, nor how long he and Claudia were married before their first child was born. On the evidence we have, they *could* have been married as late as 135, producing three sons in quick succession between then and early 132 (the posthumous one).

[33] Above, p.27 n.25. Briscoe (*JRS* 64 (1974), 125–35) sees Tiberius as one of a group of men who broke away from Scipio over domestic policy; but I am not convinced.

father and Claudius' father, who shared consulship and censorship in 177 and 169, the combination was not so very startling.[34] (In fact, it seems reasonable to suppose that Gracchus senior was on good terms with both the Claudii and the Scipiones, as Julius Caesar is found on good terms with both the old rivals Pompey and Crassus in 60-59).

The simplest statement of Tiberius' aims in 133 comes from Cicero: 'Tiberius Gracchus sought to carry an agrarian law. It appealed to the common people. It looked likely to safeguard the fortunes of the poor. The best people threw their weight against it, because they saw it was a source of discord, and believed that to remove the rich from their long-held possessions would be to rob the state of its defenders.'[35] This is the line followed in general by all our authorities, who present Tiberius as the real mover in all this and not as a mere tool of an oligarchic group, and as aiming (however ill-advisedly) to redress serious and widespread social and economic discontents by a straightforward and perfectly legal re-distribution of public land, using the illegal excess holdings of a comparatively few rich men to resettle landless peasants on small holdings.

Yet the question remains, why did he and those who collaborated with him seek to do this, and what did they hope to achieve?

Tiberius' motives have more than once been questioned. Recently, Earl, in his monograph on Tiberius, has argued forcefully against the existence of a serious economic and social crisis.[36] He seeks the answer to the question in the manoeuvrings of power politics:

Roman politics was always an unceasing and relentless struggle for position, prestige, and power waged by the various sections of the nobility. Ap. Claudius Pulcher and his associates will not have been unmindful of the possibility of obtaining the political support of the urban *plebs* and the rural proletariate, of adding these classes, or a section of them, to their *clientelae*. It was an important prize and would have given this group an important advantage in political affairs.[37]

Yet Earl himself recognizes that we have to look further than that; and he elsewhere argues that the background and impetus of the programme of

---

[34] Earl, *Ti. Gracchus,* 60 ff.

[35] *pro Sestio* 103: 'Agrariam Ti. Gracchus legem ferebat: grata erat populo; fortunae constitui tenuiorum videbantur; nitebantur contra optimates, quod et discordiam excitari videbant et, cum locupletes possessionibus diuturnis moverentur, spoliari rem publicam propugnatoribus arbitrabantur.'

[36] D.C. Earl, *Tiberius Gracchus: A Study in Politics* (Brussels, 1963).

[37] Ibid. 40.

Tiberius Gracchus and his supporters is to be sought in a desperately serious shortage of available military manpower, a situation which they aimed to exploit both because of the urgent need to do something about it and also in the expectation of stealing a march on their rivals. 'Rome was faced with a desperate military crisis'; and the alternative to doing something about it was the 'unthinkable' one of 'abdication of her position as the leading power in the Mediterranean world. . . . It therefore remained to increase the number of citizens possessed of the necessary qualification [for legionary service]. It has often been pointed out that this would be an incidental effect of the *lex Sempronia agraria*. It was, I suggest, the measure's main public purpose.'[38]

With much of that there is no cause to quarrel. The leading politicians of second-century Rome were naturally always on the look-out for opportunities to increase their influence. Tiberius himself stressed the danger that Rome's imperial gains might be wrested from her if she did not maintain her reserves of military manpower.[39] That those manpower resources had been severely strained by the imperial expansion of the second century is not in dispute. The minimum property qualification for legionary service had already been drastically reduced without curing the sickness;[40] and in 133 the Marian step of opening the legions to all citizens without regard to their census, which was seen in its own day a generation later as a radical move,[41] may not have been entertainable—Tiberius himself is reported to have held that possession of at least some property was a necessary and desirable condition of eligibility for legionary service when he asked, 'Was not a man who could serve in the army more useful than one who could not? Was not a man who had a stake in his country more likely to be devoted to its common interests?'[42] Rome's overseas wars, particularly those in Spain, were a constant drain, and during the '50s and

---

[38] Ibid. 34–5. As Badian observes (*Aufstieg u. Niedergang* I.i.681 ff.) Earl does not always make his position as clear as he should.

[39] Appian, *BC* 1.11: Κινδυνεύουσιν ἐν τῷδε περὶ ἀπάντων, ἢ κτήσασθαι καὶ τὰ λοιπὰ <τῆς οἰκουμένης> δι' εὐανδρίαν, ἢ καὶ τάδε δι' ἀσθενείαν καὶ φθόνον ὑπ' ἐχθρῶν ἀφαιρεθῆναι.

[40] See Brunt, *IM* 402 ff., who argues for a reduction to 1,600 HS in 214, and a further one to 600 HS before 129, perhaps as early as 171. There may well, of course, have been others between these two figures, which derive from Polybius 6.19.2. and Cicero, *de re pub.* 2.40.

[41] Sallust, BJ 86: 'non more maiorum'.

[42] Appian. *BC* 1.11: Καὶ χρησιμώτερος ὁ στρατιώτης ἀπολέμου, καὶ τοῖς δημοσίοις εὐνούστερος ὁ κοινωνός.

'40s they occasioned serious unrest as citizens from time to time resisted the levy.[43] From the early '30s down to 132 there were dangerous slave uprisings in Italy itself, and a major and expensive full-scale slave war in Sicily.[44] Metellus Macedonicus as censor in 131 delivered a famous speech on the urgent need to increase the birth-rate, and we may well suppose that many others were alive to the situation.[45] It is always true, of course, that it is one thing to be concerned and quite another to grasp the nettle of remedial action. Laelius, closest and most influential of Aemilianus' friends, had himself some years earlier mooted a proposal for agrarian reform, only to abandon it, allegedly under pressure from powerful and interested opposition.[46] All in all, it is no surprise that subsequently other men should have resumed the issue, and seen in proposals for agrarian reform both national utility and political advantage to themselves. After all, settlement on the land was a traditional Roman way of keeping up and increasing the number of *adsidui*, and colonies had not been founded solely as *propugnacula imperii*.

Nevertheless, we must surely question whether a distinction can properly or profitably be drawn between a recruitment crisis on the one hand and a social and economic crisis on the other. It has already been argued that in the second century they were two sides of a single coin. It was the impoverishment and proletarianizing of the peasantry which produced the shortage of *adsidui*, of men that is of sufficient property to be registered for the levy. The impact of conscription was itself an important cause of that impoverishment. The slave war in Sicily and the lesser tumults in Italy not only called for troops to suppress them, they must also have led at least some people to reflect that some revival of the free peasantry would reduce dependence on and danger from an alarmingly large servile workforce. Rome's recently acquired Mediterranean empire both occasioned much of the distress and demanded garrisons and field forces for its

[43] Above, p. 9.

[44] References in Broughton, *MRR* i *sub annis*.

[45] For Metellus' speech, see Malcovati, *ORF*² pp.107–8. Cf. Livy, *Perioche* 59, Suetonius, *DA* 89.

[46] Plutarch, *TG* 8.3. The date is uncertain. The year 140 when Laelius was consul seems likeliest. Legislation as praetor in 145 is improbable. If he held a tribunate, it would have been in the late fifties. See Astin, *Scipio Aem.* 307–10. Tibiletti (*Athenaeum* N.S. 28 (1950), 234–6) insists that Laelius' proposal need not have been for an agrarian law, but I find his argument obscure and it is not easy to see precisely what alternative he has in mind. See also Scullard, *JRS* 50 (1960), 62–6.

maintenance. Appian's account, while stressing the increasingly desperate plight of the peasantry of Italy, at the same time pictures Tiberius as aiming to produce not economic but human wealth: Γράκχῳ δ᾽ ὁ μὲν νοῦς τοῦ βουλεύματος ἦν οὐκ ἐς εὐπορίαν ἀλλ᾽ ἐς εὐανδρίαν. Δυσανδρία and εὐανδρία do not unambiguously denote shortage or plenty of men, but rather shortage or plenty of men who can do the state some service. The poor might be numerous and fertile, yet unsuited by physique as well as by lack of property for campaigns.'[47] To try to unravel these intertwined strands and discard some of them is unrealistic and captious, even if the object is the reasonable one of seeking to emphasize the pragmatism and self-interest of the reformers and to tone down a too brightly coloured picture of high selflessness and humanity, unmarred by political calculation. Whether Tiberius was merely concerned for the poor because their poverty endangered Rome's supply of soldiers, whether he was concerned for them for their own sake, or for reasons of traditional sentiment, or for what we might vaguely and generally term constructively 'patriotic' motives, we can never know for certain. That he was in some sense of the word 'concerned' about them is a plain fact.

There is no relevant force, either, in the contention that at this time Italian agriculture was in a healthy state.[48] There is indeed good reason to suppose that it was more prosperous than ever before, thanks to capital injection and improved techniques and widening markets and cheap slaves and low labour costs. But, not only is it possible for agricultural prosperity to coexist with agrarian discontent and misery, it can easily cause it. We need look no further back than our own generation to observe how greatly agriculture in western Europe has improved its efficiency and profitability since 1945, and how dramatically at the same time the numbers of those employed in agriculture have fallen both absolutely and proportionately. The expanding and prosperous 'urban economy' of modern Europe has generally (though not everywhere) led to this surplus labour's being readily absorbed elsewhere. But such has not always been the case, not with the enclosure agriculture of earlier centuries for instance; and certainly it was not true of second century Italy.[49]

[47] Appian, *BC* 1.11. Brunt, *IM* 77.

[48] Earl, *Tiberius Gracchus*, 29, 37, etc.

[49] We must note in passing that Earl's unhappy slip in confusing *ager Romanus* with *ager publicus populi Romani,* viz. the whole with part of the whole, makes his calculations worthless, and misleads him into minimizing the situation. (On the economic efficiency of slave-labour, see above, p. 18, n. 44).

It is, then, pointless, even misleading, and certainly unhelpful to try to tease out a single thread from this tangle and label it as the one sure clue which will lead us out of the labyrinth. Even at the time men were surely not nicely aware of their priorities. Human affairs, past as well as present, only too often face us at all levels with messes to be sorted out or head-aches to be coped with, rather than clear-cut problems awaiting tidy solutions: with a choice between options none of which is free from dis-advantages, all of which fall short of the ideal, and perhaps only few of which can be confidently judged to be certain to be available or practi-cable. There is no evident reason to assume that Tiberius Gracchus and his collaborators believed that all Rome's chief problems could be resolved at a stroke by his agrarian bill, or that it was the certain political 'winner' some have seen it as. Rome needed soldiers to fill the legions which policed her empire and secured her pre-eminence. That was presumably common ground among all of her politicians; but it may have seemed that the great period of foreign wars had drawn to an end, and hence to some the need could have appeared less urgent. Increased dependence on slave-labour was demonstrably not without its dangers; but it was economically attractive to the rich men who dominated affairs. The condition of many peasants was wretched; but while some leading men might be moved to compassion or concern, others might be left indifferent. Some senators may have feared for future social and political stability, while others re-mained sanguine or short-sighted. We can be quite sure that any move to recover and redistribute public land to revitalize the peasantry (for what-ever motives) would be bound to arouse vigorous opposition from the vested interests which would be threatened, and hence that political support won from the poor would be balanced by political hostility from those of the better off who would be up in arms against such a move as subversive of the rights of property and the good order of society. So, while Tiberius and his associates may have seen some advantage to themselves in pro-moting their programme, the disadvantages must have been equally appa-rent. So too, *mutatis mutandis*, with their political rivals. It is fair to assume that then, as today, men could do their political sums with much the same data available to all of them, and yet reach different conclusions about needs and priorities and possibilities. All we can hope to see is what sort of items entered into their calculations, not precisely how and why the different balances were struck.

We are to a great extent at the mercy of our sources, as some of them too were at the mercy of their own.[50] Both those who champion reform and those who oppose it can always be expected, whatever their true motives may be, to represent themselves as acting from other than self-regarding impulses, and to be tempted to portray the other side in a quite different light. Reform is always popular with those who look to benefit from it, and such popularity can scarcely fail to be politically valuable. It is true that our authorities nowhere directly suggest that the aim of the agrarian bill was to increase the political power of a faction, and that hostile comment claimed rather that Tiberius himself was building a base for personal supremacy, 'regnum parare'.[51] But that may not have been an initial objection so much as a consequence of the way the situation developed, as Tiberius became increasingly separated from his early supporters. Few would disagree that he did leave some of them well behind, most notably the consul of 133, P. Mucius Scaevola, allegedly one of the chief influences behind his legislation, who after Tiberius was killed lent his considerable talents and authority to the eloquent defence of those responsible for his death.[52] Similarly perhaps Metellus Macedonicus, who was soon with Scaevola to succeed to the leadership formerly exercised by Crassus and Claudius,[53] rounded on Tiberius at a late stage in uncharacteristic alliance with his enemy Q. Pompeius.[54] It is also worth noting that Claudius himself, Tiberius' father-in-law, the most powerful single figure on his side, and with him one of the three original agrarian commissioners, is conspicuous only by his absence when the final crisis develops. Of course, he may have been unwell, or perhaps his duties as a commissioner had drawn him far from Rome; but it is odd that we do not find him throwing his great weight as *princeps senatus* behind the threatened tribune.

It is hard to escape the fact that it was not so much the agrarian bill itself as Tiberius' own developing response to the opposition to it that created a situation so remarkable that it was then, as it has generally since

---

[50] See below, p. 37, n. 57.

[51] So Brunt (*Gnonom* 37 (1965), 191–2).

[52] Cicero, *de domo* 91: 'Scipionis [Nasicae] factum statim P. Mucius consul . . . multis senatus consultis non modo defendit sed etiam ornavit.' On Scaevola's influence over Tiberius' legislation, see above, p. 27 n. 25. On Nasica's own wariness about Scaevola, see below, p. 88.

[53] Above, p. 27 n. 24.

[54] Plutarch, *TG* 14.2. A speech of Macedonicus, *contra Ti. Gracchum,* mentioned by Cicero (*Brutus* 81) was very likely delivered on this occasion; Cicero says that it was 'preserved' in the *Annals* of C. Fannius, but tells us nothing more about it.

been, regarded as a great watershed in the history of the late Republic.[55] The consequence is that we cannot be sure how much of the reaction was due solely to dislike of the proposal in itself,[56] nor how far later interested distortion has been at work. It is clear that we are confronted by two rival traditions, the one 'popular' and favourable to the Gracchi, the other 'aristocratic' and critical.[57] The assassination of Tiberius and the pogrom against his supporters among the commons (apart from Tiberius we hear of no men of standing who suffered) engendered deep bitterness. His forceful and eloquent younger brother not only played on the pathos of his brother's martyrdom ('Pessimi Tiberium fratrem meum optimum interfecerunt. Em, videte quam par pari sim!'), he is also suspected of having fathered on him some of his own wider and larger ideas ('Quid tam aecum

[55] Cicero, de re pub. 1.31: 'Mors Ti. Gracchi et iam antea tota illius ratio tribunatus divisit populum unum in duas partis.' See too Sallust, BJ 42. (The idea was commonplace, and it would be tedious to list all references to it.).

[56] A point overlooked by some critics of Earl in their reviews of his book: e.g. Nicolet, REA 67 (1965), 144ff., Brunt, Gnomon 37 (1965), 189ff.

[57] The fundamental review of this question is that of Fraccaro in 'Studi sull' età dei Gracchi' Studi storici per l'antichità classica 5 (1912), 317–448; N. S. 1 (1913), 42–136; Opuscula ii.18–52. For a rejection of Gabba's (and others') view that Asinius Pollio was Appian's source here, see Cuff's excellent 'Prolegomena to a Critical Edition of Appian B.C. I' in Historia 16 (1967), 177–88. Appian gives no hint of which source or sources he was following. Plutarch refers on occasion specifically to Cicero, C. Gracchus' βιβλίον, the speeches of Tiberius and Gaius Gracchus, the letters of their mother Cornelia, Cornelius Nepos, Gaius Fannius, and Polybius. The particular instances, and a list of the other sources available to later historians, are conveniently set out by Holden in pp. xvii–xliii of the introduction to his edition of Plutarch's Gracchi (Cambridge, 1885). Personally, I can see little point in trying to guess which specific sources lay behind the accounts of Plutarch and Appian: there is just too little to go on. (I should certainly accept the communis opinio that Diodorus Siculus used Posidonius—for what that is worth.) It is generally easy enough to detect pro-Gracchan and anti-Gracchan and neutral points of view when they occur. On Plutarch's method in his biographical writing, see the excellent analysis of Gomme in his Commentary on Thucydides i. 58–84 (cf. Appendix 3 below, p. 226). For a justified refusal to accept Earl's distinction between 'the Latin sources' on Tiberius Gracchus and 'the Greek sources', see Brunt's review in Gnomon 37 (1965), 189–92: as Brunt observes (189), 'we have no detailed Latin account of 133 [or of 123–121 for that matter], but no reason to think that any which existed differed substantially from the histories that Appian and Plutarch [and, we may add, Diodorus and the pedestrian Latin summarizer Florus] followed.' All in all, we simply have to take what we are given, always alive to the obvious truth that the programmes and actions of the Gracchi were such as inevitably to give rise to partisan reactions which will be bound to be mirrored in the evidence which survives to some extent or other. Cf. above, Introduction, pp. 1–4.

quam inopem populum vivere ex aerario suo?').[58] But, was it really attribution, or was it a case of Gaius' inheriting and developing these ideas?[59]
We cannot be sure. The careers of the two Gracchi were to provide plentiful ammunition for the political battles of words and slogans and ideo-
logies of the next two or three generations, not the best recipe for producing sound evidence about aims and motives.[60] On top of which, the
question of how far they may have been influenced by Greek political
theory and history is at once important and elusive.[61]

What can we be certain of? There was a serious and widespread socio-
economic malaise, intimately associated with the problem of legionary
recruitment, both of them products of empire; a group of influential
politicians ready to collaborate with and stimulate (some might even say,
manipulate) an outstandingly gifted and forceful young noble of proud
and distinguished political ancestry and egregious education, a man with
good reason to harbour a keen personal resentment against a rival group
who had themselves it seems entertained ideas of agrarian reform some
years earlier only to drop them prudently in deference to affronted opposition; a bill that could certainly be represented as of national benefit and
was sure to arouse great popular enthusiasm, but was also sure to
antagonize a number of rich and powerful men; concern about the dangers
of increasing dependence on slave labour, but a lot of capital tied up in its
continuance; perhaps too a pervasive if ill-defined worry that there was
something gravely amiss with 'the state of the nation'. A nice balance of
factors. The influential Aemilianus was far away fighting in Spain. Of the
men on Tiberius' side, Scaevola alone of the two consuls for 133 was
actually on the spot in Rome, and along with the *princeps senatus* Claudius, the tribune's father-in-law, was in the key position to plot and control the course of senatorial debates; while Scaevola's brother Crassus,
already a senior pontiff, was to succeed the following year to the office

---

[58] Malcovati, *ORF*[2] pp. 178, 186. Cf. below, pp. 218 and 224.

[59] It is impossible to deny that Tiberius' contention that 'it was only just that
what belonged to all should be shared among all'—δίκαιον τὰ κοινὰ κοινῇ διανέμεσθαι
(Appian, *BC* 1.11)—has the same ring as the words just cited. But the determined
sceptic will see here yet another example of contamination.

[60] Compare how both Solon and Caesar became 'political footballs', with unfortunate consequences for historians who must try to sift the truth from the fiction.

[61] See the perceptive comments of Nicolet in *REA* 67 (1965), 142–58; Badian,
Aufstieg u. Niedergang I.i. 678–81. Plutarch reports (*TG* 8) that most of his authorities held that Diophanes and Blossius 'egged Tiberius on'—παρορμησάντων.

of *pontifex maximus* on the death of Tiberius' cousin and enemy, Scipio Nasica. A formidable trio, but scarcely 'revolutionaries'.[62] Yet Tiberius' agrarian bill was in at least one important respect 'revolutionary', since it aimed to find land to distribute to the needy by taking it, not from enemies defeated in war or disloyal allies punished for defection, but from rich Roman and allied occupiers. If there were precedents for this, they had to be sought in the misty and unreliable history of the earliest days of the Republic: indeed, such 'precedents' may only have been intruded into the tradition at this period.[63] This gave the proposal a new flavour, and its opponents a new stick to beat it with; and, certainly before very long, it touched sensitive nerves among the ruling classes of the allied communities of Italy. But Tiberius was not to be deterred or denied by criticism and opposition, however deeply felt or dangerous: he pressed resolutely ahead as the quarrel swiftly changed its nature, ceasing to be a quarrel over the rights and wrongs of a particular agrarian bill and burgeoning to embrace fundamental questions about the true nature of the governance of the Roman state, the limits of senatorial control and of popular sovereignty, the whole formulation and direction and implementation of national policy. There was nothing 'conservative' here, no mere tacking for temporary 'party' advantage: the issue of legionary recruitment and declining numbers of those eligible to serve becomes remote. Whatever we make of the beginnings, the Tiberius Gracchus who was clubbed to death in the ugly tumult of a street-battle was not the mere agent or instrument of a faction of ambitious and basically calculating nobles. He died alone.

[62] The other consul of 133, L. Piso, was away from Rome fighting the slaves in Sicily during that year. That this was going to be so may have been known some time in advance (see Badian, o.c. 690, n.51). Badian also makes the point that the brothers Crassus and Scaevola were both pontiffs, and Claudius an augur, all three evidently of some seniority in their respective colleges, and that this was likely to be useful given that the then *pontifex maximus* Scipio Nasica was known to be hostile to Tiberius, and that questions might well arise about alleged religious impediments involving the validity of his legislation.

[63] A point frequently made. See e.g. Gabba, *Athenaeum* (1964), 29–41.

III

THE *LEX AGRARIA*

Tiberius Gracchus expressed concern about the military manpower of
Rome, the general well-being of the inhabitants of Italy, the growth of
large and strictly illicit holdings of *ager publicus*, the increasing use of slave
labour on the land, and the consequent dwindling in the numbers and
vigour of the free peasantry. Appian says that he spoke of these matters
with grave eloquence—ἐσεμνολόγησε—and that he underlined his argument
by stressing the lesson to be learned from the dangerous and expensive
slave war which had broken out in Sicily two years earlier, and was still
going on. Plutarch (and Florus clearly followed the same source here) puts
into Tiberius' mouth a moving and vivid contrast between the wild beasts
of Italy, which at least had their lairs and their nests, and the wretched
men who fought and died for their country but went homeless and shelter-
less with the sky for their only covering, called on to defend a fatherland
which did nothing for them in return and in which they had no true
share.[1] This state of affairs he sought to remedy, with powerful support
from some of the leading members of the ruling nobility and with enthusiastic popular encouragement, by new legislation designed to put free
small farmers back on the land. Whether from the outset he looked further
than that there is no knowing; but we must suppose that he knew that he
was bound to run into vehement opposition from vested interests, and so
had done some serious thinking in consultation with his chief supporters
about what he might do to circumvent or overcome it.

   The bill which he promulgated was essentially simple and straightforward in substance, for all that its certainly very complex detail eludes
us. There was in Italy a considerable amount of land which belonged to

---

[1] Appian, *BC* 1.9; Plutarch, *TG* 9.4; Florus 2.2 (cited below, Appendix 2, p. 225).
All three are similar, the latter two strikingly so. We cannot rely on Appian and
Plutarch for verbatim citation; but the general gist and certain striking phrases or
images may well go back via an intermediate source to the *ipsissima verba* of Tiberius.
For speeches by Tiberius were certainly preserved: 'et Carbonis et Ti. Gracchi habe-
mus orationes' (Cicero, *Brutus* 104; and cf. Pliny, *NH* 13.26). His reputation as an
orator was eclipsed by that of his younger brother. Extant fragments and references
are in Malcovati *ORF*² pp. 145–52. See also Fraccaro, 'Stud. età Gracch', 415–38;
Nicolet, *REA* (1965), 142 ff.; Badian, *Aufst. u. Niederg.* I.i.678.

the state but which was occupied by *possessores* who lacked a formal or secure title to it.[2] By law, any individual who occupied more than 500 *iugera* of such land (a little over 300 English acres, or 125 hectares) was guilty of a punishable offence. Similarly, the number of beasts both large and small which any one man could in addition pasture on public land was restricted by law. In practice, however, these regulations had come to be widely disregarded or evaded by wealthy men. Tiberius was not content merely to reassert the existing regulations, or to vary them, or to provide for sterner penalties to deter miscreants. His bill was not just a negative *lex de modo agrorum*, but much more positive. It provided for the election of a public commission of three men whose duty it would be to conduct a thorough investigation stretching over a number of years in order to determine where holdings existed which exceeded the legally permitted limits. Anyone found to be in breach of the rules, however, was not to be charged with the offence and punished, but simply required to surrender any excess holdings. Indeed, the pill was sweetened by granting to such individuals a secure legal title to the 500 *iugera* which they were permitted to retain, together with further blocks of 250 *iugera* for any children they had.[3] What happened to those whose holdings were within the legal limits we are not told; they too may have been given a secure title, but we can be pretty sure that it was considered that those who were not called on to surrender any land had no claim to such compensation. The excess holdings thus recovered the agrarian commissioners were to distribute for settlement by small farmers—though the rich public land in Campania, the *ager Campanus*, was at least for the most part excluded from distribution under

[2] On the technical meaning of *possessio*, see Appendix 1, below p. 206.

[3] For the security of title, see Appian, *BC* 1.11.5 (τὴν ἐξαίρετον ἄνευ τιμῆς κτῆσιν ἐς ἀεὶ βέβαιον ἐκάστῳ πεντακοσίων πλέθρων), where I take ἄνευ τιμῆς to mean 'free of charge', viz. the secure title to the 500 *iugera* the occupier was allowed to retain was given free, very likely to compensate for improvements which he had effected to the excess holding he was now required to surrender. Only Appian (*BC* 1.9.3; 1.11.5) mentions the child-allowance; but it is equitable, and makes sound demographic sense. He cannot have meant only male children, for in both places he uses the neutral παῖς ('child') and not υἱός ('son'). It was once widely accepted that there was an overall ceiling of 1,000 *iugera*, and hence that extra land was allowed for only two children. But that is in itself implausible (why legislate against the philoprogenitive?), and is merely the result of trying to marry the statements of Livy, *Perioche* 58 and *de viris illus.* 65 that the limit was 1,000 with the consensus of the other sources that it was 500. The text of the *Perioche* is never reliable for figures, and in any case it is here uncertain and may well be corrupt. So caution is called for. See Badian, *Historia* (1962), 210ff.; Earl, *Tiberius Gracchus*, 17–18.

Tiberius' law. The allotments made by the commissioners were to be in-alienable, and almost certainly a small rent was charged, probably little more than a token rent and very likely a technicality connected with inalienability.[4] The first three commissioners elected under the law were Tiberius himself, his father-in-law Appius Claudius Pulcher, and his younger brother Gaius, who was serving with Aemilianus in Spain at the time: Appian says that this was at the insistence of the voters, who were afraid that the work would not be properly carried through unless Tiberius and his closest kin were given executive control and responsibility.[5]

So much in bare outline. A number of particular points require separate discussion.

To begin with, it is debatable whether only Roman citizens were to benefit from the distributions or whether Latins and Italian allies were also eligible. It is unthinkable that Tiberius proposed to evict all non-Roman occupiers from public land, no matter how small their holdings; and nothing in our evidence begins to suggest or support any such intention on his part. It is safe to assume that any rich non-Romans who were found to be occupying public land above the 500 *iugera* limit were required to surrender the excess, although under what conditions we cannot say; I should guess that they too were recompensed with a secure title to what they were allowed to retain. When it comes to actual eligibility for allotments under Tiberius' law, Appian clearly implies that non-Romans were to be eligible: his account harps on the theme of 'the Italian race', and Tiberius is presented as asserting that his work was 'of the greatest justice and benefit for the whole of Italy', and as being acclaimed on all sides as 'the founder not of one city or of one people but of all the peoples of Italy', and as aiming at 'the regeneration of the Italian race'.[6]

Many scholars have nevertheless held that Appian was wrong or mis-guided, and that his account must be taken to reflect the distortions of later propagandists, particularly his younger brother Gaius, whose pro-

---

[4] 'Nec duo Gracchi . . . nec L. Sulla . . . agrum Campanum attingere ausus est' (Cicero, *de lege agr.* ii.81; and cf. i.21). On the Gracchan marker found near Capua, see below, p. 55. For the rent, see Plutarch, *CG* 9.2.

[5] Appian, *BC* 1.13. Cf. Plutarch, *TG* 13, and below, p. 52.

[6] ἔργον ὁσιώτατον καὶ χρησιμώτατον Ἰταλίᾳ πάσῃ (*BC* 1.12.7); οἷα δὴ κτίστης οὐ μιᾶς πόλεως οὐδὲ ἑνὸς γένους ἀλλὰ πάντων ὅσα ἐν Ἰταλίᾳ ἔθνη (13.3); ἐς πολυανδρίαν τοῦ Ἰταλικοῦ γένους (7.4). Other allusions to the same theme are to be found at 1.8.1; and it is at 1.9.1 that we are told that Tiberius ἐσεμνολόγησε περὶ τοῦ Ἰταλικοῦ γένους ὡς εὐπολεμωτάτου τε καὶ συγγενοῦς.

Italian activities are notorious.[7] Above all, it is maintained that the evidence of Cicero in his dialogue *de re publica* rules out any possibility that Latins or Italians participated in the benefits of Tiberius' bill, for Cicero makes Laelius charge that Tiberius 'persevered in behalf of Rome's citizens, but paid no heed to the rights and treaties of allies and Latins'. How could the knowledgeable Cicero have written in that way if he knew that non-Romans as well as Romans were eligible for land grants from the agrarian commissioners?[8]

But that argument is far less secure than it looks. If we read the passage in question in full, we discover that Laelius is simply being made to take the predictable Scipionic line in 129, the dramatic date of this dialogue which is supposed to be taking place a few weeks before Scipio's death that year. No one denies that by 129 disputes had arisen between the commissioners and some non-Roman communities over the precise boundaries between their land and the Roman public land, and perhaps too about the rights of such communities to use the *ager publicus*. The non-Romans concerned applied for help and support to Scipio, presumably aware of his antagonism to the commission. Scipio responded to the appeal, and successfully urged on the Senate that disputes between the Roman state and its Latin and Italian allies went beyond the competence of the agrarian commission and must fall to be looked into by consuls and Senate. The consul Tuditanus was charged by the Senate to look into the matter; but he quickly abandoned it as too difficult, and took himself off to the Balkans, leaving things unresolved.[9] The initiative in these complaints can only have come from the ruling classes, who constituted the governments of the non-Roman communities; they were the very men who stood to lose heavily if large holdings of their own were held to lie within the bounds of Roman public land. That in this matter 'the poor were at one with the rich' there is no evidence;[10] nor is it even likely that they

[7] e.g. Badian, *FC* 169ff.; Earl, *Tiberius Gracchus*, 20ff. On Gaius Gracchus' βιβλιον, see above, p. 6.

[8] Cicero, *de re pub.* 3.41: 'Ti. Gracchus perseveravit in civibus, sociorum nominisque Latini iura neclexit et foedera.' The whole passage has to be read (it is cited below, p. 106 n. 73) to savour fully its vague generalizations and pompous oversimplifications. As Greenidge observed (*Hist. of Rome* i.136 n.2), it is improbable that Tiberius consciously or deliberately violated treaty rights, and 'Cicero is perhaps stating the result, rather than the intention, of the Gracchan legislation'.

[9] Appian, *BC* 1.19; Livy, *Per.* 59. On this episode, see further below, p. 92. On *ager publicus* in allied possession, see above, p. 11.

[10] Thus Earl, *Tiberius Gracchus*, 21, where no evidence is offered in support.

were, unless we suppose that the magnates took care to alarm the small men by misleading them about the implications of the commission's activities (admittedly, a fairly simple task in a semi-literate and very ill-informed society). Overall, it looks as if Laelius is simply voicing a tendentiously generalized complaint about the alleged besmirching of Rome's honour by a rival political clique; and that fits in well with the context of 129, as we should expect from the knowledgeable and sympathetic pen of Cicero three generations later. It is in tune with the outburst of Tubero earlier in the same dialogue, when he is heard claiming that the activities of Tiberius Gracchus and his associates had created division within a previously harmonious Roman people, and deploring the bad behaviour of the group opposed to Aemilianus and his friends, the upsetting of Latins and Italians, the daily new wickednesses of seditious agrarian commissioners, and the consequent perturbation of 'men of wealth' ('viri locupletes').[11]

To descry propaganda at work on one side while ignoring its probable presence on the other is disingenuous or partisan. It is only too plausible to suppose that anti-Gracchan spokesmen, and later writers influenced by them or in sympathy with them, chose deliberately to suppress or play down or ignore the truth that the Italian protests in 129 emanated not from the mass of the Italian peoples but from the magnates, and sought to mask 'party' thrusts behind a show of selfless highmindedness. The tears which Tubero, Laelius, and company were shedding in 129 over the plight of Latins and Italians were revealed within four or five years as crocodile tears by the strenuous opposition which they and their like put up to the proposals of Fulvius Flaccus and Gaius Gracchus for a wider extension of political equality and opportunity to Latins and Italians. And it was plainly not Gracchans who were responsible for the arrogant brutalities against non-Romans in Italy of which Gaius Gracchus was to complain so fervently.[12]

Arguments adduced from the extant fragments of the agrarian law of 111 (Bruns, *FIR* 11 = Riccobono, *FIRA* 8) are insecure, and the inferences drawn from it inevitably uncertain, for the inscription on which it is preserved is full of gaps and leaves wide ground for conjecture. It has been

[11] *de re pub.* 1.31: 'concitatis sociis et nomine Latino, foederibus violatis, triumviris seditiosissimis cotidie aliquid novi molientibus, bonis viris locupletibus perturbatis.' And cf. above, p. 27 n. 24 and p. 37 n. 55.

[12] Gaius' speech *de legibus promulgatis* (*ORF*[2] pp. 190–2) is quoted below, pp. 186 and 221.

urged that lines 3 ('QVOIQVE DE EO AGRO LOCO EX LEGE PLEBEIVE
SCITO IIIVIR SORTITO CEIVI ROMANO DEDIT ADSIGNAVIT') and
15 ('AGER PVBLICVS POPVLI ROMANI QVEI IN ITALIA P. MVCIO L.
CALPVRNIO COS [= 133 B.C.] FVIT EIVS AGRI IIIVIR A.D.A. EX
LEGE PLEBEIVE SCITO SORTITO QVOI CEIVI ROMA[*no agrum dedit
adsignavit* . . .') indicate that only Roman citizens had been granted assignments of land by the Gracchan commissioners. But Mommsen took these
to be references to allotments in colonies and not to individual viritane
assignments such as Tiberius Gracchus' commissioners made; he argued
that assignments by lot ('SORTITO') implied colonial assignments. Even
if some may feel that Mommsen failed to produce cogent evidence that the
lot could not also be used for viritane assignments (e.g. to resolve the
problems of a superfluity of applicants or varying quality of different plots
of land), nothing prevents the assumption that other missing sections of
the inscription may have made separate reference to non-Romans, or that
sensitivity about the *iura et foedera* of Latins and Italians led the drafters
of this law to eschew any reference to them. Again, since there are wide
gaps following the two sections just cited, it is not implausible to suppose
that somewhere in these Latins and Italians could also have been mentioned (the gaps amount to over 300 and 100 letters respectively). Finally,
it could well be that the law of 111 was concerned to convert into private
property only those allotments of public land which were held by Roman
citizens, leaving holdings of non-Romans as they were. In any case, as will
be argued later, it could be that Tiberius had legislated to provide allotments for non-Romans as well as Romans, but that these did not in the
event materialize.[13]

It is also very questionable whether we should be too readily prepared
to lend an ear to suggestions that Appian's use in this context of the words
Italiôtai or *Italia* is confused or anachronistic. As Cuff has insisted, it is
'difficult to believe that he could ever have been guilty of wilfully misunderstanding in his source the difference between Romans and Italians
before 90 B.C., especially in a section which deals inter alia with a war

---

[13] For Mommsen's analysis of the agrarian law of 111, see his *Gesammelte
Schriften* i.65–145; and, on this particular point, see especially ibid. 101 ff. For the
most recent detailed treatment, see Johannsen's dissertation *Die lex agraria des
Jahres 111 v. Chr.* (Munich, 1971), where this particular point is treated on pp.
220 ff.

between the two.'[14] It seems, moreover, unlikely that Gaius Gracchus could have hoped to get away with blatant misrepresentation of a central feature of a law which was still in operation, only nine or ten years old at most, and readily available to be consulted and cited verbatim to give the lie to any distortion of this magnitude. All in all, it is prudent to reserve judgement on this point; especially if we allow that Tiberius may originally have intended that non-Romans should benefit, but that allotments to them failed to materialize when the interested protests of wealthy occupiers succeeded in checking any redistribution of public land the proper control and destination of which was disputed by the governments of the non-Roman communities of Italy.[15]

There is also disagreement about the antecedents of Tiberius' proposal so far as concerns the date of the existing enactment *de modo agrorum* which limited permissible occupation of public land to a maximum of 500 *iugera*, which constituted the base from which he started. It is a matter of much more than academic interest: not only our own view, but surely also that of contemporaries, must take or have taken account of the question of how obsolete were the rules Tiberius now purposed to enforce. Both Appian and Plutarch refer to the existing limits,[16] and it was once customary to identify them with the Licinian laws of 367-360.[17] But the tradition about those laws is highly questionable; and in any case a limit of 500 *iugera* plus the additional right to pasture 100 large and 500 small beasts

---

[14] Cuff, *Historia* (1967), 179. Cuff's article should finally dispose of this argument, since to my mind it establishes that Appian (whether rightly or wrongly is another question) throughout the first book of his *Bella Civilia* meant 'Italians' when he wrote Ἰταλιῶται. Galsterer (*Herrsch. u. Verw. im Rep. Italien* 37ff.) shows that 'Italia' was in the second century a geographical term which comprised both Roman and non-Roman Italy; but that is irrelevant to Appian's use of the ethnic Ἰταλιῶται. See also Shochat (*Athenaeum* (1970), 25–45) for a spirited defence of Appian in this matter. Nagle's attempt (ibid. 372–94) to prove that Appian was wrong is loosely argued and too often marred by a failure to appreciate that the evidence is not as clear-cut as he makes it out to be. The description of τὸ Ἰταλικὸν γένος as συγγενές (above, p. 42, n.6) is especially to be noted.

[15] This argument I first heard from my tutor C.E. Stevens many years ago. See too Greenidge (*Hist. of Rome* i.115) and Brunt (*IM* 76), who is 'far from convinced that Gracchus did not intend to include Italians among the beneficiaries of his law'. Note also the judicious caution of Sherwin-White (*RC*[2] 217–18). I am also impressed by the arguments of Gabba (*Athenaeum* (1964), 29–41), for all that they are suggestive rather than conclusive. See also Shochat (art.cit.).

[16] *BC* 1.8. *TG* 8.

[17] See (e.g.) Strachan-Davidson's note ad loc. in his edition of Appian, and *CAH* vii.538–40. For the Licinian legislation, see Livy 6.35, Plutarch, *Camillus* 39.

on further public land is implausibly high for the second quarter of the fourth century; probably, here as elsewhere, the issues and conflicts of the late Republic have been retrojected into an earlier age either through carelessness or through a desire to uncover or manufacture precedents. To judge by the run of his account, Appian (who himself says nothing about the date of the existing regulations and certainly makes no mention of Licinius) thought that his precedent law came fairly late in the story he was telling; and the provision he records that a fixed proportion of free labourers had to be employed alongside or as well as slaves in order to keep an eye on them is surely anachronistic for Licinius' day. The rules which Tiberius took as his starting point had most probably not come into existence until the period just before the Hannibalic War, or even the early part of the second century itself.[18]

Nevertheless, however certain or uncertain that may be, it is important to stress that we do know that we are not dealing with an obsolete set of rules long lost sight of in the mist of time. The rules, whenever they had reached this final form, were being enforced in the second century. In 196 and 193 there were many prosecutions of cattlemen (*pecuarii*) for violations of the rules governing the pasturing of beasts on public land; in the earlier year only three convictions resulted, but in the latter convictions were numerous, the responsible public officers being the aediles, who may have taken action on the information of the men who farmed the grazing-tax (*scriptura*).[19] Far better evidence comes as a result of the good fortune which has preserved, for us to read, the contemporary observations of the elder Cato in 167.[20] In the course of a speech delivered in that year, Cato argued that the state of Rhodes ought not to be punished for simply having wished that Rome might fare badly in her war with Macedon, but only if—which was not the case—she had suited her actions to her wishes. To drive home his argument against the manifest injustice of such a punishment, he drew an analogy with the law governing the use of Roman public land:

Does there [he asked] exist any law so harsh as to prescribe penalties for anyone who merely wishes to exceed the permitted limits on the number of cattle which can be pastured on public land, or to hold more than 500 *iugera*? Of course, we should like to have more of everything; but so long as the wish remains unimplemented in action the law leaves us unpunished.

[18] On this point of chronology, see Appendix 1 below, p. 208.
[19] Livy 33.42, 35.10. Toynbee, *HL* ii.261.
[20] Cato cited in full in Appendix 1 below, p. 209.

It is hard to believe that Cato would have chosen to make his point (or rather weaken it) by citing obsolete regulations more honoured in his day in the breach than in the observance; and the obvious conclusion to draw is that in 167 the regulations were currently accepted as enforceable. If so, the abuse which Tiberius was seeking to check may have been little more than a generation old, at least in its more flagrant and widespread manifestations; and it could even be that Laelius' move in this matter, which he had abandoned on encountering strong opposition from influential men, had been in reaction to the early growth of this abuse in the fifties and forties.[21]

We are nowhere enlightened about the details of how Tiberius' bill affected the grazing of cattle on public land over and above the 500 *iugera* which individual *possessores* were to be allowed to retain as their private property.[22] Moreover, modern scholars disagree about the size of the allotments distributed by the Gracchan commissioners, and the number of poor citizens who received allotments. The maximum size of any allotment may have been set at 30 *iugera* (a little under 20 acres or 8 hectares); but that is no more than an inference which has been drawn from a provision in the *lex agraria* of 111 which is concerned with a special category of holdings not exceeding 30 *iugera*.[23] In practice, the sizes of allotments must surely have varied with the quality and location of the land; and there is good reason to believe that the average size would have been quite a bit smaller than 30 *iugera*, perhaps more like half that figure.[24]

---

[21] Above, p. 33.

[22] That the numbers of beasts which could be pastured on public land were additional to the 500 *iugera* which could be occupied, and not an alternative, is demonstrated by Tibiletti in his reply (*Athenaeum* (1950), 248ff) to the doubts expressed by Last (*Riv. stor. ital.* (1949), 432). I suspect that Tiberius was prepared to allow *ager publicus* which was too poor for arable farming to go on being used for cattle-raising, though with a rent or poll-tax charged to those who pastured more than only a few cattle. In general, see Appendix 1, below p. 209.

[23] So Mommsen suggested, basing himself on line 14 of Bruns, *FIR* 11: '[*sei quis tum cum haec lex rogabitur* <gap of nearly 150 letters> *agri colendi cau*] SA IN EUM AGRUM AGRI IUGRA NON AMPLIUS XXX POSSIDEBIT HABEBITVE: [*i*]S AGER PRIVATUS ESTO.' See Appendix 1 below, p. 216.

[24] Earl, *Tiberius Gracchus*, 19. Brunt (*IM* 194) assumes that a family of four needed for subsistence at least 120 *modii* of wheat (a *modius* equalled roughly 15 English gallons) a year, plus something on top to sell to buy essentials like oil, wine, etc. Some 10 *iugera* of medium-quality land would produce (allowing for fallowing) between 75 and 150 *modii* annually. Of course, peasants might supplement their

However, argument has mostly centred around the effectiveness of Tiberius' bill so far as concerns, firstly, how many people derived (or could have been expected to derive) benefit from it; and, secondly, whether Tiberius' proposed scheme was the best way to tackle the problem.

The census figures of the Roman population which are preserved in the *Perioche* of Livy are often called in aid.[25] They give the following totals of citizens for the years in question:

136	317,933
131	318,823
125	394,736
115	394,336

Prima facie, it is tempting to seek to connect the steep rise of some 75,000 citizens registered between 131 and 125—almost 25 per cent, and far in excess of any natural increase—with the *lex Sempronia agraria* of 133 and with the distributive activities of the commission which it created.

Several arguments have started from the assumption that the census recorded, not the total number of male citizens, but only the number of *adsidui*, viz. those who were registered as possessed of at least the minimum property needed to qualify for legionary service. The poorest citizens were on this view excluded from the count, so that the increase between 131 and 125 can be interpreted as due to the success of Tiberius' commission in providing tens of thousands of landless citizens with land. Others have posited a lowering of the *adsiduus* qualification about 130/129 in response to the legionary manpower shortage. Against both these explanations, however, is the consideration that it has long been questioned whether the census totals did include only *adsidui* rather than all male citizens of every class and category. Brunt's recent exhaustive examination has convincingly reaffirmed and strengthened the conclusions of Beloch, Fraccaro, and Tenney Frank that 'the census figures purport to comprise

---

livelihood by pasturing a few beasts on common land or by seasonal work on larger nearby estates. Tibiletti (*Athenaeum*, N.S. 28 (1950), 228) suggests 8 *iugera* on modern standards (say a couple of hectares). But this is just to give some sense of scale. Quality of land was very variable, and except on such soil as the Campanian 10 *iugera* would not have sufficed. See *IM* 295 for varying sizes of allotments in the past.

[25] Brunt, *IM* 78–83 for detailed arguments and references to what follows. Brunt's treatment is not only the most recent but also (in my judgement) the most convincing. On the reliability of the census totals for 125 and 115, see p. 50 n. 27, below.

all adult male citizens'.[26] Granted that this is so, and provided that the
transmitted figures are sound,[27] the increase of 75,000 between 131 and
125 cannot be used as a rough yardstick to measure how many men became *adsidui* through grants of Gracchan allotments, and other explanations must be sought. One possibility is improved registration; and a
different connection could be found with the agrarian law by supposing
that previously censors had not troubled much to seek out and register
citizens who were very poor or homeless and unsettled, and that the men
themselves did not bother to register: now some of them had been settled
on plots of land and so got counted, while others took care to be registered
so as to ensure their eligibility for land-grants. Even so, it is awkward that
there is no sign of any upswing in the 131 figures, two years after the law
had been passed; to attribute this to administrative delays and uncertainties
may account for few actual allottees being counted in 131, but does not
explain why the figures for that year were not swollen by those poor
citizens who became concerned to register once the commission had been
established.[28] The plain truth is that we move among uncertainties, and
can reach only the negative conclusion that the transmitted census figures
cannot properly or safely be used to try to quantify the practical consequences of the *lex agraria*.[29]

It is possible to doubt, too, whether Tiberius' proposals were the best

[26] *IM* 24–5. Cf. 15–25 in general. On a supposed lowering of the census qualification at about this time, see Gabba, *Esereito e società*, 13ff.

[27] Toynbee, *HL* i.471 follows Beloch *et al.* in disbelieving the accuracy of the
transmitted totals for 125 and 115 and wanting to emend them. But (Brunt, *IM* 78)
'the census totals cannot be demonstrated to be corrupt except by proving that they
are inexplicable'; and this their doubters have not done. For obvious reasons, figures
in any manuscript are open to corruption more than other elements, and it is easy to
question them if they create difficulties for particular theories. To establish that they
are correct is normally impossible; while to question their reliability is only too easy,
and hard to refute positively.

[28] Carcopino suggested (*Bull. Assoc. Budé* 22 (1929), 14: see also his *Hist.
romaine* II.i.234) that the increase can be explained by assuming unusually extensive
manumissions of slaves, and large-scale enrolments of Latins and Italians on the
census list *c.* 125 in connection or association with the franchise activity of Flaccus
as consul in 125. There is no direct evidence in support; and one would expect some
echo at least of all this in our sources. But the mere fact that this suggestion could be
made by so acute and well-informed a scholar is a measure of our ignorance.

[29] Earl's calculations. (*Tiberius Gracchus,* 26) are valueless, thanks to his unhappy major error in confusing *ager publicus* and *ager Romanus.* The truth is that we
have no information about the total amount of *ager publicus* in Italy in 133, nor how
much of it was being exploited by individuals in breach of the existing rules.

way to help impoverished peasants and strengthen the state. At first sight, it does not seem of much use to put men back onto small plots of land so long as the political and social and economic conditions that had driven them off in the first place remained substantially unchanged. Even if fresh big wars did not break out to drag them from their farms, the prospect was not bright. Of course, it may be that the allotments were to be larger and hence more viable than the peasant farms of the past. Cash crops might have been a paying proposition; but they would need capital investment, and not all the distributable land can have been the best place to raise them or market them. In so far as the agrarian 'problem' was 'solved' in the late Republic and early Empire, it was by the planting of colonies on good sites outside Italy and by the considerable unofficial emigration that went on, especially to Provence, Baetica, and Tunisia, the great Roman and Italian 'colon' areas. 'At nos hinc alii sitientis ibimus Afros' was the last resort of the landless Meliboeus of Vergil's First Eclogue.[30] The 'problem' was not easily to be 'solved' by replanting men to pursue a subsistence existence, farming land which was often better suited to other systems of exploitation, and in circumstances hostile to such a way of life. Nevertheless, rather than dismiss Tiberius Gracchus with all the easy wisdom of hindsight as a man who sought to treat the symptoms of the disease rather than its underlying causes, we should give him credit for at least recognizing that the disease existed and for setting about trying to do something about it.

A broadly similar defence can be made against charges that his measure was inequitable. The profits made out of Rome's expansion during the second century had certainly been enormous; and it was not unreasonable that the common people, so far from being impoverished, should benefit, or at least that their sufferings should be alleviated.[31] To take something from the rich to give to the poor, and at the same time help safeguard Rome's social stability and the supply of legionary manpower, does not sound so very unfair or revolutionary, especially when we reflect on how much the peasant soldiery had contributed to that expansion. But this measure did not draw money direct from public funds; and it took only

---

[30] *Eclogues* 1.64. On overseas settlement at this period, see A.J.N. Wilson, *Emigration from Italy in the Rep. Age of Rome.* I am not convinced by Brunt's doubts on this subject in *IM*, ch. 12.

[31] As Tiberius himself declared (Appian, *BC* 1.11): δίκαιον τὰ κοινὰ κοινῇ διανέμεσθαι.

from those of the rich who had invested capital in excess holdings of, or pasturage on, *ager publicus*, and did not touch those who had sunk their money into other categories of land, or urban property, or other than real property. Even in the case of the first category, the incidence of the exaction must have been uneven. Hence the measure was in some real sense inequitable, whatever the legal rights and wrongs. It was also politically delicate in so far as considerable areas of *ager publicus* were so located as to give rise to disputes with the non-Roman communities. In theory, a more effective alternative could have been to adopt the policy of using public funds to buy land for distribution, as Rullus was later to propose in 63 and Julius Caesar in 59. But once again we are being wise after the event. Quite probably such an approach was not conceivable or feasible in 133, and public funds (Asia was not yet a province) insufficient.[32] At all events, even after Tiberius' violent death, the *fait accompli* of his law was accepted, and we certainly hear of no constructive criticism of his proposal having been put forward. This may suggest that the inequity was not thought to be too serious, and that alternative ways of finding land to distribute were not believed to be readily available.

The appointment of Tiberius himself as one of the three commissioners instituted by his agrarian law seems to have been without precedent[33] — it may be noted that eleven years later Livius Drusus ostentatiously left others to be chosen as commissioners under his colonial law, and won credit thereby.[34] The precise legal powers enjoyed by the commissioners elude us; but the successful intervention of Aemilianus in 129 does not show that these powers were defective, and it certainly cannot be assumed that they were then varied or abolished, since a senatorial decree could not override a law passed by the people. The answer probably is that in 129 it was held by the Senate that disputes between the commission and allied governments went beyond the competence of the commission and fell to be settled by consuls and Senate.[35]

[32] On the low level of public funds at this time, see Astin, *Scipio Aemilianus*, 166. By the time of the Rullan and Caesarian proposals there were vastly greater revenues to exploit, and rich new revenues from Asia Minor to look forward to. All the same, Tiberius surely assumed that the Senate would make a reasonable amount of public money available to his commissioners once the bill had been carried.

[33] Badian, *Aufst. u. Niedrg.* I.i.705. Cf. Cicero, *de leg. agr.* ii.21.

[34] Plutarch, *CG* 10. Such commissionerships were of considerable political value—but Drusus may have known or suspected that his own colonies would never be founded (cf. below, p. 171).

[35] Last, *CAH* ix.44; below, p. 92.

In reporting the creation of the commission, Appian speaks of its three members as 'changing every year': ἐναλλασσομένους κατ᾽ ἔτος.[36] His wording has led to much discussion, but Carcopino's explanation seems to be the right one. He suggested[37] that what we might term the 'chairmanship' or 'presidency' of the commission rotated each year among the three members; and indeed it is hard to see what else Appian can have had in mind when he chose from among the available compound forms of the verb ἀλλάσσεσθαι the fairly rare compound with the suffix ἐν-.[38] The work of the commission was going to take several years, and its members could be expected to need time for other activities: of the first three appointed, Tiberius was himself tribune at the time, while his brother Gaius was serving with the army in Spain. It is generally accepted that the membership of the commission changed its composition only on the death of one of its members; and it is inherently improbable that they were subject to annual re-election, or that Appian would have used the language he does use to describe annual election or re-election.[39]

---

[36] *BC* 1.9.

[37] *Gracques*, 125 ff., esp. 149–53. His explanation has been widely but not universally accepted. (Badian, o.c. 704 peremptorily dismisses it as 'one of Carcopino's fancies', while offering no worthwhile argument against it.) Carcopino's argument is in my opinion a model of cogency and thoroughness, and marred only by occasional overschematism in peripheral detail. (See further below, p. 133).

[38] The instances of this compound in LSJ all point to internal or mutual exchanges or interchanges. Cf. Carcopino's own list of examples.

[39] That the office is listed along with other elective offices in the extant *repetundae* law of 123 (the Tabula Bembina: Bruns, *FIR* 10) does not tell against this. For it was an elective office of the Roman state, and there was no reason to omit it just because it was tenable for longer than most—though not all—such offices. The view that the Gracchan *IIIviri* were only annual appointees and subject to annual election is hard to accept in the face of the evidence that the same men apparently held office for several years, and were replaced only on death. Continuity was obviously desirable. The *IIIviri* who normally organized colonial foundations usually took two or three years over the job, and did not change. The Gracchan *IIIviri* had a far more complicated and lengthy task than that. I also find it significant that Cicero, in his speeches in 63 against Rullus' agrarian bill, though he several times points a contrast between Rullus' bill and the laws of the Gracchi (e.g. in the matter of the *ager Campanus*), fails to contrast the five-year term of office proposed by Rullus for his commissioners with the one-year term which some scholars would posit for the Gracchan *IIIviri*. Given that Cicero is playing every trick in the book to discredit Rullus' proposal, his failure to exploit this one is impressive support for Carcopino's reading of the situation. Finally, it must be stressed that Gaius Gracchus was one of the three commissioners initially elected early in 133, for all that he was currently serving with the army in Spain and not due back for quite some time. What would be the point of electing the absent Gaius in 133 if the elections were annual?

A small number of boundary stones (*termini Gracchani*) have been un-earthed in Italy bearing the names of the commissioners.[40] One batch gives the names in the order C. Gracchus, Ap. Claudius, and P. Crassus, which is how the membership of the commission stood after Crassus had been elected to replace the dead Tiberius Gracchus.[41] Another stone pre-sents the order M. Fulvius Flaccus, C. Gracchus, and C. Papirius Carbo;[42] Flaccus and Carbo are known to have replaced Claudius and Crassus, them-selves both dead by 130.[43] Finally, we have a stone with the names Crassus, Claudius, C. Gracchus, in that order;[44] unlike the others, it is not an original but a stone set up over fifty years later by M. Terentius Varro Lucullus when he was restoring boundaries in an area where the Gracchan commissioners had established them previously. Its evidential value has been doubted because, whereas all the original stones use the *nomina* of the commissioners, this stone mixes two *nomina* (Licinius and Claudius) with a *cognomen* (Gracchus); but that is not in itself a cogent reason for assuming that the order of names has been varied in the copying.

On Carcopino's theory, the order of the names varied as the 'chairman-ship' rotated among the three commissioners. Hence, he dated all the first batch to 131, on the reasonable hypothesis that Gaius' turn first came round in that year: when elected in 133 he was by far the junior of the three and actually out of Italy. If that is correct, his subsequent turns will have come round in 128, 125, and 122. The last date is interesting, for in 122 Gaius left Rome for Africa to see to the organization of his new colony of Carthage/Junonia, and that at a time when affairs at Rome really called for his closest attention. He had been preceded in Africa on this same business in 123 by Fulvius Flaccus, who presents us in 122 with the extraordinary spectacle of an ex-consul holding office as tribune of the *plebs*. If, as I believe to be true, the foundation of Junonia came under the umbrella of Gaius' extended *lex agraria* and so was the responsibility of the same commissioners, it could be that it was as chairman for 122 that Gaius had to go to Africa; and this could also explain the bizarre sight

---

If, however, election was for the duration of the commission's task—which would evidently take some years to complete—this puzzle disappears.

[40] *ILLRP* i pp. 269–75.

[41] Ibid. nos. 467–72.

[42] Ibid. no. 473. And see below, p. 60, n. 57.

[43] Appian, *BC* 1.18; Plutarch, *TG* 21.

[44] *ILLRP* i. no. 474.

of an ex-consul on the tribune's bench that year: knowing that Gaius would have to be away, it was arranged that his most influential, experienced, and energetic collaborator should hold the fort in his absence. One could go further, and, assuming that Flaccus was chief commissioner in 123, the year he went to Carthage himself, and hence previously in 126, try to discern a connection between the 126 chairmanship and the alien expulsion bill of Pennus in that year and the citizenship proposals of Flaccus as consul in 125. But, although we may suspect that there may be something in this, the evidence does not allow us to do more than sniff the air.[45]

The scant surviving *termini* are manifestly far too few to serve as a statistical base. But it is intriguing that one comes from quite near Capua.[46] While we cannot allow this one stone (which need show no more than that the commissioners surveyed the area, or could have some connection with Gaius' road-making) to outweigh the plain statement of Cicero that the Gracchi left the Campanian Land untouched, and the fact that it was not until Caesar's law of 59 that it was earmarked for distribution, this chance epigraphic discovery can at least remind us how ignorant we are about the details of the *lex Sempronia agraria*. Another puzzle is presented by an acephalous inscription from Polla in the Val di Diano in Lucania recording the construction of a road from Rhegium to Capua by a man who says that he had as praetor in Sicily hunted down fugitive slaves there or in southern Italy and handed them back to their owners. The inscription pretty certainly dates from 132 or 131, and was set up either by T. Annius Rufus, a praetor for 132, or (a little less probably) by P. Popillius Laenas, one of the consuls for 132. The builder of this road claimed that he was

---

[45] See further below, pp. 132 and 171. It is worth noting that Flaccus' name immediately precedes that of Gaius in *ILLRP* i no. 473. (For a full table, see below, p. 133 n. 50.) Nagle (*Athenaeum* (1970), 383-4) attempted to trace in some detail the areas where the Gracchan commissioners were most active; but the evidence he relied on is very uncertain and of heterogeneous quality, and hence much of Nagle's argument is insecure and over-speculative. I prefer the tried caution of Frederiksen in *Dial. di arch.* (1970-1), 330-57. To take just one example: the obvious temptation to rush to attribute the evidence of centuriation around Lucera and San Severo in the modern Foggiano (and other examples which may or may not fall in the same category) to the activities of Gracchan commissioners must be resisted (Frederiksen, 342-4); the dating is so uncertain that no secure conclusion can begin to be drawn.

[46] *ILLRP* i. no. 467 = ILS 24, discovered at Sant' Angelo in Formis, not far from Capua itself. On the Campanian Land, see above, p. 42 n. 4.

the first man to have caused herders to abandon public land to arable farmers.[47] Whether he did this in Sicily or in southern Italy is not made plain; the link between road-building and the assignment of land along the route for riparian settlement is well known, as too is that between free-ranging armed slave-herdsmen and slave revolts. But the claim underlines the topicality and importance of Tiberius Gracchus' own warnings and aspirations.

The provision of Tiberius' law that the allotments were to be inalienable[48] has bred much controversy, with some scholars labelling it 'an economic absurdity' and others denying this and calling in alleged parallels from Kenya or the Punjab as well as from the ancient Spartan *kleros* system. Whether these parallels help may be doubted, since it may be questioned whether they are true parallels. On the other hand, charges of economic wrongheadedness are themselves misguided if it is accepted that Tiberius was aiming not at maximizing the profitability of Italian agriculture but at resettling small free peasants on the land (οὐκ ἐς εὐπορίαν ἀλλ' ἐς εὐανδρίαν), and thereby at least *inter alia* shoring up Rome's reserves of military manpower and lessening her potentially dangerous dependence on slave-labour. If such were his aims, the inalienability provision is easy to understand and to justify: it both safeguarded the commission against dishonest applicants who planned to sell off their allotments quickly, and also shielded genuine allottees from the pressures which were otherwise only too likely to be brought to bear on them by the rich owners anxious to buy their land back. It is worth recalling that Appian refers to such pressures as a factor in the original process of dispossession of the small peasant proprietor; and he later tells us that, when after the death of Gaius Gracchus the allotments were quickly made alienable, the rich proceeded to buy the land back and even to force allottees to sell.[49] Given that failure to prescribe inalienability clearly could, and pretty certainly would, have led to such consequences, there is no need to search further for an explanation. Even if it is contended that it would be

---

[47] *ILLRP* i no. 454 = *ILS* 23: '. . . eidem praetor in Sicilia fugiteivos Italicorum conquaeisivei redideique homines DCCCCXVII eidemque primus fecei ut de agro poplico aratoribus cederent paastores.' For Annius rather than Popillius Laenas as the author of this inscription, see Wiseman, *PBSR* 32 (1964), 21–37; 37 (1969), 82–91– attractive, but not conclusive. Against Annius, see Hinrichs, *Historia* (1969), 251–5.

[48] Appian, *BC* 1.10. That a small rent-charge was levied in connection with the inalienability provision is probable; see above, p. 42 n. 4.

[49] Appian, *BC* 1.7 and 27; cf. below, p. 203.

futile—for what was the allottee to do if he simply could not make ends meet and could not raise money on the value of his holding?—it would still be necessary; and we cannot assume that Tiberius shared the view that this sort of dilemma would arise very often.[50]

A final uncertainty concerns the stages in the evolution of the agrarian bill between its first promulgation and its actual passage into law. Appian has nothing to say about this, but Plutarch reports a change. He begins by stressing the mildness and generosity of the original proposal: it not only exacted no punishment from those who had broken the law by exceeding the legal limits, simply calling on them to surrender the excess, it even added on top of that a 'reward' or 'premium', τιμή.[51] What Plutarch meant exactly, or understood, by this τιμή is far from clear: it could perhaps refer either to the grant of a firm legal title to the 500 *iugera* they were allowed to keep, or to the concession of further land above that limit in respect of children; although the 'child allowance' is not mentioned as such by Plutarch, or indeed by any other source than Appian.[52] However, it may be that Plutarch's source was referring to something entirely different such as (e.g.) compensation for improvements, a feature ignored by Appian who was content to register only the final form of the bill without retailing the preliminary stages. For Plutarch later says that Tiberius was so irritated by the selfish opposition of the vested interests that he retaliated by making his bill harsher, and simply ordered them to quit that land which they occupied in breach of the existing laws.[53] Whether this alludes to the withholding of secure title to 500 *iugera*, the cancellation of the 'child allowance', or the retraction of some other concession unknown to us, is a question to which we can give no confident answer. Granted that Plutarch was right about the bill's being modified in the direction of greater sternness to the large holders, the cancellation of the 'child allowance' may be marginally preferable as the explanation as more readily explaining the delight the poor are said to have experienced when they heard

---

[50] For recent discussions of the inalienability provision, see Badian, *Aufst. u. Niederg.* I.i.680–1. For my part, I share Frederiksen's opinion that 'the inevitable doom of the smallholder was still a long way off', and 'the evidence suggests . . . that the agrarian programme of the Gracchi was very far from being an archaizing dream' (*Dial. di arch.* (1970–1), 356).

[51] *TG* 9.

[52] See above, p. 41 n. 3.

[53] *TG* 10: κελεύων ἐξίστασθαι τῆς χώρας ἣν ἐκέκτηντο παρὰ τοὺς προτέρους νόμους.

of the amendment, since there would be more land to distribute; and perhaps too it could help to account for the silence of all but Appian about this feature of the law. But it is not the sort of detail we should expect to find outside Appian and Plutarch anyway; and any blow at the rich would no doubt have evoked popular pleasure.[54]

To conclude, a summary will be helpful.

At some time in the period just before the Hannibalic War, or (less probably) in the early decades of the second century, a limit of just over 300 acres had been fixed by law as the maximum amount of public land (*modus agrorum*) that any one man might occupy and work, and the number of large and small beasts (cattle and horses, sheep and pigs) he might additionally pasture on public land was limited to 100 and 500 respectively. Legal penalties both could be and were exacted against those who broke the law, and they were recognized as in force and enforceable in an extant speech which Cato delivered in 167. By 133, however, these regulations had come to be widely disregarded, apparently with impunity. The *lex Sempronia agraria* reasserted the legal limit of 500 *iugera* (we hear nothing about the extra pasturage provisions) and required those who actually held more to surrender the excess. Land thereby recovered was to be distributed among poor peasants, possibly in allotments not exceeding 30 *iugera* or just under 20 acres, but the size of the lots surely

[54] This is a tiresome puzzle. A little later on (*TG* 10) Plutarch tells a story of Tiberius' offering to pay out of his own pocket to his obstructive colleague Octavius the τιμή of the considerable amount of public land Octavius himself would have to surrender if the agrarian bill were carried. The surprising and scarcely credible comment that Tiberius possessed very modest personal means from which to find this τιμή smacks of later romantic colouring, for the Sempronii Gracchi can scarcely not have been well off. But the story cannot be dismissed on that ground alone: the offer could have been an effective *ad hominem* ploy, with its implication that Octavius' opposition was founded less on principle than on personal interest. However that may be, the τιμή here seems to mean the 'price' or 'value' of Octavius' threatened holdings; hence (unless Plutarch has got into a muddle, as he may well have done, perhaps at some point through misunderstanding a Latin source's nuances) it cannot mean the same as the τιμή of *TG* 9, since that would imply the bizarre conclusion that Plutarch meant that the original bill proposed to pay those illegally holding or exploiting public land the value of the illegal amounts which the bill required them to surrender. Plutarch's version of a toughening up of the original bill could just have some connection with the enigmatic notice of Livy, *Per.* 58 that Tiberius 'promulgavit et aliam legem agrariam qua sibi latius agrum patefaceret, ut idem triumviri iudicarent qua publicus ager qua privatus esset.' Given the messes the Epitomator can so readily and so often make of his original Livian material, we have to take this sort of thing

varied with the quality and location of the land. These allotments could not be alienated; and they were probably subject to a token rent. It is certainly possible—but no more than that—that Latins and Italians were eligible for lots as well as Roman citizens; but, if so, probably few if any received lots, possibly in consequence of the obstruction successfully mounted by the governing classes of the non-Roman communities to the move by the commissioners to distribute public land which they claimed to lie within their boundaries or which was otherwise the subject of argument about jurisdiction and control.

How many individuals were assisted, or were expected to be assisted, by the law we cannot say. The extant census totals cannot safely be used as a basis for calculation for several reasons. Obviously, the numbers involved were large: otherwise it would be very hard to make sense of the action of the well-informed and experienced men behind the bill, the widespread enthusiasm which it aroused, and the vigour and vehemence of the opposition it evoked. Only public land in Italy was to be dealt with; and even here the *ager Campanus* was to be left undistributed, or substantially undistributed at least. Those required to surrender land were to be recompensed by the grant of a secure title to the 500 *iugera* they were allowed to keep, and with extra land on top for any children they had. One or other of these concessions may perhaps have been withdrawn in the final form of the law.

The law provided for the people to elect a commission of three men with authority to carry through the complex work of checking, surveying, delimiting, recovering, exchanging,[55] and assigning. It would clearly take years to complete the work, so provision was made for the active executive chairmanship of the commission to rotate annually among its three members, thereby freeing the others in large part for other duties and activities. The three commissioners first elected were Tiberius Gracchus himself, his younger brother Gaius, and his father-in-law Ap. Claudius Pulcher. We know of no changes in the commission's membership other than those occasioned by the death of a commissioner. The commissioners had legal powers of adjudication and of enforcement of their decisions;[56] but a few

---

with a pinch of salt; but it does suggest that Livy's original full account may have referred to two stages in the agrarian legislation of 133, whatever they were.

[55] On exchange of lands, see Brunt, *IM* 299.

[56] The *termini* nos. 467–73 in *ILLRP* i, all originals, give the commissioners the title *IIIvir(ei) a(gris) i(udicandis) a(dsignandis)*—the last might less probably be ex-

years later, in 129, these were held to be insufficient to cover disputes which in effect involved the determination of the territorial boundaries of Latin and allied Italian communities, and the legal rights of such communities as opposed to those of private individuals.[57]

---

panded to *a(dtribuendis)*. The later restoration, no. 474, calls them *IIIvir(i) a(gris) d(andis) a(dsignandis) i(udicandis)*. Why the *dandis* was added here I cannot fathom; but nothing can be rested on it. Bruns, *FIR* 9 and 10 both use the form *IIIviri a(gris) d(andis) a(dsignandis)* in their lists of officers of state. That might be taken to show that by 123 the *IIIviri* had lost (in 129) their power *iudicare*; but, even if they had, which seems to me very unlikely, one would expect that it had been restored by Gaius Gracchus. But his *lex agraria* could have been carried later in 123 than Bruns 9 and 10: see Appendix 3 below, p. 236. On the whole I suspect that the answer is that Bruns 9 and 10 meant to include any agrarian commissioners, whether they had the power *iudicare* or not.

[57] Tibiletti in a recent essay on 'Les Tresviri a.i.a. lege Sempronia' in *Hommage à la mémoire de Jérome Carcopino* (Paris, 1977), 277ff., which has just come to my attention, accepts Carcopino's theory about internal rotation among the three commissioners, but is unhappy about the implications of talking of a rotating 'presidency'. The point is a fine one. If the word 'president' is felt to be improper, we can instead speak of 'executive commissioner' or suchlike, as in fact I have commonly done.

There has also just come into my hands an article by M. Pani (Istituto Lombardo, Acad. di Sci. & Lett., Classe di Lettere, 1977, 389–400) concerning the Gracchan *cippus* recently discovered in Apulia, in the area to the north-west of Lucera. Pani suggests that its discovery there lends strength to the view that the centuriation of which evidence has been revealed by aerial photography in this region may well be of Gracchan rather than of pre-Gracchan date. But (see above, note 45) I fail to see that this new *cippus* in any way tells against the cautiously sceptical approach of Frederiksen to such questions. Surely few, if any, scholars can have believed that the mere fact that no Gracchan *cippi* had hitherto been found in Apulia meant that none had ever existed. Even now, less than a dozen have been unearthed throughout the whole of Italy.

This particular *cippus* is substantially intact (see the photographs in Pani's article) but preserves only the names of Fulvius Flaccus and Gaius Gracchus (in that order) and their designation as *IIIviri a.i.a.* There is no room for a third commissioner's name, and Pani very reasonably suggests that the stone can therefore be dated to the period when there was a gap in the membership of the commission following on the death of Crassus and before Carbo had yet been appointed to fill his place.

I cannot myself see that this new stone adds any further relevant material to the debate about whether Carcopino was right or wrong in postulating a circulating executive chairmanship of the commission, or to the question about what happened to the adjudicatory powers of the commissioners in 129—a point also pursued by Pani in another very recent article (*Annali della Facoltà di Lettere e Filosofia*, Bari, 1976–77, 131–46), where he comes to the conclusion (on what seem to me to be inadequate grounds) that these powers were indeed lost but then quickly restored to the commission after Aemilianus' death shortly afterwards.

IV

THE TRIBUNATE OF 133

Tiberius Gracchus was one of the ten men elected to enter their year of office as *tribuni plebis* on 10 December 134. How many votes were cast for him, how many of his colleagues-elect were in any sense committed for him or against him, how much organized opposition he had encountered, we cannot say. Appian's narrative carries us straight into the tribunate itself. Plutarch starts earlier, and says that Tiberius turned to the project of agrarian reform immediately after he was elected, fired by the popular appeals and slogans which were scrawled up all over Rome calling on him to recover the public land for the poor.[1] But it is hard to believe in such appeals as the main instigation of his programme rather than as a response to his advertisement of it. It is highly likely that he had outlined his over-all programme and plans while seeking election, and that the last months of 134 which followed his election were occupied with the detailed drafting of his bill so as to have it ready for prompt promulgation, as well as with discussing tactics and options with his leading collaborators and sounding out opinion and reactions.[2] If so, it is a reasonable guess that actual or potential opponents were early alerted to what was in the offing, and that Tiberius' difficult and obstructive colleague M. Octavius may have been run as a candidate by them rather than (as Plutarch has it) only later won over by them.[3]

Tiberius took his agrarian bill directly to the popular assembly of the *concilium plebis*, without first submitting it to the Senate for discussion and consideration. The obvious explanation for this is that he knew that he could not count on the Senate's giving his bill a favourable or sympathetic hearing. Men like Claudius, Scaevola, Crassus, and Tiberius himself were admirably qualified to do that sort of calculation and get their answers right; and, if their soundings had suggested that a reasonably warm

---

[1] Appian, *BC* 1.9. Plutarch, *TG* 8. 3–4.

[2] The Rullan agrarian bill was presented to the assembly in December 64 as soon as Rullus took office as tribune. It was common knowledge at the time that the tribunes-elect had been busy on its drafting ever since their election that summer: Cicero, *de lege agr.* ii. 10–12.

[3] Plutarch, *TG* 10.1. Appian (*BC* 1.12) is not specific on this point.

response might be hoped for, it would have been at least ill advised not to try to secure it. No doubt Octavius could have deployed his tribunician veto in the Senate as he was to in the *concilium plebis*. But if the trend of debate and opinion had driven him to use his veto in the Senate, Tiberius would have been left in the favourable position of being able to point to underlying senatorial approval of his bill if he had then taken it to the assembly. Obviously, however, if such approval was not to be looked for, it was better tactics not to approach the Senate in the first place, and thus avoid the charge that he had begun by conceding that respect was due to it, only to change his tune once he found it hostile. Theoretically, one can allow that there could have been a significant number of senators who would have approved of, or acquiesced in, the agrarian proposals so long as they had first been submitted to the Senate, and who opposed the bill only because of Tiberius' high-handed treatment of that body and through apprehension of the latent long-term dangers which such bypassing threatened. But it is most unlikely that the bill's very experienced and knowledgeable backers would have been guilty of such inept miscalculation and maladroitness.

For a tribune to bypass the Senate and take a proposal straight to the *concilium plebis* was not illegal—although precisely what 'legal' or 'illegal' means or meant will have to be considered later. It has, indeed, been asserted that to act thus was, at least in certain circumstances, not even 'outrageous and quite unheard of'.[4] But we here tread uncertain ground. The surviving books of Livy take us down only to the year 167, so that we are left with a broad gap in our information on this sort of topic during the next thirty years or so. Even before 167, it has been suggested, there may have been instances of such bypassing which Livy did not trouble to record;[5] but this could conceivably have been true only of the most routine and uncontroversial of measures, and so the suggestion does not really help us, given that Tiberius' bill was both novel and contentious. What we

---

[4] Badian, *Aufst. u. Niederg.* I.i.695.

[5] Ibid. 694–5: 'Possibly, if the process was non-controversial, Livy would not even have mentioned it. (He does not report routine legislation.)' But Badian's argument here from the silence of Livy and others about the enfranchisement of all *cives sine suffragio* (which, he asserts, 'it is generally agreed' had taken place before 133) inclines to circularity. Sherwin-White in fact argues persuasively that *municipia civium sine suffragio* did still exist at least as late as 133: *The Roman Citizenship*[2] 210–14 (see below, p. 110).

do know for certain is that in 287 a *lex Hortensia* had enacted that what the *plebs* should command should bind all Roman citizens; thus as a consequence *plebsicita* were not obliged to secure senatorial approval.[6] On a famous occasion in 231, the tribune C. Flaminius carried a law to distribute the *ager Gallicus* in north Italy in small lots among Roman citizens, against keen opposition from most of the Senate; this *plebiscitum* evidently became law without winning the prior approval of the Senate, and it is the most obvious and apposite precedent for Tiberius Gracchus' own action.[7] In 188, the tribune C. Valerius Tappo promulgated a bill to grant full Roman citizenship to some Italian communities; four of his colleagues moved to veto it on the ground that it had not first secured the Senate's endorsement, but 'on being instructed that it belonged to the People and not to the Senate to grant such rights to whomsoever the People chose, they abandoned their plan', and the bill passed into law.[8] These two measures of Flaminius and Tappo are our only secure examples of such bypassing, but we can add three further later proposals which almost certainly fall into the same category: the abortive attempt of C. Licinius Crassus in 145 to have priesthoods filled by popular election, and the two ballot laws of 139 and 137, the *lex Gabinia* and the *lex Cassia*.[9]

Hence, to act as Tiberius acted was not unprecedented, for all that the precedents were few. None of these earlier proposals had sought, of course, to take possessions away from existing citizen holders, however ill founded their claims might be.[10] All in all, however, a good case can be made out for maintaining that Tiberius was not going outside accepted constitutional limits, as indeed we should expect, given the standing and experience of the established *principes civitatis* who stood at his shoulder.[11]

[6] Reff. in *MRR* i *sub anno*. Cf. Mommsen, *SR* 2.312.

[7] *MRR* i *sub anno*.

[8] Livy 38.76. 7–9.

[9] Badian, o.c. 695. *MRR* i *sub annis*. One could pretty safely add to this list a law carried in 189 or 188 by the tribune Terentius Culleo about enrolling the children of freedmen on the census lists. It is mentioned only by Plutarch (*Flamininus* 18.1), who says that Culleo ἐπηρεάζων τοῖς ἀριστοκρατικοῖς ἔπεισε τὸν δῆμον ταῦτα ψηφίσασθαι. For a list of second-century *plebiscita* known to have been carried with the approval of the Senate, see Earl, *Tiberius Gracchus*, 45.

[10] What the previous position had been of the land distributed by Flaminius' bill is unclear. It may well have been leased out; but there is no indication that, if it was, the lessees were regarded as in any way securely holding the land for which they paid rent to the state.

[11] 'Their present power and future hopes too deeply rooted in the oligarchic system and its spoils to wish to destroy it.' (So Earl, *TG* 14–15.)

If to bypass the Senate would be to give the kiss of death to his proposal, they would be revealed as foolish amateurs even to contemplate such tactics—and that they assuredly were not. It had worked in the past. No doubt, feathers would be badly ruffled and voices raised in protest; but, once the bill had gone through the *concilium plebis*, the chances may well have seemed good that opposition would eventually subside into intermittent sniping and obstructiveness.[12] Although in 145 the eloquence of C. Laelius had sufficed to balk Crassus, in 231 Flaminius' bill had gone through and stayed on the statute book, with beneficial effects in the long run for Rome's military manpower. In 188, tribunes had been talked out of resorting to the veto; and again, in 137, although the tribune Antius Briso threatened a veto and was encouraged in this by the consul M. Lepidus, he was eventually dissuaded from carrying out his threat by Aemilianus, and Cassius' bill went through.[13] But now, in 133, it was to be a different story. This time the tribune Octavius stuck to his guns, and so faced Tiberius with the cruel choice between abandoning or seriously modifying his bill, or else finding some way to override his colleague's veto. As we know, he chose the latter course, and took the momentous step of having a fellow-tribune removed from his office.[14] It may be that he and his associates had foreseen this very eventuality, and had laid plans in advance about how to deal with it if it should arise. But equally it may be that Octavius' unprecedented obduracy took them quite aback, and dislocated their arrangements, and confounded their calculations; and that behind this *bouleversement* lay a failure on their part to assess correctly just how provocative the 'confiscatory' aspect of the *lex agraria*

[12] Badian (o.c. 690ff.) develops this point well.

[13] Cicero, *de nat. deorum* 3.5 and 43 (Laelius); *Brutus* 97 (Aemilianus).

[14] Id. *de legg.* 3.24: 'Quin ipsum Ti. Gracchum non solum neglectus sed etiam sublatus intercessor evertit. Quid enim illum aliud perculit nisi quod potestatem intercedenti collegae abrogavit?' On the unprecedented character of Octavius' veto more will be said later (below, p. 78). Why Octavius did not deploy his veto to prevent his own deposition from office is an unresolved mystery. It may be that even his nerve broke at last in face of the ugly mood of the assembly on this occasion; or it may be that the vote was judged to be tantamount to an election, when a veto could not be used. Fraccaro (*Studi sull'età dei Gracchi* i.112) thought it was because he did not want to recognize the proceedings as in any way valid. It may even be that his supporters judged that the game was up, and further resistance futile. Or the answer could lie in some combination of any or all of these factors. We are simply left guessing.

was to prove.[15] On the evidence available to us, we cannot be sure either way.

The formal public confrontation over the bill must have begun with its promulgation, probably in December 134. This will have marked the start of a series of *contiones* at which its merits or shortcomings and its detailed provisions could be dilated on and argued about. The starkly economical account of Appian does not bother with all this, although echoes of these public debates may reverberate in his general narrative. Plutarch is fuller.[16] How much his account derives from later imaginative reconstruction rather than resting on firmer ground such as Tiberius' surviving speeches, we may legitimately question. In particular, we cannot place total reliance on his somewhat obscure reference to a toughening up of the first version of the bill in angry response to opposition.[17] But, for all his general tendency to paint the lily, we can readily accept from Plutarch that a fine battle of words and tempers went on before it came to the actual voting. Tiberius and Octavius, he says, engaged in almost daily contests from the speakers platform, all conducted at the highest level of serious debate (although Tiberius' alleged offer to buy his colleague off would seem to fall a little below that[18]). Tension mounted, and Tiberius used his tribunician authority to pronounce a ban on all public business, and set his personal seal on the doors of the public treasury, in an attempt to force the issue.[19] There were rumours of plots against his life, and he took to openly carrying a sword-stick.

When the day for voting on the bill at last arrived, the meeting was turbulent and noisy. When Tiberius ordered the bill to be read out, Octavius used his veto to forbid it. Tiberius berated him soundly, but had to give him best, and adjourned the assembly for a week, *in nundinum*. To

[15] See above, p. 10. To the complaints there listed may be added (Appian, *BC* 1.10.3) the fears of bankers and moneylenders who had advanced loans on the security of holdings of *ager publicus* which were now threatened.

[16] Appian, *BC* 1.11–12; Plutarch, *TG* 9–10. On procedural detail I have followed Appian's tighter account.

[17] See above, p. 57. But very likely the speech summarized at *TG* 9.4 (above, p. 40) has its roots in Tiberius' *ipsissima verba*.

[18] Above, p. 58.

[19] It is debatable whether a tribune had a formal right to proclaim a *iustitium*; but that does not much matter here, for the veto could have been deployed to much the same effect. For references to modern discussions, see Astin, *Scipio Aemilianus*, 346–7.

this second meeting he came with a powerful guard of supporters, meaning to overawe his colleague; but again Octavius vetoed the order to recite the bill, and the crier had to remain silent. The two men fell to mutual recrimination, and the crowd became restless and rowdy, until certain influential persons (Plutarch specifies the ex-consuls Manilius—or Manlius—and Fulvius) intervened and persuaded Tiberius to refer the dispute to the Senate,[20] a suggestion which (so Appian says) he seized on eagerly, convinced that all men of goodwill were bound to recognize the merits of his bill. That seems odd, else why had he not gone to the Senate in the first place? Perhaps the truth is that he now felt that the Senate would note his determination and be anxious to avoid further trouble. Either way, he was quickly disappointed, for all he got there was strong opposition and even abuse. Hurrying back to the assembly, he announced another postponement *in nundinum*: but at this third meeting the assembly was to have two items of business on which to vote—the agrarian bill itself, and a motion concerning the propriety of a tribune's remaining in office if he used that office to thwart the will and oppose the interests of the assembly by which he had been elected to hold that office.[21]

It may be that Tiberius first offered Octavius the option of having the people vote whether he himself should continue in office, undertaking to step down at once if the vote went against him. If so, Octavius was too wily to fall into so obvious a trap. So the vote began to be taken against Octavius. The first tribe to vote voted for his deposition, whereupon Tiberius begged him to give in and drop his veto. Octavius refused, and the counting continued. There were thirty-five tribes in all, and the first seventeen all went the same way. With just one more needed to produce the required majority, Tiberius desperately redoubled his appeal to Octavius to give in and not drive him to the extremity of ousting a colleague from office, insisting on the justice and the national advantages of his bill, and stressing the enormous popular enthusiasm it could plainly be seen to have aroused. It was to no avail; despite the fearful pressures on him, Octavius was not to be moved. Calling Heaven to witness his repugnance at being forced to this step, Tiberius summoned the eighteenth tribe to vote. Octavius was no longer a tribune. Appian says merely that 'he slipped

[20] Above, p. 28.
[21] Appian, *BC* 1.12.5: εἰ χρὴ δήμαρχον ἀντιπράττοντα τῷ δήμῳ τὴν ἀρχὴν ἐπέχειν. And see above, p. 64, n. 14.

away and ran off'—διαλαθὼν ἀπεδίδρασκε. But Plutarch has it that Tiberius instructed his personal freedmen attendants to drag him from the tribunal; the crowd surged forward menacingly, but those of the rich who were present linked arms to protect him and he managed to escape, although not before one of his loyal servants was blinded by the mob as he covered his master's flight, all this to Tiberius' great distress, who rushed to quiet the violence once he saw what was afoot. With Octavius gone, a new tribune was elected in his place;[22] and, free at last from the impediment of Octavius' veto, the bill was voted into law. Subsequently, Tiberius and his brother Gaius and his father-in-law Claudius were elected by the assembly as the three commissioners who were to implement the provisions of the *lex Sempronia agraria*. The election of Claudius is significant, in that it shows that the *princeps senatus* himself in effect publicly set his imprimatur on the law, and hence too by implication on the bypassing of the body whose doyen he was and on the deposition of Octavius.

Feeling ran high in the Senate, however, and Tiberius was bitterly attacked. On the motion of his own cousin, the *pontifex maximus* Scipio Nasica (consul 138), the commissioners were voted derisively trivial sums for their expenses. Nasica's hostility to his cousin knew no bounds (something worth remembering when we are confronted by modern assumptions that close kinship can be taken to imply friendship and political collaboration), allegedly exacerbated by the fact that he was himself a very large occupier of *ager publicus*. In turn, the people's indignation grew sharper; and the sudden and unexplained death of one of Tiberius' friends and the curious *post mortem* features exhibited by the corpse led to wild rumours of poisoning. Tiberius himself put on mourning, and appealed to the commons to look after his family, as if despairing of his own life.[23]

Chance now took a hand. Attalus III Philometer, whose kingdom of Pergamum was later in large part to constitute the Roman province of Asia in what is now western Turkey, had recently died, leaving a will in which he named the *populus Romanus* as his heir. The Pergamene envoy

[22] The new tribune's name is given variously as Mummius (Appian), Minucius (Orosius), or Mucius (Plutarch): the latter says he was a mere lackey (πελάτης) of Tiberius'. Incidentally, to judge by Tiberius' alleged later argument against Annius (below, p. 71) all thirty-five tribes had gone on to vote for Octavius' deposition.

[23] Plutarch, *TG* 13. Appian's sparer narrative moves straight from the election of the commissioners to the tribunician elections of 123, without referring even to the Attalus bequest.

happened to reach Rome with the will just at this moment, and he may even have stayed as a guest in Tiberius' house.[24] Be that as it may—and the envoy's seeking out Tiberius is as likely to be due to his current political eminence as to inherited family influence[25]—Tiberius was soon aware of the facts, which could not in any case have been kept secret from him and his friends, who included the resident consul in office and the *princeps senatus*. He saw an opportunity ready to hand to circumvent the opposition, and introduced a bill to appropriate the royal moneys of Pergamum to provide equipment and so on to help his new allottees get settled and to make proper provision for the commissioners' expenses.[26] That in itself need not perhaps have caused such a very great stir; one may suspect that, had the news about Attalus not turned up so opportunely, Tiberius would have brought a bill before the assembly to raise money from some other public source. But he took a long step further than that, and announced that arrangements for the future administration of the territories which made up the Pergamene kingdom would not be left for the Senate to settle. He would himself in due course bring proposals on that subject to the *concilium plebis* for the people to decide.[27]

This was to give hostages to fortune with a vengeance. Precedents could be pointed to for bypassing the Senate even with a bill as novel in many

---

[24] Badian, *FC* 174. But the story Pompeius told about what he saw the envoy doing in Tiberius' house does not entail that the envoy was lodging there; he could have been paying a call. For a brief account of the story of the 'provincializing' of Asia, see below, p. 153, in connection with Gaius Gracchus' *lex de provincia Asia*.

[25] Badian (ibid.) stresses the importance of Tiberius' father's tour of inspection in the East in 165. Professor Brunt, in conversation, has bolstered my own doubts that this was the whole story. There must have been a number of eminent Romans around who could show at least as good a claim to patronage where Pergamum was concerned. As Greenidge observed (*A History of Rome* i.129), no sane ambassador could have neglected Gracchus.

[26] Livy, *Per.* 58, reports Tiberius promising a bill to divide the Pergamene moneys among those poor citizens who could not get land grants because there was not enough land to go round. The epitomator's obtuseness and clumsiness in condensing his original, at second or third hand, is such that Livy's own authority cannot be claimed for such evidence. But behind the muddle could lie an original Livian account which had Tiberius projecting 'social benefit' measures that went beyond the *lex agraria*, perhaps using the Pergamene moneys to fund them. On such possible new proposals, see below, p. 73.

[27] Plutarch, *TG* 14.1. (Perhaps the Senate did not challenge the propriety in principle of voting proper sums to the agrarian commissioners, but argued that funds were low. The opportune news from Pergamum allowed Tiberius to get round that objection.)

respects as the *lex Sempronia agraria* was. The deposition of a tribune
could be defended as the only way to allow free expression to the people's
will in this matter. Octavius' stubborn intercession could be attacked as
itself unprecedented. The election of Tiberius as a commissioner under his
own law, and the earmarking of public funds to make the law effective,
could both be justified as essential parts of a single complex of actions and
reactions which were all inextricably bound up one way or another with
the overall agrarian programme. But matters of public finance—and, surely,
the accumulated reserves and anticipated future revenues of the Pergamene
kingdom far exceeded the conceivable needs of the agrarian programme
alone—and foreign affairs and relations lay by practice and precedent and
convention within the Senate's sphere; and the Senate was the body
which, even in the view of the neutral outside observer, was eminently
best qualified to deal with them. Polybius, in his roughly contemporary
account of the workings of the Roman state, went so far as to say that the
people had nothing at all to do with such matters: πρὸς δὲ τὸν δῆμον
καθάπαξ οὐδέν ἐστι τῶν προειρημένων.[28] Perhaps one should see Tiberius'
move into this field merely as an angry response to the harrassing tactics
of his opponents, or as a shot fired across their bows to encourage them to
sheer away and break off the engagement. To others it may look as if he
was shifting his sights to fresh targets.

One can readily believe Plutarch when he says that this really set the
cat among the pigeons.[29] Two senior consulars, Q. Pompeius (consul 141)
and Q. Metellus Macedonicus (consul 143), who were to share the censorship in 131, both weighed in with attacks on Tiberius. It is worth noting
that they were usually at odds with each other, and in particular that a
year or two later Macedonicus was along with Scaevola to step into the
places left vacant in the senatorial leadership by the deaths of Crassus and
Claudius.[30] Pompeius lived near Tiberius, and he told the Senate that it
was thanks to this proximity that he knew that the Pergamene envoy
Eudemus had presented Tiberius with a royal diadem and a robe of royal
purple for his use when he became King of Rome. We may suspect that
Plutarch, or his source, has taken too literally what was meant to be a
sardonic joke; but the humour—if humour it was—had a sharp and bitter

---

[28] Polybius 6.13.7.
[29] *TG* 14. 1–2: Ἐκ τούτου μάλιστα προσέκρουσε τῇ βουλῇ.
[30] See above, p. 27.

edge, and Pompeius' words find an echo in those which Cicero puts into Laelius' mouth in his dialogue *de amicitia*: 'Ti. Gracchus regnum occupare contatus est, vel regnavit is quidem paucos dies.'[31] Orosius reports that Pompeius solemnly pledged himself to bring an indictment against Tiberius as soon as his year of office was up and he could no longer rely on his office for immunity.[32] Macedonicus for his part drew an acid contrast between Tiberius' own father, whose austere sternness as censor had so impressed and intimidated his fellow-citizens that they used to douse their lights if he happened to be passing on his way home from a dinner for fear lest their own entertainments should seem immoderately prolonged, and the censor's abandoned son who was lighted home every night by a bodyguard of desperadoes drawn from the dregs of society. Even more senior than either Pompey or Metellus was the veteran ex-consul of 153, T. Annius Luscus, who challenged Tiberius to a formal *sponsio* that his deposition of Octavius had violated the sacrosanctity of a tribune.[33]

Tiberius proceeded to summon a meeting of the assembly, and ordered Annius to appear before it, meaning to indict him himself.[34] But Annius first asked him a question: 'Suppose you purpose to dishonour and disgrace me, and I appeal for protection to one of your colleagues, and he comes to my assistance, and you get angry, will you have him deposed?' This question is said to have left Tiberius so much at a loss for a reply that he at once dismissed the assembly. Later, he gave the people a considered answer. Admittedly, a tribune was sacrosanct, in that he was consecrated to the People and stood at their head. But, if he changed course and deprived their vote of its force, then he stripped himself of his office by failing to honour the conditions on which he had been elected to hold it.

---

[31] *de amicitia* 41. Macedonicus' speech was preserved by Fannius in his *Annales*, so Cicero, *Brutus* 81, attests. 'Purpura et diadema' occurs in a speech of Gaius', presumably in a reference to this occasion (Appendix 2 below, p. 224).

[32] Orosius 5.8.4.

[33] A *sponsio* was a sort of judicial wager. Each party put up an agreed sum and the one adjudged the loser forfeited his money. See Crook 'Sponsione Provocare' in *JRS* 66 (1976), 132–8. That Annius was a consular is revealed by Livy, *Per.* 58.

[34] Plutarch, *TG* 14.3 speaks disparagingly of Annius' character but concedes him great skill in disputation. Cicero says he was 'non indisertus' (*Brutus* 79). Later grammarians were able to cite verbatim from Annius' speech (Festus *apud ORF²* 106: 'T. Annius Luscus in ea quam dixit adversus Ti. Gracchum'). On Annius' age and seniority, see Badian, *Aufst. u. Niederg.* I.i. 715 n. 137. He could have been closely related to the Annius who was the probable author of the acephalous Polla inscription (above, p. 55).

Tribunes could imprison consuls: both were elected by the People, so surely the People itself had the right to deprive a tribune of the powers it had granted him if he abused those powers? A tribune who ordered the Capitol to be destroyed or the dockyard to be burnt down would be a wicked tribune, yet still a tribune: but a tribune who put down the People was no tribune at all. He drew analogies with the expulsion of the last Etruscan king from Rome, and with the punishment of the Vestal Virgins, who for all their sacrosanctity could be buried alive if they were found guilty of unchaste and sinful conduct. Instances had been known of tribunes resigning office or asking to be excused. Finally, if it was right and lawful that a man be elected tribune by a vote of a majority of the tribes, how could it not be more right and more lawful for him to be deprived of that office by the vote of them all?[35]

That is powerful counter-punching. Once again, how much goes back to a sound contemporary source, or how far the theme has been worked over later, it is hard to say. But it is impossible to believe that the question was not asked and argued and answered in these sorts of terms at the time. It has been maintained that there was no answer to Annius' question, and that Tiberius' arguments were irrelevant to it.[36] It can, however, equally be maintained that it was Annius' question which was irrelevant and sought to blur the issue. Annius gave an example of the overriding of the *ius auxilii*: that tribunician prerogative to extend protection to a citizen threatened by magisterial action was central to the tribunate and went right back to its traditional origins centuries earlier; and it was clearly distinguishable from the allied and derivative right of a tribune to use his *ius intercessionis* to veto an act of positive legislation, and especially an act which commanded overwhelming support from the *concilium plebis*.

[35] Plutarch, *TG* 15. The idea of destroying the Capitol turns up again elsewhere. Cicero has it that when, after Tiberius' death, Laelius was questioning Blossius in the course of the official inquiry, he asked Blossius if his devotion to Tiberius was such that he would have obeyed him if he had ordered him to fire the Capitol. Blossius replied that Tiberius would never have given such an order, but that he would have obeyed him if he had. Valerius Maximus tells much the same story, and so too does Plutarch, who erroneously substitutes Nasica's name for that of Laelius, and has Blossius adding that Tiberius would never have given such an order 'unless it were to the People's advantage'. See Cicero, *de amicitia* 37; Val. Max. 4.7.1; Plutarch, *TG* 20.2. For the likely topical relevance of Capitol and dockyard, see Badian, o.c. 708. On the role of the tribune as 'the servant of the People', see below, p. 78 n. 47.

[36] Badian, o.c. 715.

Even if it were held, as it could have been, that Octavius had been in effect extending *auxilium* to citizens who stood to lose considerable amounts of land; nevertheless, leaving aside the fact that these threatened holdings were strictly illegal, it was one thing to answer the appeal of a private citizen threatened by the executive action of an officer of state (and that was what the *ius auxilii* was basically about), and quite another to use the *ius intercessionis* to frustrate a *plebiscitum* which commanded massive public support and was designed to recover for the state what belonged to the state. Moreover, Annius chose to ignore the important truth that it was not Tiberius Gracchus who had deprived Octavius of his office, but the *plebs Romana* itself.

The conflict of opinion about the rights and wrongs of Tiberius' action is as old as politics, and recalls Burke's famous distinction between a delegate and a representative. Sides are likely to be taken in accordance with personal political conviction, or bias.[37] Given that Rome had no written constitution, it is hard to see what other criteria there could be for taking sides. A determinedly casuistical partisan could even have urged in answer to Annius that it was Octavius who had in effect been seeking to prevent Tiberius from extending *auxilium* in its broadest sense to the mass of poor citizens whose livelihood and reasonable aspirations had been for too long at the mercy of a rich, privileged, and over-influential few, who were now to be compelled to give back to the people what had been stolen from them. Certainly, the Cicero of the *pro Cornelio* would have found it no great task to embroider so promising a theme; and, only a generation or so earlier, the elder Cato in his speech *de praeda militibus danda* had drawn an acid contrast between 'the thieves who stole private property and spent their lives in gaol and the thieves who stole public property and spent their lives in luxury' (*ORF*[2] p. 91).

It was now that Tiberius took the final and in retrospect fateful step of announcing that he would be a candidate for re-election as a tribune. Once again we move into an area of controversy, both as to the reasons behind his decision and as to what steps he may have taken to win electoral support. Appian, economical as ever, merely notes the threats which were

---

[37] Compare the keen arguments currently going on in the United Kingdom about how far the Parliamentary Labour Party is, or should be, bound by the decisions of the Labour Party Conference and other extra-Parliamentary bodies; how far individual M.P.s should be regarded as 'mandated' by their constituency parties; and so on.

mounting to attack Tiberius for his alleged irregularities once he should revert to the status of a private citizen and lose that immunity from prosecution which his office conferred on him. It is unwise to argue too tightly from the silence on some details of Appian's laconic account. Plutarch, however, has Tiberius coming forward with a new programme: a bill to reduce the period of military service, another concerned with the right to appeal to the People from judicial decisions, and a third to establish 'mixed' courts composed in equal parts of *equites* as well as senators. The unquestionably confused 'fragments' of Dio Cassius (they are not really fragments but crudely condensed excerpts from his full narrative) refer to a bill about military service and another 'whereby Tiberius sought to transfer the courts from the Senate to the *equites*'. And Velleius Paterculus talks of a 'promise to give citizenship to the whole of Italy'.[38] There is smoke here, but scant chance of locating the fire which was its source. All we can safely say is that, whatever Tiberius' motives may have been for seeking a second year as tribune, it is reasonable to suppose that he put forward some sort of programme. Simply to write these reports off as infections from later propaganda designed to father on to him some of his younger brother's schemes is rather arbitrary. Gaius is often said to have learned a lesson from reflecting on the narrowness of his brother's 'power-base': it could be that Tiberius woke up to the same truth himself, albeit belatedly.

Both Appian and Plutarch are at one in stating that Tiberius' main motive in seeking re-election was his fear of what lay in store for him once he reverted to private status. Some modern writers have doubted that, at any rate as being the whole explanation; and, to my mind, with some justice.[39] It is not a subject to pontificate on. The seeking after simple reasons for anything, especially simple single motives, may only too often

[38] Appian, *BC* 1. 13–14. Plutarch, *TG* 16. Dio fr. 83.7 (Boissier). Vell. Pat. 2.2 ('pollicitus toti Italiae civitatem'). The reference in Pliny, *NH* 33.34 to what 'the Gracchi' did about the courts ('iudicum autem appellatione separare eum ordinem primi omnium instituere Gracchi discordi popularitate in contumeliam senatus') is unfortunately too loose to rely on; it could be a slip or a casual oversimplification or generalization, though on the face of it Pliny is saying that both brothers interested themselves in the question of *equites* serving as *iudices*. For a possible Livian allusion to a 're-election programme', see above, p. 68 n. 26.

[39] Thus, e.g., Last, *CAH* ix. 31–2; Scullard in Marsh, *A History of the Roman World 146–30 B.C.*[3], 407; Astin, *Scipio Aemilianus,* 351; Lintott, *Violence in Republican Rome*, 182. Badian is far too brusque (o.c. 716) in his rejection of this view.

be a quest for oversimplification. It can, one would venture to suggest, scarcely have escaped Tiberius and his associates that to stand for a second consecutive year of office would be to pile Pelion on Ossa: to sharpen yet further the knives that were already being whetted against him, to add to the list of his alleged 'crimes against the state'. Apart from his public undertaking to introduce legislation about the cities of the Pergamene kingdom—a most complicated business, and certain to absorb months of investigation and negotiation and drafting—there was surely an urgent need to buttress his position against the attacks he is said to have feared by proposing new measures; merely to hold a second tribunate would do no more than postpone the day of reckoning. The argument that he would not have had so very much to fear from a trial does not lack weight, especially if some friendly new tribunes could be elected to lend their *auxilium* or deploy their veto to protect the people's champion. His popularity with the *populus* at large needs no emphasis; and the election of Crassus Mucianus as consul by the timocratic centuriate assembly in summer 132, not to speak of Fulvius Flaccus' election as consul six years later, warns against assuming too readily that Tiberius would have been sure of a hostile reception if he had stood trial before that assembly in 132. Nevertheless, cool reason does not always explain men's actions. That Tiberius was right to be worried about his personal future, and that he made emotional appeals to the people to help save him, we have no good reason to doubt. Either way, the bid for re-election turned out to present more difficulties than it removed, and it proved to be the last straw so far as his opponents were concerned. In retrospect, it was a crass piece of misjudgement; and, if his motive was solely or chiefly self-preservation, it is a bitter irony that a move designed to save him from political extinction should have cost him his life.

The confusion which attended the last act of Tiberius' tribunate finds a small but appropriate echo in the narrative of our two main authorities. Plutarch refers to two assemblies, what seems to be an abortive one to vote on the new legislative proposals, followed by a second, electoral, assembly. But attentive reading reinforces the belief that his language is at best ambiguous and Plutarch himself badly muddled. It is preferable, on these and more general grounds, to follow Appian, who talks of two assemblies both of which were electoral.[40] As his enemies began energetically

---

[40] Appian, *BC* 1. 14–16; Plutarch, *TG* 16–19. L.R. Taylor (*Athenaeum* (1963),

canvassing for rival candidates to keep him out of a tribunate in 132, Tiberius in some nervousness started to summon supporters from the country districts. But people there were busy with summer work, so with time running out he appealed fervently to the poorer city-dwellers to use their votes to save a man whose work for the common people had put him at this great risk. On 'polling-day' the first two tribal votes declared were both for Tiberius, but the 'rich' thereupon objected that it was illegal for a man to hold the tribunate twice in succession. Rubrius, the tribune on whom the lot had fallen to preside that day, wavered; whereat the man who had been elected tribune in Octavius' place called on Rubrius to surrender the presidency to himself. Rubrius was ready to do this, but at this point the other tribunes insisted that a new president must be properly selected by lot, and everybody fell to bickering. With the tide beginning to run against him, Tiberius caused the assembly to be adjourned, and put on a public show of formal mourning, not neglecting to use his family—as indeed was customary—to heighten the pathos of his appeal.[41]

'The surviving accounts of that final day of Tiberius' tribunate'—so writes Astin, whose careful reconstruction is here broadly followed—'differ on many points, with the result that any reconstruction of the events is inevitably hypothetical in important respects. This is no cause for surprise. The events themselves were characterized by confusion and disorder, and to the difficulties confronting even a contemporary who wished to ascertain the facts must be added the patent interest of each side in ascribing to their opponents as much as possible of the blame for the catastrophe; it may be doubted if there was ever a primary account which was not tendentious.'[42] Crowds began gathering on the Capitoline after a night of tension, marked at its end (so the story went) by a clutch of sinister omens. On one version, Tiberius' supporters occupied the centre ground of the

---

51ff., (1966), 238ff.) would reconcile the two sources by taking both the last assemblies (in effect, a single, but interrupted, assembly) as legislative, the legislation in question being a bill to make re-election (*continuatio*) legal. But, apart from the consideration that one would expect Tiberius to have presided if his own bill were the subject, her arguments are unconvincing—and unnecessary, since the conflict can be explained as the result of a venial confusion on Plutarch's part better than by departing from both accounts. For arguments against Taylor's thesis, see Earl, *Athenaeum* (1965), 95 ff.; Badian, o.c. 720–1.

[41] Dio fr. 82.8 says that his mother Cornelia also was with him.

[42] Astin, *Scipio Aemilianus*, 218–26.

assembly place and the Capitoline temple even before sunrise. There was a great deal of noise and excitement. Meanwhile, the Senate was meeting in the nearby Temple of Fides. Most of Tiberius' fellow-tribunes continued to be obstructive, despite the cheers and enthusiasm which had greeted his own arrival; and the din and shoving and scuffling not only made formal procedures impossible but also served to obscure what precisely was going on and fed lively rumours, even including one that Tiberius was moving to depose all his obstructive colleagues. No doubt reports of varying completeness and accuracy kept reaching the Senate, where Scipio Nasica called on the consul Scaevola to take firm and positive action to deal with the situation. But Scaevola refused to countenance the use of force, maintaining that the best policy was to 'wait and see': if anything illegal or criminal should take place, then would be the time to overrule it. That did not satisfy Nasica, who rounded on the consul and charged him with cowardice and treachery, and called on everybody who wanted to defend law and order to follow his own lead. While all this was going on, Fulvius Flaccus slipped away, and with great difficulty ploughed his way through the press of people to reach Tiberius with a warning of the dangers that were threatening. As Nasica and a throng of senators and their personal retainers moved purposefully on their way, the crowd began to fall back, overawed by the spectacle of the *pontifex maximus* himself and so many prestigious followers.[43] It must be doubted that either side had any clear idea of what it was going to do; the only weapons employed seem to have been staves and hastily improvised cudgels wrenched from wooden benches and such. Although some 200 or 300 are reported to have died, a great many of them may well have been crushed or trampled to death in the stampede to get out of the confined meeting-place. As Tiberius himself sought to make his escape, he stumbled over men who had already fallen, and as he rose he was struck on the head by the leg of a stool wielded by his fellow-tribune P. Satureius, and at least one other

---

[43] Appian (*BC* 1.16.3) notes, in some puzzlement, that Nasica had wrapped the hem of his toga over his head. Earl (*Tiberius Gracchus*, 118–19) identifies this garb as the *cinctus Gabinus* adopted by a priest when making a sacrifice. I am unconvinced, and find it hard to believe that Nasica set out with the firm intention of killing Tiberius as a sort of sanctified public victim, let alone with his own hand. He may simply have had it in mind to impress those who saw him by his august priestly rank, and thereby intimidate obstruction. Or Strachan-Davidson (note ad loc.) may be right in hesitating to go beyond seeing the gesture as more than an arresting one to attract attention.

blow followed. His body is said to have lain at the foot of the statues of the old kings of Rome. That night, it was tipped into the Tiber with the rest of the many dead.

'The death of Tiberius Gracchus, and already before that the whole thrust of his tribunate, has divided a united people into two camps.'[44] While there is room enough for argument about the inspiration and motives of Tiberius Gracchus and the powerful men who encouraged and supported him, few would deny the essential falseness and superficiality of this picture which Tubero drew for Aemilianus and his friends of a Rome which had been a united nation until Tiberius came along with his apple of discord. The issues and the grievances which he championed or exploited were not his creations, and their origins can be traced back long before he was born. 'Any senator of respectable antecedents and moderate ability', wrote Greenidge, 'who had a stable following among the ruling classes, might have succeeded where Tiberius Gracchus failed; it was a task in which authority was of more importance than ability, and the sense that the more numerous and powerful elements of society were united in the demand for reform of more value than individual genius or honesty of purpose.'[45] It is indeed this very fact that serves to sharpen debate about what was in the minds of the reformers. The original and central issue of land reform could not fail to be highly popular, and a big majority vote in the *concilium plebis* for any properly thought out and orchestrated proposal was safely predictable, and bound to bring political profit in some measure. Powerful and persuasive arguments could be adduced to show that some regeneration of the free peasantry, quite apart from reducing the risk of slave insurrections, would help to guarantee the security of Rome's empire, and thereby in the long term prove of benefit to all classes in the state. Of course, opposition was to be expected, since wealthy men who stood to lose heavily were sure to complain vociferously and use every resource to defeat such a measure. They are not to be cheaply dismissed as short-sighted. Short-sightedness is a normal human condition; and historians owe their long sight to the fact that they look back rather than forward, as they owe their detachment to the fact that they are passing judgement on matters which do not impinge directly on their own

[44] Cicero, *de re pub.* 1.31 (cited above, p. 37 n. 55).
[45] *A History of Rome* i.101.

personal interests. Moreover, shortness of sight is relative; it is worth remembering that, leaving aside the mature politicians who sat in the seats of power in 133, young men of thirty or so from the senatorial and propertied classes were to live out another forty years and reach their full three score years and ten in secure comfort in an Italy where the refusal of the governing class to grapple seriously and sincerely with a wide range of economic and social and political grievances had resulted in no more than some scattered and transient alarums.[45 a]

Tiberius and his associates had as good a claim as any other group of men to represent the Roman 'establishment' of their day, and to share in its political expertise. The decision to take the agrarian bill straight to the people may have been unorthodox, but it was not unprecedented; and it must have seemed sound tactics. The true 'joker in the pack' turned out to be Octavius. Never since the passing of the *lex Hortensia* in 287 had there been recorded one single instance of a tribune's persisting in using his veto to block the passage of a *plebiscitum*, save in one or two cases where the tribune was essentially using his veto to give *auxilium* to individuals who were threatened by what were in effect *privilegia*.[46] The well-informed Greek historian Polybius, writing some fifteen or so years before 133, and drawing on the conventional wisdom he had learned from Aemilianus and Laelius and other noble Roman friends, observed that 'a tribune is always duty-bound to act in accordance with the people's wishes, and above all to make what the people wants his target.'[47] However far the tribunate had departed from its revolutionary beginnings over three centuries earlier, however much the tribunes themselves had drifted into becoming the *mancipia nobilitatis*, the instruments that is whereby the ruling class as a whole could readily check and control individual magistrates, Polybius attests that this basic proposition was still recognized as valid, or at least accepted as formally correct. Despite occasional posturings in the past, this was the very first time that a veto had been persisted with against a *plebiscitum* in over 150 years; and it was very probably a development

---

[45 a] Even Karl Marx, for all his exceptionally 'long' sight in historical matters, was on several occasions seriously mistaken in his estimate of how events were likely to turn out in his own lifetime.

[46] Badian, *Aufst. u. Niederg.* I.i. 699.

[47] Polybius 6.16.5: Ὀφέιλουσι δ'αἰεὶ ποιεῖν οἱ δήμαρχοι τὸ δοκοῦν τῷ δήμῳ καὶ μάλιστα στοχάζεσθαι τῆς τούτου βουλήσεως.

which the reformers had not bargained for. As Cicero expressed it, it was the stubborn resolution of Octavius that broke Gracchus: 'fregit Ti. Gracchum patientia civis in rebus optimis constantissimus M. Octavius.'[48]

What lay behind Octavius' last-ditch stand we cannot be sure. He may have been hoping to force the bill to be amended in certain important respects rather than to kill it altogether. It may well be that neither side had a fully articulated plan. The original aim of the veto could simply have been to win time for manoeuvre and discussion, to marshal forces and to test reactions. Such precedents as there were did not really match this new situation. It was above all the 'confiscatory' aspect of the bill that was especially novel, and the threat to large holdings not all that far from Rome itself, producing widespread anger and dismay among those who were directly or indirectly threatened by it. There was also its sheer scale. It is true that the first thirty years of the second century had seen 1,000,000 *iugera* of land handed out in assignments and colonizing projects to provide for some 100,000 families.[49] But it was one thing to plant settlers on lands a fair distance from Rome in a series of projects stretching over several decades, and quite another to make a massive 'one-off' direct attack on the interests of the well-to-do where these were involved in secure areas nearer Rome. At Saturnia in 183,

members of the Roman ruling class destined for a colony a territory of the old Roman domain situated near to the capital. And that same generation which witnessed in its youth, as it were with indifference, these operations was destined to witness in its old age the strenuous resistance which the same Roman ruling class put up to Tiberius Gracchus when he tried to do

---

[48] Cicero, *Brutus* 95. One may contrast the situation in 67, when the tribune Gabinius was confronted with the persistent opposition of his colleague L. Trebellius to his bill to confer on Pompey a special command against the Mediterranean pirates. Gabinius promptly fell back on Tiberius' ploy, and called for a vote to depose Trebellius from his tribunate. The latter had declared earlier that the bill would pass 'only over his dead body'; and even now he held out, because he believed that Gabinius was bluffing. But, after seventeen tribes had voted for his deposition, he climbed down and withdrew his veto, and the bill was passed. Two years later Cicero in his *pro Cornelio* was to praise Gabinius for having bravely refused to allow the lone voice of Trebellius to drown the united voice of the whole state (Asconius p.72 C): 'neque, cum salutem populo Romano atque omnibus gentibus finem diuturnae turpitudinis et servitutis afferret, passus est plus unius collegae sui quam universae civitatis vocem valere et voluntatem.' Unlike Tiberius, Gabinius survived to hold a consulship nine years later. Times had changed.

[49] See Appendix 1 below, p. 214.

much the same sort of thing. But perhaps Gracchus was not proposing to repeat something on the lines of the colonization of these preceding decades, and in this may lie the resolution of the problem. The agrarian and colonial policies of the pre-Gracchan period proceeded quietly and without collisions, seeking to respond step by step to the various necessities, and to satisfy the needs and interests of all the parties concerned, and also to conciliate the great landowners by choosing unoccupied lands, of which —at any rate in the Cisalpina—there was large abundance. This policy conformed to custom, and provoked no excitement. Not such the agrarian policy of Tiberius Gracchus. The traditional policy, which could offer in the Cisalpina a region far from hostile or miserly, did not satisfy him. To break the great estates, that was what he wanted.

So wrote Tibiletti. But we must bear in mind that very large areas of lands unoccupied at the beginning of the century had been distributed by now, and moreover had probably experienced an influx of rich exploiters in the generation or two before 133, as the regions concerned became more secure and as more and more money and slaves became available to be deployed. The earlier approaches may well have been no longer available, while the virtual abandonment of such large-scale settlement after the '70s had probably built up a massive back-log.[50]

Many leading politicians are also likely to have had grave misgivings about the appointment to a long-term commission with such very wide powers of three men who were so closely related to each other, and to have been worried about how they might exploit their opportunities. The most eminent of the three, the *princeps senatus* Claudius, was known as a tough and wilful character: ten years before, when refused a triumph for his defeat of the Salassi, he had gone ahead and celebrated one just the same, thwarting a tribunician veto by having his Vestal Virgin daughter ride arm-in-arm with him in his carriage so as to shield her father from physical arrest with her own sacrosanct person.[51] The unco-operative attitude of some of Tiberius' colleagues at the elections in summer 133, and Satureius' physical assault on him in the final tumult, suggest that Octavius may have had hopes of support from some of them from the beginning; but, once again, their mood and attitude may have changed only later, for it is not recorded that any of them intervened to try to impede Octavius' deposition. It cannot be believed that the *princeps senatus* did not

---

[50] Tibiletti, *Athenaeum* (1950), 195 ff. Below, Appendix 1, p. 214.
[51] Reff. in *MRR* i. 471. Cf. Earl, *Tiberius Gracchus*, 47–9.

command a substantial following in the Senate; and he accepted a commissionership under the law once it had been carried after Octavius' deposition. If only things had stopped there, we should be better placed to try to estimate just how close to the wind the reformers had sailed. When the dust had settled, no attempt was made to repeal or invalidate the *lex agraria* itself, and the commissioners are not known to have run into serious obstruction until complaints from Italian allies gained a hearing and a champion in 129. It is possible to surmise that a man like Metellus Macedonicus was basically in sympathy with the idea of agrarian reform, and turned against Tiberius only after the Attalus business; two years later, he was as censor to deliver a speech on the need to increase citizen numbers of such forcefulness that it became famous, and was even read out in full by Augustus to the Senate over a century later. In the few lines we can still read, we can detect an echo of a theme of Tiberius Gracchus' in the insistence on the need to ensure Rome's lasting security.[52] Nor did Crassus Mucianus' close association with the reform—he was elected to fill Tiberius' place as a commissioner after Tiberius' death—prevent his being elected consul in the summer of 132 by a majority in the *comitia centuriata*, and a little later chief pontiff by the tribes.

In the end, the agrarian issue plainly was dwarfed by issues that ran wider and deeper. The *lex de Attali pecunia* and the promise, or threat, to use the *concilium plebis* to legislate on the organization of the Pergamene territory;[53] the new programme of reform which Tiberius may have outlined when making his bid for re-election; and the very attempt to secure a second, successive, tribunate—these factors transformed the situation and made the charge that Tiberius was aiming at personal supremacy much more plausible. We come back to the question of 'legal' and 'illegal', concepts which it is very difficult to pin down for late Republican Rome. In strict law, the sovereignty of the *populus* or the *plebs* duly met together in their assemblies under their elected officers was supreme. There was no statutory restriction on the subjects to which they could be asked to address themselves. A good case could be made for the thesis that their

---

[52] Livy, *Per.* 59; Suetonius, *DA* 89.2. Citations from the speech in Aulus Gellius, *AN* 1.6.1 and 7 = *ORF*[2] p. 108. For the Gracchan echo on the theme of *salus perpetua*, see Appian, *BC* 1.11 (cited above, p. 32 n. 39).

[53] Carcopino's strained attempt to discount this tradition is unconvincing, and has not won support. See notes and discussion on pp. 306–9 of the second edition of his *Autour des Gracques* (1967).

sovereignty could allow them to depose an officer they had themselves elected. We know of no statutory barrier to re-election (*continuatio*) so far as the tribunate was concerned, although such a barrier did exist for the consulship. *Ager publicus populi Romani* was the property of the Roman People, the Roman state, and of nobody else. But to concentrate on this aspect of things would be to be guilty of a fundamental misunderstanding of the whole constitutional development and ethos of the Roman Republic over the previous three and a half centuries of its existence. The manner of its development had left it, to the schematically logical eye, riddled with contradictions and anomalies. The passage of the years and changes in accepted practice often left the letter of the laws unaltered while profoundly affecting their spirit and interpretation. Men and institutions could retain powers on paper which it was understood they would not in practice deploy, and similarly they might come to exercise powers which had no statutory basis. Statute law itself was far from self-consistent; and tradition and precedent, *mos maiorum* and *disciplina maiorum*, what we in the United Kingdom term 'constitutional conventions', certainly had a force at least equal to that of statutes.[54]

The events which led to the killing of Tiberius cannot be dismissed as the work of a totally irresponsible clique of men with no respect for legality, however little of our sympathy they may command or be thought to deserve. They had a powerful case. Tiberius was straining precedent with the novel character of his agrarian bill and his bypassing the Senate. He was breaking precedent in having Octavius deposed so as to remove his veto: no other instance of the deposition of an officer of state was ever cited apart from the apocryphal case of Tarquinius Collatinus, the man who was consul with Brutus in the very first year of the Republic. He was breaking precedent in purposing to take control of matters of finance and provincial and international affairs out of the hands of consuls and Senate. He was breaking precedent in seeking re-election as tribune.[55]

[54] See my *Cicero: A Political Biography*, ch. II, for a fuller statement.

[55] To ask whether *continuatio* of the tribunate was 'legal' or 'illegal' is to miss the point, and mislead. Earl's insistence (*Tiberius Gracchus*, 103) that 'it can be confidently stated that re-election to the tribunate had never been forbidden by law' is of little relevance, as later moves (below, p.91) to establish the point positively demonstrate. Whatever may have been the case for Licinius and Sextius nearly 250 years earlier, the question was a moot point for the Romans of 133. For recent discussion, see Astin, *Scipio Aemilianus*, 351–2.

And 'precedent' was a powerful and venerable word in a dictionary where the Latin for 'revolution' was *res novae*.[56] The tribunate of the *plebs* had been in its origins a 'revolutionary' office, designed to champion the commons against a repressive and exclusive aristocracy. But those origins were centuries old, and the small central-Italian town of the fifth century which had given birth to the tribunate, and the fourth century central-Italian state which had institutionalized it, were unrecognizable in imperial Rome of the late second century. Times had changed, and the resuscitation of long-forgotten traditions and powers and enactments was a severe shock, and contrary to the long accepted and established rules of play.[57] What made it all the worse was that the man at the centre of everything was no mere upstart, but one of the most gifted, brilliant, eloquent, and well-connected young nobles of his generation, a member of the great college of augurs, son-in-law of the *princeps senatus*, son of a man who had been consul twice and censor, grandson of Scipio Africanus, the conquerer of Hannibal.

None of this is to say that Tiberius Gracchus was criminal or wicked, nor to condemn his aims or his methods. It is simply to emphasize that he was bound for trouble 'as the sparks fly upwards'. Behind the shown of legalism he was a revolutionary, as much as the patrician noble Julius Caesar was to be, and a very dangerous one at that—whether or not he himself fully appreciated it. He founded his position on the doctrine that the will of the People was sovereign, at any rate when it spoke with a united voice; that a tribune was obliged to respect and represent that will; that he could be deposed or re-elected at the discretion of the People; that he could use the People's assemblies for legislation on any subject, whether the Senate approved or not. Whatever this was, it was assuredly not the way the Roman constitution worked in practice, or had ever worked. For the members of the ruling class, at least, what they regarded as *libertas* consisted very much in the authority of the Senate (in which

[56] Professor Brunt has observed to me that 'the Latin for "constitution" is perhaps "discriptio civitatis a maioribus nostris sapientissime constituta" (Cicero, *pro Sestio* 137)'.

[57] As Badian observed (*Aufst. u. Niederg.* I.i.669), recent studies of what L.R. Taylor termed the 'forerunners of the Gracchi' (in her article in *JRS* 52 (1962), 19–27) by herself, Scullard, Astin, and others 'collect instances of [pre-Gracchan] seditious tribunes, but fail to recognize the important differences that made their activities trivial and temporary' when compared with those of the Gracchi. See also Bleicken, *Das Volkstribunat der klass, Rep.*

they served), and rested on the twin pillars of collegiality and limitation of tenure of office: on the fact, that is, that, with the exception of the crisis office of dictator, every officer of state, no matter how wide or discretionary his powers, had at least one colleague with *par potestas* or *imperium aequum* who could impede or block him, and held his office (and here even a dictator was no exception) for a strictly defined and limited period of time. It was these twin pillars which Augustus had effectively to demolish to clear the way for his substitution of a Principate for the *libera res publica*. The nobles of the late second century were understandably appalled at the vista which seemed to be opening up of a demagogue's holding office indefinitely and directing the affairs of Rome without fear of serious impediment from colleagues and without reference to Senate and consuls. This was to strike at the roots of the security of the oligarchy; and the 'establishment' was not prepared to sit quietly by and watch itself being legislated out of power. The killing of Tiberius was not inevitable, but his collapse surely was.

It is plain that Tiberius set out to tackle a serious social ill. His motives were surely not simple but complex. That he was ambitious for power goes without saying, and was only to be expected of a Roman of his birth and ability and character. All politicians are ambitious for power, and all reform programmes win wide support. But the scattering of tens of thousands of grateful allottees on small subsistence farms was not an obviously or immediately effective way to win continuing dominance over the politics of the capital. In 133 Rome was still two generations away from the openly violent summoning of armed and organized supporters from the Italian countryside. Had Tiberius set his heart on becoming the leading politician of his day, he had no need to do more than to follow a conventional enough career: his brilliance and energy, his talents and personality and inherited standing and connections, would have assured him a smooth road to the heights. In that, he was very unlike Sulla and Pompey and Julius Caesar, all of them in their various ways men born outside the exclusive inner circle of the ruling oligarchy. Which is what tempts so many to see him as a genuine reformer—there are some about in most periods and places when large issues are looming—and to regard him as morally justified in taking the steps he did take in order to circumvent the obstruction of those who had set their faces firmly against any change, and to look to the possible influence of Greek political experience and theory for his inspiration. That Blossius of Cumae was treated by Laelius, during his interrogation of him, as a follower of Tiberius rather than as an *éminence grise* behind him does not invalidate the latter suggestion; for the Greek parallels were easily discernible by every man of good education and wide reading—as too were the differences between the two societies.[58]

In the end, Tiberius' motives, and to some extent his intentions as well, remain private to himself and his closest family and friends. Even if we are led, as much by the heart sometimes as by the head, to think highly of them, we must not forget that a Roman noble of the second century before Christ, however fine his sensibilities and however elevated his moral values, did not and could not share all or even many of the values of a modern European. Qualities which most of us might well hesitate to applaud he would have commended without reserve—for example, concern for one's proper standing and prestige, *dignitas* and *auctoritas*, and the quest for personal *gloria*. We have no grounds for supposing that Tiberius ever questioned the basic structure of contemporary Roman society with its subordinated gradations, or the extension and exercise of Rome's dominion over the cities and peoples of the Mediterranean. We must beware of allowing our sympathies to invest him with anachronistic virtues and ideals. He was a man who became more and more tightly caught up in a net of obligations and pride, the eldest son of a great Roman noble house and a famous father, with the bluest blood running in his veins; a man of manifestly stubborn character honour-bound by his public promises to the common people who looked to him for hope and succour; a prisoner of his own *dignitas* much as Julius Caesar was later to claim himself to be, set firm on a course which Sallust could represent as aiming 'to lay claim to freedom for the people.'[59] It is not easy for those who spend their lives in studies and libraries to sense the thrill and elation of wildly cheering crowds, and hearts burning with sincere and affecting gratitude, and to assign to such factors their due weight. Tiberius experienced them at first hand, as he experienced too the disdain and vituperation of many of his peers. It is impossible to believe that this gifted and ambitious young noble remained unmoved by the experience. He had known humiliation before, after the Numantine treaty, and also the

---

[58] Greenidge (*A History of Rome* i. 104–6) has some excellently crisp observations on this topic. On Blossius, see Dudley, *JRS* (1941), 94–9.

[59] Sallust, *BJ* 42.1: 'postquam Ti. et C. Gracchus . . . vindicare plebem in libertatem et paucorum scelera patefacere coepere.'

enthusiastic thanks of the soldiers he had saved and of their families.

By his actions, he inexorably began to unite the ruling oligarchy against him in defence of their common interests; with the result that in the end the more violent and extreme among them were incited and allowed to take measures into their own hands, with some show of justification. Even the consul Scaevola could not find it in him to assert his authority against them at the critical moment, and is found doing his best to 'bind up the wounds' when the final murderous tumult was over.[60] In Spain Scipio Aemilianus, when he heard the news of his brother-in-law's death, is said to have been moved to repeat the words of the goddess Athene when she heard that Orestes had murdered Aegisthus: 'So perish any other man whose crimes be like to his!' When he had returned to Rome, his public reply to the tribune Carbo was in the same vein. Tiberius' killing, he declared, was justified, if he was aiming to seize supreme power: 'Ti. Gracchum, si is occupandae rei publicae animum habuisset, iure caesum.' Such was surely not the conscious aim of Tiberius Gracchus. But his actions had made it only too plausible to insinuate that that was where his activities and arguments had been leading him.[61]

---

[60] Cicero, *de domo* 91 (cited above, p. 36 n. 52).

[61] Plutarch, *TG* 21.4. The reply to Carbo was famous, and is referred to by Cicero (*de oratore* 2.106, *pro Milone* 8); Valerius Maximus (6.2.3); and Velleius Paterculus (2.4.4), whose version is given in the text to this note and alone includes the important 'si' clause. The words of Athene are from Homer, *Odyssey* i.47:
Ὡς ἀπόλοιτο καὶ ἄλλος ὅτις τοιαῦτά γε ῥέξοι.

V

'THE DOUBTFUL TRUCE'

Thucydides insisted (somewhat testily) that the years which followed the Peace of Nicias in 421 were a time not of true peace but of what he termed an ὕποπτος ἀνοκωχή.[1] The same might well be said of the period following the death of Tiberius Gracchus. But unfortunately we have no Thucydides to guide us through these years. Both Appian and Plutarch move briskly on to December 124, when Gaius entered on the first of his two consecutive tribunates; and the odd pickings that can be gleaned elsewhere are too scanty to supply us with the material for reconstructing the course of events in any confident detail. It is more than usually true that attempts to discern political groupings and consistent policies are misguided: there is too little straw to make sound bricks. Conjecture is unavoidable, but circumspection is equally necessary. The activities of the agrarian commission must have remained of central interest, and at least from 129 they impinged on the large question of Rome's relations with the non-Roman communities of Italy; but hindsight may exaggerate the keenness of the concern which contemporaries felt about the latter. As often, the leading politicians may have been generally much more absorbed in trading in the small change of short-term wheeling and dealing; and external affairs, especially in Asia where a long and tedious war broke out early in 132 bringing many complications in its train, must often have bulked large in men's minds. We must, of course, do our best to trace back the threads which come together in 123 and 122, but it is highly likely that the sheer scale of events in those years came as a surprise to most.

Tiberius Gracchus' corpse remained unburied. Although Plutarch's story that Gaius was refused when he asked permission to collect the body and bury it at night cannot be true (Gaius was still abroad in Spain), it perhaps reflects the apprehension which the authorities felt about the danger of violent public demonstrations if there were to be a proper funeral.[2] To the same apprehension may also be ascribed the curious fact that the

---

[1] Thucydides 5.26.3. 'Doubtful truce' is Jowett's translation.
[2] Plutarch, *TG* 20.2. Cf. Carcopino, *Gracques*, 195.

expiatory rites were conducted in Sicily, of all places. Cicero tells how Tiberius' death was followed by alarming portents, and recourse was had to the Sibylline books, which revealed that 'antiquissima Ceres' was to be placated; although there was a very fine temple of Ceres at Rome, the *decemviri* sent their officers instead to the old shrine of Ceres in faraway Enna in central Sicily—a choice which may have owed more to political calculation than pious scrupulousness.[3] That Scipio Nasica became the object of popular hatred is no surprise.[4] There was, it seems, a move to set up an enquiry which involved him in some way, although what its constitution or terms of reference were we cannot say. At any rate Cicero has a good story to tell about it: when M. Fulvius Flaccus in a scurrilous attack had proposed P. Mucius Scaevola as a judge in the matter, Nasica formally demurred, saying that Scaevola was biased; when his fellow-senators murmured in loud disapproval of such words, 'Ah, gentlemen,' said Nasica, 'it is not that he is biased against me, he is biased against everybody.'[5] There is no sign that Nasica was brought before a court of inquiry; but he was sent off to Asia as a *legatus*,[6] and this could have been a way of removing him from public view or shielding him from an inquisition, for Cicero speaks of the *invidia* he had incurred and Valerius Maximus specifically states that the legateship was devised to remove him from a hostile Rome.[7] What his future prospects might have been we cannot say, since before long he died at Ephesus and had been succeeded as *pontifex maximus* by Crassus Mucianus by early 131.[8]

What stands out, of course, is that no move was made to invalidate the *lex Sempronia agraria*, although plausible grounds for invalidation were not lacking. In part we may ascribe this to a sober policy of not adding insult to injury; but again we must emphasize that the agrarian bill itself may have enjoyed stronger 'respectable' support than the other aspects of Tiberius' activity. Appius Claudius and Crassus Mucianus, men surely of

[3] Cicero, *Verrines* II.iv.108. Professor Brunt has reminded me that Ceres was patroness of the *plebs Romana*; but the month of August was *tutela Cereris*, so her choice as the goddess to be placated might indicate that Tiberius was killed in August 133. For references, see Pauly–Wissowa *RE* iii. 1975–7.

[4] Plutarch, *TG* 21.4.

[5] Cicero, *de or.* 2.285.

[6] *ILS* 8886 = *ILLRP* i. 333.

[7] Cicero, *de re pub.* 1.6; Val. Max. 3.2.17.

[8] Cicero, *Phil.* xi.18.

wide influence, were unscathed, and Crassus himself went on to secure not only a consulship for 131 from the centuriate assembly but also the succession to Nasica as chief pontiff from the tribal assembly. He had already been elected to fill Tiberius' place on the agrarian commission.[9] Scaevola, who as consul had tried to restrain violence in vain, must have acted as a moderating influence. Although Cicero tells us that he exerted himself to defend Nasica's action, the story of Nasica's reluctance to see him as a judge suggests a more neutral position, and in due course he took his brother Crassus' place at the head of the group in opposition to Scipio Aemilianus and his friends; Crassus had been killed in the fighting in the east in 130, and Scaevola also took his place as chief pontiff. The *princeps senatus* Appius Claudius was himself dead by 129, and his place and that of Crassus as *IIIviri a.i.a.* were filled by M. Fulvius Flaccus and C. Papirius Carbo.[10] The date of Scaevola's death is unknown; all we can say is that later juristic writers attest him as still alive in 121, but that he must have died at some time before December 114, when we find a different chief pontiff presiding over the first trial of the Vestal Virgins.[11] At all events, he ceases to impinge on the Gracchan scene, and apparently he devoted himself to jurisprudence and historical research. Gaius Gracchus married the daughter of Scaevola's brother Crassus, but Scaevola is nowhere reported as continuing with Gaius the involvement he had shown in the programme of Tiberius Gracchus.[12] Metellus Macedonicus, who from 130 onwards shared the leadership of the old 'Claudio-Crassan group' with Scaevola, was elected to the censorship of 131; but apart from his famous speech on the need to increase the citizen birth-rate we have nothing to show what line he took.[13] Aemilianus himself died in 129. Thus the big figures in the story of Tiberius Gracchus disappear, to be replaced by new names in the story of his younger brother. Our inability to follow them any further creates more difficulties in the way of understanding the events of 134/133 than for the future; but we are surely justified in assuming that the deaths of Claudius and Crassus greatly weakened the authority of the agrarian commission of which they were both members

---

[9] *MRR* i. 495.

[10] Cicero, *de domo* 91 (cited above, p. 36); *de or.* 2.285; *de re pub.* 1.31 (above, p. 27). Cf. *MRR* i.503, Carcopino, *Gracques*, 182–3.

[11] Asconius 45 C. Cf. *MRR* i. 534, Pauly-Wissowa *RE* s.v. Mucius (7).

[12] Above, p. 27.

[13] Above, p.81. Cf. Astin, *Scipio Aemilianus*, 237–8, 354–5.

and made it more vulnerable to attack in 129, while the untimely death of Aemilianus took some of the force out of the opposition.

In 132 the consuls P. Popillius Laenas and P. Rupilius were instructed by the Senate to hold an inquiry and take action against the supporters of Tiberius Gracchus.[14] The details once again elude us, but it looks as if no men of real standing were involved but only the smaller fry, perhaps only those who were present during the final disturbance. It was during the course of this inquiry that the interchange took place between Laelius and Blossius about the burning of the Capitol.[15] It is noteworthy that the victims of the inquiry—it was said to have been 'pitiless' and to have resulted in banishments and executions—either did not or could not avail themselves of the protection of the existing laws which gave citizens the right to appeal to the People against capital sentences imposed by magistrates; some of those punished may have been non-citizens, but they cannot all have been. When nine years later Gaius Gracchus moved to punish Laenas for his conduct in 132 and to try to ensure against a repetition of such a proceeding, he apparently found it necessary to introduce a brand new law;[16] and his attack then on Laenas makes it clear that Roman citizens had been put to death in 132.[17] Last suggested that at bottom we may have here an instance of consuls exercising the *ius coercitionis* which was inherent in their *imperium*.[18] Perhaps so; but it is likelier that the answer should be sought along different lines. It seems that from the early second century special courts (*quaestiones extraordinariae*) began to be constituted by senatorial decrees and under the presidency of magistrates with *imperium* to deal with a range of offences, including (as in the case of the famous Bacchanalian *quaestio* of 186, for example) offences which could be visited with a capital penalty. Such *quaestiones* did not have the authority of the People behind them, but nevertheless they were accepted without fuss as effective instruments of law and order which did not

---

[14] Plutarch, *TG* 20.3; Cicero, *de amic.* 37; Sallust, *BJ* 31.7; Vell. Pat. 2.7.3; Val. Max. 4.7.1. Cicero shows that Laelius was a member of the consuls' advisory committee on this occasion, though Plutarch erroneously attributes his role to Scipio Nasica (curiously, Last, *CAH* ix.36 does not spot this error): cf. above, p. 71, n. 35.

[15] Above, p. 71. Blossius went free, and took himself off to join the revolt of Aristonicus in Asia, only to commit suicide when the revolt there foundered (Plutarch, *TG* 20.3).

[16] Below, p. 119.

[17] For the fragments of Gaius' attacks on Laenas, see Appendix 2 below, p. 220.

[18] Last, *CAH* ix.56.

occasion domestic sectional political objections—that is, they were essentially uncontroversial. But the *quaestio* established by a decree of the Senate in 132 proved to be blatantly 'party political' and could be attacked as an instance of partisan repression hiding behind a show of legal propriety. Hence in 123 Gaius Gracchus felt constrained to carry a law making it a capital offence to set up any capital court which had not been specifically authorized by the People (*ne de capite civium Romanorum iniussu populi iudicetur*) and make it also retrospective in its effect. Detailed discussion will be delayed until we come to deal with Gaius' law in its due place.[19] But it is significant of the balance of political forces at the time that in 132 the 'establishment' got away with such tactics. In 123 Popillius did not wait to stand trial under Gaius' new law but quickly removed himself into self-imposed exile; he came back again to Rome soon after Gaius' death in 121, but we know nothing of the arguments in favour of the bill which authorized his return. He apparently carried the chief weight of odium, for only one writer names his fellow-consul Rupilius along with him as the object of Gaius' later attack.[20] It could seem bitterly ironic that Popillius may be the author of the acephalous inscription from Polla who claims to have been 'the first to make herders give way to farmers on the public land';[21] but he may be an example of a politician who sympathized with certain aspects of Tiberius Gracchus' agrarian policy while wanting to have no truck with his further adventures.[22]

Aemilianus was back in Rome by early summer 132, and celebrated his triumph over the Numantines.[23] In 131 or 130 we find him taking the field along with his friend Laelius to oppose a proposal of the tribune Carbo to assert the legality of iteration of the tribunate.[24] Carbo, already

[19] For a full discussion, see below, p.117, in connection with Gaius Gracchus' legislation in 123.

[20] Vell. Pat. 2.7. Rupilius may in fact have been dead by 123.

[21] Above, p. 55.

[22] He may simply have been carrying out the charge which the Senate had laid on him as consul. Valerius Maximus (4.17.1) wrote: 'Cum senatus Rupilio et Laenati consulibus mandasset ut in eos qui cum Graccho consenserant more maiorum animadverterent.' 'More maiorum' could suggest a primitively savage form of punishment; and the words 'malo cruce' ('on an evil cross') are cited from Gaius' own attack on Laenas (Appendix 2 below, p.220). But Valerius may have meant nothing so precise as that.

[23] For this date, see Astin, *Scipio Aemilianus*, 230–1.

[24] The year of Carbo's tribunate could have been either 131 or 130. Munzer (*RE* s.v. Papirius no. 33, col. 1017) prefers 131, Fraccaro ('Stud. età Grac.' 440) opts for 130. I find it impossible to choose.

or soon to become a *IIIvir a.i.a.* alongside Gaius Gracchus and Flaccus, was at this time eloquent in his defence of the dead Tiberius;[25] which makes it impossible to suppose that he so drafted his bill as to permit any inference that Tiberius' attempt at re-election had been illegal. The precise wording is irrecoverable, and the bill did not become law; although backed by the eloquence of Gaius Gracchus, it was attacked by Aemilianus in a 'masterly' speech.[26] It was during the fight over this bill that Carbo nagged Aemilianus into giving his opinion that the killing of Tiberius had been 'justified' and responding to the clamour which greeted these words with his famous rejoinder about 'mere stepchildren of Italy'.[27] Nevertheless, despite the uproar, a majority of the plebeian assembly rejected the bill. Carbo did, however, manage to carry a law which extended the use of the ballot to legislative assemblies. Why the one bill failed and the other succeeded, how the two were related (if at all) to each other or to the *plebiscitum reddendorum equorum* either chronologically or otherwise, there is no knowing.[28]

The agrarian commissioners had settled to their task, and there was a spate of contentious adjudications as arguments about boundaries and titles and improvements multiplied. Tempers rose, and the disputes were noisy.[29] It may be that by 129 the most easily reclaimable land had been dealt with, and the commissioners began to go on to the trickier work of reclaiming land from non-Roman individuals or communities. At any rate it was in that year that the latter appealed to Aemilianus to defend their interests. He successfully urged that the issues involved went beyond the competence of the commissioners, and that such weighty matters of international relationships must fall to Senate and consuls to resolve.[30] The

---

[25] Cicero, *de or.* 2.170: 'Ti. Gracchi mortem saepe in contionibus deplorasti.'

[26] Cicero, *de amic.* 96, where we also learn that the speech was 'published': 'et est in manibus oratio'. Cf. *de or.* 2.170; Livy, *Epit.* 59.

[27] Above, pp. 21 and 86. Astin (o.c. 234) has it that Aemilianus' 'outburst both signified and sealed his forfeiture of popular favour'; but one has to insist that in fact a majority of the popular assembly followed his lead and voted to reject the bill.

[28] Cicero, *de legg.* 3.35 (On the *pl. redd. equ.*, see immediately below.)

[29] Appian, *BC* 1.18; Livy, *Epit.* 59.

[30] On Aemilianus' intervention, see above, p. 52. See too the discussions reviewed by Nicolet in Carcopino, *Gracques*[2], 309–11. Some have suggested that Aemilianus provoked an *abrogatio* or *obrogatio* of Tiberius' law, or a *senatusconsultum* followed by a *rogatio*. But I much prefer to follow Last's interpretation (*CAH* ix.44). Fragment 84 of Dio Cassius certainly tells against the view that the Gracchan commissioners lost any powers in 129, since it maintains that after Aemilianus' death a

consul C. Sempronius Tuditanus—his colleague M'. Aquillius was busy with Aristonicus' revolt in Asia—apparently found it all too difficult and so left to fight a war himself in Illyria. Appian says that Aemilianus was too wary to attack the agrarian law itself openly and directly;[31] and, all in all, it is probably best to assume that a looseness or ambiguity in the original drafting concerning the commissioners' adjudicatory powers was now exploited. Tuditanus' failure to do more than touch on the problem must have largely, if not entirely, blocked any further distributions of public land the status of which was disputed by Italian and Latin governments. There is no obvious reason why assignment of other public land should not have continued, however: the assumption that it did not rests on a probably over-literal acceptance of Appian's statement that Tuditanus' inaction reduced the commissioners themselves to inactivity, which could be either a casual exaggeration or a reference essentially to the Italian and Latin land. Still, we may readily suppose a serious slowing-down, since Appian goes on to say that after Aemilianus' death not long afterwards the big *possessores* none the less continued to find multifarious pretexts for delay.[32]

Finally, also in 129, we have a tantalizing glimpse of a proposal to exclude senators from membership of the eighteen centuries of public horse, which were an important element of the centuriate assembly, which at this date numbered 193 centuries in all. Badian has seen this move as part of the idea 'later refined by C. Gracchus: to drive a permanent wedge into the governing class and split it along the one line of fissure that could be discerned. What had happened—uniquely, as far as we know—in 169, when the voters of the officer class had turned against the *auctoritas* of the Senate, was to be encouraged and institutionalized. A new class was to be created.' He also went on to guess that this measure should be linked with

---

little later the commissioners 'had the whole of Italy at their mercy to despoil as they chose'! There is extant a brief passage from a speech by Aemilianus puzzlingly (and I am sure mistakenly) entitled 'contra legem iudiciariam Ti. Gracchi' (*ORF*[2] p.133), but it is not helpful: it deplores the spread of indecent dancing among children of good families—which in some degree echoes the 'decline of public morality' theme which can be detected in the comments put in Laelius' mouth by Cicero in *de re pub.* 3.41 (dramatic date 129): cf. below, p. 106.

[31] Appian, *BC* 1.19: Τὸν μὲν Γράκχου νόμον οὐκ ἔψεγε διὰ τὸν δῆμον σαφῶς.

[32] Ibid: Οἱ δὲ τὴν γῆν διανέμοντες, οὐκ ἀπαντῶντος ἐς αὐτοὺς οὐδενὸς ἐς δίκην, ἐπ' ἀργίας ἦσαν. The unco-operative attitude of the *possessores* is noted at *BC* 1.21: Τὴν δὲ διαίρεσιν τῆς γῆς οἱ κεκτημένοι καὶ ὡς ἐπὶ προφάσεσι ποικίλαις διέφερον ἐπὶ πλεῖστον.

the institution of the equestrian privilege of fourteen special rows of seats at the public games.[33] Given the meagre evidence we have, all this is very bold speculation—though none the worse for that. Clearly, the beneficiaries of the *plebiscitum reddendorum equorum* would be well-to-do non-senators for whom places in this prestigious and electorally highly influential body would now become available. However, it is hazardous to go much beyond this obvious point. The move could have been more anti-senatorial than pro-equestrian; and in any case it is to be presumed that the censors were to continue to be responsible for enrolment in these centuries, as before. On top of that, we cannot even be certain whether the proposal passed into law (not that that fact affects the intention of the move), and we are not told who was the author of it: Cicero makes Aemilianus refer to it simply as a proposal which was being mooted shortly before his own death, characterizing it as a 'novel hand-out' foolishly desired by too many people. Apart from this single passage we have no other information on the subject.[34]

The next significant move—or, rather, the next significant move of which we are informed[35]—came in 126, in the shape of a notorious aliens expulsion act carried by the tribune M. Junius Pennus, which ordained the physical removal from Rome of all non-Romans.[36] This was also the year in which Gaius Gracchus was quaestor, and during the course of it his commissioner colleague M. Fulvius Flaccus was elected consul for 125. Gaius is known to have attacked Pennus' act, and it is tempting to tie it in in some way with the proposal which Flaccus brought forward as consul in 125 to extend Roman citizenship more widely in Italy. But it is not all that easy to see how the link works. Although Flaccus may well have given his proposal a wide airing while still consul-elect, or even earlier, he cannot have actually moved it before he took office in January 125; and Pennus' tribunate expired on 10 December 126.[37] Moreover, Gaius Gracchus must

---

[33] Badian, *Publicans and Sinners,* 55 ff.

[34] Cicero, *de re pub.* 4.2 : 'nimis multis iam stulte hanc utilitatem tolli cupientibus, qui novam largitionem quaerunt aliquo plebiscito reddendorum equorum.' This passage is of course evidence only that such a bill was proposed, not that it was carried into law.

[35] It is noteworthy that Greenidge and Clay, *Sources*[2], can find nothing worth listing under the years 128 and 127 save the names of the consuls.

[36] Cicero, *de off.* 3.47; cf. *Brutus* 109.

[37] *ORF*[2] p. 180 (Appendix 2 below, p. 218). Carcopino (*Gracques,* 194 ff.) maintained that Cicero's statement (*Brutus* 109) that Gaius Gracchus and Pennus were

have left Rome fairly early in 126, for he was assigned as quaestor to the consul L. Aurelius Orestes, who went out to campaign in Sardinia that year. Hence, if his speech against Pennus' bill was delivered in Rome before he left, that bill itself must have been put forward some eight or nine months earlier than Flaccus' entry on his consulship. On the other hand, it could be that Gaius' speech was a retrospective attack delivered after his return from Sardinia in 125 or 124.[38] But it is perhaps unwise to look for over-close links when our information is so scanty and scattered; a neat connection between Pennus' law and Flaccus' proposal may well be a mirage to tease the historian thirsty for knowledge in a desert waste.[39]

How Flaccus succeeded in securing a consulship for 125 one would dearly like to know. The centuriate assembly was a very different body from the tribal assembly of the *plebs* which elected the tribunes, and its election of Flaccus is evidence that he enjoyed substantial support among the solid citizenry of the equestrian centuries and of the first class whose votes dominated it. According to Appian, his proposal to extend Roman citizenship was tied up with the difficulties which the agrarian commission had been encountering in dealing with the disputed public land. The idea was that in return for the citizenship the Italians and Latins would give up their obstruction—and, indeed, if the communities concerned were to become part of the Roman state, the legal difficulties about the public land would be transformed, probably simplified, and perhaps entirely removed. The Italians, Appian says, were very ready to accept the proposal, reckoning that the citizenship was worth more to them than the disputed

respectively quaestor and tribune in the same year 126 ('fuit enim M. Lepido et L. Oreste consulibus quaestor Gracchus, tribunus Pennus') could mean that Gaius was quaestor for the twelve months beginning 5 Dec. 127 and Pennus tribune for the twelve months beginning 10 Dec. 126; since Carcopino would have Gaius back from Sardinia early in 125, he is able to fit neatly together the franchise proposal of Flaccus as consul in 125, the aliens expulsion bill of a Pennus who was tribune in 125, and a speech against it by a Gaius who was back in Rome early in 125. But too much is sacrificed here to schematism; the *Brutus* passage is not to be crammed into so Procrustean a bed, for it must surely mean that Gaius and Pennus were in office together for the bulk of the consular year which began on 1 Jan. 126, and hence that they both entered office in December 127. Otherwise Cicero would be guilty of a confusing and quite unnecessary solecism.

[38] For what it is worth, the one reference to this speech calls it *de lege Penni* and not *contra legem Penni*. But *Brutus* 109 points to a date in 126.

[39] The cautious conclusion of Brunt (*JRS* 55 (1965), 90) that the motives and exact nature of Pennus' law are obscure to us is here preferred to the over-confident resolution of Badian (*Dial. di arch.* (1970–1), 385 ff.; *Foreign Clientelae*, 177 ff.).

land.[40] But Flaccus ran into stiff opposition at Rome itself, and in the end he was posted off to fight a campaign in Gaul, and the proposal lapsed.[41] And that is all we know, except that Valerius Maximus, in a superficial and hostile brief notice of it, reports (plausibly enough) that the *ius provocationis* (the right of appeal against the severe penalties that a Roman magistrate could inflict) was offered as an alternative to those who might be reluctant to accept the citizenship itself.[42]

Given the paucity of our information about the whole episode, it is risky to speculate. But Flaccus does not seem to have fought very hard for his proposal, and one may suspect that it may have been something of a *ballon d'essai* designed to test the strength and direction of the wind, or a move to call the bluff of the opposition. A few years earlier, in 129, the latter had made a great play of being the real friends and champions of Latins and Italians; now they were driven to run their true colours up the mast and reveal themselves as hostile to the extension of political equality in Italy. Even if that was not Flaccus' object, it was a foreseeable consequence of his proposal, and hence may well have been taken into account by him and his associates. It is also to be noted that there is nowhere any suggestion that Flaccus contemplated using his position as consul to decide or resolve the disputes about 'non-Roman land' in favour of the agrarian commission of which he was a member. By the time that he and Gracchus came forward with their franchise programme in 123/122, the idea of extending political rights and opportunities in Italy had been given a wide airing, and he and his friends had been seen to be for it and their opponents against it.[42a]

Into all this we must try to fit the revolt of the Latin colony of Fregellae in 125. It was put down by the praetor L. Opimius, and the next year a new Roman citizen colony of Fabrateria Nova took Fregellae's place.[43] No other community joined in the revolt, and this isolation of

---

[40] Appian, *BC* 1.21: καὶ ἐδέχοντο ἄσμενοι τοῦθ᾽ οἱ Ἰταλιῶται, προτιθέντες τῶν χωρίων τὴν πολιτείαν.

[41] Ibid. 34.

[42] Val. Max. 9.5.1: 'Flaccus . . . cum perniciosissimas rei publicae leges introduceret de civitate <Italiae> danda et de provocatione ad populum eorum qui civitatem mutare noluissent.' On the *ius provocationis* as an alternative to citizenship, see below, p. 186.

[42a] See Hall, 'Notes on M. Fulvius Flaccus', *Athenaeum* (1977), 280–8; and for further discussion of this business, see below, p. 185.

[43] Evidence in *MRR* i. 510–11.

the Fregellans may be in some way connected with the unpopularity which the town had won for itself over fifty years earlier in 177 for allegedly 'poaching' too many immigrants from other towns and thereby creating 'manpower problems' for those towns.[44] The causes of the revolt, and its immediate antecedents, are obscure; but there is a suggestion that some of the Fregellan ruling class remained loyal to Rome, helped in ending the revolt, and were resettled as Roman citizens in the new colony of Fabrateria. Given that there may have been a division along socio-ethnic lines between the Fregellan ruling class and the numerous Samnite immigrants who had come to settle in Fregellae over the preceding two or three generations, it is reasonable to suppose that in at least some respects Fregellae was a special case.[45] On the other hand, the usually reliable Asconius says that Opimius' capture of Fregellae 'seemed to have cowed all the other Latins' ('ceteros quoque nominis Latini'), whom he characterizes as 'ill disposed' towards Rome.[46] It is a measure of the miserable nature of our evidence that an event so startling and noteworthy as the revolt of a *colonia Latina*, and one whose loyalty in the crisis of the Hannibalic War had been exemplary, should be enshrouded in so dense a fog.[47]

Through that fog we can, however, discern the outline of the stand which Gaius Gracchus took on some major political issues, although we have to remember that he had spent most of his adult life down to 124 on public service outside Rome and Italy: he had, so he pointed out in a speech delivered in that year, performed twelve years of military service as against the customary maximum of ten, and had spent two years as quaestor in Sardinia;[48] and he was still under thirty years old. As a *IIIvir* he was

---

[44] See Badian, *CR* (1955), 22–3. We need not assume that remembered rancour remained keen for fifty years: there could have been other comparable instances of Fregellan selfishness between 177 and 125. Much is lost with the loss of Livy's full account after 167.

[45] See Badian, *Dial di arch.* (1970–1), 389–91, and the works there cited.

[46] Asconius 17 C: 'Notum est Opimium in praetura Fregellas cepisse, quo facto visus est ceteros quoque nominis Latini male animatos repressisse.' One should not put too much weight on Plutarch's general report (*CG* 3.1) that Gaius was alleged to have sought to cause revolt 'among the allies': ὡς τοὺς συμμάχους ἀφιστάντι καὶ κεκοινωνηκότι τῆς περὶ Φρέγελλαν ἐνδειχθείσης συνωμοσίας.

[47] So Last (*CAH* ix.45): 'With the death of Scipio the fog which enshrouds the Gracchan age grows thicker.' On Fregellae's earlier outstanding loyalty, see ibid. 47–8.

[48] Plutarch, *CG* 2.6: Appendix 2, below, p. 218.

identified with, and helping to implement, his brother's agrarian policy. He had supported Carbo's proposal in 131 or 130 concerning iteration of the tribunate. He had attacked Pennus over his aliens expulsion bill, and he may safely be presumed to have seen eye to eye with Flaccus over his franchise proposal (he was actually away in Sardinia for at least a good part of Flaccus' consular year): indeed, he was charged with having stirred the allies to dissension and with having been involved in the plan which led to the revolt of Fragellae. When accused of impropriety in having refused to stay on in Sardinia with the proconsul for a third year as quaestor, his spirited defence of his decision to return to Rome turned at one point to an attack on the low level of other men's public morality: the money-belts which had been full when he set out for Sardinia were empty and hung light about him when he came back home, while others who took jars of wine out with them to the provinces brought them back empty indeed of wine but brimful of silver.[49] Although, curiously, Appian says that many in the Senate held Gaius in contempt, this must be wrong, and one suspects a mistranslation or misunderstanding here by Appian of a Latin source:[50] Gaius was clearly a formidable figure on a number of grounds, and in particular he stood head and shoulders above the other public speakers of his day; given time, he would in Cicero's opinion have developed into Rome's greatest master of that art. The fragments that survive still convey something of the power and impact of his oratory; and we can well believe Diodorus and Plutarch when the former says that Gaius was given a hero's welcome by the people on his return from Sardinia, they seeing in him his brother's successor as their champion, and when the latter insists that 'the establishment' regarded him as a very dangerous threat.[51]

'Tiberius Gracchus had come before the burgesses with a single administrative reform. What Gaius introduced in a series of separate proposals was nothing else than an entirely new constitution.'[52] Mommsen's judgement dramatically oversimplifies the tribunate of the elder of the two brothers, but it very rightly underlines the breadth and depth and

---

[49] Appendix 2 below, p. 219.

[50] Appian, *BC* 1.21.4: πολλῶν δ'αὐτοῦ καταφρονούντων ἐν τῷ βουλευτηρίῳ.

[51] Diodorus 34/5.25; Plutarch, *CG* 2–3. On Gaius' quality as an orator, and for the surviving fragments of his speeches, see Appendix 2 below, p. 217.

[52] Mommsen, *A History of Rome* (English trans.) 3.109.

complexity of the activities of the younger. The condition of the urban commons, the food supply of Rome, agrarian and colonizing and construction projects, public finance, the legal system, the army, the government of provinces, the election and tenure of public officers, the political status of Latins and Italians—all of these came within the sweep of his tribunician scythe. But before moving on to consider each in its due place in a detailed treatment of his two tribunates, it will be helpful to set out here something of the background to the importance of the two elements which bulk largest in the story: the *equites* (the 'knights' as they are often somewhat misleadingly termed), and the Latin and allied Italian communities. Although Gaius was to focus attention on both, both had a long history behind them.

The *Equites*[53]

The 'Servian' organization of the centuriate assembly of the Roman People included eighteen centuries of cavalry, *equites equo publico*, so called because their mounts were provided and maintained by the state from specially earmarked revenues. Traditionally, about the year 400 this force of 'public horse' was supplemented by men who supplied their own horses. These latter were not enrolled in the eighteen centuries, but they none the less shared some of the distinguishing dress and general prestige of the *equites equo publico*. In the year 225, according to Polybius, the *equites* of both categories numbered all told well over 20,000 men.[54] However, increasingly from the end of the third century onwards Rome's cavalry in the field came to consist largely of *auxilia* recruited from allied or friendly states; and the *equites Romani* became essentially the class from which Rome drew the officers for her armies and for the staffs of her military commanders and her governors. Nevertheless, the eighteen centuries of *equites equo publico* still retained their important voting role in the centuriate assembly; membership was controlled by the censors, and high social standing was an important prerequisite. Indeed, for a long time senators could be enrolled in them, but it is probable that they themselves —although not their sons—were specifically disbarred from membership

[53] In general on the *equites* see: Hill, *The Roman Middle Class*; Henderson, *JRS* 53 (1963), 61ff. (= Seager, *The Crisis of the Roman Republic*, 69ff.); Brunt, *The Equites in the Late Republic* (= *Crisis*, 83ff.); Nicolet, *L'Ordre équestre à l'époque républicaine*; Badian, *Publicans and Sinners*; Wiseman, *New Men in the Roman Senate*.
[54] Polybius 2.24.14. Cf. Nicolet, o.c. i. 114–15.

by a plebiscite carried in 129.[55] By now the property qualification required of an *eques*, the *census equester*, was probably a minimum of 400,000 HS; it is likely that it had not been as high as that in 225, and we should therefore assume that it had been revised upwards during the second century.[56] How many citizens possessed the *census equester* in the Gracchan period we just cannot say; indeed, how many of those who did possess it were actually enrolled in the eighteen centuries is uncertain, although it is fairly safe to assume that this latter number was either 1,800 or 2,400.[57]

During the last 150 years of the Republic, the material resources of individual *equites* obviously varied very widely: some could barely qualify at the minimum census level, others could boast of means beyond the reach of many senators. Increasingly, as has already been observed, the expansion of Rome's territorial dominion opened up new fields for what we may loosely term 'financial' activities, in the widest sense of that adjective: alongside those who drew their wealth predominantly from the land and associated sources, the number of those who did well out of these activities was constantly growing (although men who prospered in such ways were not slow to invest at least part of their gains in land).[58] Apart from private enterprise in its many forms, the execution of public contracts let out by the state (whence the name *publicani*) became more and more important. For all that the mention of 'publicans' at once leads the modern reader to think of the men who carried out the public contracts for the collection of taxes and customs-dues, down to the end of the third century these played a relatively small part, and the chief area of activity and profit for the *publicani* lay in the *ultro tributa*, the contracts for public works and supplies, especially military equipment and supplies in time of war. And even after her victory over Hannibal's Carthage set second-century Rome racing off down the high road to empire, the *ultro tributa* remained important, and involved sums of money which were enormous by the standards of the day. The system remained well under control, and despite occasional misbehaviour and ructions it can be said

[55] Above, p. 93.

[56] So Brunt (*IM* 700), against Nicolet (o.c. 46–68). A *census equester* is alluded to by Polybius (6.20.9).

[57] Discussions in Hill (o.c. 44 ff.) and Nicolet (o.c. 115 ff.).

[58] Above, p. 6. As Brunt and Nicolet and Wiseman have shown, landed property was very often the basis of equestrian wealth, as of senatorial.

to have been in excellent working order in the middle of the century.[59]

Private enterprise in the service of the state is something which we all know about, at any rate on our side of the Iron Curtain. We have our own *publicani*: sub-postmasters in village shops or café-owners who operate the P.M.U. in France; builders who erect public buildings and the contractors who clean them; companies who build frigates for the navy or tanks for the army or planes for the air force, or supply clothing and foodstuffs to the services; printers who print government pamphlets, firms who build motorways—the list is a long one, and it would be tedious to enlarge it. Even the farming of taxes went on in Europe and elsewhere until quite recently: as late as 1896, 'an eminent Professor of Law at the University of Jena . . . could report that certain municipal taxes in his city were still being farmed out for collection; and that the city of Jena was convinced that this was more profitable to it than the system of direct collection adopted by some other cities.'[60]

The two chief differences between second-century Rome and modern Europe in such matters were the virtual absence of any bureaucracy or permanent civil service and the fact that Rome had undergone no industrial or technological revolution on the scale that has transformed our own societies. The officers of state themselves held office for only one year, and both at home and abroad they were largely assisted by their own personal freedmen and slaves, which meant an absence of continuity and expertise at those lower levels as well; it was not until Augustus freed himself in effect from the limitation of annual tenure that the huge personal staff of the effective ruler of Rome, the *familia Caesaris*, could begin to develop into an embryonic imperial civil service. And the failure of industry and manufacture to expand and extend as our own have done meant that the really big money by Roman standards—leaving aside agriculture, and the fruits of office enjoyed pre-eminently by the ruling nobility—came from government contracts for building and road-making, the working of publicly owned mines and quarries and woodlands, the provision of military supplies and equipment, and of course the collection of public

---

[59] This paragraph, and what follows, borrows heavily from my review of Badian, *Publicans and Sinners* in *CR* (1975), 96–8. Chapters 2–3 of Badian's book may be consulted for references and detailed discussion.

[60] Badian (o.c. 12–13) aptly cited this observation from F. Kniep, *Societas Publicanorum* i. 92.

revenues.[61] As Rome became increasingly parasitical on the Mediterranean world, so such undertakings engrossed a larger and larger share of the wealth of a society which remained essentially agriculturally based and which lacked wide private markets for mass production. Extensive sub-contracting, and the labour thereby directly or indirectly employed, brought more and more of the Italian economy into dependence on the state and the state itself into dependence on the contractors.

Roman senators were debarred by convention and by law from engaging directly in public contracting.[62] The rich *publicani* were of course members of the equestrian class—'the flower of the equestrian order'; but none the less, as in other and later societies, 'business' was sometimes felt to be not altogether acceptable for members of the highest and governing class, and there was moreover an understandable sense that those who determined and supervised public policy and public business should not themselves be directly involved in the profitable execution of public contracts. Outstanding individuals like the elder Cato and Gaius Marius might rise from respectable local landowning equestrian rank to the heights of public office, and many others from the same sort of background to the lower foothills, but the *publicanus* was a horse of a different colour. The first consul attested as having come from the publican ranks was Publius Rupilius, consul in 132; and his background was held against him, just as some people were ready to sneer at the British Prime Minister Sir Robert Peel, whose family wealth had come from cotton-spinning.[63] We need not suppose that such attitudes were resented or questioned by the *publicani* themselves, who surely accepted such social stratifications as natural and desirable. A *publicanus* had to own lands in Italy to put up as security for a public contract, but not all well-to-do non-senators should be supposed to have wanted to make the leap to the ranks of the Senate; in his own day Cicero spoke of *equites* as men who either had not been able to attain such heights, or *had never sought to*.[64]

---

[61] Polybius, cited by Strabo 3.2.10, reported that in his day the silver mines near Cartagena in Spain employed 40,000 hands and yielded the Roman state a revenue of 100,000 HS a day = over 35,000,000 HS a year. This single instance gives an idea of the scale such operations could attain.

[62] In general, for what follows see Badian, o.c. 50 ff.

[63] For Rupilius, see Val. Max. 6.9.8.

[64] Cicero, *pro Cluentio* 150: 'Putant enim [sc. homines equestris ordinis] minus multos sibi laqueos legum et condicionum ac iudiciorum propositos esse oportere qui summum locum civitatis aut non potuerunt ascendere aut non petiverunt.'

Nevertheless, the possibilities of friction between *equites* and Senate are obvious. The story in Livy of criminal frauds which were perpetrated by *publicani* during the Hannibalic War and which the Senate was allegedly reluctant to pursue and punish through fear that such action might offend the *ordo publicanorum* can be discounted as exaggerated and anachronistic.[65] But there was clearly trouble later. In the year 184 the censors exacted very tough terms for the contracts which they let out; and the publicans, or at any rate a number of them, got the Senate to annul the contracts, probably helped in this by the bitter personal enemies within that body of the elder Cato, who was one of the two censors concerned. Little good the annulment did them, for the censors proceeded to exclude from the second round of bidding all those 'who had made a mockery of the previous letting' ('qui ludificati priorem locationem erant') and to re-let all the contracts at only slightly lower levels ('omnia eadem paulum imminutis pretiis locaverunt'). Fifteen years later, in 169, when the censors for reasons unknown to us had excluded from the bidding for public contracts all those who had secured contracts in 174, a tribune was found to propose the cancellation of the new contracts and even to prosecute the censors, Tiberius Gracchus *père* and Gaius Claudius; Claudius had a very narrow escape, for he was saved by a margin of the votes of only eight out of the 193 centuries; but, given the massive and almost decisive number of centuries which voted for his condemnation, and the contribution to his escape which was made by his colleage Gracchus, who was apparently not himself in any serious danger of condemnation, there must have been more to the affair than a demonstration of the powerful anger of an affronted *ordo publicanorum*. The Senate refused in 167 to lease to the *publicani* the working of the gold and silver mines in conquered Macedonia. That has been seen as a wary response to the growing and disturbing power of the *publicani*; but there are other and probably better explanations of the refusal, such as a sense that Rome's sinews might be overstretched and an understandable reluctance to get too closely involved in the tiresome affairs of Greece; the mines could have been exploited only under the protection of an occupying army, and there is no record that the *publicani* protested against the Senate's decision.[66]

---

[65] Livy 25.3.9 ff. (the year was 213/212). For a demolition of this version of the story, see Badian, o.c. 17 ff.

[66] Livy 39.44 (for 184); 43.16 (for 169); 45.18 (for 167—and cf. Diodorus 31.8).

Something of what lay behind the tendency to such conflicts can be discerned in Polybius' exposition of the ways in which the 'people' (by whom he here means in effect the *equites*) were subordinated to, dependent on, and controlled by the Senate round about the middle of the second century.[67]

Throughout Italy [he wrote] a great many contracts, too many to enumerate easily, are let out by the censors for works of construction and repair. And on top of those there are many revenues to be farmed from rivers, harbours, orchards, mines, and land—in short all that has come under the dominion of Rome. All these fall to be undertaken by the people; and pretty well everyone, one might say, is involved in these contracts and the profits from them: some people are the actual purchasers of the contracts from the censors, some stand surety for them, some pledge their own personal fortunes to the state for this purpose. In all these matters I have listed the Senate is supreme: it can grant extensions of time; it can provide relief in the event of some mischance; and, if a contractor finds it absolutely impossible to fulfil a contract, it can free him from it. In fact, there are many ways in which the Senate can greatly injure or conversely assist the contractors, since all questions about such matters are referred to it. Most important of all, it is from the Senate that the judges are appointed to decide most public and private suits of any magnitude. So everyone is bound to the Senate by ties of obligation and dependence to secure protection; and, uncertain and apprehensive that they may need senatorial help, they are all very wary of obstructing or opposing senatorial decisions.

So much then, in brief, to help set the general scene. In treating of the Gracchan period, we have to reckon with the existence of a class of well-to-do Roman citizens who were not members of the senatorial order, but who were marked out by their wealth and in other ways as constituting an estate superior to the bulk of the citizens. Some were actually members of the prestigious eighteen centuries of *equites equo publico*, although even after senators themselves were excluded in 129 younger members of senatorial families who had not yet entered the Senate were also enrolled in those centuries. Others, although they were registered as

---

For modern discussions, see Brunt (o.c. p. 99 n. 53, above, 138–41); Badian, o.c. 35–44.

[67] Polybius 6.17. On the equation here of 'people' and *equites*, see Walbank's *Commentary* ad loc.; Brunt, 'The Equites in the Late Republic', 119; Badian, *Publicans and Sinners*, 45. On the selection of *iudices* from the Senate, see Brunt, loc. cit. 142–5. On Polybius 6.17.4 in particular, see Nicolet, *Irish Jurist* (1971), 163–76.

owning the resources necessary to qualify them for membership (the *census equester*), were not *equites equo publico* but may still conveniently be called simply *equites*. If that sounds somewhat evasive, it needs to be emphasized that we are dealing with a period of considerable and fairly rapid change; that nearly all our evidence comes from later periods when conventions had settled down and hardened, and hence the language of writers like Cicero, let alone Plutarch and Appian, may be innocently anachronistic; and that Gaius Gracchus himself was the man who above all others gave shape and direction to the political consciousness and aims of the class. The wealth of these men varied widely, as did their backgrounds. Some were predominantly landowners and such who played a leading part in ordering the affairs of their own local communities outside Rome: the families of Marius and Cicero, with their prominence in the government of Arpinum, are representative of the type;[68] and there was a constant filtering upwards from some of these families into the lower reaches of the senatorial order. Others, although they owned land, derived their wealth chiefly from financial activities, above all the leading *publicani*, without whose resources of expertise and organization and manpower the Roman state could scarcely have limped along. These distinctions we shall have to come back to later.[69] We have already noted the possibility that Tiberius Gracchus himself began to turn his attention to the political importance and potential of the *equites* in the last few weeks of his tribunate, and the suggestion that their support was perhaps being angled for in 129.[70] But it is not until the tribunates of Gaius Gracchus that they leave the wings and take up a position right in the centre of the stage.

[68] See (e.g.) Stockton, *Cicero*, ch. I.

[69] Not all those who were commercially active in the Roman world were full Roman citizens, for numerous Italians—especially from the Grecized cities of Italy— were to be found in this field, and in the eyes of the provincials were simply lumped together with their fully Roman counterparts as Ῥωμαῖοι. See especially: Hatzfeld, *Les Trafiquants italiens dans l'orient hellénique,* 242 ff.; Wilson, *Emigration from Italy in the Republican Age of Rome,* 85 ff.; Gabba, *Le origini della guerra sociale,* 55; Sherwin-White, *The Roman Citizenship*[2], 139 ff. Of course, quite a number of these Italians will have been *cives sine suffragio,* which will have made their lumping together with full *cives* all the more understandable.

[70] Above, pp. 73 and 93.

Rome and Italy[71]

In a speech delivered to the Senate in A.D. 48, the Emperor Claudius insisted that it was one of the secrets of Rome's success in not merely increasing but retaining her power that from her earliest years she had, unlike Sparta and Athens, had the wisdom and the willingness to absorb erstwhile enemies within her own body politic: 'Quid aliud exitio Lacedaemoniis et Atheniensibus fuit, quamquam armis pollerent, nisi quod victos pro alienigenis arcebant? At conditor nostri Romulus tantum sapientia valuit ut plerosque populos eodem die hostis, dein civis habuerit.'[72]

Although that claim enshrined an important truth, for Rome had been notably liberal in extending her citizenship in the period down to the Hannibalic War, it would have sounded false to the ears of many of the non-Romans of Italy who belonged to the two or three generations preceding the outbreak of the Social War in 90. Increasingly, from the early years of the second century we can discern a marked change in the attitude of Rome towards the other communities and peoples of Italy. Laelius was made to remark on this disturbing tendency by Cicero in the dialogue *de re publica*; after his complaint that Tiberius Gracchus, though persevering in behalf of the citizens of Rome, had neglected the rights and treaties of allies and Latins, he continued:

If this practice, this lack of self-restraint, should begin to become more widespread; if our dominion should cease to be based on law and come to rely on force, so that those who have until now given us their willing obedience should be held subject through fear. . . . I am concerned for our posterity and for Rome's own immortality, which could abide for evermore if only we were to live by our ancestral institutions and practices.[73]

In the early second century, 'Rome was beginning to govern Italy in a

---

[71] On the matters discussed in this section, see above all the full treatment by Sherwin-White in the second edition of his *The Roman Citizenship* (1973), where he was able to take account of and discuss the literature on the subject which appeared in the thirty or so years following the appearance of the first edition in 1939.

[72] Tacitus, *Annals* 11.24. For the same general idea, cf. Cicero, *pro Balbo* 31 etc.

[73] Cicero, *de re pub.* 3.41: 'Quae si consuetudo ac licentia manare coeperit latius imperiumque nostrum ad vim a iure traduxerit, ut qui adhuc voluntate nobis oboediunt terrore teneantur, etsi nobis qui id aetatis sumus evigilatum fere est, tamen de posteris nostris et de illa immortalitate rei publicae sollicitor, quae poterat esse perpetua, si patriis viveretur institutis et moribus.'

sense not far removed from the modern.' At the same time, 'the more one considers the status of the allies the more inevitable their incorporation and the municipalization of Italy appears.'[74] In these twin processes lies the explanation both of the growing tensions and hostilities between Roman and non-Roman Italy, and of their eventual resolution in the two or three generations which followed the Social War.[75]

The non-Roman communities of Italy fell into three broad categories: the Latins, the *civitates sine suffragio*, and the allied or federate Italians.

Rome had first come to prominence as singly the most powerful of the small towns and peoples of Latium, and as such *prima inter pares*, the natural leader of the joint enterprises of the *Latini*, 'the men of the plain'. This relatively small region shared a community of language, religion, and culture; and the incorporation of the bulk of its inhabitants into the Roman state in the latter half of the fourth century was an event as easily predictable in its way as, say, the synoecism of Attica, and in itself not particularly remarkable. Indeed, other towns in Latium had been at the same game before 338, for by then the original 'Thirty Peoples', the *triginta populi* which had constituted the original Latin confederation, had been replaced by a mere dozen or so independent *populi*, a development in part due to the absorption of the smaller members by the larger.[76] None the less, it is important that all this happened in a historical period, the fifth and fourth centuries, and not so far back in the mists of prehistory that the Romans could ever be tempted to deceive themselves into thinking that things had always been thus since time began. The incorporation of most of Latium into the single state of Rome was a remembered political act. As Claudius reminded his audience, places which were in his day virtually suburbs of Rome had once been independent foreign states.[77]

As Roman power extended in Italy, so she began to plant colonies. Given both the limited technology and the political assumptions of the time, it was essential that these new towns with their attendant territories should be given their own local administrations. And, given too that the great majority of the *coloni* were themselves drawn from Rome and

[74] Sherwin-White, o.c. 105, 127.

[75] By 'Italy' in this section is meant, effectively, 'Italy south of the River Po'.

[76] Sherwin-White, o.c. 31.

[77] *ILS* 212 (= *FIRA* i.43, Bruns, *FIR* 52) lines 9–11: 'Supervenere alieni et quidem externi, ut Numa Romulo successerit ex Sabinis veniens, vicinus quidem sed tunc externus.'

Latium, it was pretty well inevitable that their organization should have been based on the old Latin pattern, and that the *coloni* should enjoy certain reciprocal rights which followed the practices of the relations between Rome and the communities of old Latium. The most important of these rights were (a) the *ius commercii*, the right to acquire a legal title to land, to buy and sell, to conclude valid contracts with Roman citizens which will be recognized and upheld by the courts; (b) the *ius connubii*, closely connected with the preceding, the right to contract a marriage with a Roman which will be recognized as of full legal validity with attendant testamentary and paternity rights; and (c) the *ius migrationis* giving a Latin the right to acquire Roman citizenship by simply establishing a domicile in Roman territory. These rights were, it must be insisted, reciprocal. A further right was the privilege accorded to Latins to cast their votes in one tribe of the Roman tribal assembly selected by lot, although this limited *ius suffragii ferendi* inevitably diminished in value as the total number of tribes rose to thirty-five. It is possible that, in certain instances, the *ius migrationis* was restrictively modified in some way in 268; and, between 187 and 177 apparently, a law was passed limiting the exercise of this right to Latins who left sons behind in their colonies of origin. Later, the right of acquiring Roman citizenship in this way seems to have disappeared altogether by the time of the Social War, but when and in what circumstances we cannot say.[78]

The Latins were frequently referred to as *socii Latini*, but they were not 'allies' in the strict sense that the Italian *civitates foederatae* were 'allies'. Rome had no *foedus* with any *colonia Latina*, for such colonies owed their existence, status, organization, rights, and duties to a unilateral act of the Roman state. They could pursue no separate foreign policy of their own, and were bound to follow Rome's; and they were required to supply troops for Rome's armies in accordance with regulations laid down by Rome, *ex formula togatorum*. For their own part, the *coloniae Latinae* early 'appear to imitate Roman institutions with riotous abandon; there are tribunes and aediles, even consuls, and *conscripti*, while at Cales and Ariminum the state is organized, like Rome, in *vici* bearing Roman names. Cicero adds (*pro Balbo* 21) that the Latins sought to assimilate their institutions and customs to those of Rome by

---

[78] Sherwin-White, o.c. 32–7, 102–4, 214–18. The final disappearance of the *ius migrationis* has by some been connected with the *lex Licinia Mucia* of the year 95; but the argument is unconvincing (see ibid. 110–11).

the adoption of 'innumerabiles leges', a statement which can only refer to the period before the Social War.'[79]

The incorporation of most of the *prisci Latini*, the old Latin communities of Latium itself, into Rome in 338, and the subsequent development of the *coloniae Latinae* in other parts of Italy transformed Latium from a geographic into a juristic term, so that by the second century 'the presence of some *Latini* in Latium is incidental'.[80] *Latinitas*, so to say, had become divorced from Latium, foreshadowing how ultimately *Romanitas* was to become divorced from Rome itself. A Latin individual or community was a person or a place with a certain juristic status, a bundle of particular rights and obligations. The new concept can be very clearly discerned in the establishment of a *colonia Latina* outside Italy, at Carteia in Spain, in the year 170. Here Latin rights were given to the 'illegitimate' children of Roman soldiers, the issue of their unions with native Spanish women; a status was accorded to these people which represents 'a modification or diminution of Roman citizenship from which it originates and with which it partially coincides'.[81] Even more remarkable, in its way, was a further development of the *ius Latii* whereby men who held local magistracies in their own Latin communities were *ipso facto* admitted to Roman citizenship; thus these men and their families became *cives Romani* without any change of domicile and while still remaining citizens, indeed leading citizens, of their own Latin communities. The date of the institution of this new *ius adipiscendae civitatis per magistratum* (which may possibly be connected with the final demise of the *ius migrationis*) is unfortunately unclear. It was certainly as established feature of the *ius Latii* by 89; it is generally held to have been an innovation of the Gracchan period, but that is something which will have to be discussed later.[82] What needs to be stressed here is how completely Roman citizenship has been divorced from the assumption that citizenship of a state must involve physical residence in, and direct participation in the affairs of, the inevitably restricted confines of a *polis*.

[79] Ibid. 99.

[80] Ibid. 101.

[81] Ibid.

[82] Asconius 3 C, speaking of the extension of Latin rights to the region north of the Po (the Transpadana) in 89 through the agency of Pompeius Strabo tells us that Strabo 'veteribus incolis manentibus ius dedit Latii, ut possent habere ius quod ceterae Latinae coloniae, id est ut petendo magistratus civitatem Romanam adipiscerentur.' See further below, p. 189.

Coloniae civium Romanorum. Finally, before moving on to say something about the other non-Romans, a momentous change in the character of colonization itself must be noted. Apart from the Latin colonies, there had been Roman citizen colonies, *coloniae civium Romanorum*, from very early times. But they were quite different from the *coloniae Latinae*, their main purpose being to provide small-scale security by controlling the few harbours and anchorages within the old Roman territory: thus Antium had been planted in 338 close by an old pirate stronghold to help defend the coastline and make up for Rome's lack of a proper fleet to guard these shores. The scale of these citizen colonies was tiny—300 families was apparently their standard complement—and far too small to constitute or support the life and organization of a proper 'state'; and they lacked the material basis for the development of an autonomous municipal organization. As late as 194, five citizen colonies which shared the size and purpose of colonies like Antium were being founded; but out of immediate contact with Roman territory. That may be a straw in the wind; eleven years later, in 183, when the foundation of a colony at Aquileia was being discussed, the question was raised whether it should be a Latin or a citizen colony (Livy 39.55.5). In fact, two years later Aquileia was founded as a *colonia Latina* with over three thousand families (Livy 40.34.2); but it was the last Latin colony of the epoch, and at this very same time three Roman citizen colonies were planted at Mutina, Parma, and Saturnia: there was no question of a mere 300 families, but of 2,000.[83]

That this development represented a conscious assimilation of the citizen colony to the Latin colony is shown by the parallels in magisterial systems and general constitutional arrangements. In short, these new citizen colonies were in every important respect the sisters of the older Latin colonies with the vital difference that the *coloni* themselves were full *cives Romani*. While sheer distance from Rome meant that even the richer among them could make only rare trips to the capital to use their *suffragium* there, they all enjoyed the legal status and rights of a citizen. Here again, the divorce of *Romanitas* from Rome itself is as clear as could be.

Civitates sine suffragio. While some scholars have held that the *municipia civium sine suffragio* had all disappeared in consequence of their promotion to full citizen status before the Gracchan period, the evidence

---

[83] Sherwin-White, o.c. 76–8. Cf. Appendix 1 below, p. 214.

is circumstantial and inconclusive, and it is safest to assume that some were still in existence then, and may well have survived right down to the time of the Social War.[84]

Although the concept of *civitas sine suffragio* had some affinity to the Greek concept of isopolity, it was at bottom a very Roman one. It involved no merely diplomatic exchange of citizenship; the designation of such communities as *municipia civium sine suffragio* underlines the basic importance of the fact that the members of such communities shared the duties, the *munia* or *munera*, of Roman citizens, most notably the obligation to military service *in legione*. Further, like the Latins, they enjoyed the *ius commercii*, the *ius conubii*, and probably also the *ius migrationis*. There is thus a real sense in which the extension of this status to communities in central Italy outside Latium was essentially an extension of the *ius Latii* to non-Latins. Yet at the same time they could sometimes be referred to as 'allies', *socii*. They each continued with a separate state or *res publica* of their own. As Aulus Gellius put it: 'municipes . . . sunt cives Romani . . . legibus suis et suo iure utentes . . . neque ulla populi Romani lege adstricti nisi in quam populus eorum fundus factus est'—they kept their own laws and were only bound by a Roman law if their own community had specifically adopted it.[85] Trouble arises because of later developments after the fourth century, for there then emerges a 'depressed' or 'inferior' grade of *municipia c.s.s.*, which had rebelled against Rome, been brought to heel, and subjected to limitations on their autonomy, the most notable of which was the sending out from Rome each year of *praefecti iure dicundo* to oversee their administration, which probably spelled the effective demise of their local self-government.[86] But not all of them travelled that road; and 'thanks to the way in which the *civitas sine suffragio* developed, the Romans were able to conceive the idea that citizenship was not entirely incompatible with membership of another, secondary community.'[87] Arpinum, for instance, was a Volscian town which had been given the status of a *municipium civium sine suffragio* at the end of

[84] Sherwin-White, 210–14. And in general on the *civitas s.s.* see ibid. 39–58, 200–14.

[85] Aulus Gellius, *NA* 16.13.6.

[86] Brunt argues (*IM* 525ff.) that these prefects 'need not have entrenched on the administrative functions' of the local magistrates. But in my view they did represent a serious erosion of local autonomy.

[87] Sherwin-White, o.c. 57.

the fourth century, and which was raised to full citizen status in 188; thereafter, Arpinum continued to exercise control of its own local affairs —seventy or eighty years later its voting laws, for example, differed from those of Rome itself[88]—although its citizens were now also full citizens of Rome with the right to vote at Rome on laws and at elections and to hold Roman magistracies. Marius, a member of the local aristocracy of Arpinum, became consul and commander-in-chief in North Africa against Jugurtha three generations after his native town had received full Roman citizenship; he was an exceptional man, but had he risen no higher than the praetorship his career would have constituted a shining example of the opportunities which were open to a man from such a background, given the necessary ability and determination.

Civitates Foederatae. The 'allies' proper, the *civitates foederatae*, of Italy had mostly concluded treaties (*foedera*) and entered into alliance with Rome after serious fighting and resistance. Rome and her federate allies were bound by treaty to assist each other in defensive wars; sometimes an allied state was specifically required to join in safeguarding the might of Rome (*maiestatem populi Romani comiter conservare*).[89] So long as Rome was engaged in securing the hegemony of Italy, all her wars were in effect, or could easily be seen as, defensive wars. Indeed, the Romans in their own estimate never fought aggressive wars; and the Romans were, of course, the interpreters of the treaties which Rome had made with her Italian allies. Hence, in practice, they could call on them for assistance even in what were in reality, if not in name, non-defensive wars. But by this time 'Rome was beginning to govern Italy in a sense not far removed from the modern'.

There was some tendency towards the Romanization of institutions among the federate states of Italy. Umbrians and Oscan—speaking peoples in particular were close to Romans and Latins both in race and in language. On the other hand, the Etruscans were not, and it is notable that Rome treated them with great wariness throughout the Hannibalic War. In theory autonomous, the *socii* were obliged to follow Rome's foreign policy and to furnish troops for her wars. Although by the early second

---

[88] Cicero, *de legg.* 3.36.

[89] An example of a *foedus iniquum* with the *maiestatem p. R. comiter conservanto* clause, albeit with an extra-Italian state, can be found in Polybius 22.15 (treaty with the Aetolians in 189): ὁ δῆμος τῶν Αἰτωλῶν τὴν ἀρχὴν καὶ τὴν δυναστείαν τοῦ δήμου τῶν Ῥωμαίων διαφυλαττέτω χωρὶς δόλου.

century the *ius commercii* and the *ius conubii* seem to have been wide-spread among the *socii*,[90] these *iura* were but a selection from those of the Latins, and the allies owed them not to their status but to individual separate grants. For all that Rome exercised the functions of a central government of Italy by working formally through the local authorities of the states concerned—the repression of the Bacchanalian excesses is a well-known example—or couched a decision in the form of a recommendation (*oportere videtur*) rather than a command (*iubet*), the area of competence and initiative of the local governments grew more restricted, and their dependence on Rome and conversely Rome's responsibility for their well-being grew larger—in 196 it was a Roman praetor who intervened to suppress a serf-insurrection in allied Etruria.[91]

The complaint of the allies [writes Sherwin-White] which in effect was that while performing the *munera* of citizens they were treated only as subjects, was true, but it could have been raised at many stages of Rome's history by any of her most barbarous allies. In Italy it took its force largely from the geographic fact that these particular allies formed part of a territorial unit, largely administered by Rome, which was being rapidly romanized and latinized in law, speech, and custom, and from the partial overlap of the true type of ally, the *civitas foederata*, with the informal allies of the *Latinum Nomen* [and, he might have added, with the *municipia civium sine suffragio*], who bridged the gap which at this period existed outside Italy between the *foederati* and Rome.[92]

But the details of the complaints of the non-Romans of Italy in general, their causes and depth and extent, is a topic which will be put aside for the moment, to be resumed when we come to investigate Gaius Gracchus' proposed legislation on the subject of Latins and allies.[93]

[90] This seems to me to follow from Livy 35.7.5 and Diodorus 37.15.2, and I should suppose that both these *iura* were almost or totally universal throughout Italy by the Gracchan period. But Sherwin-White (125–6) is more cautious. Certainly, so far as concerns the *ius commercii*, the more advanced Romans would have had the better of the mutual exchange over the less advanced peoples of rural Italy. One may note how the fifth century Athenians exploited to their own material advantage the right to acquire real property (ἔγκτησις, ἐγκτήματα) in the territory of their allies. Compare too the interesting case of the Centuripani in Sicily, as described by Cicero in *Verr. II*, iii. 108.

[91] Livy 33.36.

[92] Sherwin-White, o.c. 133.

[93] Below, pp. 185 ff.

VI

THE LEGISLATION OF GAIUS GRACCHUS

By his public advocacy of the suppression of aristocracy and the establishment of democracy [wrote Diodorus Siculus] Gaius Gracchus was able to
draw on the willing support of all classes. Indeed, they became not just
willing supporters, but virtually the prime movers in his bold plans. Each
and every one of them, inspired by his own selfish hopes, was ready to
face any risk to defend the laws which began to be introduced, as if he
were defending his own private advantage. By stripping the senators of
their right to sit in judgement, and appointing the *equites* to serve as
iudices, he made the inferior element in the state master over the superior
(τὸ χεῖρον τῆς πολιτείας τοῦ κρείττονος κύριον ἐποίησεν); and, by shattering
the harmony which had existed hitherto between Senate and *equites*, he
exposed both of them to the pressures of the mob. He split the state into
two, thus paving the way for personal supremacy. He squandered the
public treasury on disgraceful and ill-judged expenditures and bribes, so
ensuring that he became the focus of all eyes. By sacrificing the provinces
to the reckless greed of the public contractors, he wrung from the subject-
peoples a justified hatred for the dominion of Rome. By currying favour
with the soldiery through laws to relax the strictness of the old discipline,
he opened the gates to mutiny and anarchy. For a man who comes to lose
respect for those set in authority over him comes to lose respect for the
laws as well; and such patterns of behaviour breed fatal disorder and
national destruction.[1]

This passage is representative of one ancient view of Gaius Gracchus:
that he was out to substitute 'democracy' for 'aristocracy'; that he sowed
discord where there had been harmony; that by a clever and calculated
appeal to selfish sectional interests he bade fair to make himself a sort of
popular tyrant of a well-known Greek type. A similar ring can be detected
in some of the criticisms which we have seen were directed against his
elder brother. The prejudiced and hostile elements in such a view are
obvious enough; but it does not altogether lack truth. The characteristically
Greek concepts of 'demokratia' and 'aristokratia' could not readily or
appositely be transposed into an alien Roman context; but no more can
they be so transposed into a modern European context, where our own
use of these words which we have borrowed from ancient Greece could

---

[1] Diodorus Siculus 34/5.25.1 (probably drawing on Posidonius).

surprise a Thucydides or an Aristotle. Diodorus was not a subtle thinker; but even Polybius found his Greek terminology intractable when he turned to analyse the constitutional ethos and organization of Rome in his Sixth Book. Gaius does not seem to have set out to annihilate the power of the Senate and the ruling oligarchy of his day, to usher in an egalitarian millennium or a 'benevolent dictatorship'. But he clearly did purpose to tame that power, to discipline it and make it function more responsibly and equitably, to curb its most flagrant excesses and remedy its grosser failings, to make the voice of the non-senatorial classes more urgently audible. If his brother's brief career and ugly death had taught him nothing else, he had surely learned that his political appeal and support must be more broadly based; and such support was scarcely to be counted on without some inducement in the shape of legislation which offered a tangible *quid pro quo*. Which at once brings us up against the teasing question: which of his many proposals were ends in themselves, and which means to other ends? And one and the same proposal might serve both purposes.

That question is not one that can be answered easily or confidently. It is rarely easy to give a confident appraisal of the deeper motives which underlay any ancient statesman's policies; and Gaius Gracchus is no exception to that rule. Had we a substantial body of his published speeches extant or reliably summarized, we should be far better off. If we could be sure of the details of each particular law or proposal, and of its place in his general scheme of legislation and its temporal relation to other proposals and other events, we could expect a wide measure of agreement about the answer. But we lack both these aids in anything like the completeness which we need.[2] So, for the moment, I propose to shelve any discussion of underlying motives and overall objectives, and to begin with an examination of his laws and proposals in themselves, trying to elicit what sort of intentions or objectives he must have had in mind in bringing them forward. Even here, there is room enough for argument.

The *lex de abactis*

Plutarch records, apparently as one of the earliest measures which Gaius introduced, a law which laid it down that anyone who had been removed

---

[2] The extant fragments of Gaius' speeches are reproduced in Appendix 2 below, pp. 217ff. The chronology of his legislation is discussed in detail in Appendix 3 below, pp. 226ff.

from public office by the People should be disbarred from ever again
holding any further public office (*CG* 4.1). He notes that it was aimed at
M. Octavius, the man whom Tiberius Gracchus had persuaded the plebeian
assembly to depose from his office as tribune of the *plebs* in 133; but he
adds that Gaius later ἐπανείλετο the law, stating publicly that he extended
this favour to Octavius at the request of his own mother, Cornelia. The
Greek verb here used can be taken to mean that Gaius 'withdrew' the proposal (cf. Plutarch's use of it at *TG* 10.2), although its more normal
meaning would be that he 'repealed' or 'rescinded' it. Diodorus (34/5.25.2)
has a confused reference to this measure, giving it as an instance of Gaius'
'overweening arrogance': although the People had judged that Octavius
should go into exile, Gaius reprieved him, saying that he did so in deference to Cornelia's intercession on Octavius' behalf.

It seems likeliest that Gaius did publish a proposal on the lines given by
Plutarch which not only laid down this rule for the future but was also
retrospective in its effect, but later amended the original draft to remove
the retrospective element. Either he had had second thoughts, or he had
intended to do so all along. Whichever way it was, he did not neglect to
make capital out of the generosity of spirit which his family was dis-
playing towards the man who had done so much to drive his brother
Tiberius to destruction.

Whether the law applied to all magistrates, or whether its application
was restricted to those officers who were elected by the *plebs* as opposed
to the *populus*, it would be very rash to decide on the basis of the evidence we have. The second alternative could well be preferable, since the
bill was passed by the plebeian assembly and not by the *populus*; but that
point is not decisive.[3]

That Gaius was chiefly moved by a desire for revenge is very unlikely. If

---

[3] Plutarch speaks of ὁ δῆμος, and not of τὸ πλῆθος: εἴ τινος ἀφῄρητο τὴν ἀρχὴν
ὁ δῆμος. Strictly, δῆμος = *populus Romanus* and πλῆθος = *plebs Romana*; but Plutarch and other Greek writers are careless about observing the distinction. The
Romans themselves seldom bothered to distinguish between the tribal assembly of
the *populus* and the tribal assembly of the *plebs*; and even official texts like the
Tabula Bembina can treat *lex* and *plebiscitum* as wholly interchangeable terms, for
all that only the *populus* could pass a *lex* and only the *plebs* a *plebiscitum*. 'There is
evidence enough to show that capital rights were controlled at will by all the Roman
assemblies indifferently in the later Republic' (Sherwin-White, *JRS* (1952), 52).
That may have been an innovation due to Gaius Gracchus himself (Greenidge, *Legal
Procedure*, 324ff.).

that had been his main aim, he would be revealed as an extremely rash and volatile character; for we can suppose that his mother must have had ample opportunity to make her feelings about Octavius known to him before he published the original draft. The intercession of Cornelia looks like a calculated and carefully publicized move to win public respect and sympathy for a magnanimous action which was in pointed contrast with the behaviour of Tiberius' own enemies. The chief purpose of the law was surely to deter opposition; to try to ensure that Gaius should not find himself confronted with a second Octavius; to make it plain that the plebeian assembly had an indisputable right to depose any of its officers who failed to retain its confidence; to insist that Tiberius had been in the right when he had moved the deposition of Octavius, whatever Annius Luscus and his like might aver.[4] Without the text of the law to guide us, we cannot say whether this last point was made explicitly or only by implication, although we can rely on it that it left no opening for the inference that it was establishing a totally new principle: the law must have been so worded as to assert, not only that nobody could possibly challenge the legality of such depositions henceforth, but also that there should never have been any doubt about this point hitherto. Otherwise, it might have been taken to show that Tiberius' action ten years earlier had itself been questionable.

It is just possible that a fragmentary inscription from Lucania (Bruns, *FIR* 9: the *lex Latina tabulae Bantinae*) preserves part of the text of the *lex de abactis*. Bruns 9 could well be an early law of Gaius Gracchus;[5] and the first few broken lines that survive well suit the nature of this particular *lex*. The remaining fragments, it is true, do not suit so well; but, given that Plutarch and Diodorus concentrate on the drama of Octavius' personal danger and reprieve, and are not concerned to go into detail about the full scope of the *lex de abactis*, we cannot rule the identification out of court. It is, however, no more than a possibility, and no deductions can safely be drawn from it. The Bantia tablet is such treacherous shoal-water that no prudent navigator would risk his ship in it.

The *'lex de provocatione'*[6]

Gaius, so Cicero tells us (*pro Rab. Post.* 12), passed a law which enacted

---

[4] Above, p. 70.
[5] See further Appendix 3 below, p. 236.
[6] I have chosen this title solely for brevity and convenience, as will soon be

that only the Roman People themselves could authorize a capital sentence against a Roman citizen: 'C. Gracchus legem tulit ne de capite civium Romanorum iniussu vestro [sc. populi Romani] iudicaretur.' Anyone passing such a sentence without such authority was himself liable to suffer the same penalty.[7]

Mommsen's views about *provocatio* long held the field virtually without challenge. He maintained that all criminal law at Rome had its roots in an initiative taken by a magistrate who held *imperium* in exercising his *ius coercitionis*, his formal power to enforce order and secure obedience to his commands in the interests of public safety and security. In due course the *provocatio* legislation gave every citizen the right to appeal to the People against a capital sentence imposed by a magistrate; and out of this right there developed the regular process of capital trials before the centuriate assembly—there being in effect two stages in such trials: the trial itself, followed by the hearing of the appeal if the magistrate condemned the accused. But recently Kunkel and others have argued convincingly that Mommsen was mistaken; and it is Kunkel whom I prefer broadly to follow. On his view, under early Roman law non-political or non-public criminal offences did not require or engender any magisterial initiative in their repression: they were left to be pursued by private citizens bringing private prosecutions or suits. The origins of *provocatio* had nothing to do with ordinary crime, but were essentially political in character. Ordinary crimes did not come within the province of *coercitio*, for this was a power which magistrates used only against crimes of a public or 'official' or political nature. About the beginning of the second century, however, the older practice whereby a magistrate would use his *ius coercitionis* (usually with the help of a *consilium* or panel of advisers) began to give way to a new system: special courts (*quaestiones extraordinariae*) were set up by senatorial decrees to deal chiefly with public or 'political' offences but also sometimes with other offences when the latter aroused widespread interest or concern and involved numerous offenders (the Bacchanalian *quaestio* of 186 is a good example). These *quaestiones* reached decisions which were clearly not the *ipse dixit* of the presiding magistrate; no interventions were made against them and no recourse had to *provocatio* because in general

---

apparent. I do not like it, but it is to some extent conventional. I prefer to call it '*lex de capite civium R.*' or '*de capite civis*'.

[7] Cicero, *pro Sestio* 61; Plutarch, *CG* 4.

they enjoyed public agreement with or acquiescence in their proceedings. But the latent danger inherent in allowing the Senate to act in this way and to assume this sort of power became startlingly clear when the special court was set up by the Senate in 132 to deal with the alleged crimes of Tiberius Gracchus' supporters. It is a mystery why we hear nothing of any attempted recourse to the *ius provocationis* in 132 (this is equally a difficulty for the Mommsenic view); we are driven to assume that the political balance was decisively in favour of the 'establishment' at the time, or else that the *quaestio* procedure somehow or other put technical difficulties in the way of exercising a right of appeal. Early in his first tribunate of 123 we find Gaius Gracchus reacting forcefully and carrying a law which did not challenge the propriety or advantages of the *quaestio* procedure but which laid it down that henceforth any such *quaestiones* could be set up only by direction of the Roman People—i.e. capital sentence could not be passed on a Roman citizen *iniussu populi*. To mark indignant condemnation of the 132 proceedings, the new law was made retrospective as well as prospective in its force.[8]

The connection of this law with the elimination of a large number of the supporters of Tiberius Gracchus nearly nine years earlier is clear. Popillius Laenas, who had presided over those proceedings as consul in 132, now withdrew into self-imposed exile rather than stay and face trial under Gaius' law, which shows that it contained a retrospective element (as did the similar law which Clodius was to carry in 58); he was duly publicly outlawed by Gaius, but returned to Rome later after one of the tribunes of 121, L. Calpurnius Bestia, had passed a bill enabling him to do so.[9] What Bestia's arguments were we are not told. Diodorus, in a very tendentious passage, says that Gaius had had to resort to massive bribery to get rid of Popillius and that great crowds of people escorted him from Rome with tears in their eyes;[10] but his notice is very condensed and

---

[8] Mommsen, *Römische Strafrecht*; Kunkel, *Untersuchungen zur Entwicklung des röm. Kriminalverfahrens in vorsullanischer Zeit*. An excellent summary and discussion of both accounts (especially that of Kunkel) is to be found in Nicholas's third edition of Jolowicz, *Hist. Intro. Roman Law*, 305–17. Jones's treatment of Kunkel in his own *Criminal Courts* is very unsatisfactory: see Brunt's review of Jones in *CR* (1974), 265–7.

[9] Above, p. 90. Cicero, *de domo* 82: 'ubi enim tuleras ut mihi aqua et igni interdiceretur? quod C. Gracchus de P. Popillio tulit.' *Brutus* 128: 'L. Bestia P. Popillium vi C. Gracchi expulsum sua rogatione restituit.'

[10] Diodorus 34/5. 26. But Professor Brunt suggests to me that Diodorus may have meant crowds of the 'best people' and their dependents.

erratic—he seems clearly to imply that Popillius' exile was not self-imposed, though Plutarch is clear that it was—and it is impossible to feel any confidence in the picture of the 'butcher of the Gracchans' as the lamented idol of the common people of Rome: Cicero suggests nothing at all of this when he talks of the 'hostility of an angry multitude' having been aroused against Popillius by Gaius.[11]

Plutarch seems to suggest that only the magistrate who actually pronounced such a sentence *iniussu populi* was liable under the law; and Diodorus also concentrates on Popillius. But Cicero in the *pro Sestio* claims that Cato's action in December 63 in moving for the death penalty during the senatorial debate on the arrested Catilinarians had exposed Cato himself to the danger of a capital prosecution; and Dio reports that the law which P. Clodius passed in 58 against any one who executed citizens without the People's authority, although it was in fact directed specifically against Cicero, who as consul had ordered the executions, was so worded as to apply to all and sundry, and in particular to any senator who had voted for the *senatus consultum ultimum* under cover of which Cicero had ordered the execution of the arrested conspirators.[12] It is quite possible that Gaius' law too had not been so worded as to confine its sanctions to those presiding magistrates who actually pronounced such sentences or ordered such executions.

In his speech *de legibus promulgatis*, Gaius spoke out in strong condemnation of certain (unnamed) Roman magistrates who had used their authority to order the flogging of some local magistrates of non-Roman communities in Italy, in anger or pique at imagined slights or oversights. The date of the speech is nowhere stated. Many scholars assign it to a date early in Gaius' second tribunate, linking it above all with the franchise proposals of 122. But some features do not fit that date so well, and it is at least as likely—I should say a shade more likely—that it was delivered early in the first tribunate.[13] The vivid examples which Gaius here gives of the arrogant and brutal misuse of magisterial authority could have been

[11] Cicero, *de legg*. 3.26: 'si nos multitudinis furentis inflammata invidia pepulisset tribuniciaque vis in me populum sicut Gracchus in Laenatem incitasset.' For Gaius' speeches attacking Popillius Laenas, see Appendix 2 below, p. 220.

[12] *pro Sestio* 61: 'dixit [Cato] eam sententiam cuius invidiam capitis periculo sibi praestandam videbat.' Cf. Dio 38.14.

[13] See Appendix 2 below, p. 221, for citations from this speech and discussion of its date.

introduced to underline and reinforce that general attack on the abuse of public office which is in large part the burden of the earliest of Gaius' bills in 123. It could even be that his law extended some sort of protection against such mis-treatment to Latins and Italians as well as to Roman citizens: Cicero's reference in the passage from his *pro Rabirio Postumo* just cited is to citizens alone; but that could simply be because he is here interested only in that particular aspect of the law, and in any case all Italians south of the Po and all local magistrates in the towns north of the Po in Italy were full Roman citizens when Cicero delivered this speech. But, whether the law did or did not affect non-citizens, the instances of arbitrary cruelty which Gaius paints so graphically in his speech would have served well to help drive his central point home. The precise scope and application of the *'lex de provocatione'* are very debatable. The old view of Mommsen, that the Gracchan *lex ne quis iudicio circumveniatur* should be closely associated or even identified with the *'lex de provocatione'*, has recently returned to favour. Strachan-Davidson's 'disproof' of this argument is far from cogent.[14] And 'the important thing is that these two laws, even if not one, were probably meant to supplement and strengthen each other'.[15] It will therefore be necessary to postpone further discussion of Gaius' object in passing the *'lex de provocatione'* until we have dealt with the *lex ne quis*.

[14] Strachan-Davidson, *Problems of the Roman Criminal Law* i.244. But (so Ewins in *JRS* 50 (1960), 98) 'this criticism only shows that it is impossible to identify the *clauses* as we have them, but this is surely impossible anyway? What, then, is to prevent us from supposing that these were separate clauses of a single law?' But later she 'wonders if Sulla would have excerpted one clause from a general Lex Sempronia *de provocatione* and put it in his Lex *de sicariis et veneficis*, particularly since there is no reason to suppose that this Lex Sempronia *de provocatione* had been abrogated by Sulla's time?' But how do we know that Sulla excerpted only the one clause? And the subsequent fate of the so-called *'lex de provocatione'* is a mystery. It seems that Clodius had to pass a new law on similar lines to that of Gaius in order to attack Cicero for his execution without trial of the arrested Catilinarians in December 63—why, if the law which had been good enough against Popillius in 123 was still on the statute book?

[15] Ewins, loc. cit. The mere fact that we have only Cicero's (accidental) evidence in his *pro Cluentio* for any reference to the very important *lex ne quis* is a strong argument in favour of the view that it was very closely linked with, or part of, the *'lex de provocatione'* which does find a place in Plutarch's and Diodorus' accounts.

The *lex ne quis iudicio circumveniatur*[16]

This law has often been discussed in connection with Gaius' *repetundae* law rather than with the *lex de provocatione*.[17] Stated briefly, the former approach starts from the premiss that the *lex ne quis* was a law which made it a capital offence for any senator or minor magistrate to accept a bribe while acting as a *iudex* in return for delivering a verdict of guilty against an innocent defendant.[18] If that premiss is correct, and assuming that the *quaestio perpetua repetundarum* (whose *iudices* were before Gaius Gracchus drawn exclusively from among the members of the Senate) was the only standing court in existence at this time, it can be taken to imply one of two conclusions: (a) at the time when Gaius introduced his *lex ne quis* he believed that it would or might in itself suffice to correct the existing defects of the *repetundae* courts of his day by deterring the senatorial *iudices* who alone sat in judgement there from any malpractice and ensuring that they would bring in only honest condemnations; (b) even if Gaius was already contemplating the introduction of non-senators as *iudices* in the *repetundae* court, he must nevertheless have had it in mind that these new *iudices* should not monopolize the court but that senators should continue to constitute some proportion of the *iudices* who manned it. In this way the *lex ne quis* has been used to buttress the view that Gaius had more than one shot at reforming the *repetundae* court: to begin with, he either planned to leave the court exactly as it was, relying simply on his *lex ne quis* to remedy its shortcomings, or he was purposing before long to double or treble the number of senators by adlecting into the Senate some three or six hundred new members from the equestrian order, or he was intending to established mixed panels of *iudices* for the *repetundae* court drawn partly from members of the Senate and partly from members of the equestrian order. Whichever way it was, Gaius' final decision to entrust the *repetundae* court exclusively to non-senatorial *iudices* must represent a later stage in his thinking and one to which he had not advanced at the time when he proposed and carried the *lex ne quis iudicio circumveniatur*. For otherwise the *lex ne quis* would have been pointless, since no senatorial *iudices* would henceforth

---

[16] See especially the discussions by Sherwin-White, *JRS* 42 (1952), 43–55; Miners, *CQ* (1958), 241 ff.; Ewins, *JRS* 50 (1960), 94–107.

[17] See, e.g., Last in *CAH* ix.53.

[18] That the *lex ne quis* applied only to magistrates and members of the Senate is clear from the *pro Cluentio*, and is not in dispute.

be left to be corrupted once the court had been handed over lock stock and barrel to non-senatorial *iudices*; and it would also have been defective in that it neglected to expose the new non-senatorial *iudices* to prosecution and punishment if they too should be guilty of accepting bribes to bring in unjust condemnations. In brief, then, on this view the provisions of the *lex ne quis* inescapably entail the conclusion that at the time when he proposed and carried it Gaius had not as yet thought of moving to the total exclusion of senators from serving as *iudices* on the *repetundae* court.

Some of these points will have to be resumed when we come to consider the *repetundae* law itself in its due place—and especially the (to my mind) unjustified assumption that in 123 there existed no other *quaestiones perpetuae* apart from that *de repetundis*. But, as it happens, the initial premiss from which all the above conclusions are held to flow has been undermined by the careful review of the evidence which has taken place during the last twenty-five years or so. It is unnecessary to repeat here the fine detail of arguments which have been set out elsewhere and which have won general acceptance.[19] It will suffice to outline their main gist.

Pretty well all our evidence about the *lex ne quis* comes from the *pro Cluentio*, a forensic speech of Cicero's delivered in the year 66, nearly sixty years later. From this speech we learn that the *lex ne quis*, originally the work of Gaius Gracchus, had been taken over by Sulla and incorporated in his own judicial legislation (much of which was in fact of a consolidating nature), and that it was still in force at the time of the trial of Cluentius (*Clu.* 151). Only members of the Senate and some minor magistrates could be arraigned under the *lex ne quis*, and non-senators were not subject to its provisions and penalties (*Clu.* 145 etc.). It provided for the trial and punishment of any magistrate or member of the Senate who conspired or co-operated with anyone in order to secure the condemnation of an innocent defendant in or by means of a public court of law: 'DEQVE EIVS CAPITE QVAERITO . . . . QVI TRIBVNVS MILITVM LEGIONIBVS QVATTVOR PRIMIS QVIVE QVAESTOR TRIBVNVS PLEBIS—deinceps omnis magistratus nominavit—QVIVE IN SENATV SENTENTIAM DIXIT DIXERIT . . . . QVI EORVM COIIT COIERIT CONVENIT CONVENERIT QVO QVIS IVDICIO PVBLICO CONDEMNARETVR'

[19] See p. 122 n. 16, above.

(*Clu*. 148).[20] Cicero's use here of *condemnare* rather than *circumvenire* is merely a casual variation of language, either on his own part or in the text of the law which he is citing; elsewhere he several times uses the verb *circumvenire*, and at one point in direct citation from the text of Gaius Gracchus' law: 'hanc ipsam legem "NE QVIS IVDICIO CIRCVMENI-RETVR" C. Gracchus tulit' (*Clu*. 151).

Circumvenio can sometimes imply 'to outwit', 'overcome', 'afflict'. But we come closest to its meaning here with the somewhat slangy modern English-American verb 'to frame'. This was a law which made it a capital offence for any magistrate or senator to participate in any way in a judicial 'frame-up', in a scheme to 'frame' an innocent party. It was not just a case of the giving and taking of monetary bribes, since we know that the giving—and no doubt the procuring also—of false testimony was punishable under the law: 'FALSVMVE TESTIMONIVM DIXERIT' (*Clu*. 157); indeed, there is no reason why we should suppose that Cicero's citations from the *lex ne quis* exhaust all its provisions.

Cicero attests that in the post-Sullan period the normal law under which a charge would be brought against a senator who was alleged to have accepted a bribe as a *iudex* was the *lex repetundarum*. Technically, it seems, he might also be liable to indictment under the *lex ne quis* if there was some element of active agency or conspiracy beyond the mere taking of a bribe.[21] We cannot be sure whether that was the position in Gaius Gracchus' time, for the *repetundae* law had undergone very considerable modifications since then, and it is possible that in his day the *lex ne quis* was the only law under which such a charge could be brought. But, be that as it may, it is clear that the *lex ne quis* and not the *lex repetundarum* was the law under which Cicero's client Cluentius could have stood trial (and thereby, so Cicero has it, been given the chance to clear his name once and for all of a grave calumny) if only Cluentius had been a senator (which he was not). But the allegation against Cluentius was not that he had accepted a bribe as a *iudex*, but that eight years earlier he had handed out bribes to

[20] We can add 'CONSENSIT CONSENSERIT' from *Clu*. 157.

[21] Sherwin-White 46, Ewins 99–100. (I have expressed this view perhaps rather more decidedly than they might.) For the *lex repetundarum* as the normal relevant law, see *pro Cluentio* 104, where Cicero is discussing the alleged bribery of Fidiculanius, one of the *iudices* at the trial of Oppianicus in the year 74: 'Fidiculanius quid fecisse dicebatur? Accepisse a Cluentio HS C̄C̄C̄C̄. Cuius erat ordinis? Senatorii. Qua lege in eo genere a senatore ratio repeti solet, de pecuniis repetundis, ea lege accusatus honestissime est absolutus.'

corrupt a court of senatorial *iudices* in order to secure the conviction of his stepfather Oppianicus; and Cluentius was debarred from standing trial under the *lex ne quis*, not because his alleged offence did not come under that law (for it did), but merely because that law could be invoked only against magistrates and senators (and Cluentius was neither): (*Clu.* 143–5).

Thus the *lex ne quis* stands revealed as a law which was not directed, or at least not exclusively directed, against senatorial *iudices* who accepted bribes to convict innocent men. It was a law which was designed to prevent or punish the abuse of court procedures in any of a variety of ways in order to falsely convict or 'frame' the innocent. That only magistrates and senators could be charged under the *lex ne quis* is perfectly understandable, and the connection with the '*lex de provocatione*' is obvious. It matters very little whether the provisions *ne de capite civium Romanorum iniussu populi iudicetur* and *ne quis iudicio circumveniatur* formed separate sections or chapters of a single law, or whether they were parts of separate enactments—although the former seems to me the more economical and hence the preferable alternative. Either way, both can be seen as part of a move to close gaps and remove obscurities in earlier legislation which had sought to safeguard the individual against the abuse of judicial or quasi-judicial proceedings on the part of the senatorial ruling-class, but which had proved ineffective against (*inter alia*) the sort of tribunal which the Senate had set up in 132 under the presidency of the then consul, Popillius Laenas. The aim of Gaius was to exact condign retribution from Popillius himself, and to provide a further deterrent—like the *lex de abactis*—against the use of similar tactics against himself and his supporters and future popular reformers and theirs. The *lex ne quis* has no particularly close connection with the *repetundae* law; indeed, the complaint against the senatorial *iudices* who had hitherto manned that court was a complaint that too many guilty men had been allowed to escape conviction, not that too many innocent defendants had been unjustly and corruptly condemned.[22] Even if Gaius had from the start been planning to introduce a bill to man the *repetundae* court (or all existing standing courts) with non-senatorial *iudices*, such a measure, even leaving aside its retrospective effect, was anything but supererogatory. His evident object was to prevent the establishing in the future of any capital inquisitions which did not have the explicit authority of the People behind them, and to deter or

[22] Appian, *BC* 1.22.2.

punish any move on the part of members of the senatorial ruling-class to use the courts—no matter who the *iudices* of those courts might be—to eliminate those whom that ruling-class disliked or feared. Any officer of state who imposed a capital sentence on a citizen without the explicit authority of the People behind him was to be liable to a capital prosecution; the same was true of any magistrate or senator who set out or helped in any way to pervert or corrupt a capital court, or perhaps even participated in setting up such a court or inquisition which did not rest on the People's authority. Power had of course to be given by the People to its elected magistrates, the Senate had an important role to play in the direction and formulation of public policy; but henceforth any abuse or misuse of those powers and of that role was to be sternly checked.

The *lex frumentaria*

Several authors allude to this law, the first of its kind in Roman history. It provided for regular monthly distributions of grain to Roman citizens at the fixed price (if we can trust our manuscripts) of 6 1/3 *asses* for a modius.[23] What the allowance for each individual was fixed at we do not know, nor whether the size of his family was taken into account. Nor can we say how that price compared with the normal price of grain at Rome, partly because such information as we do have shows that prices could fluctuate widely: the quality of the harvests in various areas of Italy and the provinces, the varying cost of transport from different surplus areas, and so on, all had their effect. Moreover, it happens that in 123 special factors affected the supply of grain to the capital adversely: the slave war in Sicily must have injured production there, and in 124 a huge swarm of locusts had devastated the crops in Africa.[24] It seems clear that there was some element of cheapness or subsidy in the price which Gracchus fixed, although the mere fact that the price was fixed and regular must in itself have helped to shield the poor from the impact of fluctuations and

[23] Plutarch, *CG* 5.1; Appian, *BC* 1.21; Livy, *Epit.* 60; Vell. Pat. 2.6.3; Schol. Bob. 135 St; etc. Cheap distributions had been known in the past on rare occasions, as for instance at the triumph of L. Metellus, *cos.* 251 (Pliny, *NH* 18.3 (4).17). The curious price of $6\frac{1}{3}$ *asses* for a *modius* might represent, with 16 *asses* to the *denarius*, the nearest rounded equivalent of a price of 1 denarius for 2½ *modii*.

[24] In general, see Tenney Frank, *ESAR* i.402–3; Last, *CAH* ix.58–9; Brunt, *IM* 376. For the locusts, see Livy, *Epit.* 60, Orosius 5.11. In England between 1812 and 1825 the average yearly price of wheat varied from as low as 44*s*. 7*d*. to as high as 126*s*. 6*d*. a quarter.

profiteering. Cicero later spoke of the measure as 'a massive give-away, which consequently was a continuing drain on the treasury';[25] and he uses the same sort of language when he tells the story of how Gaius' old enemy L. Calpurnius Piso Frugi (whose *cognomen* bore witness to an Aberdonian parsimony) turned up to claim his allowance of grain under the law; Piso had himself spoken out against the law, but when now reproached for his inconsistency he replied: 'I do not care for this fancy of yours, Gracchus, to divide my goods among every Tom Dick and Harry; but, since that is what you are doing, I shall claim my share.' The story may be apocryphal, but it makes no sense unless the distributed grain was in some sense 'a bargain'. Yet, in this same passage, Cicero tells us that Gaius spoke as if he were a guardian of the public purse ('verbis tamen defendebat aerarium'); and a little later he adds that any reader of Gaius' speeches would declare him to be the watchdog of the treasury ('lege orationes Gracchi: patronum aerarii esse dices').[26]

We are evidently faced with a hostile tradition about this measure, which represents it as a massive and calculated bribe to win popular support, not as a genuinely disinterested social reform. As Cicero put it quintessentially in his *pro Sestio*, it greatly pleased the common people, for it generously provided them with the means of subsistence without the need to do any work to earn it: 'iucunda res plebei; victus enim suppeditabatur large sine labore.'[27] That sort of comment is far from unbiased— one is reminded of the complaints of well-to-do critics nowadays that over-generous provision of national assistance payments makes the world a paradise for idlers and scroungers, and that such measures are introduced by interested politicians simply as a means to buy votes. However, as we have seen, the huge profits which Rome had made out of her extending power had been very unevenly distributed, and the claim that it was only right that the poor should have some share was not unreasonable. The work which could have paid the wages to buy the means of subsistence was not easy to come by in the Rome of the late Republic; and Gaius surely realised that land distributions and colonial plantations must still

---

[25] *de off.* 2.72: 'C. Gracchi frumentaria magna largitio, exhauriebat igitur aerarium.' Cf. Diodorus 34/5.25, Orosius 5.12.

[26] *Tusc. Disp.* 3.48: ' "Nolim" inquit "mea bona, Gracche, tibi viritim dividere libeat. Sed. si facias, partem petam." '

[27] *pro Sestio* 103.

leave the capital housing large numbers of poor citizens. He had special magazines built to store grain, and that must have helped with careful management to flatten out the worst effects of price-fluctuations.[28] He also provided new public revenues to help meet expenditure in the shape of new levies and customs-dues, *vectigalia* and *portoria*, as well as re-organizing the collection of the enormous revenues of the new province of Asia.

The rich no doubt resented the inroads which the corn-law would make on one method by which they had themselves been able to buy the dependence and political support of many of the poor citizens, what Tacitus later called the 'pars populi integra et magnis domibus adnexa';[29] under Gaius' law the poor would be less impelled to look to the rich for such doles. They were also bound to claim that the law was 'a bribe on the largest scale, and a measure which could not fail to make paupers of the great mass of independent, self-supporting citizens'.[30] Yet the regular supply at a fixed and reasonable price of a staple basic food is scarcely in itself destructive of society, and such remarks came as unconvincingly from the lips of the rich as did the famous recommendation from Marie Antoinette about eating cake if bread was not to be had. It is attractive to suppose that some brief citations which we chance to have from Gaius' speech *de legibus promulgatis* were answers to such criticisms. We find him talking scathingly of 'things which *they* say are provided as luxuries', denying that 'words like "self-indulgence" can be applied to the basic necessities of life', and protesting against the suggestion that 'what is a necessity for *them* is for *us* a display'.[31]

At the same time, the corn law cannot have failed to swell the size of Gaius' popular following and win votes for other measures; and Gaius must have been well aware of this. Thus this measure is undoubtedly one which, even if it was an end in itself and inspired above all by humanitarian concern for the wretchedness of the city poor, was also a means to further ends, among them the building up of his own political support and the

[28] Plutarch, *CG* 6; Festus p. 392 L.

[29] Tacitus, *Histories* 1.4. Cf. Brunt, *The Roman Mob*, 21.

[30] So wrote Holden in his note on p.115 of his excellent edition of Plutarch's *Gracchi* (Cambridge, 1885). Here a late-nineteenth-century conservative reflects the attitude of the rich Romans of Gaius' day and later. But, as Last sensibly observed (*CAH* ix.59), 'the penniless could no more pay $6\frac{1}{3}$ asses for a modius of wheat than they could pay whatever wheat had cost in the days before control.'

[31] See Appendix 2 below, p. 222.

weakening of the political hold which the great noble houses exercised over the urban commons. Predictably, it excited a hostile and denigrating response from the ruling-class, and from those like Cicero who later shared their point of view. A stray comment from Cicero's contemporary Varro to the effect that Gaius 'implanted in people the hope that they would not have to pay more than they themselves determined or decreed' ('in spem adducebat non plus soluturos quam vellent') probably belongs in this context.[32] It has been suggested that we may have here a reference to a Gracchan law aimed at relieving debtors, but such a law is nowhere else attested, or even hinted at, and the corn law fits well enough:[33] the People were now given the idea (so it could be alleged) that in future they themselves could fix the price they were prepared to pay for corn, or indeed anything else.

The *lex de provinciis consularibus*

None of the surviving continuous accounts so much as mentions this law; but it rests on the secure evidence of Cicero and Sallust, although not surprisingly they tell us nothing of the exact time or circumstances of its passing.[34] Under its provisions the Senate was to continue, as hitherto, to determine which provinces the consuls of any given year were to hold; but the two provinces in question had to be named in advance of the elections which would disclose who the two consuls in question would be. To take an example: the provinces for the consuls of the year 121 would fall to be determined by a decree of the Senate before the consular elections were held in 122, and so before anyone could know for certain who would be the two men who as consuls in 121 would hold those provinces. And, since the use of a tribunician veto to delay the passing of the necessary decree was specifically forbidden by Gaius' law, no interested parties could drag the business out until after the elections.

It may be that there was a connection between this law and the fact that one of Gaius' collaborators, C. Fannius, was a candidate for one of the two consulships of 122; and that Gaius was anxious that, if elected,

[32] Cited by Nonius Marcellus p. 728 L.

[33] Brunt, *Social Conflicts*, 90. But, in Brunt's defence, it is admittedly hazardous to argue from the silence of the sources in such matters; we owe a lot of our information to stray allusions.

[34] Cicero, *de domo* 24, *de prov. cons.* 3 and 17, *ad. famm.* 1.7.10; Sallust, *BJ* 27.

Fannius should not be removed from Rome (where a friendly and co-operative consul could be of immense help in 122) by being sent off to govern a distant province.[35] It is true that the consuls of any given year in fact drew lots to discover which of the two should have which province, so that it would not be possible for the Senate to assign a specific province to one or other of them.[36] But none the less it might have been open to the handful of great nobles who controlled the Senate to try to do a deal with Fannius, with the co-operation of his fellow-consul, to win him away from Gaius by holding out the prospect of a plum province. We know that Fannius, who was duly elected a consul for 122, did in fact break with Gaius and go over to the side of his opponents; hence it is also conceivable that Gaius may have been not altogether sure of Fannius earlier in 123, and so was concerned to minimize the risk of his defection by getting the consular provinces for 122 settled well in advance.

On the other hand, we must remember that this particular law was not repealed after Gaius' downfall, and indeed remained in force until superseded by a *lex Pompeia* in 52; which shows that it cannot have been anathema to the ruling nobility. So it may well be that other explanations should be sought, such as that Gaius was concerned with a point of principle, in that he believed that the People should know before they elected their consuls what sort of jobs they were going to have to do. It is important that he recognized that the Senate was the only body with the necessary experience and knowledge to decide the allocation of provinces, and that he made no attempt to take this function from them. His main concern may simply have been to try to ensure that the choice of provinces should be as free as possible from personalities and intrigue, to shield the consuls from improper influences and from any temptation to dance to a particular tune in order to ensure a desirable choice of provinces.[37] The law might fall into a period of co-operation between Gaius and the Senate such as Plutarch has been taken to attest for the latter months of 123.[38] It is, however, noteworthy that the law apparently had nothing to say about the selection of praetorian provinces, and in this respect it differed from the *lex Pompeia* of 52 which dealt with both categories and brought them

[35] See Appendix 3 below, p. 236.

[36] 'Rigging' of the lot was known (cf. Cicero, *ad famm.* 5.2.3), but normally required the collaboration of all concerned.

[37] So Last, *CAH* ix. 63–4.

[38] Plutarch, *CG* 6.1. But see below, p.174, for argument against.

under the same set of general regulations. In the end, we have to admit that we can ask more questions about the *lex de provinciis consularibus* than the meagre evidence which we have allows us to answer.

The *lex agraria,* and the colony and road-building laws

Gaius' agrarian law is something of a puzzle. Indeed, Appian does not so much as mention it;[39] and Plutarch's notice is curt and uninformative, as also are those of the other authorities who allude to this measure.[40] Yet the surviving epigraphic text of the *lex agraria* of 111 does not anywhere cite the agrarian law of Tiberius Gracchus as a relevant antecedent law but only that of Gaius, which indicates that Gaius' law must have done more than merely supplement or strengthen his brother's: it must itself have constituted a new enactment which stood alongside or even superseded the law of 133, while no doubt incorporating much of its substance.[41]

We saw how in 129 the intervention of Scipio Aemilianus had had the effect of preventing the agrarian commissioners from proceeding with the reclamation and distribution of public land in cases where it could be alleged that Latin and allied rights were in danger of being infringed, and that Scipio had probably been exploiting a looseness or ambiguity in the drafting of Tiberius' law in connection with the adjudicatory powers which it conferred on the commissioners who were to operate it.[42] If Gaius' law now 'enacted nothing new save the restoration to the commissioners of the jurisdiction which they had lost',[43] or alternatively did

---

[39] He perhaps assumed its existence in his general account in *BC* 1.27 of the history of the agrarian question after 122.

[40] Plutarch, *CG* 5.1 (cited below, p. 229); Livy, *Epit.* 60: 'tulit legem agrariam quam et frater eius tulerat.' Vell. Pat. 2.6.3: 'dividebat agros, vetabat quemquam civem plus quingentis iugeribus habere, quod aliquando lege Licinia cautum erat.' Auctor *de viris illustribus* 65: 'agrarias et frumentarias leges tulit, colonos etiam Capuam et Tarentum mittendos censuit, triumviros agris dividendis se et Fulvium Flaccum et C. Crassum constituit' (where 'Crassum' is presumably a mistake for 'Carbonem'). The statement of Siculus Flaccus that Gaius 'legem tulit ne quis in Italia amplius quam ducenta iugera possideret' is rightly discounted by Last (*CAH* ix.67), given that nobody else refers to any such savage reduction in the amount of land existing *possessores* might retain. Flaccus' figure of 200 *iugera* is either a slip on his part, or a copyist's error, or perhaps refers to the maximum size of allotments in Gracchan colonies ('amplius iugera CC' occurs in line 60 of the agrarian law of 111 in connection with land at Junonia).

[41] Bruns, *FIR* 11, line 22.

[42] Above, p. 92.

[43] So Mommsen, *History of Rome,* 3. 110.

no more than clarify and confirm that jurisdiction, the scant attention paid to it by our sources would be more easily explicable. But that way out seems to be barred by the authoritative evidence of the text of the 111 law. Moreover, given Gaius' attitude towards the Latins and Italians, it seems unlikely that he would have chosen to reopen old wounds in this way, and set the commissioners busy surveying and distributing this contested land, or that we should hear no echoes of the sort of protests which were loudly advanced six years earlier if he had in fact done so.[44]

As Last observed, 'it is plain that, in his attempt to carry on the work of Tiberius in providing for the unemployed, the means on which Gaius relied was the establishment of colonies';[45] which makes it tempting to suppose that there was a very close connection between his agrarian bill and the colonial foundations for which he was responsible. I incline to believe that Gaius' agrarian law made two major innovations with respect to that of his elder brother: he gave the commissioners power to deal with public land, *ager publicus populi Romani*, outside Italy, and also empowered them to plant colonies as well as to make individual (*viritim*) assignments. Under the umbrella of this general law, particular colonies could be founded by separate enactments like the *lex Rubria* which established Junonia/Carthage, and this I take to be the sense behind the notice in the Livian *Epitome* (60) that Gaius 'legibus agrariis latis effecit ut complures coloniae in Italia deducerentur et una in solo dirutae Carthaginis, quo ipse triumvir creatus coloniam deduxit.'[46]

It is significant, in this connection, that Fulvius Flaccus, whose term as executive commissioner came round in 123, seems in that year to have gone out to see to the preliminaries of the Carthage colony. Appian in fact says that it was in 122 that Flaccus sailed to Africa, in company with Gaius.[47] But Appian has evidently got into a muddle, as is indicated by his

---

[44] That the census figures show no appreciable increase in the number of citizens registered after 125 is neither here nor there. Cf. above, p. 49, for the difficulty of using these figures.

[45] *CAH* ix.68.

[46] On this whole question, see the excellent discussion of Carcopino in *Autour des Gracques,* 244ff. Line 24 of the agrarian law of 111 refers to *IIIviri* founding colonies. It could well be that the reference is to the Gracchan *IIIviri,* and (if it is) it supports the view that Gaius' agrarian law enlarged their powers so as to give them such a function. (Cf. also p. 204 n. 69, below.)

[47] Appian, *BC* 1.24: ἐς Λιβύην ἅμα Φουλουίῳ Φλάκκῳ, κἀκείνῳ μεθ' ὑπατείαν διὰ τάδε δημαρχεῖν ἐλομένῳ, διέπλευσεν.

comment that it was 'for this reason' (διὰ τάδε, apparently to help Gaius with the settlement of Junonia) that this ex-consul had extraordinarily assumed the office of tribune—there was not the slightest reason why Flaccus needed to be elected a tribune so as to accompany Gaius to Africa. Plutarch makes it plain that Flaccus stayed behind in Rome to hold the fort while Gaius was away,[48] and he is obviously to be followed here. Appian has misunderstood his source. Quite probably Flaccus had gone to Africa himself in 123, and the fact that both he and Gaius went out to Junonia separately but at a close interval lies behind the notion that they both went out together; in 122 Gaius was due to be the executive land commissioner, and in that capacity it was known that he would have to spend some time at Junonia, which is why his most experienced and influential associate, the ex-consul Flaccus, stood for and was elected to a tribunate of 122 so as to be in a position to take over charge of their programme.[49] It is indeed probable that originally Gaius had not planned to be tribune himself in 122, preferring to remain free for other tasks.[50]

If that approach is accepted, it is not hard to see why our sources should have so little to say about the *lex agraria* and more about the colonies. The question is, however, very much an academic one. As with the '*lex de provocatione*' and the *lex ne quis*, the agrarian and colony activities have to be taken together as parts of a single whole, whatever our view of their precise statutory relationship. Even if it was not as executive agrarian commissioner that Gaius went out to Africa in 122 but as a specially elected colonial commissioner or *IIIvir coloniae deducendae*, the importance which he attached to being closely involved in the colonial programme and his readiness to accord it some priority over the need for his presence in Rome are still clear. For, granted that he did carry a substantive *lex agraria* in 123 and that his turn as executive commissioner was due to come round again in 122, it would be surprising if he nevertheless accepted the onerous appointment of founding commissioner for

---

[48] Plutarch, *CG* 10. 1–2. Cf. 11.2 (below, p. 173, n. 31).

[49] I suspect this is the true explanation of Appian's confused διὲ τάδε.

[50] See below, p. 169. The rotation of the 'executive chairmanship' among the *tresviri a.i.a.* is set out by Carcopino (whom I have followed) in Table I on pp. 182–3 of his *Gracques*. Briefly, it goes thus: 133 Appius Claudius; 132 P. Crassus (*vice* Tiberius Gracchus); 131 Gaius Gracchus; 130 Appius Claudius; 129 Fulvius Flaccus (*vice* Crassus); 128 C. Gracchus; 127 C. Carbo (*vice* Claudius); 126 Flaccus; 125 C. Gracchus; 124 Carbo; 123 Flaccus; 122 C. Gracchus; 121 Carbo; 120 C. Sulpicius Galba (*vice* Flaccus—C. Gracchus' place being filled by L. Calpurnius Bestia).

Junonia/Carthage if that task was essentially a separate and independent one.[51]

Apart from Junonia, we hear specifically of colonies at Scolacium and Tarentum—to be renamed Minervium and Neptunia—and at Capua.[52] Appian names only Junonia, but says that Gaius projected 'many' colonies. The *Liber Coloniarum* attests Gracchan foundations at Ferentinum and Tarquinii in Tuscany, and at Abellinum, Cadatia, Suessa Aurunca, and Vellitrae in Latium and Campania;[53] but whether any or all of these were actually founded or projected by Gaius, or whether they later laid claim to this historic lineage when they had grown up as centres for *viritim* Gracchan settlement in their areas, as Telesia and Grumentum so grew up, the authority of the *Liber Coloniarum* is too uncertain to establish.[54] The Livian *Epitome* (60), like Appian, talks of 'several' ('complures') colonies. All in all, it seems that Gaius did project quite a number of colonies, which is not to say that all were in fact founded in 123 or 122.

We hear of no colonies planted in Italy after Auximum in 157, itself the first since the 170s, until we come to Gaius' tribunate.[55] So the latter's resumption of colonization after a gap of over thirty years was something

[51] Plutarch says (*CG* 10.1) that Gaius went out to Junonia in 122 'because the lot had fallen to him': Ῥουβρίου τῶν συναρχόντων ἑνὸς οἰκίζεσθαι Καρχήδονα γράψαντος. . . κλήρῳ λαχὼν ὁ Γάιος ἐξέπλευσεν εἰς Λιβύην ἐπὶ τὸν κατοικισμόν. But that is consistent, I think, with the suggestion that it was his turn to serve as executive land commissioner in 122.

[52] Plutarch, *CG* 8.2. Vell. Pat. 1.15. Bloch and Carcopino (*Histoire romaine* II.i.243 n. 16) say that 'nothing proves that Scolacium Minervium was a Gracchan rather than a Livian colony (Vell., 1,15,4), since the tribune Livius Drusus entered on his office on 10 December 123.' That seems strained. Though Velleius merely dates Scolacium to 123 without saying who was responsible, it is hard to accept that Drusus carried a colony law in the first two or three weeks of his office and that a measure of this nature introduced and carried so swiftly went unremarked by Plutarch and Appian. I prefer to treat Scolacium as a Gracchan colony.

[53] Appian, *BC* 1.23.1: καὶ ἀποικίας ἐσηγεῖτο πολλάς. The *Liber Coloniarum* 'colonies' can be found in *Gromatici Veteres* (ed. Lachmann) i. 216, 219, 229, 233, 237, 238. All are said to have been established 'lege Sempronia'—except Cadatia 'lege Graccana'.

[54] For Telesia and Grumentum, and in general on this topic, see Beloch, *Roem. Gesch.* 505ff. and the article by Nagle in *Athenaeum* 48 (1970), 372–94, esp. 385ff. where this question is gone into in some detail with full references to earlier work such as that of Pais. Cf. Brunt, *IM* 527.

[55] Salmon (*Roman Colonization under the Republic*, 112–15) would date Auximum to 128 and not 157, and he suggests a colony at Heba in Tuscany in 128 as well, both perhaps part of a move by the anti-Gracchans to counterbalance the popularity won by Tiberius' land law. But I do not find his arguments convincing.

of an innovation. How we should account for this gap is a matter for speculation. But the absence of any serious military threat in the north of the peninsula, private hostilities within the ruling nobility whose members might look askance at the advantages that could accrue to rival families or cliques who would acquire large *clientelae* as founder-patrons of a new colony, and probably most of all the determination of the wealthy to exploit the public land for their own personal profit must all have played their part.[56] And Gaius' programme was also novel so far as concerns the character of at least some of his colonies; he was not concerned to establish strongpoints to guarantee Rome's military control—*propugnacula imperii*—nor just to settle small farmers; he 'recognised that the industrial spirit might be awakened by new settlements on sites favourable to commerce'.[57] Scolacium lay on the wide bay which cuts into the underside of the 'toe' of Italy below the Iapygian promontory; and Tarentum (the modern Taranto) offered a harbour in the northern corner of the 'instep' —both well-chosen sites for the development of urban centres which could do much to revive the economies of the areas in which they stood and remedy the run-down character of the once prosperous regions which they would serve.[58] Capua had ceased to exist as a city—and she had been a great one—since the dreadful penalty which Rome had visited on her disloyalty in 211; although Gaius apparently cast no covetous eyes on the bulk of the rich *ager Campanus* itself,[59] the commercial potential of the town was obvious. As for Junonia, the novelty was all the sharper in that it was not only a great natural commercial centre but lay outside Italy on the site of Carthage itself.

Plutarch says, with particular reference to Tarentum and Capua, that Gaius looked for colonists from among the 'most respectable' elements of the citizen body;[60] and at Carthage the size of the land-grants ran up to 200 *iugera*.[61] We need not assume that all Gaius' projected colonies were of this nature; but any colony, as opposed to a scheme of individual

---

[56] See Chapter 1 and Appendix 1.

[57] Greenidge, *History of Rome* i.224. This feature of Gaius' colonies is universally recognized.

[58] On the 'emptiness' of the extreme south of Italy, see Brunt's chapter XX ('Italiae Solitudo') of his *Italian Manpower*, esp. pp. 353 ff.

[59] Cicero, *de lege agr.* ii.81: 'Nec duo Gracchi . . . nec L. Sulla . . . agrum Campanum attingere ausus est.'

[60] *CG* 9.2: τοὺς χαριεστάτους τῶν πολιτῶν.

[61] Bruns, *FIR* 11, line 60. Cf. Mommsen in *CIL* i pp. 75 ff.

land-grants such as Tiberius' bill had provided for, required from its inception some sort of established social hierarchy: a governing class, and below that the various graduations of the rest of the population; a need which had been regularly reflected in the differing sizes of the land-grants made to different categories and classes of colonists in the past. We need not suppose that the poor had no part in such Gracchan foundations, though it may be that these comprised many settlers likely to settle down to 'urban' as opposed to 'agricultural' livelihoods; and Plutarch's 'most respectable' citizens surely included small craftsmen and tradesmen and shopkeepers as well as the men of real substance whose capital and expertise and connections were vital to the success of the new foundations. Not all, alas, came to anything. Scolacium and Tarentum, so Velleius attests, were founded; but Capua came to nothing, and Carthage was very short-lived; and which, if any, of the others listed in the *Liber Coloniarum* actually materialized, either now or in the years immediately following, we cannot confidently assert.

Both Plutarch and Appian refer to Gaius' road-building projects, Appian commenting on the large numbers of craftsmen and contractors he gathered for this purpose, and Plutarch on the remarkable energy which Gaius displayed in personal supervision of this work and other tasks like the construction of granaries.[62] It is reasonable to take the road-construction along with his colonial plans, as providing an improved network of communications not merely for them but also for rural Italy in general. It has even been suggested that Gaius may have been laying the foundations of an Italian postal service, a project which in the end had to wait for Augustus and his successors to bring it to fruition;[63] and it is not indeed far-fetched to discern in a man like him a keen interest in improving the channels of governmental intelligence and supervision.

In shifting the emphasis away from *viritim* assignments of land to this sort of development, Gaius showed himself a pioneer in a field which was to be more fully developed in succeeding generations. The benefits to the regions concerned are obvious, and the appeal to a wider section of the citizen body is also clear. The delicate susceptibilities of the non-Roman communities in Italy seem to have been respected in so far as we hear of no resumption of the complaints of 129—though what might have ensued

[62] Plutarch, *CG* 6.2; Appian, *BC* 1.23.1.
[63] Ramsay, *JRS* 10 (1920), 84 ff.

with regard to that contested public land had Gaius' franchise proposals gone through is another matter. Moreover, leaving aside any worries about the growth in his personal prestige and influence and following, his sheer political power, it is hard to see in these constructive works of statesmanship any direct affront by Gaius to the ruling nobility. Certainly, one might expect that the colonies and the great construction works will have been generally welcomed by the *publicani* and all those to whom they gave employment.

The *lex militaris* and the *lex de tribunis militum*

Plutarch attests a *lex militaris* (νόμος στρατιωτικός) which required clothing and equipment to be provided for soldiers free and without any stoppage from their pay, and which also forebade the enlisting of any recruits under the age of seventeen. A curious pair of clauses if they constituted the whole law—but we have to work with the material we are given. Diodorus, as we saw, had it that 'by currying favour with the soldiery through laws to relax the strictness of the old discipline, Gaius opened the gates to mutiny and anarchy'; which (if the reference is in any part to a *lex militaris*) suggests rather more.[64] So far as the age-limit on recruiting is concerned, Gaius may have been resuming a proposal made ten years earlier by his elder brother;[65] the abuse must have been prevalent enough to require statutory correction, and must reflect an overall shortage of men available as well as a shortage of *adsidui* who could afford to equip themselves or put up with stoppages from their meagre rate of pay.

It is hard to avoid suspecting that Diodorus' language, however partisan and casuistically rhetorical, indicates that there was more to Gaius' *lex militaris* than the two items which Plutarch chooses to highlight, and that he did something to ensure against the abuse of authority in the army as he did in the matter of abuse of power by magistrates and Senate at Rome. But exactly what, we have no means of knowing.

For the suggestion that Gaius passed a law (connected with, or part of, the *lex militaris*) providing that the military tribunes of the first four legions should be elected by the People rather than selected or nominated, the reader is referred to the discussion in Appendix 3.[66]

[64] Plutarch, *CG* 5.1; Diodorus 34/5.25 (above, p. 114).
[65] Above, p. 73. (For a suggestion that Gaius' law may have reduced the period of service, see Brunt *IM* 401, n. 4).
[66] Below, p. 236.

The *lex de repetundis* and the *lex iudiciaria*[67]

The evidence concerning these two laws—if indeed there really were two laws and not one—is difficult and confused, and has led to much disagreement among modern scholars. As Balsdon observed,

it is improbable that all Roman historians would agree upon any more precise statement of certainty than the following: that C. Gracchus, whether by a *lex Sempronia iudiciaria*, or by a *lex Sempronia de repetundis*, or by a *lex Acilia de repetundis* which may, or may not, be reproduced in the *lex repetundarum*, fragments of which are preserved at Naples and at Vienna (*CIL* I², 583), established *equites* (selected either from owners and past owners, within certain age limits, of the *equus publicus*, or from all those who possessed the equestrian *census*) *either* in place of, *or* in association with, senators as jurors in the *quaestio de repetundis*.[68]

In the discussion which follows, I take it as established that the epigraphic *repetundae* law (*CIL* i². 583=Bruns, *FIR* 10), often known as the 'Tabula Bembina', does preserve the (fragmentary) text of Gaius Gracchus' *repetundae* law; that it was carried into law in 123; and that, while it may be that it was in fact a *lex Acilia* or perhaps even a *lex Rubria et Acilia*, it is best to avoid any possible misunderstanding or confusion or circularity of argument by referring to it simply as 'the Gracchan *repetundae* law', or 'Bruns 10', or in some other similarly neutral fashion.[69]

Cases which were brought *de pecuniis repetundis* are commonly called 'extortion cases'; but, strictly speaking, they involved actions for the *recovery* of money or property (*pecunias repetere*) which had been improperly acquired. The first occasion when complaints from provincials on this score were brought to the attention of the Senate and acted on seems to have been in the year 171, when representatives of a number of Spanish

---

[67] The modern literature on these laws is vast, and impressive in quality. Note especially the following: Mommsen, *Ges. Schr.* i. 1–64, iii. 339–55; Greenidge, *Legal Procedure of Cicero's Time*, 435–504; Strachan-Davidson, *Problems of the Roman Criminal Law* ii. 75–152; Carcopino, *Autour des Gracques*, 205–35; Balsdon, *PBSR* 14 (1938), 98–114; Fraccaro, *Opuscula* ii. 255 ff.; Gelzer, *Kl.Schr.* i. 222–7; Sherwin-White, *PBSR* 17 (1949), 5–25, *JRS* 42 (1952), 43–55, *JRS* 62 (1972), 83–99; Henderson, *JRS* 41 (1951), 71–88; Miners, *CQ* (1958), 241 ff.; Ewins, *JRS* 50 (1960), 94–107; Jones, *Proc. Camb. Phil. Soc.* (1960), 39 ff.; Badian, *AJPh* (1954), 374 ff., *Historia* (1962), 205 ff.; Brunt, *The Equites in the Late Republic*, Appendix II, pp. 141–8 (=Seager, *Crisis*, 107–14).

[68] Balsdon, o.c. 98.

[69] For detailed discussion of these points, and other connected issues, see Appendix 3 below, p. 230.

peoples complained of the rapacity and arrogance of certain Roman magistrates in Spain. It having become clear to the Senate that, apart from any other considerations, money had been taken from the Spaniards ('cum et alia indigna quererentur, manifestum autem esset pecunias captas'), a praetor, L. Canuleius, to whom the province of Spain had already been allocated, was put in charge of the affair and instructed to appoint five *recuperatores* ('recoverers') chosen from among the members of the Senate for each of the magistrates complained about, while the provincials were directed to nominate Roman *patroni* to handle their case for them.[70] The object seems to have been simply to secure that, should the allegations be found to be true, the individuals concerned should repay to the Spaniards what they had taken from them. The action was thus what we would term a civil action, but naturally the concomitant circumstances were such as to give the whole proceedings something of a political colour. The procedure was modelled on that of private recuperatorial actions, and was based on the principle of *condictio*: viz. no cause of action was specified, or in other words no account was taken of exactly how it was that that which the plaintiff was seeking to recover for himself had come to be in the possession of the defendant.[71]

A little over twenty years later, this *ad hoc* procedure was superseded by a permanent court of *recuperatores* chosen from among members of the Senate. This was effected by a law which was passed in 149 by the tribune L. Calpurnius Piso Frugi,[72] the man who turns up as an enemy of Gaius Gracchus a quarter of a century later.[73] The *lex Calpurnia de pecuniis repetundis* retained the essential character of the 171 proceedings: the penalty remained simple restitution or repayment of the sums involved, and there was apparently no further penalty beyond that, not even the penalty of *infamia* with its consequent disqualification from active political life. That makes it probable that the *repetundae* court was not at this time regarded as a true *iudicium publicum*: L. Lentulus seems to have gone on to be elected censor in 147 for all that he had been an early victim of the new *lex Calpurnia*.[74] Some time between 149 and 123 the *lex*

---

[70] Livy 43.2.

[71] Sherwin-White, *PBSR* (1949), 6. On *condictio*, see Jolowicz, *Hist. Intr. to Roman Law*[3], 214ff.

[72] Cicero, *Brutus* 106; *de off.* 2.75; *Verr.* II.iii.195, iv.56.

[73] Above, p. 127; below, p. 220.

[74] Sherwin-White, loc. cit. For the 'poena simpli', see Bruns, *FIR* 10, line 59.

Calpurnia was modified or expanded or supplemented by another tribunician law, the *lex Junia*; but of the latter we know nothing but the name.[75]

Gaius' *repetundae* law, in large part preserved in the Tabula Bembina, marked a very considerable change. In particular, the *iudices* of the *quaestio perpetua repetundarum* were henceforth to be recruited exclusively from outside the ranks of the Senate; and the penalty was no longer to be simple restitution, but was increased to twofold restitution.[76] Both were significant departures from what had gone before: the latter from the plain principle of *condictio* and simple restitution in that it introduced a positively penal element into the decisions of the court, the former in that the introduction of *iudices ex plebe*—which is what the new *iudices* were, however their qualifications may have been expressed in the law—assimilated the *repetundae* court to the category of *iudicia publica*, with the consequence that the disability of *infamia* inevitably became attached to an adverse verdict, a consequence surely arising from Gaius' intention in general to stiffen the penalties and thereby strengthen the deterrent element in the *repetundae* law.[77] Inasmuch as men convicted by this court henceforth often took themselves off into exile, and we hear talk of their *caput* being at stake, this was simply the consequence of a wish on their part either to evade the severe financial penalty, or to escape indictment on capital charges arising out of the facts revealed at the *repetundae* hearing, or perhaps even out of shame; the law did not make *repetundae* itself a capital offence, although for a prominent and ambitious politician the disbarment from membership of the Senate and from tenure of any public office which was entailed by *infamia* could easily be represented as virtually the loss of his *caput*, his existence and identity as a citizen.[78]

Valerius Maximus (6.9.10) says 'L. Lentulus consularis lege Caecilia repetundarum crimine oppressus censor cum L. Censorino creatus est'; after Mommsen (*CIL* i. p. 55), 'Caecilia' has generally been taken to be a slip for 'Calpurnia'.

[75] Against the view that the *lex Junia* may itself have been 'Gracchan' see Appendix 3 below, p. 231.

[76] Bruns, *FIR* 10, line 59: 'QVOD POST HANCE LEGEM ROGATAM CO [*nsilio probabit*]VR CAPTVM COACTVM ABLATVM AVORSVM CONCILIATVMVE ESSE, DVPLI'.

[77] Sherwin-White, *PBSR* (1949), 6–8. He is not however as positive as I am that this was Gaius' deliberate intention: he writes (p. 7) that the introduction of *infamia* 'may have resulted from the court's change of status, and not from any intention of the legislator to stiffen the penalties in this respect.'

[78] That the penalty under Gaius' law was not capital is definitely established by Sherwin-White in his answer (*JRS* 1952, 83–99) to the objections of Mrs. Henderson (*JRS* 1951, 71–88).

Of course, the most startling feature of Gaius' law was that it meant that from now on errant senatorial officers of state would no longer be 'tried by their peers' but by a panel of *iudices* drawn from the ranks of the equestrian class. Hence Diodorus could speak of Gaius as thus having 'made the inferior element in the state master over the superior'; and similarly Appian could write that he made the *equites* 'as it were rulers over the senators and the senators virtually their subjects'.[79] Such language could scarcely be in sharper contrast to what Polybius had written not long before about the dominance of the Senate over the whole of the rest of the citizen body and over the *equites* in particular.[80]

Gaius' *repetundae* law was not a simple measure with three or four clauses. It dealt, exhaustively and at length, with every detail of the process: the officer who was to preside over the court; the definition of the offence, and of who was liable to be charged with it; the assignment of *patroni* (counsel), if desired, to assist the plaintiffs; the qualifications and selection of the *album* or pool of 450 *iudices*; the drawing and challenging of the one hundred *iudices* who were to be initially charged with hearing any given case; the procedure for bringing a charge, and what was to happen if the man charged had died, or taken himself outside the jurisdiction of the court; the conduct of a hearing; the security of witnesses and of written evidence; the oath to be taken by the *iudices*, how they were to proceed to a decision, the reporting and counting of their votes; the giving of securities, assessment of the sums involved, method of payment, and the handling of these moneys; rewards for successful prosecutors—and so on. Here, however, we shall for the moment confine ourselves to the question: Who exactly were the *iudices* who were to sit in judgement in the court?

The ancient writers all speak of them simply as *equites* (or, in Greek, as ἱππεῖς). But that leaves open the question of what *equites* is to be taken to mean in this context. To that question there are two possible alternative answers: either they were present or former members of the eighteen centuries of public horse; or they were those citizens who, regardless of whether they were or had been enrolled in those centuries, were

---

[79] Diodorus 34/5. 25.1. Appian, *BC* 1.22.4: τοὺς μὲν ἱππέας οἷά τινας ἄρχοντας αὐτῶν ὑπερεπῆρε, τοὺς δὲ βουλευτὰς ἴσα καὶ ὑπηκόους ἐποίει.
[80] Above, p. 104. (Whether Appian and Diodorus were thinking solely of the *repetundae* court is a question which will be examined later.)

registered by the censors as possessing the *census equester*.[81] The Tabula
Bembina preserves sufficient of the negative criteria of the law to reveal
that magistrates and past and present members of the Senate (and their
fathers and sons and brothers as well) were excluded even if qualified
under the positive criteria; that the *iudices* had to be aged between thirty
and sixty, and had to have a domicile either in Rome itself or within a
close distance (perhaps as close as one mile) of the capital. There were
further exclusive provisions which have disappeared, possibly including
one which barred anyone who had fought as a gladiator.[82] Unfortunately,
however, in both sections where the law set out the positive qualifications
of the *iudices*, we are faced with wide gaps in the extant inscription which
can be as well filled with a supplement specifying possession of the 'public
horse' as with one which requires simply possession of the *census
equester*.[83]

Given the state of our evidence, it is too much to hope that everyone
will agree which of the two answers is the correct one. On the whole I incline to believe, but without any really warm conviction, that the qualification was expressed in money terms, since the elder Pliny does say that
quite some time was spent in finding a settled name for this class, and that
it was only in Cicero's day that the name *equites* became 'stabilized',
which can be taken to suggest that Gaius had not drawn his *iudices* from a
group which already enjoyed this official designation.[84] But this argument,

---

[81] Above, p. 100.

[82] Line 16: 'QVEIVE MERC[*ede conductus depugnavit depugnaverit.* . . .]'.

[83] Lines 12–14, 16–17.

[84] See Nicolet *L'Ordre équestre* i. 163–88 for the fullest recent discussion of the
qualification question. He comes down in favour of the answer's being possession of
the public horse (membership of the eighteen centuries) and not of the *census
equester*. But I cannot share his confidence on this. I should agree with him that
probably the *equites* of the *lex Aurelia* of 70 were members of the eighteen centuries, and the *tribuni aerarii* of that law in effect men who enjoyed the *census
equester* without being members of those centuries; but that does not necessarily
prove anything about the Gracchan law fifty years earlier. His argument (pp. 511 ff.)
from a very fragmentary section of the law (line 28), where there is a reference to
not depriving certain persons of the public horse (NEIVE EQVOM ADIMITO), that
this shows that the *iudices* did possess the public horse is very weak, for even if the
qualification was expressed solely in terms of possession of the *census equester*,
many if not most of the *iudices* will also have been *equites equo publico*. (The
comment of the elder Pliny comes from his *NH* 33.8.34: 'Iudicum autem appellatione separare eum ordinem primi omnium instituere Gracchi . . . . M. Cicero demum
stabilivit equestre nomen in consulatu suo.')

like all the others on both sides, is far from being water-tight. I do not, however, propose to go into the question here in detail, because in the final analysis it does not really matter which of the two answers is the right one: either way, Gaius is revealed as having elected to draw his *iudices* from among the non-senatorial well-to-do who lived in or near Rome. That is the important thing, and precisely how he defined this category in his law is essentially only a subsidiary question.

Having got this far, we must pause for breath: we have not reached the summit, and there still remain further and higher peaks to scale. That we have uncovered the substance of Gaius Gracchus' final reform so far as concerns the *repetundae* court is a proposition that would win general assent. But we have now to face two further and interconnected questions: (a) Can we trace an earlier stage in his plan to reform the *repetundae* court; and (b) Was he concerned to pass not simply a new *lex repetundarum* but a general *lex iudiciaria* embracing other courts as well?

Notoriously, the evidence of the ancient writers on these points is, at least at first sight, conflicting and imprecise. Appian says that the courts, which had acquired a bad reputation for being corrupt, were taken from the Senate and handed over by Gaius to the *equites*; and he cites three recent instances where accused men had bought an acquittal on charges relating to provincial misgovernment. Diodorus says that Gaius stripped senators of their right to sit in judgement and appointed the *equites* to serve as *iudices*. Florus speaks of the influence (*auctoritas*) of the equestrian order as having rested, thanks to Gaius, on its domination of the courts: *iudiciorum regno niteretur*. Velleius on three occasions talks of the courts as having been transferred from Senate to *equites*. Tacitus has it that the Gracchan legislation established the equestrian order in possession of the courts; and Cicero, delivering his Verrines in 70, refers to an unbroken period of almost fifty years during which the equestrian order has served as *iudices*. Not one of these writers in any way hints that under the Gracchan arrangements the *equites* shared their judicial function with senators, and not one of them specifically limits that function to the *repetundae* court alone.[85]

Two others, however, have a different tale to tell. The Epitome of Livy

---

[85] Appian, *BC* 1.23. Diodorus 34/5.25.1. Florus 2.1 (cited below, p. 225). Vell. Pat. 2.6.3, 2.13.2, 2.32.3. Tacitus, *Annals* 12. 60 (cited below, p. 233). Cicero, *Verr.* I.38: 'cum equester ordo iudicaret annos prope quinquaginta continuos.'

reports Gaius as having carried a law to add 600 *equites* to the existing 300 senators, thus producing a Senate with a total membership of 900.[86] This law is not here in any way connected with any court or courts; but it is plain that we must study what the Epitomator has to say in connection with the notice in Plutarch of 'a judiciary law whereby Gaius cut away most of' (or, 'did most to curtail') 'the power of the senators. For they alone sat in judgement in the courts, and for this reason they inspired dread in both people and *equites*. Gaius enrolled three hundred of the *equites* alongside the senators, themselves three hundred in number, and made them jointly responsible for judgements'.[87]

The Epitomator's notice is plainly a very confused variant of the account in Plutarch.[88] Plutarch's *equites* are added to the senators qua *iudices* and not as themselves new senators. It passes belief that Gaius could have proposed to flood the Senate with new members—and the Epitomator says that he did not simply propose to do this, but actually carried a law which did it—and that no ancient source should anywhere so much as allude to so momentous a move with the single exception of the notoriously and consistently inaccurate and confused and unselective Epitomator of Livy.[89] We can safely take it that what lay behind his muddled notice was something in Livy along the lines of what we find in Plutarch.

---

[86] Livy, *Epitome* 60: 'tertiam (legem tulit C. Gracchus), qua equestrem ordinem tunc cum senatu consentientem corrumperet, ut sescenti ex equite in curiam sublegerentur et, quia illis temporibus CCC tantum senatores erant, DC equites CCC senatoribus admiscerentur, id est ut equester ordo bis tantum virium in senatu haberet.'

[87] Plutarch, *CG* 5.1. In the *comparatio* (2) of the brothers Gracchus with Agis and Cleomenes he expresses it clearly: Γαΐῳ μῖξαι τὰ δικαστήρια προσεμβαλόντι τῶν ἱππικῶν τριακοσίους.

[88] Despite Last (*CAH* ix.69–71), who most surprisingly accepts the Epitomator's account as true as it stands.

[89] On the grievous shortcomings of the Epitomator, who was almost certainly working from an already existing abbreviation of Livy and not from his full text, see Balsdon, *PBSR* 14 (1938), 100. His record of accuracy for this period, when it can be checked, is very bad indeed. And in dealing with the *lex Aurelia* of 70 (the details of which Livy himself cannot have got wrong) he represents a law which established in effect courts which were two-thirds equestrian and one-third senatorial as having established instead wholly equestrian-manned courts (*Epit.* 97: 'iudicia ... ad equites Romanos translata sunt'). In the course of reduction (which can shrink a whole book of Livy to half a page) the original notice that the Senate lost its Sullan monopoly and had to be content to share the courts with *equites* and *tribuni aerarii* has been garbled.

It has generally been assumed that Plutarch, and in his own garbled fashion the Epitomator as well, must have rescued from oblivion an early stage in Gaius' approach to judicial reform, later abandoned in favour of the final version of his legislation which totally excluded senators from serving as *iudices*. Gaius began by planning for mixed courts, half-senatorial and half-equestrian. (It has been argued that the *lex ne quis iudicio circumveniatur* supports the conclusion that there must have been such an earlier approach; but that argument, as we have seen, does not hold water.)[90] He probably did not actually pass such a law—the Epitomator is quite unreliable on such points, and Plutarch can use the word νόμος to mean 'a proposal' as well as 'a law'—but he at least made such an intention public. On this view, we are left with two questions to answer: why did Gaius change his mind, and why did Plutarch and the Epitomator fail to report the final version of the law.

There is, however, an alternative way of looking at the evidence as we have it.[91] We can suppose that Gaius did pass a general *lex iudiciaria* which provided for the establishment of a mixed *album iudicum* composed both of senators and of *equites*, and that it was only the specific law on the *repetundae* court which insisted that the *iudices* for these trials should consist wholly of non-senators—and for understandable reasons: *repetundae* was a charge which could be brought only against senators, and hence it could be maintained that it was proper that senatorial *iudices* should be barred from sitting in judgement on their peers in that court. It would be remarkable, on the assumption that there were two stages in Gaius' approach to judicial reform and hence that there must have been an important change of mind on his part, that Plutarch should have failed to comment on this in his biography, especially given that he recorded Gaius' change of mind over the *lex de abactis*. Moreover, Appian writes that:

Soon after the court law had been passed, so they say, Gracchus declared that he had totally destroyed the Senate. And, as time passed, experience showed his words to be more and more true. For the power to sit in judgement over all Romans and Italians and over the senators themselves to any degree concerning money and *infamia* and exile elevated the *equites*

[90] Above, p. 122.

[91] The argument summarized in this paragraph was fully developed by Brunt in his *Equites in the Late Republic*, 141–8 (= Seager, *Crisis*, 107–14). It was hinted at by Gelzer in his review of Hill, *The Roman Middle Class* in his *Kleine Schriften* i. 222–7.

to be as it were their masters, and made the senators virtually their subjects.

Appian must have had in mind more than just the *repetundae* court. Further, the other authorities do not speak *totidem verbis* only of the *repetundae* court, but of 'the courts'. There is no certainty that the *repetundae* court was the only *quaestio perpetua*, the only 'standing court', in Gaius' time: it simply happens to be the only one whose existence we can be sure of. Others already existed, so Cicero suggests, in the days when C. Carbo was a young man: since Carbo was consul in 120, this must mean well before 123.[92] One distinct possibility is a *quaestio perpetua de ambitu*, for we know that Marius was tried for electoral malpractice at some time before 114 (probably in 116 or 115); that could have been an *ad hoc* tribunal, but it is more likely to have been a *quaestio perpetua de ambitu*.[93] The idea that as late as Gaius' tribunate common murderers were inevitably cumbersomely tried by the centuriate assembly and not by a *quaestio perpetua inter sicarios* is hard to stomach.[93a] The evidence which we have for the period down to Sullan and post-Sullan times is full of holes, so that wide gaps in our information on this sort of topic are only to be expected. Even apart from any *quaestiones perpetuae*, the pre-Gracchan Senate had in general a near monopoly of jurisdiction in those trials, both public and private, where the charges were heavy: so Polybius observed,[94] and that fits in well with what Plutarch said about the dread which the senators consequently inspired in all other citizens. So perhaps Plutarch meant that the *equites* were to be given a share in jurisdiction where (unlike charges of *repetundae*) non-senators might be defendants; and they may plausibly be supposed to have been enabled now to fill the role of the *unus iudex* or of a *recuperator* or *centumvir* by the inclusion of *equites* in the appropriate albums from which these judges were drawn.

---

[92] Cicero, *Brutus 106*: 'nam et quaestiones perpetuae hoc (C. Carbone) adulescente constitutae sunt, quae antea nullae fuerunt; L. enim Piso tr. pl. legem primus de pecuniis repetundis Censorino et Manilio consulibus [= 149 B.C.] tulit.'

[93] Mommsen, *Röm. Strafr.* 866–67.

[93a] Cicero tells us (*de fin.* 2.54) that in 142 the praetor L. Hostilius presided over a *quaestio inter sicarios*; he does not say that it was a *quaestio perpetua*, but it might well have been, since there is no hint in Cicero's language that it was a *quaestio extraordinaria*.

[94] Cited above, p. 104.

To this way out there are, inevitably, objections. So far as concerns the Appian passage (on which this view lays considerable stress), Appian here seems to me clearly to be looking ahead to the long-term consequences of Gaius' reform, not seeking to analyse its immediate import; not only does the section just quoted point that way, but so too do the lines which immediately follow, beginning as they do with Appian's observation that 'the *equites* took their stand alongside the tribunes [note the plural] when it came to voting, and in return they got from them anything they wanted.' Thus Appian may simply have meant to take Gaius' reform of the *repetundae* court—and that this was the court which he had particularly in mind is strongly suggested by his specific reference to the three recent scandalous acquittals in this court—and use it as a peg on which to hang an excursus about how their control of the courts came as time passed to prove a very potent political weapon in the hands of the *equites* right down to the end of the Republic.[95] Plutarch's 'law' has provision for 300 *equites* to be available for service as *iudices* (the Epitomator's number of 'new senators' is 600); but Bruns 10 provides for a pool of 450—not an insuperable difficulty, but a difficulty all the same.[96] On one occasion Cicero seems to be saying that mixed senatorial-equestrian courts did not exist before the *lex Plautia iudiciaria* of 89, although it must be granted that the passage in question can be interpreted differently.[97] While it is true that none of our authorities limits Gaius' activity to the *repetundae* court alone, it is equally true that all of them, save Plutarch, certainly suggest, even if they do not explicitly state, that all his *iudices* were *equites*, and give no hint of mixed courts.[98] The Epitomator's omission of

[95] I have discussed this passage with Professor Brunt, and he accepts that this is in fact the proper way to take Appian here.

[96] Bruns, *FIR* 10, line 12: 'FACITO VTEI CDLVIROS LEGAT QVEI IN HAC CIVIT[*ate* etc.'] The fact that Bruns 10 spells out the qualifications of its *iudices* in full is no proof that they cannot also have been so spelled out in an earlier general *lex iudiciaria* of Gaius Gracchus; Roman legal drafting techniques were far from economical, and frequently downright repetitive.

[97] Asconius 79 C: 'Memoria teneo, cum primum senatores cum equitibus Romanis lege Plotia iudicarent, hominem dis ac nobilitati perinvisum Cn. Pompeium [probably to be corrected to 'Pomponium': Badian, *Historia* (1969), 475] causam lege Varia de maiestate dixisse.' Balsdon (*PBSR* 1938, 101), whom Brunt follows, pointed out that 'cum primum' can mean 'as soon as' as well as 'when for the first time'. That is certainly true, but it does not 'feel right' to me in this context—but that is rather subjective.

[98] Of course Cicero knew that mixed courts had existed under the *lex Plautia* of 89 (I do not myself share the prevalent view that the *lex Servilia Caepionis* of 106

any reference to what we may conveniently term Bruns 10 can be put down to sheer incompetence, which led him to omit from his thirty-one-line condensation of Livy's sixtieth book a very important item which must have been in Livy's full text, while wasting five of those lines on a garbled and repetitive version of the Plutarch law. But Plutarch's omission of any mention of this law and of its total exclusion of senators from this court is surely at least as remarkable as a supposed omission to notice a change of mind on Gaius' part.

It is impossible to claim certainty for any one solution where the available evidence is so difficult to fit together and has suggested different answers to many different scholars. But, on balance, the objections just rehearsed seem to make it preferable to adhere to the earlier view that Plutarch's 'law' was in fact not a law but an initial proposal that was aired and subsequently discarded in favour of a more radical approach, and that it was for that reason that it was lost sight of and neglected or ignored by all save Plutarch in his detailed biography of Gaius and by the lost full text of Livy. As to why Plutarch omitted to refer to and discuss the final version, I can only suggest that he must have got into a muddle. The chapter immediately following begins by saying that 'the People not only accepted this law, but also empowered Gaius to select the *iudices* from among the *equites*', and that this made Gaius' strength 'almost monarchical', with the consequence that even the Senate now had to listen patiently to the advice which he gave.[99] That Gaius was empowered to choose himself which *equites* were to serve as *iudices* passes belief. The *repetundae* law entrusts the selection of the *album* in its first year of operation to the praetor peregrinus and thereafter to the praetor to whom the presidency

---

established 'mixed courts' as opposed to wholly senatorial courts; but this is not the place to argue the point). So when Cicero spoke (*Verrines* i.38) of 'nearly fifty years during which the *equester ordo* were sitting as *iudices*', he must have included in this sweeping statement (I take it he is exaggerating to fifty the actual forty-two years from 123 to Sulla's reform of 81, which gave senators a monopoly of the courts) some periods of time when the *equites* did not sit alone, or did not sit at all (though Caepio's law, which may have confined the courts to senators, was very short-lived). I think that all Cicero meant to indicate here was the record of (so he brazenly alleges) total incorruptibility which the equestrian *iudices* had enjoyed in the period between Gaius Gracchus and Sulla.

[99] CG 6.1: Ἐπεὶ δὲ οὐ μόνον ἐδέξατο τὸν νόμον τοῦτον ὁ δῆμος, ἀλλὰ κἀκείνῳ τοὺς κρίνοντας ἐκ τῶν ἱππέων ἔδωκε καταλέξαι, μοναρχική τις ἰσχὺς ἐγεγόνει περὶ αὐτόν, ὥστε καὶ τὴν σύγκλητον ἀνέχεσθαι συμβουλεύοντος αὐτοῦ.

of the *repetundae* court shall fall in any particular year.[100] The language of Plutarch here may perhaps veil what ought to have been a reference to the final version of Gaius' law which confined the selection of *iudices* to the equestrian class, and the effects which that had on heightening Gaius' political power and his domination over the Senate.[101]

Why Gaius changed his mind in this matter (assuming that he did), we can only guess. Possibly the response to his initial proposal—the hostility which it aroused in the Senate or the enthusiasm with which it was received by everyone else—led him to plump for the more radical approach. Perhaps his re-election to a second consecutive term of office (whether part of his original plans or not), and the appearance of Drusus as a colleague likely to cause trouble, had something to do with it. A growing awareness of just how tough a fight was going to develop over the franchise proposals of 122 may have impressed him with the importance of securely cementing his support among the equestrian class, or cowing senatorial opposition. Perhaps it was simply that he had come to appreciate that even a half-share in the control of court decisions would leave too much power in the hands of the Senate. All we can be sure of is that the final form of his law must have been welcome to all those voters who wanted to see the Senate's power cut back, and in particular to those of the non-senatorial well-to-do who could look forward to being selected as *iudices*.

That Gaius passed not just a *lex de pecuniis repetundis* but a general *lex iudiciaria* seems likely on a number of grounds. As we have already observed, none of our authorities specifically limits his activity to the *repetundae* court—though it would perhaps be as well not to rest too much weight on this point. However, the lucky accident that has preserved the Tabula Bembina from destruction should not of itself trick us into supposing that only the *repetundae* court was affected; the epigraphic law is not concerned solely with the selection of the *iudices* who

---

[100] Lines 12, 15–16.

[101] The mention of his 'law' by the Epitomator immediately precedes what must be a reference to Gaius' re-election. Plutarch's 'law' also precedes his own reference to Gaius' re-election. But Appian's judiciary law follows his notice of the re-election. Just how much strength all that may add to the case for an earlier and a later stage in the judiciary legislation is however far from clear: see Appendix 3 below, p. 228. In any case, it proves nothing either way against Brunt's view that Plutarch's law was additional to and separate from the *repetundae* law, since there is every reason to suppose that it would have been carried earlier, if it was carried.

were to try *repetundae* cases, but also with the penalty and the procedures of the court, where it also introduces major changes, so that nothing forbids us to suppose that a general *lex iudiciaria* would have made such a specific measure relating to a single court any the less desirable or necessary. If Gaius was concerned to make the *equites* a balancing factor against the Senate, he needed to relieve them of that dependence on senatorial jurisdiction which Polybius stressed, which was quite another matter from cases of *repetundae*, a charge which could not in fact be brought against any non-senator. There is no good ground for holding that *repetundae* was the sole offence for which a *quaestio perpetua* had been established before 123. And Gaius could have enacted that any future *quaestiones* which might be established should be serviced by equestrian *iudices*. The special *quaestio* set up in 110 on the initiative of the tribune C. Mamilius to investigate and punish the Jugurthan scandals and their perpetrators was manned by what Cicero called 'Gracchani iudices'; perhaps Mamilius so specified in his bill, but it may have been a consequence of Gaius' law that they had to be *iudices* of that sort.[102] Gaius himself may have contemplated legislation to establish new *quaestiones* or to reform existing ones, though diverted from that object by the pressure of events in 122. It would certainly be consistent with his thinking in the matter of the '*lex de provocatione*' and the *lex ne quis iudicio circumveniatur* to picture him as a man who—for whatever reasons —saw in senatorial control and manipulation of judicial processes a dangerous arrogation of power and influence by the ruling-class which called for correction and counterbalancing.

In theory, that counterbalance could have been found by insisting that all trials of any gravity should be heard and decided by the People. But such *iudicia apud populum* were by now obsolescent and cumbersome— just how cumbersome can be seen in the Rabirius affair of 63, a prosecution

---

[102] Cicero, *Brutus* 128: 'invidiosa lege [Mamilia] C. Galbam sacerdotem et quattuor consularis, L. Bestiam, C. Catonem, Sp. Albinum, civemque praestantissimum L. Opimium, Gracchi interfectorem . . . Gracchani iudices sustulerunt.' Brunt (*The Equites*, 142 n. 2) says that 'Gracchani iudices' in this passage '*means* only "*iudices* whose sympathies were Gracchan"; but presumably they were Equites'. This I do not believe to be true. I take Cicero to be underlining here the irony of the fact that Opimius, 'the man who killed Gaius Gracchus', although he had several years earlier (as Cicero notes) been acquitted when tried for this act by the *Populus*, was now belatedly brought to book by a court manned by *iudices* on the Gracchan pattern.

designed to focus public attention in a sensationally archaic way rather than to secure a conviction. The *quaestio perpetua*, which began its evolution in 149, offered a much superior alternative, and came to be accepted as a preferable procedure on all sides. Such a *quaestio* could be established only by the People, and accordingly no appeal to the People could lie from its decisions. The definition of the offence and details of procedure and punishment were set out in the law which established the *quaestio*; and these could be varied only by another law. For the rest of the life of the Republic, contention came to be focussed, not on whether or not *quaestiones perpetuae* were desirable, but on the definition and extension of what constituted criminal acts, the penalties to be exacted, and the nature of the *iudices* who were to decide the cases.

It is clear, as we have seen, that Gaius' choice fell on those prosperous citizens who either were enrolled in the eighteen centuries of public horse or had sufficient wealth to be eligible for enrolment. They had to be 'neither too young, nor too old'. Certain individuals who would otherwise have been eligible for selection as *iudices* may well have been excluded because they had acquired their substance in ways which were generally regarded as being unacceptable or discreditable: there were certain professions or callings which Roman opinion commonly held to make those who followed them unfitted for office even at comparatively lowly levels.[103] Since senators and their closest kin were excluded, it is understandable that Gaius turned to a class of men whom he judged to have sufficient standing, education, and knowledge of affairs to cope with a task, the duration and complexity of which called not only for those qualities but also for the possession of some reasonable means. The *iudices* were not to be remunerated for their services, which obviously ruled out those who could not afford to work for nothing; while the fact that the men he chose were far from poor would minimize the risks of bribery and corruption, and also of improper pressures from the ruling aristocracy. Whatever we make of the influence on Gaius of radical Greek ideas, he had no thought, it seems, of turning Rome into an Athens where random selection by use of the lot from all citizens, and payment for public service to those so selected, were the order of the day.

---

[103] Thus, even if otherwise qualified, auctioneers or funeral directors or undertakers could be barred from local municipal office or even membership of a local council: see the *lex Julia Municipalis* (Bruns, *FIR* 18) lines 94–6.

It is important that those qualified to serve as *iudices* had to have a domicile at Rome itself. Thus it was from the well-to-do citizens of the capital alone that Gaius was going to draw the men who were to hear and decide the cases that came before a *quaestio*. Given that the time and inconvenience involved in travelling any considerable distance, and the consequent long and possibly not infrequent absences from attention to local affairs and private preoccupations, could have made recruitment from a wider area both difficult and unpopular, this factor alone may have governed Gaius' decision in this matter. But, however that may be, the result was that the courts would be in an important sense in the hands of those whose wealth was more likely to be drawn from public contracting and usury rather than agriculture and cattle-raising and smallish local manufacture and such. Putting it crudely, the rich Romans of the capital were bound to be favoured. Not only were men from that sort of background—above all the *publicani*—more closely involved with the policies of the central government and the management of its affairs in that they had an obvious and direct interest in them and in exercising some influence in those areas,[103a] their wealth and their importance were valuable assets to any politician who could win their favour and support, as the history of the later Republic clearly demonstrates. Whether Gaius deliberately angled to win them or not, the consequence must have been that he did secure the favour and support of this important body of men, who might be expected to see in him someone they needed to continue to back so as to safeguard their own new gains as well as someone from whom they might hope for further advantages which they were unlikely to have any real hope of securing from the ruling nobility. That is not to say that Gaius callously sacrificed the interest of the provincials and others in order to buttress his own political strength: had his continued for any long period of time to be the most important voice at Rome, he might have taken steps to correct any serious abuse by the *equites* of their newly won power in this and other fields. But any politician, however 'pure' his motives or objectives, must in practice involve himself to some extent in 'horse-trading', since in general men will only support those politicians who offer them some tangible benefit in return for their support. Disinterestedness and concern for the well-being of others at some sacrifice to one's own are no doubt admirable qualities, but sadly they have never been widespread.

[103a] Cf. *Verrines* II.iii.94.

If Gaius believed that he could kill two birds with one stone, that he could cut back the power of the ruling oligarchy and at the same time acquire important political backing for the successful implementation of his programme, that is no ground for moral reprobation. It was a question of priorities. If Gaius was of set purpose beginning to marshal the political force of the non-senatorial rich in order to pave his way to large reforms which he judged to be necessary and desirable, he was doing no more than setting a precedent which had to be followed later by all those Roman politicians who, regardless of their motives, were confronted with the need to overcome the vested interests and settled authority and power of the ruling oligarchy if they were to push through programmes which that oligarchy could be expected to rally itself to oppose and defeat.

Finally, before leaving this long and involved examination of Gaius' judiciary legislation, two further points remain to be noted.

The *repetundae* law did not debar non-citizens from themselves initiating a prosecution. On the contrary, it offered rewards or incentives to successful prosecutors who were not already citizens (and to their families) in the shape of the grant of either Roman citizenship or *provocatio*.[104] The absence of any requirement for non-citizens to proceed only through the agency of a citizen *patronus* may well be an innovation of Gaius', and an important one; the matter of the grant of citizenship or *provocatio* will be resumed when we come to treat of the larger matter of Gaius' enfranchisement policy.[105]

The law probably offered, to any aggrieved party who wanted to avail himself of it, an alternative and quicker process for simple recovery which did not involve any further penalties or disabilities for the defendant beyond mere repayment.[106]

The *lex de provincia Asia* and the *lex de vectigalibus et portoriis*

Attalus III, the last king of Pergamene Asia, had died unexpectedly, aged only thirty-six and childless, after a reign of five years, probably in September 134. That he had bequeathed his kingdom, should he die without issue, to the Roman People was very likely due simply to a design to protect himself against the ambitions or hostilities of others by ensuring

---

[104] Bruns, *FIR* 10, lines 76ff. Cf. Sherwin-White, *JRS* 62 (1972), 93–4.
[105] Below, p. 186.
[106] This I take to be the import of Bruns 10, lines 7ff., though admittedly the lacunae render any interpretation speculative.

that they would gain nothing by engineering his own removal.[107] The contents of his will are obscure; we know that it granted freedom to the city of Pergamum; and it may have made similar provision for all the Greek cities of his realm. Tiberius Gracchus, as we have seen, moved to make the royal moneys available to finance his own projects in Rome and Italy, and declared his intention of organizing the affairs of the whole area.[108] But Tiberius' death and the revolt of Aristonicus which promptly broke out in Asia threw things into confusion. The Roman government did not move with any great haste, and it was not until three years after Attalus' death that a Roman consul, Crassus Mucianus, reached Asia Minor. The revolt had been quashed by 129. Rome did not show any marked keenness to extend her dominion in the area, and large tracts of the kingdom were handed over to neighbouring client kings, or left independent. The nucleus of the kingdom was, however, organized as a new Roman province of Asia; the details of the organization elude us, though it is clear that the revenues were collected on a local basis until Gaius Gracchus came forward with his *lex de provincia Asia*.

What Gaius did was to ensure that the revenues of this immensely rich province should be contracted out, not locally, but by *censoria locatio* at Rome itself.[109] It may be that he had already blocked an earlier move towards different arrangements, perhaps in the year 124, by a certain Aufeius.[110] Rome was generally ready enough to take over existing systems if they worked well; and the system of tithing, if properly ordered, had obvious advantages over a requirement to pay a fixed sum irrespective of agricultural yields in any given year. The Pergamene kingdom was an advanced one, and had developed a taxation system on a tithe basis, as had also been the case in the advanced Grecized island of Sicily. But in the Roman province of Sicily the tithes were auctioned off separately in each local community under the supervision of the Roman governor; as to Asia, under Gaius' law the revenues due to Rome were to be let out *en bloc* by the censors at Rome (*censoria locatio*).

The wealth of Asia was proverbial in the late Republic. Cicero's speech

---

[107] Sherwin-White, *JRS* 67 (1977), 67–8. That whole article (pp. 62–75) supplements the exhaustive work of Magie, *Roman Rule in Asia Minor*, published in 1950. For all details reference should be made to those works, especially the latter.

[108] Above, p. 68.

[109] Cicero, *Verr.* II.ii.12 for the classic statement.

[110] See Appendix 2 below, p. 221.

pro lege Manilia, delivered in 66, abounds with evidence to this effect. He notes how Mithridates' sudden irruption into Asia in 88 had led to the overnight collapse of the Roman credit-market, and goes on: 'Believe me— you know it yourselves—the Roman money-market, the Roman credit-market, are inextricably interlocked with those Asiatic funds. If they collapse, they cannot but bring the Roman market down in the same ruin.'[111] Even in 123, the sums involved were enormous; and by his requirement that the revenues be auctioned *en bloc* at Rome itself Gaius effectively guaranteed that the rich profits were bound to fall into the pockets of the great joint-stock undertakings of the wealthy *publicani* of the Roman equestrian class. The enthusiasm with which they must have greeted this move needs no underlining.

Here again, however, we are not constrained to the simple conclusion that Gaius' sole concern was to buy the political support of these powerful interests. Granted that the sensible procedure was to adapt the efficient existing fiscal system of the Pergamene kingdom, the alternative would have been to follow the Sicilian precedent. But that would have meant that the revenues would have been auctioned far away from Rome under the supervision of the governor of the province; and there was no need to wait for the trial of a Verres to appreciate what depths of corruption and malversation of public moneys that might lead to: the scandalous acquittal of the former governor of Asia, M'. Aquillius, by the *repetundae* court was a vivid and recent reminder. An auction at Rome could serve two purposes. It would involve the wealthy Roman financiers, and it would take place under the vigilant eyes of the Roman People and their officers, in particular under the eyes of the tribunes, who might be expected to be quick to spot and check any flagrant corruption. Gaius was launching some expensive projects, and at the same time he insisted that he was no spendthrift of public moneys;[112] the *lex de provincia Asia*, while no doubt winning valuable support for Gaius from the *publicani*, can also be taken to have been an effective measure for securing that the rich new revenues of Asia would be maximized and available to help finance other parts of

[111] *pro lege Man.* 19. Note too ibid. 14: 'Nam ceterarum provinciarum vectigalia tanta sunt ut eis ad ipsas provincias tuendas vix contenti esse possimus, Asia vero tam opima est ac fertilis ut et ubertate agrorum et varietate fructuum et magnitudine pastionis et multitudine earum rerum quae exportentur facile omnibus terris antecellat.'

[112] Above, p. 127, on the corn law.

Gaius' programme. Certainly, had Gaius not intervened, there is no good reason for supposing that the tithes and customs-dues of Asia would not have been farmed by publicans—Rome had no other means available for collecting such revenues unless she resorted to the less sophisticated system of a fixed lump-sum payment from each community (as in Spain), which there are no grounds for suggesting she would have done anyway—and open to corrupt practices on the part of collectors and governors alike, and with less of a guarantee that such misdoings would be kept to a minimum so that the public treasury would gain the maximum profit.

It is convenient here to look briefly at Gaius' introduction of new revenue-charges and customs-dues. Velleius Paterculus has a rather abrupt notice to the effect that Gaius introduced new customs-dues—and that is all.[113] Whether these new *portoria* were in Italy, and connected with his colonization programme, or in Asia, or indeed where and what they were, we have no means of knowing. Aulus Gellius cites a long passage from a speech of Gaius, in the course of which Gaius says that he is advocating the increasing of public revenues (*vectigalia*). Here again, the reference may be either a general one or specifically concerned with the prospective reorganization of the Asian arrangements. But, whichever way these matters stood, it is noteworthy that Gaius has it that the object of securing such an increase is to facilitate the provision of benefits to the Roman People and to improve the administration of Rome: 'Ego ipse, qui aput vos verba facio ut vectigalia vestra augeatis, quo facilius vestra commoda et rempublicam administrare possitis.'[114] Reform is seldom cheap, and often expensive—or, at least, that is generally true of the sort of reforms with which Gaius was associated. The money had to be found from somewhere, either by the more efficient management of existing resources or by the provision of new sources of public income.

The *lex de sociis et nomine Latino*[115]

The name given to this law is derived from Cicero's reference to the speech which Fannius delivered against it as 'de sociis et nomine Latino', a speech which he describes as 'decidedly fine and noble': 'sane et bonam et nobi-

---

[113] Velleius 2.6.3: 'nova constituebat portoria'.

[114] Cited from the speech of Gaius *contra legem Augeiam*: Malcovati, *ORF*[2] 187–8 = Aulus Gellius, *NA* 11.10. (The fragment is cited in full in Appendix 2 below, p. 221).

[115] See also Appendix 3 below, p. 237.

lem'.[116] The single excerpt from it which happily has survived makes it clear that Gaius was offering full citizenship only to the Latins, and not to the rest of the peoples of Italy.[117] Hence, unless we take refuge in the assumption that at some time after Fannius had attacked his proposal Gaius modified it and extended its range, we can quickly dismiss the testimony of Velleius, in what is in any case a markedly careless and rhetorical summary, that Gaius 'was for giving the citizenship to all the peoples of Italy and extending it almost as far as the Alps': 'dabat civitatem omnibus Italicis, extendebat eam paene usque Alpis'.[118]

Appian's report fits in well with the assumption implicit in the passage from Fannius' speech: he writes that Gaius 'invited the Latins to share fully in all the rights of the Romans, assuming that the Senate could not with any show of decency hold out against Rome's own kindred. As for the rest of the allies, who lacked the right to vote at Rome, he was for granting them the right to do so henceforth, hoping to have them too on his side when it came to voting on laws'.[119] Although he does not fully grasp it, Appian must here be alluding to the old right (long dead by his own day) which the Latins possessed that any Latin who happened to be in Rome might cast a vote there in that one tribe out of the thirty-five which was selected by lot for this purpose. So Appian is in effect saying that the Latins were to be given the full citizenship, and the *socii Italici* the *ius Latii*.[120]

Plutarch's account is more confused, but it can be sorted out so as to come into line with Appian's.[121]

Flaccus, in his abortive proposal of 125, had apparently offered the *ius provocationis* as, in at least some cases, an alternative to the grant of Roman citizenship; and the Gracchan *repetundae* law also seems to have offered a similar choice to successful prosecutors.[122] Whether the same choice was available under Gaius' proposal *de sociis et nomine Latino* we are not told.[123]

This proposal never, of course, became law; and to a large degree it constituted the rock on which Gaius finally came to grief, in that by

---

[116] Cicero, *Brutus* 99. [117] Cited in full below, p. 239.

[118] Vell. Pat. 2.6.2. [119] *BC* 1. 23. 2

[120] See e.g., Sherwin-White, *The Roman Citizenship*², 136; Badian, *Foreign Clientelae*, 299–300.

[121] See Appendix 3 below, p. 237.

[122] See above, pp. 96 and 153. [123] On this point, see further below, p. 186.

persisting with it in the face of growing hostility or apathy he forfeited a lot of the political support at Rome on which he had to be able to rely for continuing success. It was not an obviously popular measure, and Fannius' attack demonstrates how the mass of ordinary citizens could be persuaded that it ran counter to their own interests; and at the same time Livius Drusus was making good headway in eroding Gaius' following among the commons. The examination of the full significance of the franchise proposal will be postponed until it comes to be considered within the whole pattern of his political programme.[124] But some preliminary observations can conveniently be made here.

The Italians had no voice at all in Roman legislation; and the Latins could only influence the way in which a single tribe out of the total of thirty-five voted on any given occasion. Hence, any enthusiasm which the prospective beneficiaries of this proposal might feel for it could not be translated into support in the assembly for its passage into law. Of course, if it went through, grateful Latins might be counted on in future as loyal and dependable voters of Gracchan proposals and candidates. It is almost certain that by now magistrates in Latin communities automatically received Roman citizenship *ex officio*, so that the leading men of the Latin towns did not need Gaius' law for themselves;[125] still, they could well have been attracted by the idea that their own local citizenries, over whom they exercised great influence, would be able to deliver a directed vote at Rome on occasions when their own special interests were involved, directly or indirectly. As for the Italian allies, Appian's implication that Gaius could hope in future to have the Italian vote on his side is careless or mistaken, since the grant to the mass of them of the *ius Latii* could do virtually nothing to affect assembly decisions. It is true, however, that the magistrates and former magistrates of the (now Latin) towns of Italy would themselves become Roman citizens, and that the vote of these well-to-do men could be important in the centuriate assembly.

In 125 Flaccus' franchise proposal had apparently been closely linked with the circumvention of the obstructions which had been put in the path of the agrarian commissioners: if the non-Romans became citizens, not only might they willingly surrender their protected position *vis-à-vis ager publicus* (and they could not be sure in any case how long they could

---

[124] See below, p. 185. For Fannius' attack, see p. 239.
[125] Below, p. 189.

count on its remaining protected), but the mere fact that they were now citizens would have transformed the technical and legal arguments in this matter.[126] Similar considerations may have lain, at least in part, behind the move in 122.

At another level, the recent revolt of Fregellae was a warning of the sort of trouble that might be expected if some radical transformation of the political structure of Italy was not soon to be effected. That the non-Roman peoples of Italy did not take up arms to achieve their aims until just over thirty years later is a fact known to us; but in Gaius' day it was not known, and it would perhaps not have been unreasonable for some thoughtful men to judge that the danger was more urgent. In the end, Rome did have to yield reluctantly to the inexorable pressure which had built up for an extension of equality of rights and standing and opportunity to the non-Romans of the peninsula; and after a dangerous and bitter and exhausting war Roman citizenship was extended throughout Italy right up to the line of the Po, and in some instances beyond. Gaius and Fulvius Flaccus and those who thought like them may then have been more far-sighted, more flexible, even simply more generous of spirit in seeking to move with the tide rather than battle against it. Certainly, Rome would have been spared much travail, and Italy too, and Greek Asia and Spain and Sicily and Africa, if this issue had been settled by other means than recourse to arms.

At the level of city politics, such a proposal, had it been carried into law, as Gaius surely must have hoped would happen, would have greatly strengthened his hold over the assemblies, and weakened the influence of the ruling oligarchy still further. What Gaius would have gone on to do with that sort of strength and prestige behind him is a question best left to the historical novelist. It as as impossible to answer confidently as it would be if we had to try to guess what the young Octavian might have done in the fulness of time had he been killed at Actium.

On electoral procedure

The author of the pseudo-Sallustian second letter to Caesar wrote that 'in the matter of the elections of magistrates, I am rather taken with the proposal which Gaius Gracchus put forward when he was tribune, that the votes of the centuries should be called for by random selection from

---

[126] Above, p. 95.

among all the five classes jumbled together': 'magistratibus creandis haud mihi quidem apsurde placet lex quam C. Gracchus in tribunatu promulgaverat, ut ex confusis quinque classibus centuriae vocarentur.'[127]

The voting-procedure in the centuriate assembly, where the highest officers of the Roman state—the censors, consuls, and praetors—were elected, greatly favoured the well-to-do citizens. The seventy centuries of the first class together with the eighteen centuries of public horse numbered not far short of one half of the overall total of 193, and they each contained fewer members than did the centuries of the lower census-classes—indeed, the very poorest citizens were all lumped together in a single century of *proletarii*.[128] These prosperous citizens voted first; and, since the total vote of the centuries in each class was reported successively and the elections continued only up to the point where the necessary number of candidates had achieved the required majority of ninety-seven centuries, not many elections needed to go beyond the count of the centuries of the second class, and even that must often have been a formality when particular candidates had already established such a commanding majority among the first eighty-eight as to put the issue beyond doubt. Hence, to suggest that the votes of the individual centuries should be called for by random selection was distinctly 'levelling' or (in some sense of the word) 'democratic'.

Granted that Gaius did make such a proposal (we have no other information apart from that already set out), we do not know when and in what circumstances he made it. The story may be apocryphal, the sort of scheme plausibly to be attributed to that great leveller and innovator, Gaius Gracchus. But it might have been one of that last batch of proposals to which Plutarch refers without specifying their precise nature.[129] There may be some connection with, or confused echo of, the row which broke out at the tribunician elections of 122, when it was protested that Gaius had been gerrymandered out of being declared re-elected for a third successive term as tribune.[130] For all that the tribunes were elected by the tribes and not by the centuries, the story of the row in 122 implies that in

---

[127] [Sallust] *ad Caesarem senem* 2.8.   [128] Above, pp. ix & 7.

[129] *CG* 12.1 (below, p. 238).

[130] *CG* 12.3: ἐκ τούτου καὶ τὴν τρίτην ἔδοξε δημαρχίαν ἀφῃρῆσθαι, ψήφων μὲν αὐτῷ πλείστων γενομένων, ἀδίκως δὲ καὶ κακούργως τῶν συναρχόντων ποιησαμένων τὴν ἀναγόρευσιν καὶ ἀνάδειξιν. ἀλλὰ ταῦτα μὲν ἀμφισβήτησιν εἶχεν. ἤνεγκε δὲ οὐ μετρίως ἀποτυχών.

the tribal assembly, too, the order of the voting of the units of which it was composed, or the reporting of their votes, could be a decisive factor in elections there as well as in the centuriate assembly.[131] Perhaps, then, Gaius did bring in a bill after his return from Africa with the intention of reforming the electoral procedures not only of the centuriate assembly (which pseudo-Sallust happened to have particularly in mind at this point) but also of the tribal assembly. By now such a bill might well have seemed attractive to a Gaius who was aware that his support was falling to a critical level, and who was less worried about the consequence that it would give offence so far as the centuriate assembly was concerned to the *equites* since he could now see that they had in any case been won away from him.[132]

[131] On the whole question of 'Voting Procedure in Roman Assemblies', see the article with that title by Hall in *Historia* 13 (1964), 267–306.

[132] On the defection of the *equites*, see below, p. 191.

VII

ANNUS MIRABILIS

There is a well-authenticated story of a dream which Gaius Gracchus is said to have had, and which he spoke of to many of his friends at the time. It happened in 127, when he was a candidate for the quaestorship. In his dream his dead brother Tiberius had appeared and said to him: 'However much you may try to delay, you are fated to meet the same death as I did'.[1]

As Cicero observed, there is no good reason to doubt the story. Nothing could be more natural than that the younger brother should have felt strongly drawn, even honour-bound, to follow in his elder brother's footsteps. The perils of that path must have been obvious, and very likely they did from time to time set up a conflict in his mind, if only at the subconscious level. But at the level of conscious action there is little sign of any hesitation, unless we choose to make something here of the fact that he spent twelve years in military service before becoming a quaestor, as opposed to the customary ten.[2] It is true that, in a fragment from his speech *de legibus promulgatis*, possibly delivered late in 124 or early in 123, he spoke movingly of how he was almost the last surviving male heir of Scipio Africanus and Tiberius Gracchus, and perhaps could properly ask the Roman people to allow him some peace and quiet: but that may have had more of oratory in it than true conviction.[3] Since 133 he had been an agrarian commissioner. In 131 or 130 he had publicly supported Carbo's bill about re-election to the tribunate. He attacked Pennus' aliens expulsion bill of 126. When his appointment in Sardinia was extended for a third year, he insisted on returning to Rome, where he had to defend himself before the censors for this alleged dereliction of duty, and where an attempt was also made to implicate him in some way in the recent

[1] Cicero, *de div.* 1.56. Where detailed references have already been given in the preceding chapter, they will not be repeated here.

[2] Gaius' twelve *stipendia* may appear to clash with his duties as an agrarian commissioner. But we can easily suppose that several of these 'years of service' were spent in Italy and not abroad, and may have occupied only half the year or less and often been fairly nominal.

[3] Appendix 2 below, p. 221.

revolt of Fregellae: there may have been little or no substance in the latter allegation, but it was significant none the less. This same year of 124 saw him standing for election as tribune for 123. And, when we contemplate the legislative programme of 123, it is impossible to resist the conclusion that it must have been the fruit of years of careful thought and detailed planning.

Something at least of what he had it in mind to do must have been public knowledge—perhaps that was why the attempt was made to keep him away from Rome a little longer, and to smear his reputation with the Fregellae allegation. Huge and enthusiastic crowds converged on Rome from all over Italy to attend the elections, so numerous that the city could not house them or the voting-place contain them. The ruling nobility rallied its strength to oppose him, and to such good effect, we are told, that his expectation of being returned at the head of the poll was disappointed, and he came only fourth out of the ten elected.[4] Yet there is no hint that as tribune in 123 he had to face any noteworthy obstruction from any of his colleagues, whose number did not include an Octavius or a Drusus; even if the 'establishment' did succeed in getting some of its own men in, they were evidently quickly reduced to silence and ineffectiveness. It could be, however, that Gaius, knowing that his own election was assured, was more concerned to make sure that he had the right colleagues than to win the first place for himself.[5]

Whether from brotherly feeling, or concern for the principles involved, or calculation, Gaius was at this time eloquent in deploring the outrage of his brother's murder.[6] His bills *'de provocatione'* and *ne quis iudicio circumveniatur* were directed against the sort of savagely repressive actions which had been taken against Tiberius and his followers, and aimed also to punish those like Popillius Laenas who had been responsible. Laenas prudently withdrew into voluntary exile until the storm blew over: he clearly knew, and his powerful friends knew too, what the outcome of a formal trial would be, especially when faced with the devastating brilliance of Gaius' rhetoric. A few years later Opimius could secure an acquittal from

---

[4] Plutarch, *CG* 3.1-2. Hall (*Athenaeum* 1972, 15) suggests that 'probably the opposition was able to see that some tribes did not include Gaius in their selected ten names at all'.

[5] Appian (*BC* 1.21.5) notes merely that Gaius' success was very clear-cut: περιφανέστατα αἱρεθείς.

[6] Plutarch *CG* 3.2. Cf. Appendix 2 below, p. 220.

the People when charged with similar excesses against Gaius and his followers; but by then Gaius was dead and his cause in ruins. These two bills were also and chiefly designed to ensure against the repetition of such tactics. If we take them along with his other judicial legislation, altogether such measures constituted a carefully thought out pattern for grappling with the problem of the growing accumulation of power in the hands of the ruling nobility, a process which had been going on apace over the past three or four generations, and the abuses and injustices which had resulted. The *lex de abactis* sounds a similar note. Octavius had been wrong to allow himself to be induced to abuse his office as tribune to seek to thwart the clear wishes and interest of the commons by whom he had been elected. Men guilty of such conduct were quite properly liable to be removed from office by those who had conferred that office on them; and it was right, too, that they should also be debarred from ever holding any public office again. In the end, Gaius withdrew the noose from Octavius' own neck. But his point had been made, the warning plainly given. Through all these measures there runs a common thread. Time-tabling and tactics imposed their own priorities and temporal disjunctions; but Gaius was not simply promoting and carrying one bill and then sitting down to think of another.

The corn law, another early measure, points in a different direction. Its popular success was guaranteed, and the support and gratitude which it engendered were very valuable. Tiberius had perhaps made a mistake in neglecting to cultivate the urban *plebs*. Gaius' provision for regular distributions of the basic necessity of life at a fixed and reasonable price was bound to endear him to those voters who had been too long accustomed to surviving on the edge of subsistence, at the mercy of the vagaries of harvests and weather and the profits of speculators, dependent too often on the occasional largesse of the great houses. There was to be a new agrarian law, and the colonies which Gaius planned to found (whether under that law or a separate one) would offer new hopes and opportunities to small peasants and ex-peasants, help to revive declining areas of Italy, and also find room for an 'urbanized' element of small traders and shop-keepers and city-workers. But Gaius no doubt appreciated that 'the poor are always with us', that not all of the *faex Romuli* could be decanted out of the capital. He insisted that he was not a spendthrift of public funds—his speeches were those of a Gladstonian guardian of the public purse.[7] Some public funds would need to be expended; but careful

[7] Above, p. 127.

management and the proper provision of great storehouses would ensure that they were not wasted carelessly. Nor were the provinces to be exhausted for Rome's replenishment. He had already had some trenchant remarks to make about such exploitation for personal gain by too many of Rome's officials; and when in 123 the governor of one of the Spanish provinces, Q. Fabius, had a large gift of corn sent from there to Rome, Gaius secured a decree of the Senate ordering that the corn be sold and the money repaid to the Spanish peoples concerned and censuring Fabius for his burdensome and intolerable behaviour towards them.[8] It may be that Fabius' action had been intended as a counterblast to Gaius' corn bill, which Gaius caused to backfire on him and his friends at Rome. It is interesting that, if Plutarch is correct, Gaius proceeded by way of a senatorial decree and not a tribunician bill; but that need not mean that he could generally command majority support in the Senate, since it could be that the senators simply appreciated that to attempt to oppose him in such a matter would be pointless.

In connection with the corn law, Appian specifically comments on the assistance which Gaius received from Fulvius Flaccus.[9] Flaccus is a tantalizingly elusive figure. Considerably senior to Gaius in age and standing and of enormously distinguished ancestry, he had been consul in 125. Of his earlier career we are largely ignorant. He was almost certainly the Flaccus who tried to warn Tiberius Gracchus of what was brewing on the tumultuous day of the tribune's murder.[10] He had probably been a quaestor before 136, and enrolled in the Senate by the censors of that year; only a close association with Tiberius and his collaborators could explain his taking Claudius' place as an agrarian commissioner when the latter died in 130. In 129 he had been loud in his vilification of Aemilianus and his limitation of the commission's activities.[11] He must have been a praetor by 128 at latest, but we know neither the precise year nor which province he held. As consul in 125, he came forward with his franchise proposal, but whether it ever came to a vote or was abandoned when its passage came to

---

[8] Plutarch, *CG* 6.1. And see above, p. 98.

[9] *BC* 1.21.5: καὶ ὁ μὲν ὀξέως οὕτως ἐνὶ πολιτεύματι τὸν δῆμον ὑπηγάγετο, συμπράξαντος αὐτῷ Φουλουίου Φλάκκου.

[10] Above, p. 76. In general on Flaccus, see Hall, *Athenaeum* (1977), 280-8.

[11] Plutarch, *CG* 10.2. Incidentally, Cicero's opinion of Flaccus as an orator was that he was no better than 'mediocre' (*Brutus* 108).

look hopeless there is no telling.[12] There is no suggestion that he tried to use his office as consul to adjudicate between the commissioners and the non-Roman communities over the disputed public land. Why that was we can only guess; but it could be that Flaccus and his friends had come to see that the way forward must now lie in two new directions. An extension of Roman citizenship could bring the communities concerned into a frame of mind to accept the commission's activities more co-operatively; and, indeed, the 129 business may have revealed that Tiberius' land law had served to trigger off the vocal expression of a number of other unconnected grievances which the non-Roman communities had come to feel deeply. Secondly, colonization projects may already have been emerging as a preferable approach to the problem of how to deal with the needs of the poor. Perhaps time was needed to think these ideas out in greater detail, and a tribune with Gaius' energy and magnetism and oratorical power to carry them into law. But Gaius was away in Sardinia, and would not be eligible for a year or two. Flaccus' franchise proposal dropped out of sight, and he went off to Provence to fight the Salluvii. But he was back in 123 to celebrate a triumph and lend his experienced support to the tribune Gaius.[13]

As I have argued earlier, Gaius' agrarian law probably introduced two particularly novel features as compared with that of his brother.[14] It empowered the commissioners to dispose of public land outside as well as within Italy, and it specifically envisaged the plantation of colonies as well as the making of *viritim* assignments. Since we hear of no objections from the non-Romans of Italy, it would appear that they were satisfied that they had nothing to fear from any new powers which the law gave to the commissioners; and perhaps they were already being encouraged to look forward to an extension of political rights and opportunities. New categories of voters could be expected to be won to Gaius' following, including men of some substance from the class outside the Senate. The road-building projects which are conveniently to be associated with this facet of Gaius' activity would also not only benefit Italy in general and improve communications, but also provide work for a large number of men, and

[12] Above, p. 94. Flaccus' cousins, consuls respectively in 135 and 134, may well have still been alive, and leant their influence to his candidature.

[13] Hall (*Athenaeum* 1977, 287) very properly discounts the view that expansion or colonization in Provence was part of a 'Gracchan programme'.

[14] Above, p. 132. Molthagen (*Historia* 1973, 449 ff.) has a similar approach.

profitable business for the public contractors who took the job on. Indeed, it is hard to see how any one, from wealthy landowners downwards, would fail to benefit from the advantages of more and better roads in Italy; and these roads, and the colonies which were planned, would also help to revive decaying areas of the peninsula.

A lot of money was needed for all these projects. Gaius was accused of squandering public funds on political bribes, of bidding fair to drain the treasury dry. But his own public position was not that of a spendthrift. He may well have argued that in the long run his projects would more than pay for themselves, since by his new arrangements for the farming of the revenues of the province of Asia, and by the institution of new imposts and customs-dues—if these latter were in fact separate from the Asian arrangements—he could also maintain that he was making prudent and sufficient provision for the outlays which his other measures would engender. Here again, the enthusiastic support of the rich and influential *publicani* who could look forward to securing the contracts for farming these considerable revenues must have been of great importance.

The law on the consular provinces may have had a connection with Fannius' candidature for a consulship of 122, and the risk that he might be posted off away from Rome; but more probably we should simply see it as one of Gaius' moves against the improper use of senatorial prerogatives. The proposal attributed to him that the voting procedure at centuriate assembly elections should be changed and put on a more egalitarian footing fits in with that pattern of thinking. But it is doubtful that it really belongs here, and the evidence for it is not of the best. Such a proposal certainly never became law, and it would clearly not have been at all pleasing to the well-to-do citizens whose support for Gaius was at this stage important, if not vital. There may have been a law requiring military tribunes to be elected by the People: such posts were not to be left in the gift of influential relatives and *patroni* to distribute to favoured young men, but assigned by the People to men of worth and experience. Certainly, the recruiting of under-age boys was to stop, and soldiers provided with clothing and equipment at public cost; and quite possibly other military reforms, which hostile critics represented as undermining true discipline, were also carried through and reflected Gaius' determination to reduce or eradicate arbitrary and excessive misuse of authority.

Something of that determination must also have lain behind the judiciary legislation. The modern Englishman is brought up to believe that the judicature is, and must properly be, separate from and independent of the legislative and executive arms of government. But, historically speaking, that is a parochial point of view; for such a state of affairs has always been uncommon in human experience. Polybius had no doubt that the Senate's domination of judicial decisions was a central element of its power. Gaius' move to deprive the members of the Senate of some or all of that domination was a direct assault on that power, and especially on the inner circle of families within the nobility which dominated the Senate itself. Some conception of the scale of that dominance can be got from a study of statistics. Of the 200 consuls who held office between 233 and 133, thirteen noble *gentes* provided 113, and five *gentes* sixty-two of those 113. If we combine those figures with our information about the praetorship, we can talk in terms of a dozen or so *gentes* which constituted the inner circle of the ruling nobility of the second century, with another dozen or so making up what virtually amounts to the ruling oligarchy as a whole.[15]

It is just possible that Gaius passed no general judiciary law at all, but confined his attention to the *quaestio de repetundis*. It is also possible that he did pass a judiciary law which provided for *equites* and senators in general to share judicial powers, while insisting that in *repetundae* trials the *iudices* should number no senators among the panel that heard and decided the cases. Even if either of these views is true, the assault on senatorial power was a heavy one. But the view preferred here is that which sees his final legislation as insisting on the exclusion of senatorial *iudices* from all *quaestiones perpetuae*, both those already in existence and any which might henceforth be established, and recruiting the *iudices* to sit on these *quaestiones* exclusively from the non-senatorial well-to-do who were registered as having a domicile in the area of Rome itself and its immediate environs. That final enactment or enactments had probably been preceded by an earlier proposal to institute mixed panels of *iudices*, part-senatorial and part-equestrian. But the earlier scheme was abandoned in favour of the final version, which may well have been carried into law not long after Gaius' election to the tribunate of 122. Either Gaius must have formed the view that, for whatever reasons, 'mixed courts' were impracticable or undesirable, or—perhaps because of a change of plan reflected by his originally unsought-for-election to a second tribunate—he decided that he

---

[15] *Histoire romaine* II.i.33. The Fulvii Flacci alone produced five of these consuls.

must now make an all-out bid for equestrian support.

Around Gaius' re-election for a second year of office as tribune there hangs yet another mist of contention.[16] In the first place, it both is now and was then notorious that, whatever the legal or conventional rights and wrongs of the matter, it was Tiberius Gracchus' attempt to secure a second, consecutive tribunate for 132 that had detonated the final explosion which led to his death. There is no need here to go into the issues involved, for they have been set out earlier.[17] In 131 or 130 Papirius Carbo, with Gaius Gracchus among his supporters, had tried to settle the question by legislation, and failed.[18] But now in 123 Gaius secured a second term, and lived to tell the tale.

Appian, in a somewhat confused notice, has it that by 123 a law had been passed to the effect that, if fewer than ten candidates put themselves up for election, the People could make up the full ten by electing anyone they chose.[19] But he does not specify the law in question, and I find it hard to believe that such a law could have been carried—even if Appian is muddled about its precise provisions—between 130 and 123 without some ripple being caused by it in our sources. It has long been pointed out that, if Appian's account is correct, all that Gaius' opponents had to do to prevent his re-election for 122 was to see that there were at least ten other normally qualified candidates—a task of childish simplicity. Hence some, like Strachan-Davidson in his note on this passage of Appian, have held that Appian has mistranslated or misunderstood a Latin source, and should have talked, not of an insufficient number of candidates for election, but of an insufficient number of candidates who received an absolute majority of the thirty-five tribal votes on the first ballot. But that is not only not what Appian says, it still leaves us wondering why the opposition did not put up at least ten other candidates, all of whom could be guaranteed to pick up at least a sufficiency of votes in most tribes. The 'fixing' of votes may not yet have reached the heights of organization and sophistication which were to be attained in the Ciceronian period, but it would have needed little enough manipulation to achieve so simple an object. And, as Last pointed out, the fact that in 110 'public business in Rome suffered

---

[16] For a full discussion, see Hall, *Athenaeum* (1972), 3–35.

[17] Above, p. 72.

[18] Above, p. 91.

[19] *BC* 1.21.6: καὶ γάρ τις ἤδη νόμος ἐκεκύρωτο, εἰ δήμαρχος ἐνδέοι ταῖς παραγγελίαις, τὸν δῆμον ἐκ πάντων ἐπιλέγεσθαι.

long and serious delays from the wranglings which were started when two of the tribunes tried to secure office for a second year' makes it 'not easy to believe that disputes so protracted as these could have occurred if the subject was one on which legislation had been passed less than twenty years before. Appian may be obscure; but the law itself, had it existed, must have been capable of interpretation in less than the months that were spent in argument'.[20] Which led Last to conclude that

though confidence on such a point is impossible, it is by no means unlikely that no measure on this subject had been passed so recently as the Gracchan age. It was custom, not law, which stood in the way of a tribune seeking to remain in office; and where convention is the obstacle prestige is the strength of an attack. Gaius Gracchus, a man whose personal influence was far greater than his brother's, may well have succeeded where his brother failed; and it is possible, though by no means certain, that Appian's story of a law which authorized this re-election is a mere inference made by some historian who failed to understand that custom was the barrier and that Gaius had authority enough to break it down.[21]

It may well be that Last was right to cut through this Gordian knot in so magisterial a manner.[22] But he did not discuss what Plutarch had to say about the re-election, and how that may affect our approach to the question. Plutarch records the active canvass which Gaius conducted to secure the election of Fannius to one of the consulships of 122, and then notes that Gaius was himself elected to a second tribunate for 122 'although he neither announced himself to be a candidate nor canvassed for election, but because of the enthusiastic insistence of the People'.[23]

It has very reasonably been pointed out that

it is hard to reconcile this statement with the theory that a law had been passed in the Gracchan interest unequivocally allowing the re-election of tribunes (whether there was a shortage of candidates or not). If such a law had been passed, why should Gaius not have been a candidate? The passage

---

[20] For the wrangling, see Sallust, *BJ* 37.2: 'P. Lucullus et L. Annius tribuni plebis resistentibus conlegis continuare magistratum nitebantur, quae dissensio totius anni comitia impediebat.'

[21] *CAH* ix.61–2.

[22] Writing this book, as I am, in the room which was for several years Hugh Last's study, and at the table at which he composed his chapters for the *Cambridge Ancient History*, I am particularly sensitive to the influence of that great scholar.

[23] *CG* 8.1: κἀκεῖνος μὲν ὕπατος, Γάιος δὲ δήμαρχος ἀπεδείχθη τὸ δεύτερον, οὐ παραγγέλλων οὐδὲ μετίων, ἀλλὰ τοῦ δήμου σπουδάσαντος.

of the law would in itself suggest an anxiety to hold a second tribunate.
  However,
if a law had been passed in the Gracchan interest that existing tribunes
could be elected if there was a shortage of candidates [—which is very improbable—] then of course by the very terms of the law Gaius could only
be elected if he were not a candidate. He might yet have been very eager
for election. In this case the circumstances reported by Plutarch would be
right, but the impression would be wrong.[24]

But, if we suppose that there had been no recent legislation which clearly
resolved the issue, and that it was as disputable in 123 as it had been ten
years earlier, then Gaius' tactics could have had advantages. If the *plebs*
could be relied on to vote for him overwhelmingly at the last moment,
even though his name was not formally before them, and provided that
his fellow-tribunes could be counted on as either co-operative or intimida-
table, his re-election could not be challenged until it was an accomplished
fact. Given a massive demonstration of electoral support, and with a far
wider power-base than Tiberius had enjoyed, Gaius would be very hard to
'unseat' once he had been elected. To that extent Last was right to insist
that the younger brother's prestige and authority were greater than his
elder brother's had been, and that here we may find the key to unlock this
puzzle. Moreover, it is certainly easy to assume that some existing but
long-disused electoral convention may have been cited in pedantic or
casuistic justification of the propriety of such a re-election, and that
Appian or his source managed to garble it.[25]

  But, though we may have found how it was that Gaius managed to
succeed where his brother had come to grief, it may nevertheless be true
that Gaius really had never intended to secure a second tribunate. The
storm which had broken over Tiberius' attempt to secure one may well
have made him ponder the wisdom of such a step.[25a] Better, perhaps, to
proceed by a different route altogether, and let the powerful and energetic and experienced Fulvius Flaccus take over the helm and steer
through the franchise legislation. Gaius' own turn as executive land commissioner was due to come round again in 122, and he was also going to
have to spend a lot of time away from Italy seeing to the affairs of the new

[24] Hall, o.c. 27.
[25] Ibid. 22–7 for a full examination of this possibility.
[25a] The failure of Carbo's proposal served to underline the dubiety of such *continuatio*.

colony of Junonia/Carthage (either as an agrarian commissioner or as a specially appointed *IIIvir coloniae deducendae*). Tribunes were not allowed to be absent from Rome for any period exceeding twenty four hours;[26] although it was possible to obtain dispensation from that rule—and Gaius must later have secured such dispensation to cover his absence when he made his seventy-day trip to Junonia in 122[27]—he may well have thought that not just Junonia but other colonies in Italy and other work generated by his legislation in 123 would give him more than enough to occupy his energies in 122, without being tribune as well.

Plutarch reminds us, if we should need reminding, just how busy Gaius was, and what great calls his legislation made on his energies.

He passed other measures for sending out colonies, for building roads, for constructing granaries. For the execution of all these projects he had himself appointed supreme controller and director, and despite the number and magnitude of these tasks he showed no signs of being fatigued by anything. On the contrary, his quickness and energy were so amazing that it was as if he had each time only one single thing to attend to, so that even those who detested him and feared him were astonished by the dispatch and thoroughness which he displayed in everything he set his hand to. The mere sight of him filled the people with wonder, when they observed him surrounded by a crowd of contractors, technicians, ambassadors, magistrates, soldiers, and literary men. All of them he treated with graciousness, showing to everyone affability without loss of dignity, giving to each man a personal attention appropriate to his character and standing. He thus demonstrated how overharsh were the criticisms of those who sought to label him as a frightening or arrogant or bullying individual. For he was an even more accomplished winner of popularity in conversation and business than he was in his speeches from the rostrum. He took especial pains over the roads he built, having regard to their beauty and attractiveness as well as their utility. They ran straight and unswerving through the countryside; they were paved with hewn stone, and built up with firm-rammed sand. Depressions were filled in; and where they were intersected by torrent-beds or ravines bridges were built to carry the roads over. With the height thus levelled on each side and perfect alignment attained, a regular and elegant appearance was achieved throughout the whole work. In addition, the whole road was measured off in miles, and stone milestones set up to mark the distances. Other stones were set up on both sides at lesser intervals to help travellers to mount their horses without the need for other assistance.[28]

---

[26] Aulus Gellius, *NA* 3.2.11.

[27] Plutarch, *CG* 11.2. On this, see further below, p. 173, n. 31.

[28] *CG* 6–7.

Thus there seem to be two alternative possibilities. Gaius may have intended all along to hold a second tribunate, but was careful to keep this secret for tactical reasons. Or he may originally have preferred, for more than one reason, to go out of office in December 123 and leave Fulvius Flaccus to steer through the franchise legislation, a project with which Flaccus had been publicly associated at least since 126/125, with a solid base of political support behind him which had been built up by the legislative programme of 123. If the latter is the true answer—as I suspect it is, though compelling proof is lacking—then Gaius' re-election must represent a very late change of plan. What caused that change we can only try to guess—as so often. It could be that a forceful wave of popular insistence, spontaneous and uncontrived, did leave him with no real choice but to bow to the wishes of the plebeian assembly. Or perhaps he began very late in the day to have doubts about Gaius Fannius' reliability as consul in 122, or Flaccus' shortcomings, or the threat posed by Livius Drusus, or a toughening in the mood of the Senate. Immediately after recording the elections of Fannius and Gaius, Plutarch goes on to say that Gaius could see that the Senate was openly at war with him, and that Fannius' goodwill towards him had become lukewarm.[29] Fulvius Flaccus was a turbulent and in some ways unattractive character, hated by the Senate and suspect because of his attitude towards the non-Romans. No better than a 'moderate' public speaker, while Gaius was away in Africa in 122 he played into the hands of their opponents by his clumsiness and violence, and some of this inevitably rubbed off on Gaius himself.[30] If Plutarch is right, Gaius had meant to spend more than seventy days away from Rome at Junonia—which, if true, reinforces the view that he would have been happier to have avoided the calls of a tribunate in 122—but had to cut his trip short and return to the capital when he heard that Flaccus was hard put to hold his own against Drusus and that affairs there urgently demanded his own presence.[31] What lay behind Gaius' change of plan, then, about a second tribunate we cannot say for sure; but it is not difficult to suggest explanations which could account for it, and to suppose

---

[29] *CG* 8.2: ἐπεὶ δὲ ἑώρα τὴν μὲν σύγκλητον ἐχθρὰν ἄντικρυς, ἀμβλὺν δὲ τῇ πρὸς αὐτὸν εὐνοίᾳ τὸν Φάννιον.

[30] *CG* 10. 2–3. Cf. above, p. 165, n. 11.

[31] *CG* 11.2: οὐ μὴν ἀλλὰ πάντα συντάξας καὶ διακοσμήσας ὁ Γάιος ἡμέραις ἐβδομήκοντα ταῖς πάσαις ἐπανῆλθεν εἰς Ῥώμην, πιέζεσθαι τὸν Φούλβιον ὑπὸ τοῦ Δρούσου πυνθανόμενος, καὶ τῶν πραγμάτων τῆς αὐτοῦ παρουσίας δεομένων.

that the ebb and flow of rumour and informed gossip and visible activity in certain quarters which attended the final run-up to the elections did cause a last-minute revision of earlier calculations.

What cannot be questioned is the ascendancy which Gaius had achieved by the autumn of 123. His superb oratory, personal charm and magnetism, indefatigable energy and attention to detail, immense practical ability and drive were harnessed to a wide range of political support, not from one section of the citizen-body alone, but from the urban and rural poor, from small tradesmen and craftsmen and suchlike, from financial and business interests, from all who had no strong personal commitment to the mainte-nance of the status quo or felt that Rome stood in pressing need of a man who could 'strike his finger on the place, And say, *Thou ailest here, and here*', probably too from many of the leading men of the Latin and Italian communities who were looking for a significant improvement in their own position. The legislation of 123, leaving aside any arguments about its exact dating and sequence and interconnections, was monumental and majestic in its quantity and range and relevance and importance. Small wonder that Plutarch should report that Gaius' power became almost monarchical, so that even the Senate itself had no option but to hold its hand and listen with such patience as it could muster whenever he was on his feet there with some advice to give or recommendation to make. What he had to propose was, however, always something suitable to the dignity of the House (like the proposal to send back the money for the Spanish corn and censure the governor Fabius).[32] It must have seemed that, with a second tribunate under his belt, Gaius' pre-eminence was assured for several years to come. But twelve months later he had little to show for

---

[32] *CG* 6.1: μοναρχική τις ἰσχὺς ἐγεγόνει περὶ αὐτόν, ὥστε καὶ τὴν σύγκλητον ἀνέχεσθαι συμβουλεύοντος αὐτοῦ. συνεβούλευε δὲ ἀεί τι των ἐκείνη πρεπόντων εἰσηγούμενος. οἷον κτλ. That the paraphrase in the text above represents the correct meaning of Plutarch's Greek I am sure; and I have been confirmed in this belief by Mr. Donald Russell of St. John's College and a number of other Oxford Grecists. As far as I can make out, it must be a misunderstanding or mistranslation of Plutarch's Greek here (thus, Langhorne: 'Even the senate in their deliberations *were willing* to listen to his advice'; and Perrin's Loeb translation: 'even the senate *consented* to follow his counsel') that lies behind the quite widespread assumption or implication that Gaius and the Senate enjoyed a 'honeymoon' period at some time in 123. That cannot be extracted from what Plutarch says here, where all that is stated or implied is that the Senate, faced with the inescapable fact of Gaius' over-whelming predominance, had no option but to make the best of a bad job and 'grin and bear it'. I know of no other evidence that could support the 'honeymoon' idea.

all his efforts, and his attempt to win a third tribunate miscarried; and twelve months after that both he and Flaccus were dead, and their cause lay in ruins.

VIII
DECLINE AND FALL

It is impossible to establish the precise chronology of the Gracchan moves of 122.[1] That something was going to be offered to the Latins and the Italians must have long been predictable; but it is not clear when a specific proposal was first published, nor how far its detailed provisions were in line with informed expectation. Appian's account is condensed and extremely unsatisfactory.[2] After a longish excursus on the judiciary law, he briefly notes Gaius' road-building and colony proposals and then proceeds to summarize the franchise proposal. (He gives no indication that we have now moved into the second tribunate, but his mention of Livius Drusus makes it plain that we must be at least very close to it.) The Senate's response was a decree forbidding any non-voter to come within 5 miles of the capital while Gaius' measures were being voted on. (The Senate was probably concerned about the risk of widespread personation—it must have been almost impossible to check the credentials of every voter when large numbers were involved—and in particular about the danger of violent demonstrations and physical intimidation.) The tribune Drusus was persuaded to block Gaius' proposals—it is not clear which ones Appian has in mind—and empowered to offer twelve new colonies in order to win popular support. In consequence, the commons looked down their noses at what Gaius was offering. Whether Drusus actually used his veto we are not told; the impression is rather that Gaius let his proposals drop for the moment, and sailed away to Junonia to see to things there (accompanied, so Appian wrongly has it, by Fulvius Flaccus); but he did first try to win back popular support by increasing the provision for the number of settlers at Junonia from an unknown smaller figure to a total of 6,000, and on his return from Junonia set about recruiting them from all over Italy. Meanwhile trouble arose about sinister signs and portents at the new colony on the old-accursed site of Carthage, and the Senate proposed to call for an assembly vote to repeal the law and abandon the colony. Gaius and Flaccus were distraught, and set in motion the chain of events which led to the final fighting and their own deaths.

[1] See Appendix 3 below, p. 237.   [2] *BC* 1.23–26.

We know that Gaius and Flaccus in fact met their deaths in 121, when both of them were out of office. Not only does Appian give no hint of this, he passes over in silence Gaius' unsuccessful bid to be re-elected to a third tribunate for 121. Plutarch is happily a lot fuller.[3] After noting the open hostility of the Senate towards Gaius after his re-election in 123, and the change in the attitude of the consul-elect Fannius, he says that Gaius introduced a bill for colonies at Tarentum and Capua in order to bind the commons to him, and then offered the Latins Roman citizenship. At this point the Senate arranged with Drusus to counter Gaius, not by meeting him head on, but by setting out to lure popular favour and support away from him. Thus Drusus capped Gaius' offer of two colonies with an offer of twelve, each to provide for 3,000 needy citizens. Whereas under Gaius' arrangements those who received public land were to pay a rent-charge to the state (presumably a continuation of Tiberius' arrangement, and with a similar object[4]), he proposed a relief from this payment—though whether this was merely in connection with his own projected foundations or in amendment of the Gracchan *lex agraria* Plutarch does not make plain. In answer to Gaius' offer to the Latins, Drusus aired an alternative proposal to give them exemption from flogging even when on military service with the Roman army. In all this Drusus was seen to enjoy the support and goodwill of the Senate. Moreover, he was careful to see that he was given no executive responsibility for the measures he proposed, in pointed contrast to Gaius' approach in such matters: other men were to be responsible for the organization of the Drusan colonies and for the expenditure of public moneys. With Gaius away in Africa, Drusus gave Flaccus a hard time of it. The news from Junonia itself did not help, for there were reports of how the standard being borne at the head of the military procession formally taking possession of the new colony was blown from the hands of the standard-bearer and shattered, that sacrificial victims were scattered beyond the boundary-markers by a sudden gale, that the markers themselves were dug up and carried off by wolves.

Gaius did what he could to arrange things in Africa, and then hurried back to Rome to lend his aid to Flaccus. The elections were not too far off, and it seemed highly likely that Lucius Opimius, the suppressor of the revolt at Fregellae, who had failed to beat Fannius the previous year,

---

[3] *CG* 8–12. Cf. Appian's confusion about the trips to Junonia above, p. 132.
[4] Above, p. 42.

would be elected consul for 121. Opimius was expected to be a forceful counter to Gaius, whose popular influence was now waning. On his return, Gaius moved out of his house on the Palatine and took up residence in the poor quarter in the neighbourhood of the Forum, ostentatiously identifying himself with the commons. He formally published 'the rest of his bills', with the intention of calling for a vote on them. One of these bills seems to have been the franchise bill, now resumed; at any rate, a massive influx of support was expected from all parts of Italy, and Fannius was persuaded to issue an edict barring all non-Romans from the capital during the voting period. Gaius issued a counter-edict denouncing the consul and promising that he would extend his own tribunician *auxilium* to protect anybody prepared to defy Fannius' ban. But, when it came to the test, he did nothing. Even when he himself saw one of his own supporters and personal acquaintances—evidently a non-citizen of some social standing—being haled away by Fannius' officers, he 'passed by on the other side', either because he mistrusted his own power or because he was afraid of giving his opponents the chance to blow the incident up into the sort of bloody explosion which had been the end of his elder brother.

On top of everything else, he contrived to antagonize some of his fellow-tribunes over the arrangements for a gladiatorial show. They and several other magistrates had had temporary stands built which they planned to hire out for profit. Gaius ordered them to be taken down, so that the poor who could not affort to rent seats would have a chance to enjoy the display. When his instructions were disregarded, he collected a gang of men from among those working on some of the public projects which he was supervising and dismantled the stands the night before. The poor were pleased, but his colleagues were out of pocket and took a more jaundiced view of what they saw as a violent and high-handed action. There was a story that the incident cost Gaius himself even more. When he stood soon afterwards for a third tribunate he allegedly secured a majority of the votes cast, but his colleagues so manipulated the returns as to rob him of his election.

So much, then, for Plutarch, who now moves on to record the election of Opimius and deal with the events of 121. These will be left on one side for the time being, while we turn to examine what lay behind the movement of events in 122.

Plutarch says that by its support of Drusus' proposals the Senate 'made it plain as plain could be that they did not disapprove of the actual measures which Gaius proposed but that what they wanted was by hook or by crook to break or humble Gaius himself'.[5] It is not clear whether Plutarch means his readers to take this literally, or whether he is describing the impression which the Senate set out to create. But, whichever way we take his words, we must consider what it was in Gaius' programme that may have most run counter to the interests of that body and its leading members, or what it was in the man himself that aroused their alarm.

That Gaius was politically ambitious goes without saying. But it perhaps does need saying that political ambition is in itself no more a vice than it is a virtue. There is no need to picture him as a power-seeking politician who was cunningly exploiting other people's grievances merely to suit his own ends. Nothing in our evidence or in his actions justifies such a conclusion. He was a man of exceptional energy and talents, born like his elder brother into the heart of a ruling class to which political activity was as natural as the air it breathed, whose members regarded the pursuit of *dignitas* and *auctoritas, honores* and *gloria*, as a sort of hereditary métier; a proud class, often conscious of a high sense of noblesse oblige and of the majesty of the *res Romana*. That by the time he stood for election as tribune in 124 Gaius had come to see himself and be seen by others as the champion to whom many of the poorer citizens looked, and along with Fulvius Flaccus as the patron on whom the aspirations of the non-Romans of Italy centred; that he was in an important sense the prisoner of his own position; that he was proud and confident of his own abilities and policies; that he was infected with a restless, but not necessarily reprehensible, urge to arrange and organize and improve; that he was aware of the power of his oratory; that he felt called on to push further along the trail which his brother had blazed, and had inherited from Tiberius a whole string of obligations and enmities—none of these propositions is likely to be a matter for serious controversy. It is credible enough, too, that, while one need not and probably should not see in this his main driving force, among the motives which inspired him should be numbered a sense of compassion for the underdog and a sense of justice which combined with a remarkable political shrewdness. Such a man, with such a background, growing up in a period when so many of

---

[5] *CG* 9.1: ᾧ καὶ καταφανεστάτην ἐποίησεν ἑαυτὴν ἡ σύγκλητος οὐ δυσχεραίνουσα τοῖς τοῦ Γαίου πολιτεύμασιν, ἀλλὰ αὐτὸν ἐκεῖνον ἀνελεῖν ἢ ταπεινῶσαι παντάπασι βουλομένη.

the old political and social and economic landmarks were shifting or disappearing, when (so to say) the call for 'Overture and beginners' was going round as the curtain was about to rise on the drama of the late Republic, is not at bottom difficult to fathom. Except that it is never easy for historians to accommodate themselves to the failure of a brilliantly gifted and forward-looking politician for whom they themselves feel admiration or respect. Knowing what the end will be, we sense too little of the high hopes that went before, are deaf and blind to the thrill of the gamble, the vagaries of chance, the heady intoxication of popularity, the excitement of the clash of wills and tactics and personalities, the deep streak of stubborness which can make a man or a woman too proud to turn back, to eat words once uttered, or to desert or disappoint trusting supporters, even when the very great dangers involved in pushing on are plain for all to see.

Of Gaius' measures it can be said that they achieved three broad effects: they corrected past sins of commission and omission on the part of the Roman government; they won him powerful political support from their beneficiaries; and they threatened the control which the ruling oligarchs had long exercised over public affairs—and, to a great extent, to their own material advantage. His opponents might conceivably have overlooked the first of these, in so far as it is realistic to separate it from the other two: as we have seen, there was much that was advantageous to the whole state, including its leading members, in Gaius' programme. But the other two were bound to arouse their alarmed antagonism. The '*provocatio*' law disarmed them of one weapon of repression of opposition, the *lex de abactis* of an important means of at least obstructing and delaying unpalatable proposals, the *lex ne quis* of a potentially useful method of deterring or removing those who incurred their displeasure. The military reforms shut the door on an easy way of keeping legionary numbers up without doing anything positive to remedy the declining numbers of the free peasantry; valuable nominations to military tribunates were removed from the gift of the powerful; the use of the assignment of consular provinces by the men who controlled the Senate to reward friends and discomfort the hostile or unco-operative was to be stopped; the Senate's traditional monopoly of provincial affairs was challenged by the law on the province of Asia; the poor were to be freed by the corn law from dependence on the calculated largesse of the rich. All in all, the citizen assemblies were being encouraged to become accustomed to the dangerous

idea that they had a right to a say in the government of their country, and
to acquire a taste for securing for themselves a larger share of the material
advantages which stemmed from Rome's power and dominion, and which
had hitherto been very much confined to the ruling class. Gaius, the tem-
pestuous and fiery orator who riveted attention and swayed the multitude
as he strode restlessly up and down across the speakers platform, tearing
his toga from his shoulder in the passion of his delivery,[6] made it his
practice to face always towards the Forum, unlike those who before him
had looked towards the Senate House, to underline the fact that it was the
People and not the Senate to whom the speaker should address himself.[7]
Others disagreed. As Cicero makes Aemilianus' great friend Laelius express
it, with the way things were going it looked as if the weightiest affairs of
state were being determined by the caprice of the mob: 'multitudinis
arbitrio res maximas agi'.[8]

In this connection, it is worth asking why it was that, both now and
later, the ruling nobility persistently resisted plans for overseas colonization, as at Junonia/Carthage; resistance to such activities in Italy is more
easily understandable, given the land distribution that would be involved
there. Down to the Gracchan period, the Senate had largely been left to
run foreign affairs itself, and its leading members had done very well out
of this arrangement. Tiberius Gracchus first gave the People a taste of
provincial control in the matter of the Attalid bequest and his proposal
to introduce to the assembly a bill to regulate the affairs of Asia. Gaius
rubbed this in with his *lex de provincia Asia* and his general purpose to use
public revenues to finance social measures. Clearly, it would not suit the
'establishment' that the People should develop too sharp an appetite for
and interest in exploiting the potential profits of empire, for that would
increase the tendency for assemblies to interfere in foreign affairs and take
control through popular leaders. Of course, more respectable and less
nakedly selfish arguments both could be and were advanced in public; and
indeed many of the nobles, like Laelius, may have honestly believed them.
But, while one may grant that the nobility of the pre-Sullan period did not
ruthlessly exploit the empire for the material benefit of Rome, they clearly

---

[6] *TG* 2.2.

[7] *CG* 5.2. Plutarch says that Gaius was the first to do this, but Cicero gives the
primacy to C. Licinius Crassus who 'primus instituit in forum versus agere cum
populo' (*de amicitia* 96).

[8] Cicero, *de amicitia* 41.

did derive great personal benefit from it, as the vast fortunes and *clientelae* of the leading families testify. Their declining to let the People become too interested in it may more safely be attributed to indifference to popular needs and aspirations than to the high moral standards which were often on their lips and even frequently in the front of their conscious minds. The Roman aristocracy is by no means unique in history in equating the continuing supremacy and wellbeing of a particular class with the best interests of their country. One may usefully compare what Ensor had to say about the die-hard Conservative resistance to the Liberal programme of the late-Edwardian period:[9]

The psychology of it was that both Balfour and Lansdowne were aristocrats born in the purple. They belonged to, they led in, and they felt themselves charged with the fortunes of, a small privileged class, which for centuries had exercised a sort of collective kingship, and at the bottom of its thinking instinctively believed that it had a divine right to do so. Passionately devoted to the greatness of England, these men were convinced that she owed it to patrician rule. In their view her nineteenth-century parliamentarism had worked successfully, because the personnel of parliaments and cabinets was still (with a few much-resented exceptions like Bright) upper-class, and the function of the lower orders was limited to giving the system a popular *imprimatur* by helping to choose which of two aristocratic parties should hold office. Tory democracy, as Disraeli put it forward, and as it was exemplified in his 1867 franchise extension, did not depart from this view; its assumption being that the wider the electorate, the less chance it would have of behaving as anything but an electorate, and that the more the poor voted, the stronger would be the position of the popularly-revered old families as against middle-class upstarts run by dissenting shopkeepers. It was the personnel elected to the 1880 parliament which first seriously disturbed this assumption . . . But from their standpoint the house of commons elected in 1906 was far worse than that of 1880. Not merely were there the fifty-three Labour M.P.s—nearly all of whom had been manual workmen, and all of whom without exception had been reared in working-class homes—but a large proportion of the huge liberal contingent consisted of men with small means, and in the cabinet itself sat Lloyd George, the orphan son of an elementary school-teacher, brought up by his uncle who was a village shoemaker. To persons born like Lansdowne and Balfour (and only a little less to Rosebery) it appeared out of the question that a house of commons so composed and led should effectively rule the nation; and scarcely distinguishing in their minds between the Constitution and the dominance of their own order, they felt justified in using any resource of the former,

[9] Ensor, *The Oxford History of England, 1870–1914*, 387–8.

however unfairly one-sided it might otherwise have appeared, in order to crush the challenge to the latter.

Gaius Gracchus was not aiming to entrust the government of Rome to the ancient equivalent of dissenting shopkeepers and manual workmen. But he was scathing in his denunciation of the sins and shortcomings of the ruling class of his time. 'Too many states', he warned, 'had come to ruin through greed and shortsightedness.' He contrasted his own conduct in Sardinia with the low standard of the behaviour of other Roman officials abroad:

I so comported myself in my province as I judged to be to your advantage, and not as I thought would best suit my own interest. I kept no extravagant table, no strikingly pretty boys surrounded me, your own children conducted themselves in my company more properly than even at army headquarters;

I so conducted myself in my province that no one could truthfully say that I had accepted a penny more than was my proper due, or that anyone had been put to expense on my account. I spent two years there. If ever a prostitute crossed my threshold, or anybody's serving-boy was solicited on my behalf, then you may reckon me the most worthless man alive. When I held myself back so chastely from their servants, by that token you can reflect how you should think I behaved myself with your own children.

The money-belts which I took out with me full of silver were empty when I brought them home; others took out great jars full of wine, and brought them back home again stuffed with silver.[10]

He warned the citizens to beware of self-seekers:

If, men of Rome, you are prepared to use your intelligence and common sense, you will realize that there is not one of us politicians who comes here without having his price. All of us who address you are looking for something, no one comes before you on any matter except to take something away with him. As for myself, who advocate that you should increase your revenues in order that you may the more easily meet your own needs and those of our country, I am not here for nothing. But what I seek from you is not money but your good esteem, and honour. Those who come here to persuade you to reject this bill are not after honour from you, but money from Nicomedes. And those who seek to persuade you to accept this bill are not after your good esteem, but a rich reward

[10] The original Latin of Gaius is cited in Appendix 2 below, pp. 217 ff.

from Mithridates to put in their pockets. As for those from our same place and our same order who hold their peace, they are the most cunning of all: they take their price from everyone, and cheat everyone. You suppose that they are far above such things, you give them your confidence as being high-minded men. But the agents of King Nicomedes and King Mithridates think that it is in their rulers' interests that they maintain silence, and so they shower them with gifts and money. There is a story that once upon a time in Greece a dramatist was preening himself on being paid a whole talent for one play he had written; but Demades, the finest public speaker in the land, replied: 'So you think it wonderful that your words have earned you a talent? Let me tell you that I have been paid ten talents by a king just to keep my mouth shut.' It is just the same now: these gentlemen are being very highly paid for their silence.[11]

Probably the most serious blow which Gaius struck against the power of the Senate was his judiciary law. It is sometimes said that this bill was carried into law by only one vote, eighteen tribes having voted for it and seventeen against, so that 'though it was well calculated to gain him equestrian support, it was not widely popular'.[12] That is, however, not a certain conclusion. The excerpt in question from the full text of Diodorus neglects to specify which particular law it was that passed by only one vote. It goes on to say that Gaius was on tenterhooks as he awaited the count, and when the result was known cried out exultantly that 'the sword hangs over the heads of my enemies—for the rest I shall be content to abide by what Fortune may decree.'[13] In a later excerpt we are also told that 'when the Senate threatened to open war on Gaius because of the change in the *iudices*, he boldly answered that, even if he died, he would not loose his grip on the sword which had been plunged into the Senate's side.'[14] The two similes are close, but not so close as to compel us to the belief that the narrowly-carried unnamed law of the first excerpt is the judiciary law of the second; a sword that hangs over the head is not also plunged into the side, and the imagery of 'drawn swords' and 'daggers of contention' is too obvious and hackneyed to be tied down so tightly.[15] But the judiciary law was carried, by whatever margin, and it is undeniable that it was a very bitter blow to the Senate.

[11] Appendix 2 below, p. 221.
[12] So Brunt, *The Equites in the Late Republic*, 147.
[13] Diodorus Siculus 34/5. 27.
[14] Ibid. 37.9.
[15] See Appendix 2 below, p. 224.

The threat posed by Gaius himself is plain to see. It was one thing for constructive, albeit controversial, measures of reform to be proposed and carried, and quite another for this to be done by the outstanding genius and energies of a single young and talented member of the ruling class who seems to have had no considerable bloc of support among the leading members of the Senate itself and who made his opinion of the grave defects and failings of many members of his class eloquently clear. He was in process of building up a wide and unchallengeable power base both inside and outside Rome. He moved without serious challenge to a second consecutive tribunate (and was nearly to get a third). He held the view that the plebeian assembly, under the presidency of forward-looking tribunes, was a proper body to help shape and direct the affairs of Rome—'multitudinis arbitrio res maximas agi'. Such a point of view could never be anything but anathema to the great noble families; and, if we put to one side any distaste or reprobation which we may feel for their selfish or insensitive neglect of urgent calls for action to alter and improve much that stood in need of remedial effort, it is possible to feel some sympathy for their response. Gaius was setting a pattern of personal dominance which ran against the grain of their most treasured beliefs about government; and not all those who in the future might take a leaf from his book could be counted on to match his own character and ideals. The spectre of the demagogue was part of what was for them not ancient but recent history. As with Tiberius, so now the younger Gracchus was stretching out far beyond the limits of what the ruling nobility saw as properly constitutional behaviour; and the threat which he was posing to their own continued supremacy must be forcefully resisted.

The franchise proposal gave them an opening. It was not immediately attractive to the ordinary Roman, and it could easily be rendered positively unpopular by selectively stressing some of its alleged consequences. Fulvius Flaccus made a poor job of holding the fort while Gaius was away in Africa. Most important, Gaius' stubborn persistence in remaining actively committed to a bill whose chances of becoming law grew thinner as the weeks went by threatened to prick the bubble of his invincibility at a time when public confidence in him was being undermined by the seductive counter-proposals of Livius Drusus.

The tide of history had certainly been bringing closer the day when something would have to be done to re-order the relations between Rome   and   the   non-Roman   communities   and   peoples   of

Italy.[16] Rome had needed Italy as a base from which to conquer the Mediterranean world; and without the manpower of Italy she could not hope to maintain her far-flung influence and dominion. To try to hold down half of Italy while keeping a fast grip on her overseas territories would be an impossible task. So long as the Latins and Italians were reasonably satisfied with their condition—or not too dissatisfied—all would be well. But there were a number of causes of dissatisfaction which could lead to trouble unless they were taken note of and treated. And for that treatment there lay to hand an instrument which Gaius proposed to use: the extension of Roman citizenship itself, the incorporation of non-Roman Italy within the Roman state. Not that he proposed to effect this all at once. Only the Latin communities were to be fully incorporated; the Italian allies were to be given the status and rights and protection hitherto enjoyed by the Latins. He had chosen the right path. Rome had indeed been following it for centuries; and forty years later it was the extension of the Roman state to include all the free inhabitants of Italy south of the Po which was the only effective answer which could be found to still the grievances which had finally led so many of the Italian allies to take up arms against Rome.

Not that we should assume that all the non-Romans were eager to become Romans. But they all wanted to be treated as in some sense at least the equals of Romans, and not as subjects. Fulvius Flaccus in 125 had apparently offered the *ius provocationis* as an alternative to citizenship; so at least Valerius Maximus reports, and although Appian does not mention this alternative there is no good reason to doubt it.[17] The Tabula Bembina, which we have seen preserves the fragmentary text of the Gracchan *repetundae* law, also almost certainly provided (in lines 78–9) that successful prosecutors should have the *ius provocationis* if they preferred it to a grant of Roman citizenship. This right of appeal against the sort of cruel and arbitrary exercise of magisterial authority of which Gaius gave some vivid instances would be an attractive prospect to those who did not possess it. The chief local magistrate of the Italian town of Teanum Sidicinum was publicly scourged on the order of a Roman consul who chanced to be there because the local baths had not been cleared quickly enough for the use of his wife and even when cleared were reported to be not clean enough for her. The neighbouring Latin colony of Cales on

---

[16] Above, p. 106 ff.   [17] Above, p. 96.

hearing of what had happened at Teanum issued a by-law forbidding its citizens to use its baths if a Roman magistrate should happen to be in the town. A similar incident at Ferentinum resulted in one of its two chief magistrates hurling himself from the town wall and in the other's being seized and flogged. On yet another occasion, a young Roman staff officer had a Venusian ploughman flogged to death on the spot for making what he took to be an insolent remark: the officer was being carried along in a closed litter, and the poor rustic had jokingly asked the bearers if it was a funeral. These are invaluable glimpses of the sort of excesses in which some Roman officials were indulging at the time—Gaius says that the incident at Teanum had occurred 'not so long ago' ('nuper')—and their misconduct was surely not confined to such acts as these: the underlying attitude of mind is clear and significant.[18] But to argue that the *ius provocationis* was what the non-Romans really wanted rather than the Roman citizenship itself is to go beyond the evidence, which simply informs us that some individuals or communities were thought likely to prefer the *ius provocationis*. Although the example of a vigorous local life at towns like Arpinum—which had not withered away after becoming a *municipium civium Romanorum* in 188 and whose burgesses had since then enjoyed all the advantages and opportunities of full citizenship—might be supposed to have sufficed to overcome any reluctance to be fully absorbed into the Roman state, we know that in some places such a reluctance did persist even a generation later. We happen to learn from an aside of Cicero's that in the year 90 the strongly Greek towns of Naples and Heraclia came close to declining the offer of Roman citizenship which was made to them under the *lex Julia*, the reason being that in both places a large body of the inhabitants were afraid that the separate identity of their towns might disappear.[19] Such reservations were only to be expected in towns with their sort of background of Greek traditions, and were much more unlikely to be found in the Latin communities and in the less politically sophisticated country towns of Italy.

It is relatively easy to draw up a list of some of the grievances which the non-Romans of Italy may well have come to entertain and want to see

---

[18] For the extant fragments of the *de legibus promulgatis*, see Appendix 2 below, pp. 221–2.

[19] *pro Balbo* 21: 'magna contentio Heracliensium et Neopolitanorum fuit, cum magna pars in iis civitatibus foederis sui libertatem civitati anteferret.'

remedied. We have already noticed the tendency of Rome's own magistrates to display an arrogance and harshness in some of their dealings with
them more appropriate towards subjects than towards allies and comrades
in arms. The fact that no more Latin colonies were planted in Italy after
Aquileia in 181, but only Roman citizen colonies, may indicate an awareness on Rome's part that her position *vis-à-vis* the rest of Italy should not
be weakened, or a reluctance on the part of Roman citizens to forego a
status that seemed increasingly superior to the *ius Latii*; it certainly boded
ill for the chances of non-Romans to share in the advantages of colonization. There were the worries connected with Rome's recovery of public
land for distribution: Tiberius Gracchus may well have not meant to exclude non-Romans from any benefit, but in the event they almost certainly
got little or nothing out of his law; and the big proprietors among them
stood to lose a lot by it. The burden of conscription pressed at least as
heavily on the non-Romans, and probably more heavily; the violent protests which Roman citizens themselves could and did make against the
draft, with the assistance of their tribunes, did something to mitigate its
severity—to the cost of those who were called on to make up any defi-
ciency.[20] There were instances of mean unfairness in the distribution of
booty; and the non-Roman towns of Italy shared scarcely at all in the improvement of material amenities on which money was lavished at Rome
itself by her successful generals.[21] Allied troops were liable to be kept with
the colours for longer stretches than the Roman legions, and more exposed
to situations of danger and heavy battle losses;[22] and the field punishment
meted out to non-Romans was harsher.[23] Overall, a growing awareness of
relative prestige and standing, and an understandable desire to share more
equitably in the profits and advantages of empire by acquiring a direct
political say in the government of Rome and Italy and the empire, were
both it seems features of the Gracchan period.[24]

The different social classes among the Latins and Italians were, of

---

[20] Toynbee, *HL* i.433, 481; ii.107, 132; Brunt, *IM* Appendix 26. Polybius 2.24.
3–4, 9, 13. On Roman resistance to the draft, see above, p. 9.

[21] Not explained away by Göhler, *Rom und Italien*, 50–2. Against Göhler see
Last, *JRS* 30 (1940), 81 ff.; Badian, *FC* 150; and cf. Livy 41.13.7; 42.4.4.

[22] Toynbee, *HL* ii. 134–5.

[23] Livy, *Epitome* 57.

[24] In general, see Sherwin-White, *The Roman Citizenship*², 214–18, and the
works there cited. For a rejection of the view that there was also a strong commercial motive, see ibid. 141–4.

course, sensible of such grievances to varying degrees. In particular, the governing classes must have placed a far higher value on possession of the right to vote and to hold office at Rome. Only the well-to-do could afford the time and expense of travelling to the capital to cast their votes, and only they would be enrolled in the equestrian centuries or the first and highest census class which counted for so much in the elections of consuls and praetors and censors; only they could entertain the hope of climbing at least the lowest rungs of the senatorial ladder of office. But there were items in the list of grievances which affected all alike, at least potentially, and it cannot have been difficult for the upper classes to count on local solidarity, or at least excite it, in such matters. In any case, it was the governing classes who really counted, and on whose co-operation Rome depended. When the Social War broke out just over thirty years later, it was the *principes Italicorum populorum* who took the lead in raising Italy against Rome;[25] and there is little or no sign of internal disunity in the rebel states.

It was almost certainly during the twenties of the second century that an important new avenue of approach to the Roman citizenship was opened to the governing classes of the Latin communities. Any Latin who held one of the local magistracies in his own town became *ipso facto* a Roman citizen, and his wife and direct descendants as well. This *ius adipiscendi civitatem per magistratum* was an established feature of the *ius Latii* by the year 89.[26] Unfortunately, we are nowhere told the date and circumstances of its institution. But it probably antedates the passing of the *repetundae* law of 123: lines 78-9 of the Tabula Bembina can scarcely be restored and interpreted except as offering certain privileges associated with the Roman citizenship as an optional alternative to the citizenship itself as a reward to successful prosecutors from Latin communities who had not held a local Latin magistracy; from which it must surely follow that Latin magistrates already had the citizenship, since it is impossible to suggest why else they should have been ineligible for these rewards for which non-magistrates were eligible.[27] But the new right was probably not introduced much earlier than 123. Gaius Gracchus, telling

---

[25] Asconius 68 C.

[26] Asconius 3 C. (cited above, p. 109, n. 82)

[27] See Sherwin-White, *RC*[2] 215–16 for a refutation of attempts to date the *ius adip. civ. per mag.* much later; cf. *JRS* 62 (1972), 95–6.

the story of the savage punishment inflicted on the chief magistrate of Teanum Sidicinum, adds that, when Cales heard what had happened there, steps were promptly taken to make sure that the same thing would not happen to a magistrate of Cales; yet Cales, unlike Teanum, was a Latin town; and, if the new Latin right already existed, the magistrates of Cales should have had a defence against such mistreatment, since they would themselves possess all the rights of a Roman citizen. All this happened, so Gaius said, 'nuper'; and, though 'recently' or 'not so long ago' is a vague expression, it must surely mean not more than at most two or three years earlier. So it seems reasonable to date the new right to about the mid-'20s. Beyond that we cannot go, except to say that it is an attractive guess that its institution could have had a connection with the revolt of Latin Fregellae in 125, when Asconius notes that 'all the other' Latin communities were also ill disposed towards Rome ('ceteros quoque nominis Latini socios male animatos'[28]), and when such a concession may have been though necessary to placate them. At any rate, it is important to bear it in mind that, if this dating is roughly correct, in offering the Italian allies the *ius Latii*, Gaius was thereby offering their ruling classes a clear road to the Roman citizenship itself.

If we ask why Gaius' proposal in 122 to give Roman citizenship to the Latins and Latin status to the Italian allies ran into such heavy weather, we cannot come up with any simple answer. At one level, the Roman ruling class itself was bound to view with great disquiet the enormous political support which Gaius and Fulvius Flaccus would acquire from the grateful beneficiaries of their bill. And such a drastic change in the political and electoral map of Italy would gravely disturb the existing balances: new blocs of voters would have to be wooed and won, especially in the first class of the centuriate assembly; new interests would have to be consulted and satisfied, involving extra time and trouble and expense, and dissipation of patronage. There was pretty certainly no good reason to expect an immediate rush of rival candidates for office from among the wealthier and more energetic and ambitious of the new citizens; but in the long run considerably increased competition for public office and the fruits of office would plainly be unavoidable. The poorer Romans would scarcely lose any sleep over all that, but they could easily be persuaded that a large increase in the numbers of the citizen body must inevitably involve a

[28] Asconius 17 C. Above, p. 97.

dilution of their own existing advantages. 'Let all these Latins in', said Fannius, 'and you will find that they will crowd you out of places at games and shows.'[29] It was easy enough to add further arguments in the same vein; and there were those who later believed that many hands had contributed to the construction of Fannius' speech, for Fannius was reckoned to be only an indifferent orator and this a truly outstanding performance.[30]

Thus Gaius' persistence in the matter of his franchise proposal was bound to win him the strong hostility of the establishment and at best only lukewarm support from the popular assembly, who were at the same time being dazzled by the tempting prospects which Livius Drusus, with the open support of the Senate, was laying before them. Simultaneously, his support among the *equites* was also being eroded. So at least Sallust tells us. The nobility, he says, reeled back under the initial assault of the brothers Gracchus, but then counter-attacked, on the one occasion through the agency of the allies and the Latins, on the other through that of the Roman *equites* 'whom hope of association had split away from the commons'.[31] The first reference must be to the blocking of the activities of the agrarian commission in 129, when Scipio Aemilianus championed the cause of the non-Romans. The second must refer to 122, and indicate that in some way or other the leading senatorial opponents of Gaius had reached a *modus vivendi* or *entente* with the *equites*. Had it been clear that the collapse of Gaius would involve the loss of the advantages which he had won for them, his supporters could have been counted on to back him to the limit, even in helping him get through his franchise bill. But the fickle and short-sighted commons could be seduced by the promises of Drusus and the scare-tactics of Fannius; and the *equites* could also be won away if they received satisfactory assurances that their own gains would not be clawed back if Gaius fell. Which is what Sallust implies did happen, and is borne out in the event. After Gaius fell from power, no move was

[29] *ORF*[2] p. 144; cited below, p. 239.
[30] Cicero, *Brutus* 99–100.
[31] Sallust, *BJ* 42.1: 'Nam postquam Ti. et C. Gracchus . . . vindicare plebem in libertatem et paucorum scelera patefacere coepere, nobilitas noxia atque eo perculsa modo per socios et nomen Latinum, interdum per equites Romanos, quos spes societatis a plebe dimoverat, Gracchorum actionibus obviam ierat, et primo Tiberium, dein paucos post annos eadem ingredientem Gaium, tribunum alterum, alterum triumvirum coloniis deducendis, cum M. Fulvio Flacco ferro necaverat.'

made by his victorious opponents to repeal the judiciary or *repetundae* laws or the new arrangements for the collection of the Asian revenues, although the first of these must have been a specially hard mouthful for the Senate to swallow.

In the end, his opponents seem to have shown more flexibility and realism than Gaius had bargained for. To tackle him head on they realized was unwise, and perhaps impossible. So they settled down to sapping and mining. The consul Fannius had been won away from him to such good effect that he was actually prominent in leading the opposition to the franchise bill, for all that he surely was aware of Gaius' and Flaccus' plans to introduce such a bill at the time when he was being backed by them against Opimius for his consulship of 122. The very capable Livius Drusus set to work to win the assembly's favour with lavish promises, promises which were apparently never realized—though whether Drusus knew that they were empty is another matter: he could have been sincere enough, but have lost the Senate's backing once it was clear that Gaius' threat had been removed.[32] For the time being, at any rate, the Senate adopted a posture of seeming interest in the material well-being of the ordinary Roman, but open hostility to Gaius himself. Gaius' own absence from Rome for over two months, the brash clumsiness of Flaccus, and the unattractiveness of the franchise proposal all played into the Senate's hands. The neutralizing of the *equites* involved a heavy sacrifice, for they had to be assured that they could safely leave Gaius in the lurch without loss to themselves; but half a loaf was reckoned to be better than no bread, and the sacrifice was duly made. Gaius was thrown back onto the defensive. Whatever his reasons were, however, he refused to drop his franchise bill or set about outbidding the opposition with cheap promises. Whether he was acting out of principle, or pride, or whether and how far he still had hopes that the bill might be carried, we cannot say. But the bill was lost; and Opimius' election for 121 was the writing on the wall. Gaius tried for a third tribunate to give himself the chance to recover lost ground, and he may in fact have won enough tribes to secure election

---

[32] Cf. Last, *CAH* ix. 72. But to say of the Drusan colonies, as he does, that 'nothing is heard of them again' is perhaps to go too far. Appian (*BC* 1.35.2) reports that in the year 91 the younger Drusus, son of the tribune of 122, himself sought as tribune to win the support of the commons with 'many colonies in Italy and Sicily, long ago promised but never yet founded.' These were perhaps the colonies promised by Drusus *père* in 122.

had he not been robbed of it by a shady manoeuvre; but the suggestion that he was thus 'gerrymandered' out of a third tribunate indicates that he no longer enjoyed much better than a marginal superiority even in the plebeian assembly itself, since the sort of support which he had commanded in 124 and 123 could not have been so easily sidetracked.[33]

Although the franchise bill did not become law, there was no violent reaction from the disappointed Latins and Italians. Indeed, it was not until the mid-90s nearly thirty years later that the moves began which culminated in the rebellion of many of the allies late in 91.[34] Which naturally suggests the possibility that Gaius and Flaccus may have misjudged how far there was in their own day a really strong and articulate desire for an extension of citizen rights on the part of the non-Romans. Indeed, some have seen the agrarian legislation of the Gracchi, and the sort of complaints and disputes which it aroused and which came to a head in 129, as lying at the root of the issue in the twenties; hence, and not surprisingly, the issue faded into the background when any further danger of Rome reclaiming public land for distribution disappeared after 122.[35] But it is hard to accept the agrarian laws as the sole or principal factor rather than as the one element in a complex of elements which served to focus the rest, a proximate cause rather than an underlying explanation; the other deep causes of discontent which have been reviewed existed independently of the agrarian issue.[36] The decision to offer full Roman citizenship to Latin magistrates must reflect an awareness on the part of the Roman government that some action was called for in this area; and the offer must itself have gone quite some way to take the steam out of the franchise issue so far as the Latin upper classes were concerned, since it would not take many years before the enfranchisement of local Latin magistrates every year together with their children would effectively mean that the whole local governing class was of Roman citizen status.[37] In this

[33] Plutarch, *CG* 12.3; above, p. 160.

[34] For recent discussions of the background to the Social War, see: Gabba, *Le origini della guerra sociale*; Badian, *Foreign Clientelae*, chs. 8–9; Brunt, *JRS* 55 (1965), 90–109; Salmon, *Samnium and the Samnites*, chs. 9–10; Sherwin-White, *The Roman Citizenship*[2], 139–49.

[35] This is broadly Badian's position (see previous note).

[36] So Last, *CAH* ix.45: 'The activities of the land commission were not the only grievance of the allies. They were merely the occasion on which the long-standing discontent found expression.' So too Sherwin-White, *RC*[2] 139 n. 1.

[37] In fact it is almost certain that the new *ius* will have been extended to all those who had already held such magistracies as well as to all future magistrates.

connection, it is to be remarked that the loyalty to Rome of the Latins was never in serious doubt during the Social War, and often outstanding. The disappearance of the agrarian issue will certainly have helped to quieten things down. But we should also take it into account that Rome was now entering on a period during which no really big wars were to be fought, which meant an abatement of calls on allied troops and of heavy losses or resentment about unequal treatment; and, when in the last decade of the century the dreadful threat of the German invaders loomed over Italy, non-Romans as well as Romans were equally in danger and equally concerned to make every effort to win victory. And we should not neglect the probability that the Roman ruling class, which had proved adaptable enough against Gaius, may well have learned a lesson from experience; aware of how close they had come to defeat, it is reasonable to guess that they resolved to be more circumspect in future and much less arrogant in their dealings with the Latins and Italians than they had been hitherto.

Nevertheless, the time factor is of great importance. 'A new constitution,' wrote Walter Bagehot, 'does not produce its full effects as long as all its subjects were reared under an old constitution, as long as its statesmen were trained by that old constitution. It is not really tested till it comes to be worked by statesmen and among a people neither of whom are guided by a different experience.'[38] So Bagehot explained why it was that the Reform Act of 1832 did not at once transform the English political scene, and why its consequences can only begin to be clearly discerned a generation or so after its passage. What we may loosely term 'the Bagehot law of delayed reaction' is very important, and by no means confined to formal or constitutional changes. It reflects a central truth of human nature of which we become more conscious as we grow older and more set in our ways and assumptions; it is not just that 'one cannot teach an old dog new tricks' (though that is a considerable part of it), but that we become impatient of change and nurture a vested interest in the continuance of a state of affairs with which we have learned to live and which we may even have learned to manage to our own advantage, 'old fogies' rather than the 'young Turks' we may once have been. The franchise issue first comes to the fore in the Gracchan period; and, true to the prediction of

[38] *The English Constitution,* p. ix, very aptly cited and exploited by Hignett, *The Athenian Constitution,* 252.

our 'Bagehot's Law', it matures almost exactly a generation later when those who were mere boys or young men in the 120s have grown up to become the mature leaders of their communities, the *principes Italicorum populorum* of the 90s. Gaius Gracchus was only about thirty years old, and for all his brilliance perhaps too young and too impatient to appreciate how long it may take to effect any far-reaching changes in society. Octavian, it is true, came to great power even younger; but that was in a period of active revolution, and in many ways he was set on bringing to fruition seeds which had been planted many years earlier.[39] Octavian, it sometimes seems, was born middle-aged; and his favourite motto was 'Make haste slowly'. He became Augustus Caesar at much the age Gaius Gracchus was when he died; but by 'making haste slowly' Augustus emulated Mithridates, and died old.

After the tribunician election of 122, we know nothing of what was happening until we come to the final bloody issue. Gaius may have tried to keep the franchise proposal alive in the last few months of his second tribunate, but it seems likeliest that he accepted defeat and immersed himself in the executive direction of the various projects which he had fathered in 123. However that may be, the scene rapidly shifts to 121 and to the incidents which led up to his death.

Once again, as with the brawl which led to Tiberius' death in 133, we are faced with the sort of partial and divergent evidence only to be expected of such tumultuous events.[40] The consul Opimius and some of the tribunes set about undoing Gaius' work; according to Plutarch, there was a deliberate plan to provoke Gaius to the violent reaction which the unstable Fulvius Flaccus was already urging on him.[41] In particular, the tribune Minucius Rufus was advocating the repeal of the Junonia law, and it was this which triggered off the final explosion. While Rufus was holding a public meeting to urge the merits of his proposal, Gaius and Flaccus

[39] It was well said by Momigliano that 'the triumph of Augustus was the triumph of Italy'. In that respect, Augustus reaped where Gaius Gracchus and others had sown.

[40] The evidence is set out in Greenidge and Clay, *Sources*[2], pp. 44–7. The account which follows is avowedly eclectic, and I have not sought to accommodate or reconcile all the minor and essentially peripheral details.

[41] *CG* 13.1. (For Gaius' speech against Minucius, see Appendix 2 below, p. 222.) The opportune presence of a force of Cretan archers supports the view that Opimius was 'spoiling for a fight'.

arrived at the head of a very large following, and a fracas developed during which a certain Quintus Antullius, who was employed as a crier in the service of the Consul Opimius, fell dead, perhaps thereby paying the price of his calculatedly provocative behaviour. That was what Gaius' enemies had been waiting for, and they moved in for the kill. A meeting of the Senate was called, while every effort was made to excite emotion by a sanctimonious and carefully staged display of Antullius' corpse, which was paraded on its bier through the Forum and into the Senate House past loudly grieving and indignant spectators—though not all were so moved, for there were those in the crowds who did not fail to contrast this hypocritical charade of public grief for a mere attendant of the consul who had got no more than he deserved with the callousness of the nobles who had murdered the tribune Tiberius and thrown his dead body into the Tiber. Gaius and Flaccus were summoned to appear before the Senate, but were too wary to answer the call; instead Flaccus' young son was sent as an intermediary. Opimius thereupon took decisive action: Rome had no police force or home military garrison, so the wealthy citizens, senators and *equites*, were called on to present themselves with their servants to take up the defence of the state—the importance of winning the *equites* away from Gaius could hardly be more obvious.[42]

Flaccus, who is said by Plutarch to have 'taken to the bottle', together with a composed but reluctant and despondent Gaius, proceeded to occupy the Aventine Hill with a large body of supporters; they hoped, said Appian, to influence the Senate to some sort of compromise.[43] The Aventine lay just outside the city boundary, the *pomerium*, and had originally been *ager publicus* which was given over to the *plebs Romana* for settlement in 456; thither the plebeians had regularly withdrawn in a body in the course of the formal seccesions which had occasionally punctuated their struggles with the patricians in the very early Republic; there was on the hill a pre-Republican Temple of Diana as the patron goddess of the old Latin League, and it had other strong Latin connections.[44] How far such historical associations influenced or dictated its choice now by the Gracchans as the place to make their stand, we can only surmise. Plutarch

[42] *CG* 14.4. Cf. events in 100 and in 63.
[43] Plutarch, *CG* 14.3; Appian, *BC* 1.26.1.
[44] See *The Oxford Classical Dictionary*[2] s.vv. 'Aventine' and 'secessio'.

says that a number of senators were not disinclined to a non-violent solution but Opimius would have none of it: there must be no treating with insurgents through intermediaries, they must come down off the hill and surrender and submit themselves to justice if they wanted to find mercy; he had Flaccus' son placed under arrest; and, though Gaius may have been in favour of going to speak to the Senate, none of his companions would agree.[45] No concessions were offered by Opimius, and the attack went in; after a stiff initial struggle the defenders were overwhelmed, thanks largely to Opimius' employment of a body of Cretan archers whose volleys threw the close-packed Gracchans into disorder.[46] It is hard to believe, incidentally, that these specialized troops just 'happened' to be on the spot; it seems likely that Opimius had had them brought to Rome specially. Flaccus and his elder son were killed while hiding in a vain attempt to escape (his younger son, the intermediary, was later allowed the concession of taking his own life). Gaius himself got away as far as the Sublician bridge; deserted by all, he ordered his personal slave to kill him so as to avoid being taken alive. The savagery of Opimius was manifested in his public promise to reward with its weight in gold anyone who brought him the head of Gaius; the man who came to claim the reward is said to have first removed the brains and filled the cavity with lead to make it weigh the heavier.

It is in 121 that the *senatus consultum ultimum*, the 'ultimate decree' so well known to all students of the political history of the late Republic, first makes its appearance.[47] The Epitomator of Livy says that 'Opimius called the people to arms on the authority of a decree of the Senate', and Plutarch that 'the Senate passed a decree charging the consul Opimius to save the state'.[48] The definitive evidence comes from Cicero. In his *First Catilinarian* he told how 'the Senate had once decreed that L. Opimius the consul was to see to it that the state took no harm'; and in his *Eighth Philippic* how 'L. Opimius the consul having introduced the question of

---

[45] Plutarch, *CG* 16. 1-2; Appian, *BC* 1.26. In general Flaccus tends to be cast in the role of the active precipitator of the final dénouement. Orosius (5.12) even credits him with a desperate attempt at the last minute to win the support of the slaves with a promise of freedom.

[46] Plutarch, *CG* 16.3; Orosius 5.12.

[47] The actual words 'senatus consultum ultimum' are first found in Caesar, *BC* 1.5.3.

[48] *Epitome* 59; Plutarch, *CG* 14.3.

national security, the Senate in this matter decreed that L. Opimius the consul was to defend the state'.[49] He went on to add: 'Senatus haec verbis, Opimius armis': apart from the actual armed suppression of the Gracchans on the Aventine, Opimius' savagery after the victory was terrible. In all, 3,000 or more are said to have perished, many not in the fighting itself, but subsequently put to death, often without having been given the chance to make a case in their defence. The bodies of Gaius and Flaccus followed that of Tiberius Gracchus into the Tiber, and their property was declared confiscate to the state; their widows were forbidden to go into formal mourning, and Gaius' wife Licinia was even deprived of her dowry.[50] It thus seemed to some a cruel mockery when the butcher Opimius later dedicated a temple to Concordia; one dark night, an unknown hand scrawled alongside its superscription the words

Concordia's temple by mad Discord built.[51]

Had the consul Scaevola in 133 been prepared to listen to Nasica's appeal and act on it, the 'ultimate decree' might have been devised twelve years earlier. He had turned a deaf ear, preferring to wait on events, and the attack on Tiberius had been an irregular affair, best not looked into too closely. But in 120 Opimius, out of office and no longer protected by his *imperium*, was brought to trial before the People by the tribune Publius Decius.[52] The choice of the People to hear the charge, rather than a prosecution before a *quaestio*, may indicate that Decius had little hope of securing a conviction from equestrian *iudices*.

Senatorial decrees could not alter or set aside laws. Even the 'ultimate decree' could add nothing to the powers which Opimius already enjoyed as consul.[53] Should a civil emergency be judged to have passed—or to be about to pass—the point at which it could be contained by normal legal powers and procedures, there was nothing for it but for the magistrates, and above all the consuls as the chief magistrates, to assume powers to

---

[49] *Cat.* 1.4: 'Decrevit quondam senatus ut L. Opimius consul videret ne quid res publica detrimenti caperet.' *Phil.* 8.14: 'Quod L. Opimius consul verba fecit de re publica, de ea re ita censuerunt, uti L. Opimius consul rem publicam defenderet.'

[50] Sallust, *BJ* 16.2; Vell. Pat. 2.7; Orosius 5.12; Plutarch, *CG* 17.4.

[51] Plutarch, *CG* 17.5: ἔργον ἀπονοίας ναὸν 'Ομονοίας ποιεῖ.

[52] On Decius, see Badian, *JRS* 46 (1956), 91–6.

[53] On the 'ultimate decree' see Last, *JRS* 33 (1943), 93–7; Stockton, *Cicero: A Political Biography*, 92-6, 133–40; Ungern-Sternberg von Pürkel, *Unters. zum spätrep. Notstandsrecht*, 55 ff.

take whatever steps they thought necessary to cope with it.[54] And, as Last observed, 'about the action taken by the agents of society during such an interruption it is futile to ask whether it was legal; for legality means conformity to law, and when law has ceased to run there is no law to which to conform.'[55] The resources of the consular *imperium* were vast, indeed in origin monarchic: a tough and resolute consul like Opimius could deploy them with decisive effect (it was apparently in the expectation that he would be ready to do so that he had been elected), trusting that once the dust had settled he could justify his conduct as having been unavoidable if the security of the state and the well-being of society were to be safeguarded against attack by those who drew their strength from illegality, violence, and terrorism: 'The safety of the nation must be the highest of all the laws.'[56] What the 'ultimate decree' therefore really amounted to was that by passing it the Senate—which was powerless to act by itself—put on formal public record its conviction that there had arisen, or was imminent, a threat to society of such magnitude that it required Rome's magistrates to take whatever steps might be needed 'to see to it that the state took no harm'. In consequence, if the legality or propriety or wisdom of his action were subsequently to be challenged, a man in Opimius' position could urge in his defence that his judgement that extraordinary measures had had to be taken had been neither personal nor partial nor arbitrary, but on the contrary had been shared by the Senate itself, the *summum consilium rei publicae*. Thus, while the 'ultimate decree' could not authorize a consul to do anything that was illegal, it served to reinforce his authority, strengthen his resolve, and arm him with a respectable and powerful defence against the day when he might be called to account for his conduct. It could even be argued that any citizen who had resisted a consul while he was carrying out his duty of keeping the state from harm had thereby abjured his citizenship and placed himself in the position of being an enemy of Rome, *hostis rei publicae*, and hence no longer entitled to the protection of the law. It was, of course, one thing to cut down men who were engaged in armed insurrection, and quite another to execute citizens who had surrendered or been taken into

[54] The other consul of 121, Q. Fabius Maximus, was away north of the Alps fighting the Allobroges in Provence.
[55] Last, art. cit. 94.
[56] 'Salus populi suprema lex esto': Cicero, *de legg.* 3.8.

custody. So Cicero was to discover to his cost some sixty years later. But Opimius was luckier. C. Papirius Carbo, now one of the two consuls of 120, and ironically enough the man who ten years before had been so loud in his laments over the killing of Tiberius Gracchus, spoke out vigorously in Opimius' defence: the killing of Gaius had been 'a just act'; and playing on the word 'consul' itself he asked, 'If a consul is someone who takes counsel for his country, was that not precisely what Opimius had done?'[57] The centuries acquitted Opimius. It was only in the year 110, and on a totally unconnected charge of corruption concerning Rome's dealings with Jurgurtha of Numidia, that Opimius was condemned by a Roman court. That court was manned by men whom Cicero designated 'Gracchani iudices'; and he also characterizes the condemned man as 'Gracchi interfectorem', 'the man who killed Gracchus'.[58] But by 110 *equites* and Senate were once again drifting into hostility.[59]

It is generally easier to baulk or delay reform than it is to reverse it. Some of Gaius' measures survived intact. In particular, the *equites* had to be allowed to hold on to what they had gained by his judiciary and financial legislation. It was not until 106 that their hold on the courts was prised loose by the *lex Servilia Caepionis*; and for five or six years before that their relations with the Senate had been becoming increasingly sour, culminating in 108/107 with Marius' election to a consulship and his appointment by plebiscite to the command against Jugurtha. Caepio's own rapid subsequent disgrace after the terrible defeat at Arausio, the recall of Marius to take command against the Germans, and the recreation by Saturninus and Glaucia of a 'plebeio-equestrian axis' quickly saw Caepio's law reversed. To follow the course of the political fighting over the courts any further would be out of place here. But it cannot be denied that the

---

[57] 'iure factum' (Cicero *de oratore* 2.106); 'si consul est qui consulit patriae, quid aliud fecit Opimius?' (ibid. 2.165). (Cf. ibid. 2.170.)

[58] Cicero, *Brutus* 128; cf. Sallust, *BJ* 40.

[59] In 119 Papirius Carbo was himself prosecuted on some charge or other by the brilliant young Lucius Crassus, who later became Cicero's mentor; Carbo took his own life by poison. Livius Drusus, tribune in 122, went on to be consul in 112, celebrate a triumph for his successes in Macedonia, and become censor in 109 (he died while holding the latter office). The activities of his famous son who was tribune in 91 perhaps suggest that there was a genuine liberal and reforming tradition in the family, and that the father may not have been a mere unscrupulous tool of Gaius' opponents in 122.

equestrian *iudices* of the late Republic often had a bad reputation for corruptibility and unfairness (though senatorial *iudices* were no better), or that the Roman *publicani* were noted for their avarice and disruptive influence. Only too often their wealth seems to have been used to support magistrates who favoured their interests, and to oppose those who threatened them or showed indifference to them, at the expense of justice and sound finance and the wellbeing and loyalty of the provinces. Their votes in the courts, or their money to buy votes, could be employed to serve the selfsame ends. Even Cicero, in his public and published utterances the champion and apologist for the *publicani* and *equites*, can be highly disparaging of their standards and their behaviour in the privacy of his personal correspondence. Usually—a man like Sulla is largely an exception—the nice balance of political strengths and the weakness of the 'central government' were such that politicians had little option but to go a considerable way in placating a class whose aspirations and self-consciousness and awareness of its own identity and potential influence Gaius had done so much to shape and direct. How much blame Gaius deserves for all this is debatable. At worst, he could be seen as a practical and realistic politician who appreciated that the end may sometimes justify the means, that in public life it is almost impossible to keep one's own hands clean. If he saw that he needed a broad base of support if he was to get his measures through and safeguard them against repeal, then if the support of the *equites* was vital to his chance of success he would have to pay the price to buy it. Politics, it has been said, is the language of priorities;[60] something which Gaius surely understood well enough. So he may have been aware of the sort of evils that these measures might lead to, and yet have thought them essential if his other objects were to be achieved.

But there is another approach. There is no good reason to believe that non-equestrian courts would have been any better: the record of the senatorial *iudices* of the pre-Gracchan *quaestio repetundarum* was tarnished by corruption and favouritism; and the senatorial courts of the post-Sullan decade were riddled with sin, as even Quintus Catulus was driven to concede.[61] And, so long as Rome had to manage without a large

---

[60] I believe that this was said by Clement Attlee. However that may be, the apophthegm is an excellent one.

[61] Cicero, *Verr.* I.44: 'patres conscriptos iudicia male et flagitiose tueri'.

and competent body of permanent and salaried public servants, the *publicani* were essential to the state, and could be relied on to use their wealth and influence to best serve their own interests, whatever Gaius did or did not do about the revenues of Asia. The only hope of remedy in either area lay in strong government and enlightened self-interest on the part of that government. In the end, Rome had to wait for Augustus to provide such a government. But Gaius is likely to have hoped that he would succeed in remaining a power in Roman politics for many years to come; and, had that happened, and had Rome's government been given a new spirit and direction by him, the worst of the later faults might either never have arisen, or have been sternly corrected if they showed signs of arising. In this, as in so much else, we must judge Gaius' actions not in the light of hindsight after his failure, but in the light of the circumstances likely to have obtained had his expectations of lasting success been realized.

The *lex de provinciis consularibus* remained on the statute book till the year 52. No doubt many of the junior members of the Senate itself may not have been averse to a law which promised them some greater freedom from interference from the established *consulares* if and when they should themselves reach the consulship. We know of no move to repeal the *lex militaris* (not that the *argumentum ex silentio* is worth all that much when our evidence is as thin as it is); and the fate of the *lex frumentaria* is uncertain. It may be that there was some limitation of it before 119, in which year Marius is reported to have opposed a corn law too.[62] But it is easy to see how the Senate may have accepted that to try to get rid of this law altogether would give rise to far more trouble than it was worth; probably the traditional weapons of inefficiency and a lack of wholeheartedness in administering measures which they did not much care for were fallen back on instead.

Where the commons did suffer was in respect of colonies and land. Junonia was killed off, although the actual settlers were not dispossessed; and it is pretty certain that a number of other colonies projected by Gaius came to nothing. As for the *lex agraria* itself, where the whole story began back in 133 to be continued by Gaius in 123, little time was lost in undoing it. Soon after Gaius' death, the land grants were made alienable, and the result was that the rich 'straightaway began to buy their allotments

---

[62] On the corn laws, see Brunt, *IM* 377, and his index s.v. 'grain'; Schneider, *Wirtschaft u. Politik*, 361–91. On Marius in 119, see further below. On possible repeal or variation of the *lex militaris*, see Brunt *IM* 401, n. 4.

from the Gracchan smallholders or bring pressure to bear on them to make them sell'.[63] Next came a law which ended any further distribution of public land, and confirmed security of tenure for existing *possessores* on payment of a rent to the state; this revenue was to be used to pay for corn-distributions, Appian tells us, 'which was some solace to the poor, but did nothing to help increase the population.'[64] Appian is somewhat obscure here; for it is not clear from his text whether these were to be additional or cheaper distributions of corn, or whether the new income was represented as essential if the existing distributions were to be maintained on their present scale and at their present price, in the hope that this argument would make the assembly more receptive to the ending of land grants. The latter alternative, or something like it, is *a priori* much more attractive, and may receive some support from a passage in Plutarch's *Life of Marius*. As tribune in 119 Marius begins by championing a new law designed to make the ballot more genuinely secret and thereby diminish the influence of the rich and powerful; despite the opposition of the Senate and the consul Cotta and his own patron Quintus Metellus (the young brother of the other and absent consul) he pushes his bill into law, not hesitating at one point to throw Quintus into gaol. Later, however, he does a right-about-turn and successfully blocks a bill for corn distributions.[65] I suspect that Plutarch is wrong about this alleged volte-face (his account of Marius is extremely jejune hereabouts), having been taken in by a misunderstanding, and hence misinterpreting his evidence. The bill in question may well have been the proposal to link the cessation of land distributions with the corn-dole, in which case there is no obvious inconsistency in Marius' behaviour. Blocked by Marius, the bill could have been resumed and carried in 118, when he had left office.

However that may be, the third and final stage was reached when not long afterwards yet another tribune abolished these rents (and, for all we

---

[63] Appian, *BC* 1.27.1: νόμος τε οὐ πολὺ ὕστερον ἐκυρώθη, τὴν γῆν, ὑπὲρ ἧς διεφέροντο, ἐξεῖναι πιπράσκειν τοῖς ἔχουσιν. . . καὶ εὐθὺς οἱ πλούσιοι παρὰ τῶν πενήτων ἐωνοῦντο, ἢ ταῖσδε ταῖς προφάσεσιν ἐβιάζοντο.

[64] Appian *BC* 1.27.2: τὴν μὲν γῆν μηκέτι διανέμειν, ἀλλ' εἶναι τῶν ἐχόντων, καὶ φόρους ὑπὲρ αὐτῆς τῷ δήμῳ κατατίθεσθαι, καὶ τάδε τὰ χρήματα χωρεῖν ἐς διανομάς. ὅπερ ἦν μέν τις τοῖς πένησι παρηγορία, διὰ τὰς διανομάς, ὄφελος δ᾽ οὐδὲν ἐς πολυπληθίαν.

[65] Plutarch, *Marius* 4: νόμου γὰρ εἰσφερομένου περὶ σίτου διανομῆς τοῖς πολίταις ἐναντιωθεὶς ἐρρωμενέστατα καὶ κρατήσας. (On the ballot law, see also Cicero *de legg.* 3.38: 'pontes etiam lex Maria fecit angustos.')

know, the corn distributions that they financed) and left the commons with nothing.[66] That happened in 111, and we have substantial fragments of this final 'agrarian law of 111' inscribed on the reverse side of the Tabula Bembina which preserves on its obverse the Gracchan *repetundae* law.[67] Some have argued that this is in fact the second and not the third of the measures listed by Appian, but I cannot believe that they are right.[68] Not that it matters either way for our purposes; for even if it is the second, that second measure marked the end of the activities of the agrarian commissioners. The last we know of their activities is a fragment of white marble from the territory of Carthage bearing the names of C. Sulpicius Galba, C. Papirius Carbo, and L. Calpurnius Bestia, apparently in their capacity as *IIIviri a.i.a.*[69] It must be earlier than 118, for Carbo had committed suicide in 119.

[66] Appian, *BC* 1.27.3: καὶ ὁ δῆμος ἀθρόως ἁπάντων ἐξεπεπτώκει.

[67] Bruns, *FIR* no. 11.

[68] For recent discussions, see Badian's article in *Historia* 11 (1962), 211–14. Nothing of any moment has been added since then. For what it is worth, my own view is that the 'fifteen years' of Appian, *BC* 1.27.4, can perfectly well be taken to refer to the period between the agrarian law of Tiberius Gracchus in 133 and the second of the reactionary measures listed by Appian, which could well belong to 118. But Appian's text at this point is very shaky, and the concluding words 'seem peculiarly hopeless' (so Strachan-Davidson wrote in his note ad loc.). It is wasted effort to spend much time on worrying out the significance of a text so corrupt that Schweighäuser prudently stopped short of it rather than attempt a translation.

Much the same is true of the puzzle about Spurius Thorius. Cicero (*Brutus* 136) wrote: 'Spurius Thorius satis valuit in populari genere dicendi, is qui agrum publicum vitiosa et inutili lege vectigali [there is a variant MS. reading 'vectigale'] levavit.' Controversy over the meaning of Cicero's Latin here—or even the correct reading of the text of the *Brutus* here, where Douglas has suggested 'vectigalem' as a possibility —has raged endlessly and inconclusively around whether Cicero's *lex Thoria* (we know nothing of it or of its author beyond what he tells us here) is the second of Appian's laws (which stopped further distribution and imposed a rent), or the third (which abolished the rent). The second of Appian's laws he attributed to a man whose name is given in all Appian's manuscripts as Σπόριος Βόριος; and it is virtually impossible to deny that this must conceal a true reading = Σπόριος Θόριος. If Cicero was attributing the third law to Thorius, then Appian made a mistake in giving him authorship of the second; but Cicero may have meant to indicate the second as being the *lex Thoria*. Last (*CAH* ix. 100) sensibly dismissed the whole business in a footnote far shorter than this one. For a full recent treatment, see Douglas' edition of the *Brutus*, Appendix C.

[69] Degrassi, *ILLRP* no. 475. Cf. Cichorius, *Roem. Studien* (1922), 113 ff.; Carcopino, *Gracques,* 181–4. The text runs as follows:

[Ex auctoritate]
[C. Sulpici] GALBAE
[C. Pa]PIRI CARBONIS

Of the fate of the *lex de abactis* we know nothing. All we can say is that the principle that the People could vote their officers out of office does not seem to have been challenged subsequently; but such instances were very rare, and there seems to have been no later case such that we could judge whether or not Gaius' law was still on the statute book. The *lex ne quis iudicio circumveniatur* (whether or not it was separate from the *'lex de provocatione'*) certainly survived, to be taken over by Sulla and incorporated in his own legislation.[70] Not that it did any good in saving Gaius Gracchus and Fulvius Flaccus, or later men like Saturninus and Glaucia, from a violent and bloody death. The 'ultimate decree' was devised to deal with the likes of them. The Roman constitution was very flexible and adaptable; and, like Balfour and Lansdowne and Rosebery, the ruling nobility of late Republican Rome, 'scarcely distinguishing in their minds between the Constitution and the dominance of their own order, felt justified in using any resource of the former in order to crush the challenge to the latter.'[71]

[L. Calpur]NI BESTIA[e]

[III vir (orum) a.i.a.]

Thus enough of the three names survives to make identification secure, but the designation of the three men is wholly a supplement. Yet it is hard to see what alternative exists. Minucius' bill to repeal the Junonia/Carthage law must surely be assumed to have gone through very soon after the deaths of Gaius and Fulvius Flaccus; thus Galba and Bestia are scarcely likely to have been appointed to replace them in their supposed capacity as colonial commissioners for a now defunct colony (though it is not impossible). It seems, however, best to assume that Galba and Bestia were elected to fill the two vacant agrarian commissionerships alongside Carbo (who had been *IIIvir a.i.a.* with Gaius and Flaccus since 129). Since the agrarian commission certainly survived for a few years after 121, new elections must have been held to replace the two dead commissioners. If the above argument is accepted, it affords strong support to the view that Gaius Gracchus' agrarian law did bring public land outside Italy within the scope of the agrarian commissioners.

[70] The sentence of outlawry which Gaius had caused to be passed against Popillius Laenas after Laenas had left Rome rather than face trial for his actions as consul was quickly repealed, and Laenas was back in Rome in the course of the year 120. But that does not in any way involve the conclusion that the 'lex de provocatione' had itself been repealed. (On Laenas' recall, see Cicero, *Brutus* 128.)

[71] We may here recall Mommsen's judgement that 'what Gaius introduced was nothing else than an entirely new constitution.'

APPENDIX 1

AGER PUBLICUS POPULI ROMANI[1]

We are not here concerned with the earliest history of Rome. No doubt the Roman state disposed of some public land from its beginnings; but the overwhelming bulk of the public land which Rome had acquired by the early years of the second century, when the acquisition of public land in Italy itself ceased, was the product of confiscation either from defeated enemies or from rebellious allies who had been brought to heel. Over the years much of this land was distributed, either in connection with colonial foundations or in individual (viritane) allotments; and land thus distributed passes out of our reckoning, for it ceased to be public land and became the private property of the assignees. Occasionally also—the best-known example is the *ager Campanus*—some public land was regularly let out on formal lease by the censors.

We are here concerned only with the public land which had not been thus assigned or formally leased, and which was still the property of the state in the Gracchan period. As we shall see, we shall also have to take account of tracts of land which constituted part of the total *territorium* of particular colonies and municipalities in Italy without such land having been assigned to specific individuals to hold as their private property.

It is best to begin by clearing up any possible misunderstandings about the technical terms *possidere / possessio / possessor*, which occur in this context.

Possessio did not mean what we mean by 'ownership'; for '*possessio* meant physical control of a corporeal thing . . . in contrast to ownership and other kinds of rights. *Possessor* was a person who had physical control of a corporeal thing, whether or not he had any right to have the thing under his control' (Schultz, *Class. Rom. Law,* 428). 'The Roman probably understood by "possession" not simply the holding of a thing but rather the holding of a thing in the manner of an owner, the exclusive holding of a thing. It was therefore not a matter needing explanation, as it would be for us, that the borrower or lessee had no possession . . . The borrower does not hold in the manner of an owner' (Nicholas, *Intro. to Rom. Law*, 111). *Possessio* of public land is thus a paradigm case: given that the occupier and user of public land exercised *de facto* control of that land *in the manner of an owner*, he was the *possessor* of that land and could pass it on to his sons—but he did not 'own' it.

---

[1] The three lengthy articles by Tibiletti in *Athenaeum* 26–8 (1948–50) are fundamental. They are cited here as T.26, T.27, and T.28. I am indebted to Professor P.A. Brunt for many helpful suggestions.

It is during the middle and late Republican period that

> there emerges the clear distinction between ownership and possession
> which is one of the characteristic features of classical Roman law.
> And to understand the Roman idea of possession it is necessary to
> understand the interdicts by which it was protected. The character-
> istic of these interdicts is that they protected possession as an existing
> state of fact without reference to its rightfulness or wrongfulness
> (except that it must not have been obtained *vi, clam,* or *precario*
> from the other party). (Jolowicz, *Historical Introduction to the
> Study of Roman Law*[3], 259).

The theory of Niebuhr, which is still widely held, was that the possessory
edicts 'were originally developed for the protection of the interest in
public land which settlers had acquired by occupation; such interest was,
of course, not ownership, and consequently an occupier deprived of his
enjoyment could not avail himself of the *vindicatio*' [a process open only
to an owner *sensu stricto*]; 'the praetor therefore, according to this view,
provided protection by interdict' (ibid. 261). Although Niebuhr's view has
been challenged, it still remains an attractive one. So far as interdicts—or
at any rate the specific interdict *unde vi*—are concerned, 'the obvious
suggestion is that it began as a police measure, and, as such, it might even
when first introduced have been available against persons who disturbed
existing enjoyment of land without regard to the question whether such
land was or was not capable of ownership *ex iure Quiritium*' [viz. on a
clear freehold title]. 'The *de facto* nature of possession is often stressed
by the jurists, and legal niceties would have no place in what was originally a matter of public order.' Three of the possessory edicts are plainly
attested as in existence before 161 B.C. at latest, and the edict *unde vi* is
mentioned in the *lex agraria* of 111 B.C. (ibid. 262-3).

Possessio was, then, not at all the same as *ownership*. And a secure title
to public land could not be acquired by a *possessor* by *usucapio*, that is
by usage and enjoyment of such land, of however long duration. That
negative fact is sufficiently attested by Cicero (*pro Sestio* 103):

> Agrariam Ti. Gracchus legem ferebat. Grata erat populo: fortunae
> constitui tenuiorum videbantur. Nitebantur contra optimates, quod
> et discordiam excitari videbant et, cum locupletes possessionibus
> diuturnis moverentur [cf. Appian, *BC* 1.8: ἐκ τοσοῦδε χρόνου
> κτῆσιν τοσήνδε ἀφελέσθαι], spoliari rem publicam propugnatoribus
> arbitrabantur.

Cicero would assuredly have spoken far more strongly had *usucapio* given
these *possessores* a secure title to the land they were having to surrender.
Tibiletti noted too the foundation of the citizen colony of Saturnia in
183: the land was of reasonable quality and must have been in the hands
of *possessores*; given that it was only 70-80 miles from the capital, there

must have been some exploitation of it by wealthy Romans for a considerable period. Yet the government resumed the land to found a colony apparently without any fuss or difficulty (Livy 39.55.9), which indicates that the essentially precarious nature of the possession of public land was clearly recognized and accepted at the time (T. 26, 176-8).

As Tibiletti argued (T. 26, 173 ff.), the regulations which in the Gracchan period laid down the conditions governing the occupation and use of the public land pretty certainly represented only the final stage in a long historic process. In the earliest days of Rome there probably was no law on the subject, but only customary practice, designed to obviate or diminish any chances of collision or conflict between different occupiers and users, and to secure some agreed measure of fairness. It could well be that by custom individual citizens could occupy only so much of this land as they could cultivate with their own family resources. Such a custom may perhaps be discerned being alluded to by later writers on agrarian matters. Thus Columella (*RR* 1.3.11): 'agros novo more civem Romanum supra vires patrimonii possidendo deserere'; Siculus Flaccus (136. 10-13 Lachm.): 'intellegebat enim [Ti. Gracchus] contrarium esse morem, maiorem modum possidere quam qui ab ipso possidente coli possit.' And Professor Brunt has drawn my attention to a passage in Aulus Gellius (*NA* 4.12) where Gellius lists some remarkable instances of disgrace or punishment inflicted by censors 'si quis agrum suum passus fuerat sordescere eumque indiligenter curabat neque araverat neque purgaverat' etc.: the explanation of this is surely to be traced back to the community's need to make the best use of its land even when it was in private freehold ownership, let alone its public land, to secure its food supply in times when it could not depend on imports. Ancient writers on the early history of the land tend to be confused and unsystematic; but the primitive practice here attested is probable enough in itself. There may also be allusions to a subsequent development whereby possessors or occupiers were allowed a claim to land which they did not actually cultivate, but which they planned to bring under cultivation in the near future. Thus Siculus Flaccus (137. 19-20 Lachm.): 'singuli terram, nec tantam occupaverunt quod colere potuissent, sed quantam in spem colendi reservavere'; Hyginus (115. 6-8 Lachm.): 'quia non solum occupabat unus quisque quantum colere praesenti tempore poterat, sed quantum in spem colendi habuerat ambiebat'; (cf. Frontinus *de agrorum qual.* 2. 21-4 Lachm.; Siculus Flaccus 138. 11-15 Lachm.). Such a concession would clearly be desirable and necessary if the land to be brought under cultivation needed clearing or draining or other comparable preparatory work.

Tibiletti held (T. 26, 174-5, 222-3) that probably the right to occupy and cultivate public land was to begin with restricted to members of the patrician class, and that plebeians had to wait for the *lex Licinia* of 367 before they too could share in this right, as in other rights hitherto confined to the patricians. That is very speculative, but of no moment either way so far as we are here concerned.

We are on firm ground when we come to the year 298. By that year there was certainly already in existence a *law* which governed the amount of public land any individual might 'possess'—a *lex de modo agrorum*—which no doubt set out the conditions attached to such possession or occupation, and prescribed penalties for infringements of the rules. That is shown by Livy (10.13. 14): 'Eo anno [298] plerisque dies dicta ab aedilibus plebis quia plus quam lege finitum erat agri possiderent; nec quisquam ferme purgatus est vinculumque ingens immodicae cupiditatis iniectum est.' This notice makes it eminently reasonable to accept that a *lex de modo agrorum* did in fact date from the time of the activities of the tribune Licinius in 367, as Livy asserts (6.35 ff.). Precisely what limits the Licinian law laid down is a matter of dispute: were they the same as those which obtained in Tiberius Gracchus' day over two hundred years later, or were they less generous? Before tackling that question, however, it is best to set out just what the limits which obtained in the Gracchan period were.

The oldest first-hand evidence which we have of a *lex de modo agrorum* comes from a surviving extract from the speech *pro Rhodiensibus* which Cato the Elder delivered in 167 (Malcovati, *ORF*² pp. 65-6: see above, p. 47). The passage in question runs as follows:

> Quid nunc? Ecqua tandem lex est tam acerba, quae dicat: si quis illud facere voluerit, mille minus dimidium familiae multa esto: si quis plus quingenta iugera habere voluerit, tanta poena esto; si quis maiorem pecuum numerum habere voluerit, tantum damnas esto? Atque nos omnia plura habere volumus, et id nobis impoene est.

This tallies well with what we read in Appian *BC* 1.8:

> Ἔκριναν μηδένα ἔχειν τῆσδε τῆς γῆς πλέθρα πεντακοσίων πλείονα μηδὲ προβατεύειν ἑκατὸν πλείω τὰ μείζονα καὶ πεντακοσίων τὰ ἐλάσσονα. καὶ ἐς ταῦτα δ' αὐτοῖς ἀριθμὸν ἐλευθέρων ἔχειν ἐπέταξαν οἳ τὰ γιγνόμενα φυλάξειν τε καὶ μηνύσειν ἔμελλον.

Thus Appian, who is in general accord with Cato, says that the *lex de modo agrorum* in the form in which it existed in 133 allowed any individual (a) to hold, occupy, 'possess' (ἔχειν) a maximum of 500 *iugera* of public land; and (b) to pasture on public land a maximum of 100 large beasts (oxen, horses) and 500 small beasts (sheep, pigs). These maxima, Tibiletti argues (T. 27, 3–12), were not alternatives: an individual could cultivate his 500 *iugera* of public land and on top of that pasture on other public land both 100 large and 500 small beasts. Apart from the fact that there was a less obvious need to 'possess' the land on which animals roamed, it would in fact quite simply have been impossible to pasture anything like so many animals on as few as 500 *iugera* (some 300 acres or 125 hectares): the quality of the land must obviously have varied widely, but using modern Italian data Tibiletti calculated that 100 head of oxen would have needed 200–400 *iugera* of top-class land, 800–1,300 of moderate land, and 2,000–4,000 of poor land, while for 500 sheep the comparable figures are 330–400, 440–660, and 1,000–2,000 (figures rounded off from tables in T. 27, 9–11).

Personally, I agree with Tibiletti and others that figures of this size are very difficult to accept for the mid-fourth century. Moreover, the provisions about employing a certain number of free workers alongside slaves, to keep an eye on them and give warning of any possible danger from that quarter, is surely anachronistic for so early a date—although it could be argued that that feature of Appian's account is itself anachronistic colouring and therefore to be discounted. If it is accepted that the figures are probably too high for the age of Licinius, then their association with the Licinian legislation of 367 as found in Livy must be explained as a consequence of later contamination, which often sought to retroject the burning controversies of the late Republic into what were believed or alleged to be broadly comparable issues and incidents of early Roman history. Nevertheless, it would be foolhardy to dogmatize on this point, and it must be recognized that other scholars (e.g. Tenney Frank, *ESAR* i.26 ff; Burdese, *Studi sull' Ager Publicus*, 56–7) have not found the figure of 500 *iugera* unacceptable for 367.

Tibiletti himself argued (T. 26, 215 ff.; 27, 30 ff.; 28, 185–8) that Livy (like the source of Plutarch's *Camillus*) knew only part of the Licinian story, and that too influenced by what happened in the time of the Gracchi and by the deliberate slant which Tiberius Gracchus himself gave it in an attempt to minimize the novelty of his own proposal by representing it as being in an important sense only a restatement of the existing *lex de modo agrorum*. Yet Tiberius not only threw in his novel douceur of a secure title to the 500 *iugera* individuals would be allowed to retain, he also (so Tibiletti held) cut out the generous further provision for pasturing beasts, and—most important innovation of all—he made specific provision for the recovery and distribution of the excess holdings. Earlier rules *de modo agrorum* seem not to have aroused serious controversy (save in 367 in connection with the extension to the *plebs* of the right to occupy public land); and the rich and copious evidence of Livy down to the year 167, not to speak of other sources, reveals no great political fireworks about such matters in the first half of the second century. Very likely (so Tibiletti continues) there were various detailed changes in the regulations between 367 and 167, but such changes were understandably ignored by our sources since they were not contentious. In Tibiletti's judgement, the true home of the final version of the regulations as attested by Cato and Appian should be sought in the early decades of the second century. Livy's failure to register the enactment of this final version anywhere in his extant account down to 167 is to be accounted for by the assumption that at the time it was regarded as of little importance, and occasioned no controversy; hence Livy did not bother to mention it.

While one may agree that the Cato–Appian figures are almost certainly too high for 367, it is difficult to follow Tibiletti in dating them as late as the early second century. Livy's sources for the latter period were reasonably rich and secure; and, given that he has shown interest in Licinius' activities, and went on to deal with Tiberius Gracchus in later books which are no longer extant, it would be remarkable if he has eschewed all reference to and interest in the final form of the rules which Tiberius set out to enforce—as Tibiletti's view implies. It would seem safer to date the final form to not long before 218, that is to say within the last part of the long period covered by the missing second decade of Livy.

But, however that may be, it is essential that we remember that, whatever answers we give to such questions, the plain fact remains that the rules which Tiberius moved to enforce in 133 were not archaically obsolete, at whatever date they had been reduced to this form. The evidence of Cato presents these rules to us as in existence, as recognized as enforceable at law, and as involving penalties if they were transgressed, little over thirty years earlier (above, p. 47). Cato did not specify the maximum numbers of beasts permitted by law; but his acreage figure is identical with Appian's, which makes it reasonable to assume that Appian's maxima for beasts were also the figures that obtained in 167.

Neither Appian, nor Plutarch, nor indeed any other source, tells us specifically what action Tiberius Gracchus proposed concerning the pasturage provisions of the *lex de modo agrorum*, as opposed to what we may term the 'occupatory' provisions. We read simply of a rigid restriction to 500 *iugera* for any individual *possessor*. No doubt a fair amount of the land which was regularly used for pasturage and droving was quite unsuitable for cultivation, or would have required a lot of time and effort and money to make it suitable. Hence it is very likely that Tiberius was content, where the land was unsuited to exploitation by small peasant farmers, to leave things as they were, insisting merely on the proper observation of the legal limits of the numbers of beasts that individuals could pasture on such land, and thereby giving the small man a chance to pasture his few animals in places where the big cattlemen had effectively created an exclusive preserve for themselves—often, one may suspect, by violent means or by intimidation; for although in theory the praetors could have given the small men protection against such disturbance, as they could the small *possessores*, in practice peasants probably did not venture to try to avail themselves of such protection with all its legal complexities, through ignorance, poverty, despair, or fear. There was little or nothing to be gained by simply driving the big cattlemen away and leaving such land to go to waste; and strict enforcement of the *scriptura*, the rent which the herders were obliged to pay to the state for making use of public pasturage, would produce useful revenues which would otherwise have been fore-gone. No doubt some of the big cattlemen with herds pasturing on public land in numbers far in excess of the legal limits sometimes had. put up *termini* (boundary-markers) to illicitly delimit certain tracts as their own; if so, they will have been required to remove them. But usually it will have been the cultivable public land that a *possessor* thus marked off as 'his own', thereby in principle at least making it possible to avail himself of the protection of the possessory interdicts against interference or ex-trusion, so long as his holding was within the limits specified by the *lex de modo agrorum*. We can be pretty certain that the only check on ex-cessive exploitation of land which was neither distributed nor in the hands of *possessores* practising arable or mixed farming were the livestock pro-visions of the *lex de modo agrorum*, which in practice were a less effective safeguard for small men even than the possessory interdicts.

Further, public land which was originally uncultivated but potentially fertile may have come to be cleared and drained etc. by the well-to-do and thus brought into cultivation. The effect must often have been to deprive neighbouring small farmers of the use of such land for grazing, feeding pigs, wood-gathering, and so on, thereby making their own holdings less viable. Such a process, eminently plausible in itself, is cer-tainly found going on in later times: Frontinus attests it in connection with *subseciva* and other categories of land which were not any one man's possession but were meant to be open to common local or riparian use (20,4; 20,9; 48,25; 53,22; 56,9 Lachm.).

Generally, when public land was divided, and assigned to individuals by colonial or *viritim* assignation, various bits and pieces were not assigned to any individual to hold as his own property but were left available for the communal use of the local farmers. Paulus (cited in Lachmann, *Gromatici Veteres* ii.395) defines *ager compascuus* thus: 'Compascuus ager appellatur qui a divisoribus agrorum relictus est ad pascendum communiter vicinis.' Other terms might be employed. Thus Frontinus (15. 7-8 Lachm.) tells us that "'compascua' multis locis in Italia 'communia' appellantur." *Subseciva*, the odds and ends of land left over after survey and division, also fall into the same general category of 'common land', access to and use of which must often have made all the difference to the small peasant farmer (it may help to account for the small size of some of the allot-ments themselves: cf. Brunt, *IM* 193-4). Improvement and enclosure of such land by the better off could have had serious effects on the chances the peasant farmer had to stay at subsistence level. (For reff. to *ager compascuus*, see Lachmann i. 15,6; 116,21; 120,16; 157,9; 201,14; 202,3.)

As can be seen in, for example, the cases of Bononia (founded in 189) and Mutina (founded in 183), the *territorium* of a colony did not consist simply of the sum total of the lands assigned to the colonists (T. 28, 227-31; above, p. 10). At Bononia, only one-third (some 400 out of

1,200 sq. km) was distributed; at Mutina, as little as about one-eightieth (25·2 out of 2,000 sq. km). Of the unassigned land which remained public, it is reasonable to suppose that some was *ager compascuus* reserved for use by colonists assigned farms nearby; some remained in the hands of the native population; some consisted of uplands of little or no use for cultivation but sometimes useful for pasturage; and some may have been left available for *occupatio*. We later find Italian towns deriving a substantial community revenue from the renting or leasing of their public land (Hyginus 116. 5 Lachm; cf. Brunt, *IM* 710); lines 29–32 of the agrarian law of 111 (Bruns, *FIR* 11) concern public land in the hands of non-Romans, and lines 31–3 make it clear that Latin towns in Italy as well as Roman towns had been corporately granted use and enjoyment of *ager publicus*. It is probable that the municipal land of later times had originally been *ager publicus populi Romani*, and consisted in large part of the originally undistributed areas of a colony's *territorium*. Whether such land had remained *de jure* the property of the Roman state, which had established the colony on lands belonging to the Roman state; whether it became either *de jure* or *de facto* either the property or in some sense at the disposal of the colony once it had been founded; whether, if the latter is true, the rules of the *lex de modo agrorum* still applied to it: these are questions to which we cannot give a secure answer. Similarly, whenever Rome confiscated lands from a defeated Italian community without immediately or subsequently founding a colony or making viritane distributions or arranging for it to be specially and formally leased out like the *ager Campanus*, was the exploitation of the confiscated land left to the Italian community concerned or to the original Italian owners, could Roman citizens occupy or otherwise use it subject to the rules of the *lex de modo agrorum*, were special provisions concerning this land included in the agreement made between Rome and her defeated enemy or rebel subject? Again, these are questions to which there are no sure answers. But it is likely enough that it is to this general area that we should look for the background to the tensions and arguments which arose between Latin and Italian governments and the Gracchan land commissioners in the years after the passing of Tiberius' *lex agraria* in 133. In particular, it is plausible to suppose that the original Italian owners of confiscated land did not clearly grasp the full import of the change in the legal status of their land consequent upon confiscation if they were in fact allowed to continue or quickly resume cultivating it as before.

Rich Romans had probably not been much concerned when the state from time to time earmarked for distribution the less profitable public land or public land in regions distant from the capital. It probably was not all that attractive to them to cultivate large estates or run large herds in remote regions which were not yet fully pacified or secure. Thus, for example, there was serious trouble in the early second century from Insubres, Boii, and other Celtic tribes in the Po valley and in the Carnic and Julian Alps; and in 181 Aquileia was founded 'as a permanent barrier across the raiding path' (*CAH* viii.328). The planting of colonies in such areas would effect pacification and guarantee security, and thus be in the interests of the rich as well as the colonists. It is worth noting that a generous colonizing policy was being pursued in the early decades of the second century, the first thirty years of which saw at least 1,000,000 *iugera* of decent land handed out to provide for some 100,000 families. The particulars are (T. 28, 195 ff; *ESAR* i. 109 ff.):

201-199	Assignments of land in Samnio-Apulia to veterans
200-198	Colonists restored to Placentia and Cremona
200	Supplement to Venosa
198	300 new colonists to an unidentifiable place (? in Campania)
199-197	Supplements to Narni and Cosa
194	Foundation of Puteoli: Volturnum: Liternum: Salernum: Buxentum: Sipontum: Tempsa; Croton—each with 300 families, not counting the Latin colonists each received
192	Foundation of Thurii and Vibo, with 3,300 and 4,000 families respectively
190	Supplement of 6,000 families to Placentia and Cremona
189	Foundation of Bononia with 3,000 families
186	Supplements to Sipontum and Buxentum
184	Foundation of Potentia and Pisaurum with (probably) 300 families apiece
by 184	Supplement to Cales
183	Foundation of Mutina (2,000), Parma (2,000), and Saturnia
181	Foundation of Aquileia (3,000) and Graviscae
177	Foundation of Luna (2,000)
173	Citizens and Latins settled in Piedmont and Emilia
172	'Many thousands' of Ligurians settled in the Transpadana
165	Supplement to Aquileia
157	Foundation of Auximum

(Tibiletti (T. 28, 234) mistrusts the confidence of Carcopino and others that Auximum was the only colony founded after 177 and before the Gracchi; in his view, 'much may have perished with the shipwreck of Livy' —whose account is, of course, lost after 167. Yet it may reasonably be doubted that we should not hear of other foundations after 167 from other sources, however poor our information on other matters.)

The question of the charges made for the use of public land is a baffling one. Some of this land—the Campanian Land is the best known instance— was specially reserved to generate revenue for the state, and regularly let out on formal contract by the censors. But, according to Appian (*BC* 1.7.3) and Plutarch (*TG* 8.1), a rent or charge had also been imposed on the public land which was simply thrown open to occupation or use by *possessores*. Indeed, Appian is also specific that, alongside this charge on the produce of such land (a tithe of one tenth on arable products and one fifth on the produce of vineyards, orchards, and market-gardens), a poll-tax was also levied on livestock pasturing: ἐπεκήρυττον ἐν τοσῷδε τοῖς ἐθέλουσιν ἐκπονεῖν ἐπὶ τέλει τῶν ἐτησίων καρπῶν, δεκάτῃ μὲν τῶν σπειρομένων, πέμπτῃ δὲ τῶν φυτευομένων, ὥριστο δὲ καὶ τοῖς προβατεύουσιν τέλη μειζόνων τε και ἐλαττόνων ζῴων. Tibiletti argued (T. 26, 182 ff) that the imposition of this charge was a latish development; but his argument is not easy to follow and lacks cogency, and his proposition cannot be proved either way. Last sensibly noted (*CAH* ix.17) that if all public land, and not merely certain selected areas, was to be let effectively at the appropriate level for its value, a survey of the thoroughgoing imperial type would have been needed, something quite beyond the capacity of the relatively unsophisticated administrative machinery of the second and earlier centuries; yet some less refined system of collection by *publicani* could have been managed. It is hard to say how regular and rigorous the collection of the charges attested by Appian and Plutarch had been. The distant and widely scattered areas involved, the attendant difficulties of communication and the problems in the way of reaching agreement about just what sums were properly due—such factors would make the task both laborious and daunting. Certainly, the disputes about boundaries which attended the work of the Gracchan commissioners (above, p. 92) indicate that payments for the holdings in question had not been regularly or carefully collected for some considerable time. When charges were specifically levied on *possessores* of public land under the second of the three laws which were passed in the years following the tribunates of Gaius Gracchus (Appian, *BC* 1.27; above, p. 202), legislation seems to have been needed. It is barely possible that between 133 and 119/118 (the probable date of the law in question) some unrecorded remission of such charges had taken place, but that seems a rather far-fetched and desperate recourse. And I should certainly follow Last (*CAH* ix.25; cf. above, p. 177) in doubting the suggestion that Plutarch (*CG* 9.2) can be taken to mean or imply that in 122 Livius Drusus had abolished *vectigal* on all the old *possessiones*, as opposed to making no provision for any rent to be paid on the new colonial allotments which he projected himself.

The question is puzzling; but it is best to assume that the collection of the charges to which Plutarch and Appian refer had lapsed or had become very slack and erratic in the years before 133. There may just possibly be a connection here with the abolition of *tributum* on Roman citizens in 167. Moreover, it seems to me very reasonable to suppose that a *vectigal* or tithe or poll-tax had never been demanded from the small farmer or grazier—the charge would in any case scarcely have been worth the trouble of collecting it—but only from men who exploited large acreages or ran large herds and flocks; and, if these latter included (as they surely did) many members of the Senate, it is not at all surprising that the 'government' was content to allow the collection of payments to lapse. The agrarian law of 111 (Bruns, *FIR* 11, lines 14–15) seems specifically to exempt from any payments anyone who pastured no more than ten full-grown cattle and their young on the public land; and the specially favoured treatment of any holdings of less extent than 30 *iugera* (lines 13–14) points in the same direction. Even if, as is very far from certain, this class of holdings represented the maximum size which the Gracchan commissioners could allocate (above, p. 48), the figure of 30 *iugera* was probably tralatician.

This Appendix makes no claim to be a complete treatment of the history of the *ager publicus* of the Roman Republic: that would require a substantial monograph of its own. It merely aims to resume some of the more important features and issues and questions in so far as a study of these is needed to illuminate the activity of the Gracchi. The length and complexity of the extant agrarian law of 111, admittedly made even more difficult to unravel by the fragmentary state of the inscription which preserves its text, are a chastening and salutary reminder that in treating of the *lex Sempronia agraria* of 133 we can do no more than aim to recover its chief and most striking feature, that is its insistence that the state should recover public land which individuals had come to exploit in excess of the legal limit of 500 *iugera* in order to redistribute this land to smallholders. That Tiberius' own law was significantly less cumbersome and complicated than its successor of twenty-two years later is a proposition so implausible as to make no claim whatsoever on our serious consideration.

APPENDIX 2
THE SPEECHES OF GAIUS GRACCHUS[1]

Of the power and persuasiveness of Gaius Gracchus as a public speaker there can be no doubt whatsoever. He belongs to the highest class. We can have no better judge than Cicero, unquestionably the greatest master of the art that Rome produced. He knew what he was talking about at the practical as well as at the theoretical level; and, despite his lack of sympathy for Gaius the politician, he frequently spoke or wrote of his outstanding gifts with admiration and enthusiasm. Many examples could be cited, but one may here stand for them all. It comes from Cicero's own masterpiece on the development of Roman oratory, the *Brutus*, which was written in the early months of 46, some three and a half years before his death. In *Brutus* 125-6 we read:

> Sed ecce in manibus vir et praestantissimo ingenio et flagranti studio et doctus a puero C. Gracchus. Noli enim putare quemquam, Brute, pleniorem aut uberiorem ad dicendum fuisse. . . . Damnum enim illius immaturo interitu res Romanae Latinaeque litterae fecerunt. Utinam non tam fratri pietatem quam patriae praestare voluisset! Quam facile ille tali ingenio, diutius si vixisset, vel paternam esset vel avitam gloriam consecutus! Eloquentia quidem nescio an habuisset parem neminem. Grandis est verbis, sapiens sententiis, genere toto gravis. Manus extrema non accessit operibus eius; praeclare incohata multa, perfecta non plane. Legendus, inquam, est hic orator, Brute, si quisquam alius, iuventuti; non enim solum acuere sed etiam alere ingenium potest.

Although comparatively numerous fragments and references and citations of Gaius' speeches survive, hardly any are long enough to give us a full taste of his qualities, and far too many are mere snippets, cited by later grammarians to illustrate this or that point of philological interest, quite out of any context. This appendix lists all the verbatim citations, however brief; one or two Greek passages which seem to be straight translations from Gaius' original Latin; and references to speeches delivered by Gaius even when no fragments survive. (References are given both to Fraccaro's discussion and to *ORF*[2].)

1. *Pro Vettio*

Probably not long after his return from Spain in 132, Gaius is said to have

[1] See especially the masterly survey of Plinio Fraccaro in his *Studi sull 'età dei Gracchi* in *Studi storici per l'antichità classica* N.S. i (1913), 42–136, esp. 66–122 (here cited simply as Fraccaro).

made a great impact with a speech in defence of his friend Vettius; but we know nothing of either Vettius himself or the issue. (Plutarch, *CG* 1.3; Fraccaro, pp. 71–3; *ORF*² pp. 177–8.)

2. *Pro Rogatione Papiria*

(a)   pessimi Tiberium fratrem meum optimum interfecerunt. Em! videte quam par pari sim.

(b)   qui sapientem † eum faciet, qui et vobis et rei publicae et sibi communiter prospiciat. non qui pro † suilla hominem † trucidet.

(c)   nequaquam iniuriose nobis contumeliam imponi sinatis.

(d)   usquequaque curavit

The speech delivered in support of Papirius Carbo's proposal concerning the legality of iteration of the tribunate in either 131 or 130 is referred to by Livy, *Perioche* 59. The four citations printed above all were taken from this speech by the grammarian Charisius to illustrate Gaius' use of the words *em, communiter, iniuriose,* and *usquequaque.* (Fraccaro, 73–6; *ORF*² 178–9.)

3. *De Lege Penni et Peregrinis*

eae nationes cum aliis rebus per avaritiam atque stultitiam res publicas suas amiserunt

Either early in 126, or at some time after his return from Sardinia in 124, Gaius delivered a speech on the aliens expulsion bill of Pennus, tribune in 126. Häpke (*C. Semproni Gracchi oratoris Fragmenta,* 48) suggests that the speech was composed by Gaius while he was in Sardinia and posted to Rome to be read there; but that seems implausible, and her argument from Festus' words 'orationem quam conscripsit' is weak (cf. Carcopino, *Gracques*, 195). It is known only because the philologist Festus commented on Gaius' use in the speech of the plural form of *res publica*. (Fraccaro 77–80; *ORF*² 179–80.)

4. *Apud Censores* and *Ad Populum cum ex Sardinia rediit*

(a)   abesse non potest quin eiusdem hominis sit probos improbare qui improbos probet.

(b)   cum galeare ursici.

(c)   versatus sum in provincia quomodo ex usu vestro existimabam esse, non quomodo ambitioni meae conducere arbitrabar. nulla apud me fuit popina, neque pueri eximia facie stabant, et in convivio liberi vestri modestius erant quam apud principia.

(d)   ita versatus sum in provincia uti nemo posset vere dicere assem aut eo plus in muneribus me accepisse, aut mea opera quemquam sumptum fecisse. biennium fui in provincia. si ulla meretrix domum meam introivit, aut cuiusquam servulus propter me sollicitatus est,

omnium nationam postremissimum <me> nequissimumque existi-
matote. cum a servis eorum tam caste me habuerim, inde poteritis
considerare quomodo me putetis cum liberis vestris vixisse.

(e) itaque, Quirites, cum Romam profectus sum, zonas quas plenas
argenti extuli eas ex provincia inanes retuli. alii vini amphoras quas
plenas tulerunt eas argento repletas domum reportaverunt.

(f) Ἐστρατεῦσθαι μὲν γὰρ ἔφη δώδεκα ἔτη, τῶν ἄλλων δεκα
στρατευομένων ἐν ἀνάγκαις, ταμιεύων δὲ τῷ στρατηγῷ παρα-
μεμενηκέναι τριετίαν [?διετίαν], τοῦ νόμου μετ' ἐνιαυτὸν ἐπανελθεῖν
διδόντος. μόνος δὲ τῶν στρατευσαμένων πλῆρες τὸ βαλάντιον
ἐξενηνοχὼς κενὸν εἰσενηνοχέναι, τοὺς δὲ ἄλλους ἐκπιόντας ὃν
εἰσήνεγκαν οἶνον ἀργυρίου καὶ χρυσίου μέστους δεῦρο τοὺς ἀμφορεῖς
ἥκειν κομίζοντας.

Plutarch (*CG* 2.4) reports that when Gaius returned to Rome from Sardinia in 124, he was charged with dereliction of duty in having not stayed
on there with the governor, L. Aurelius Orestes, whose proconsular
appointment had been prorogued. Whether on this occasion Gaius delivered two speeches or only one is disputed; but the suggestion that there
was only one speech, entitled *oratio apud censores in contione ad populum*, is not attractive or convincing. Of the passages printed above, (a) is
cited from a speech *apud censores* by Cicero (*Orator* 233) to illustrate a
point of word-order; (b) from the same speech by the grammarian Charisius. The three longer passages (c)-(e) Aulus Gellius (*NA* 15.12) cites from
a speech *ad populum in contione*; but (f) Plutarch quotes as having been
delivered *apud censores*. The suggestion that Gaius may have used virtually the same words in two separate speeches is fanciful, and on the
whole it is likeliest that Plutarch has slipped up here. But comparison of
(d), (e), and (f) shows how plausible it is to suggest that other remarks or
comments attributed by Plutarch and Appian to the two brothers Gracchi
may reflect—as (f) manifestly does—the *ipsissima verba* of their speeches.
(Fraccaro, 78-87; *ORF*[2] 180-2.)

5. *Pro Se*

si nanciam populi desiderium, conprobabo rei publicae commoda

Plutarch (*CG* 3.1) tells us that Gaius was next accused of complicity in the
revolt of Fregellae, but acquitted. No surviving fragment can be reliably
assigned to any speech by Gaius on this occasion, but both Fraccaro and
Malcovati would place here the few words printed above cited by the
grammarian Priscianus from a speech of Gaius 'pro se' in order to illustrate
the use of the verb *nancio*. But this attribution to the Fregellan context is
extremely conjectural, little better than a wild guess. (Fraccaro, 87-8;
ORF[2] 183.)

6. In P. Popillium Laematem: pro Rostris, circum Conciliabula

(a) Ὑμῶν δὲ ὀρώντων, ἔφη, Τιβέριον ξύλοις συνέκοπτον οὗτοι, καὶ διὰ μέσης τῆς πόλεως ἐσύρετο νεκρὸς ἐκ Καπετωλίου ῥιψησόμενος εἰς τὸν ποταμόν. οἱ δὲ ἁλισκόμενοι τῶν φίλων ἀπέθνησκον ἄκριτοι. καίτοι πάτριόν ἐστιν ἡμῖν, εἴ τις ἔχων δίκην θανατικὴν μὴ ὑπακούει, τούτου πρὸς τὰς θύρας ἔωθεν ἐλθόντα σαλπιγκτὴν ἀνακαλεῖσθαι τῇ σάλπιγγι, καὶ μὴ πρότερον ἐπιφέρειν ψῆφον αὐτῷ τοὺς δικαστάς. οὕτως εὐλαβεῖς καὶ πεφυλαγμένοι περὶ τὰς κρίσεις ἦσαν.

(b) quae vos cupide per hosce annos adpetistis atque voluistis, ea si temere repudiaritis, abesse non potest quin aut olim cupide adpetisse aut nunc temere repudiasse dicamini.

(c) homines liberi nunc in oppido occisitantur

(d) credo ego inimicos meos hoc dicturum

(e) poteratur

(f) malo cruce

(g) antecellant

(h) eo exemplo instituto dignus fuit, qui malo cruce periret

Plutarch (*CG* 3.4) gives (a) what seems to be a Greek paraphrase of part of a speech delivered by Gaius as tribune (December 124/January 123) on the subject of his brother's murder and the execution without a proper trial of his supporters. It seems clearly to belong in the context of the attacks on Popillius Laenas, against whom Gaius delivered at least two speeches. (b) is cited by Aulus Gellius (*NA* 11.13) simply as from an 'oratio in P. Popillium', but the grammarian Festus cites (c) as from an 'oratio pro rostris in P. Popillium'. Gellius (*NA* 1.7) cites (d) as coming from a speech 'cuius titulus est de P. Popillio circum conciliabula'; and (e) and (g) are cited by the grammarians Festus and Diomedes from the same source. (f) Festus describes as from the 'oratio quae est in P. Popillium posterior', while (h), also from Festus, evidently also comes from the same speech against Laenas, though the text has been garbled into 'in Pompilium et matronas', whatever that may conceal. (Fraccaro, 88-97; *ORF*² 183-5.)

7. In L. Calpurnium Pisonem Frugi

Cicero (*pro Fonteio* 39) refers to an attack by Gaius on his old enemy Piso Frugi 'qua in oratione permulta . . . turpia ac flagitiosa dicuntur'. He also says that once when Gaius at a *contio* told an attendant to summon Piso and the man inquired which Piso he meant (there were several Pisones), Gaius replied: 'Cogis me dicere, inimicum meum Frugi'. No attributed citations from this speech survive, and those tentatively assigned to it by Fraccaro and Malcovati I prefer to include among the fragments *incertae sedis*. (Fraccaro, 98-9; *ORF*² 186-7.)

8. *Dissuasio Legis Aufeiae*

nam vos, Quirites, si velitis sapientia atque virtute uti, etsi quaeritis, neminem nostrum invenietis sine pretio huc prodire. omnes nos qui verba facimus aliquid petimus, neque ullius rei causa quisquam ad vos prodit nisi ut aliquid auferat. ego ipse, qui aput vos verba facio ut vectigalia vestra augeatis quo facilius vestra commoda et rem publicam administrare possitis, non gratis prodeo; verum peto a vobis non pecuniam sed bonam existimationem atque honorem. qui prodeunt dissuasuri ne hanc legem accipiatis, petunt non honorem a vobis verum a Nicomede pecuniam. qui suadent ut accipiatis, hi quoque petunt non a vobis bonam existimationem verum a Mithridate rei familiari suae pretium et praemium. qui autem ex eodem loco atque ordine tacent, hi vel acerrimi sunt; nam ab omnibus pretium accipiunt, et omnis fallunt. vos, cum putatis eos ab his rebus remotos esse, inpertitis bonam existimationem; legationes autem a regibus, cum putant eos sua causa reticere, sumptus atque pecunias maximas praebent. item uti in terra Graecia, quo in tempore Graecus tragoedus gloriae sibi ducebat talentum magnum ob unam fabulam datum esse, homo eloquentissimus civitatis suae Demades ei respondisse dicitur: 'Mirum tibi videtur si tu loquendo talentum quaesisti? ego ut tacerem decem talenta a rege accepi'; item nunc isti pretia maxima ob tacendum accipiunt.

This substantial fragment is cited by Gellius (*NA* 11.10) from a speech of Gaius 'qua legem Aufeiam dissuasit', and along with the fragments from the *de legibus promulgatis* gives us a real chance to savour the quality of his rhetoric. The proposal of Aufeius (some would emend to Saufeius, or even Aufidius, but on weak grounds) was concerned with a quarrel involving two kings, Mithridates V of Pontus and Nicomedes II of Bithynia, over the proposed grant of Phrygia to Mithridates. The Aufeian proposal was defeated, it seems, and in the end neither king got Phrygia (*CAH* ix 106-7). There may well be a close connection between this speech of Gaius and his own arrangements for the handling of the revenues of the new province of Asia. (Fraccaro, 99–103; *ORF*² 187–8.)

9. *De Legibus Promulgatis*

(a)   si vellem aput vos verba facere et a vobis postulare, cum genere summo ortus essem et cum fratrem propter vos amisissem, nec quisquam de P. Africani et Tiberi Gracchi familia nisi ego et puer restaremus, ut pateremini hoc tempore me quiescere, ne a stirpe genus nostrum interiret et uti aliqua propago generis nostri reliqua esset, haud <scio> an lubentibus a vobis impetrassem.

(b)   nuper Teanum Sidicinum consul venit. uxor eius dixit se in balneis virilibus lavari velle. quaestori Sidicino M. Mario datum est negotium ut balneis exigerentur qui lavabantur. uxor renuntiat viro parum cito sibi balneas traditas esse, et parum lautas fuisse. idcirco palus destitutus est in foro eoque adductus suae civitatis nobilissimus homo M. Marius. vestimenta detracta sunt, virgis caesus est. Caleni, ubi id audierunt, edixerunt ne quis in balneis lavisse vellet cum magistratus Romanus ibi esset. Ferentini ob eandem causam praetor noster quaestores abripi iussit: alter se de muro deiecit, alter prensus et virgis caesus est.

(c) quanta libido quantaque intemperantia sit hominum adulescentium, unum exemplum vobis ostendam. his annis paucis ex Asia missus est qui per id tempus magistratum non ceperat, homo adulescens pro legato. is in lectica ferebatur. ei obviam bubulcus de plebe Venusina advenit, et per iocum, cum ignoraret qui ferretur, rogavit num mortuum ferrent. ubi id audivit, lecticam iussit deponi, struppis quibus lectica deligata erat usque adeo verberavit dum animam efflavit.

(d) ea luxurii causa aiunt institui

(e) non est ea luxuries quae necessario parentur vitae causa

(f) quod unum nobis in ostentum, ipsis in usum adportatur

All these passages are cited from a speech of Gaius *de legibus promulgatis*: (a) is from the Bobbiensis scholiast on Cicero's *pro Sulla* (p. 81 Stangl); (b) – (e) are from Aulus Gellius, *Noctes Atticae*, the first two at 10.3 and the second two at 9.14; (f) is from a comment of the grammarian Festus on *ostentum*. Many scholars have assigned the speech *de legibus promulgatis* to a date early in Gaius' second tribunate, impressed by the concern here shown for the treatment of non-Romans in Italy, which they think fits best with the 'Italian programme' of that second tribunate. I am inclined to side with those who would date the speech early in the first tribunate: (b) and (c) could fit in well with the context of the '*lex de provocatione*' and the *lex ne quis iudicio circumveniatur*, pretty certainly passed early in 123 (see above, p. 122); (a) is appropriate enough to such an early date, though it could admittedly fit early 122 as well; and (d), (e), and (f), while defying any specific pigeon-holing, would certainly suit the *lex frumentaria*, also a bill of early 123. On the whole, then, I prefer a date early in 123 (or very late in 124), with the *leges promulgatae* being the earliest Gracchan proposals. But certainty is clearly unattainable. (Fraccaro, 104–13; *ORF*[2] 190–2.)

10. *In C. Fannium*

As Fraccaro (113) pointed out, Cicero, *Brutus* 100, clearly implies the existence of a speech in which Gaius attacked C. Fannius after the latter had turned against him in 122. No fragments survive.

11. *De Lege Minucia*

mirum si quid his iniuriae fit; semper eos osi sunt

A scrap cited by Festus from the last datable speech of Gaius, attacking a proposal of M. Minucius Rufus (tr. pl. 121) to abrogate the *lex Rubria* which had authorized the founding of Junonia/Carthage (Fraccaro, 113–14; *ORF*² 103). Nothing can be deduced from this tiny fragment: Festus was merely interested in the form 'osi sunt'.

12. *In Q. Aelium Tuberonem*

utrum inimicorum meorum factio an magis sollicitudo te impulit ut in me industrior sis quam in te?

Tubero, son of Scipio Aemilianus' sister Aemilia, is attested as a consistent opponent of Gaius by Cicero (*Brutus* 117), and he mentions speeches by Tubero against Gaius and a speech of Gaius against Tubero. From the latter the passage above is cited by the grammarian Priscianus. The date and circumstances are unknown. (Fraccaro, 114; *ORF*² 171–2.)

13. *In L. Metellum*

usque adeo pertaesum vos mihi esse

The grammarian Diomedes cites the above from a speech of Gaius *in L. Metellum*. Which particular L. Metellus this man was, and date and circumstances, are unknown. (Fraccaro, 114–15; *ORF*² 194.)

14. *Adversus Furnium*

quibus ego primus quo modo auxiliem?

Again from Diomedes. Furnius is unknown, and Furius (viz. L. Furius Philus) has been suggested. But date and circumstances of delivery are unknown. (Fraccaro 115; *ORF*² 194.)

15. *In Maevium*

considerate, Quirites, sinistram eius; en, quoius auctoritatem sequimini qui propter mulierum cupiditatem ut mulier est ornatus.

A fine example of Gaius' invective, directed against an unknown Maevius in unknown circumstances, and cited by the antiquarian Isidorus, who was interested in the point about men wearing rings. (Fraccaro, 116; *ORF*² 195.)

16. *In Plautium*

The speech is referred to by Valerius Maximus (9.5) as containing a reference to the arrogance of the ruling-class at Capua, where the members of the local senate used a separate forum from the commons. No citations survive, and date and circumstances are not given. (Fraccaro, 116–17; *ORF*² 195.) Carcopino's elaborate hypothesis (*Gracques*, 193 ff.) dating the speech to 125 I find unconvincing.

17. *In Rogatione Cn. Marci Censorini*

si vobis probati essent homines adulescentes, tamen necessario vobis tribuni militares veteres faciundi essent.

This tantalizing fragment we owe to the interest of the grammarian Charisius in the use by the elder Cato and Gaius of the adverbial form *necessario*. The occasion of the speech and the nature of the *rogatio* of this unknown Censorinus are not stated. (Fraccaro, 117-18; *ORF*² 196.)

18. *Fragmenta Incertae Sedis*

(a)   aerarium delargitur Romano populo

(b)   pueritia tua adulescentiae tuae inhonestamentum fuit, adulescentia senectuti dedecoramentum, senectus rei publicae flagitium.

(c)   quo me miser conferam? quo vortam? in Capitoliumne? at fratris sanguine redundat, an domum? matremne ut miseram lamentantem videam et abiectam?

(d)   purpura et diadema

(e)   patres familiae

(f)   misereri vestrum

(g)   tu matri meae maledicas, quae me peperit?

(h)   σὺ γὰρ Κορνηλίαν λοιδορεῖς τὴν Τιβέριον τεκοῦσαν;

(i)   suos parentes amat

(j)   a reference to the inhabitants of Nursia as *scelerati*.

(a) and (b) are cited by Priscianus and Isidorus respectively just as utterances of Gaius, with no indication of context. Fraccaro and Malcovati attribute them to the speech against Piso Frugi—a mere guess. (c) is cited by Cicero (*de or*. 3.214) and others, similarly without context: it sounds as if it comes from one of Gaius' last public utterances. (d) – (j) are similarly unlocated scattered tags: (g) and (h), from Seneca (*Dial*. 12.6.6) and Plutarch (*CG* 4) are interesting, not merely because of the slight variation between them, but in that they suggest that the stories about Cornelia's involvement in her sons' political activities may not be quite unfounded, given that Gaius felt driven to defend her publicly (*in contione*, says Seneca). (Fraccaro, 98-9, 118-22; *ORF*² 186-7, 196-8.)

19. *Dubia*

(a)   sicas in forum

(b)   quid tam aecum quam inopem populum vivere ex aerario suo?

(c)   quid ad ius libertatis aequandae magis efficax quam ut senatu regente provincias ordinis equestris auctoritas saltem iudiciorum regno niteretur?

The famous remark about 'daggers in the Forum' occurs in varying forms in Cicero (*legg.* 3.20), Appian (*BC* 1.22) and Diodorus (34.37; cf. 37.9). Cicero writes: 'C. vero Gracchus ruinis et iis sicis, quas ipse se proiecisse in forum dixit quibus digladiarentur inter se cives, nonne omnem rei publicae statum permutavit?' It is generally held to have come, not from a speech, but from the historical tradition about Gaius: see Fraccaro 103 and the reff. cited there, n. 4. If not from a speech, its authenticity is perhaps doubtful.

(b) and (c) both come from Florus (*Epit*, 2.1). Häpke, in her edition of the fragments of Gaius (Munich, 1915), suggested that they might well come from Gaius' own mouth, a view which Malcovati (*ORF*^{2} 186, 189) adjudged 'non inmerito' and 'non sine iure'. To my own ears, the first has the truer Gaian ring. But it is noteworthy that both these sentences quoted follow immediately on a sentence which closely resembles another in the next chapter (2.2) where Florus writes that Tiberius Gracchus 'depulsam agris suis plebem miscratus est, ne populus gentium victor orbisque possessor laribus et focis suis exularet': this last seems clearly to echo the *ipsissima verba* of Tiberius (above, p. 40, n. 1). Further, (c) seems to be echoed somewhat in Appian (*BC* 1. 22.5): τοὺς μὲν ἱππέας οἶά τινας ἄρχοντας <τῶν βουλευτῶν> ὑπερεπῆρε.

It is best simply to set out the passage from Florus 2.1 fully. The heading in the text is *De Legibus Gracchanis*, and the material may ultimately derive from Livy:

> Seditionum omnium causas tribunicia potestas excitavit, quae specie quidem plebis tuendae, cuius in auxilium comparata est, re autem dominationem sibi adquirens, studium populi et favorem agrariis frumentariis iudiciariis legibus aucupabatur. Inerat omnibus species aequitatis. Quid tam iustum enim quam recipere plebem sua a patribus, ne populus gentium victor orbisque possessor extorris aris ac focis ageret? Quid tam aecum quam inopem populum vivere ex aerario suo? Quid ad ius libertatis aequandae magis efficax quam ut senatu regente provincias ordinis equestris auctoritas saltem iudiciorum regno niteretur? Sed haec ipsa in perniciem redibant, et misera res publica in exitium sui merces erat.

Postscript

Several passages, notably from Appian and Plutarch, could be (and have been) cited as evidence of the public utterances of Gaius Gracchus. Of these I have cited above only two or three, where the evidence is of the strongest that the original Latin of Gaius must lie behind a Greek version. Personally, I have little doubt that several more do genuinely derive from Gaius' actual speeches; but caution is necessary, and it would be misleading to include such passages in an appendix devoted to the *ipsissima verba* of Gaius that fortunately have survived. For those of more adventurous disposition, reference may be made to the excellent work of N. Häpke, *C. Semproni Gracchi oratoris Romani fragmenta collecta et illustrata* (Munich, 1915).

APPENDIX 3

THE CHRONOLOGY OF C. GRACCHUS' LEGISLATION

Facts are the first need of the student of history. He must know
"who did what when". Indeed, if he knows the facts in the order
which they occurred, he can often reconstruct and interpret the
history for himself. There is a vast deal more value in dates than the
most early Victorian schoolmistress ever suggested to her classes.
Half the mistakes and misunderstandings in our current notions of
history arise from some belief that events happened at other than
their actual dates.

What Haverfield had to say to Oxford undergraduates over sixty years
ago (*The Study of Ancient History at Oxford*: O.U.P., 1912, pp. 6-7) has
a very close bearing on the study of the political career of Gaius Gracchus.
It bristles with difficulties and arguments about chronology. As in the case
of the Pentecontaetia, we are presented with a lot of facts in search of a
timetable; and historical reconstruction of Gaius' tribunates can begin
only when we have first sorted out his actions into their proper chronological sequence and interrelation. Inevitably, we must often fall back on
speculation and circumstantial evidence. In part, the problem arises because there is no single account to which we can entrust ourselves with
confidence. Appian and Plutarch mention only a selection from the total
of the attested bills of Gaius;[1] and to the thirty crowded months of his
activity Appian devotes three-quarters of the space which he allotted to
the six months of Tiberius. Plutarch is fuller than Appian, but less well-
ordered and more rhetorical; and it is hazardous, thanks to his method of
composition (on which see the observations of Gomme in his *Commentary
on Thucydides* i. 54-84), to take his apparent chronology at its face value:
Plutarch sometimes, and quite properly, arranges his subject-matter by
type (κατὰ γένος) rather than by chronological sequence (κατὰ χρόνους).
Much additional and valuable information comes to us in the form of dis-
connected snippets—references to something which Gaius did by later
writers like Cicero, or brief citations from speeches of Gaius by later
grammarians interested in Latin usage rather than in Roman history. Thus
we should not even know about the very important *lex ne quis iudicio
circumveniatur* were it not that Cicero found it relevant to refer to it
nearly sixty years later in his defence of Cluentius, where all he tells us is
that Gaius passed this law, and not when or why or in what circumstances
—just as we ourselves might on occasion refer to, say, 'the granting of

---

[1] A full list can be found at the end of this appendix.

independence to India by Clement Attlee' without going into any detail. Even the very important *repetundae* inscription which has survived owes its survival to chance, and as well as shedding light on other problems presents us with puzzles of its own, thanks to the large gaps in its text.

However, to begin with Appian. The first measure he mentions after Gaius' election to his first tribunate (and in view of the problem concerning his dating of the judiciary law of Gaius, which we shall soon have to grapple with, it is worth noting that he indicates no time-gap between that election and the introduction of Gaius' first bill: καὶ περιφανέστατα αἱρεθεὶς εὐθὺς ἐπεβούλευε τῇ βουλῇ) is the corn law (*BC* 1.21.5). He then records Gaius' election to a second tribunate (21.6), and follows this with a notice of the judiciary law (22. 1-7), of the road-building programme and colonizing proposals (23.1), and of the franchise bill and with it the first mention of the opposition of Livius Drusus, who was one of Gaius' colleagues in his second tribunate beginning in December 123 (24. 1-5). The colony of Junonia/Carthage is then referred to as having been already authorized at some unspecified earlier point in time, brought in by Appian at this stage in his narrative in connection with Gaius' trip to Africa to see to affairs at Junonia (24. 1-5). Thereafter we move on to a highly compressed and patchy account of the sequence of events which led up to Gaius' failure and death in 121.

All that is little enough; and a particular difficulty arises over the timing of the judiciary law. What Appian wrote was:

> (21. 5-6) In this way, by a single measure [the corn law] , Gaius wasted no time in winning the People over to his support. In this he had the collaboration of Fulvius Flaccus. And straight away after this he was elected tribune for the coming year as well. For by this date a law had been passed to the effect that, if there should be an insufficiency of candidates, the People should be free to elect anyone they chose.

> (22.1) So Gaius Gracchus ἐδημάρχει τὸ δεύτερον, having the People on his pay-roll, so to say; and he set about winning over the so-called *equites* as well . . . by means of another measure of the following nature. [the judiciary law] .

Some take the opening words of 22 to show that Appian has now moved on to Gaius' entry on his second tribunate in December 123, and hence they take the judiciary law to be later than that and so a measure which belongs in that second tribunate. Others accept this reading of Appian's Greek, but argue that Appian must have slipped up somehow, and must have confused Gaius' election to a second tribunate in summer or early autumn 123 with his actual entry on his second term in December; accordingly, they date the judiciary law to the period immediately following the elections in summer/autumn 123. With this latter view I should myself agree, adding that Appian's opening clause in 22 perhaps need not, however, be translated 'So Gaius Gracchus began his second tribunate', but rather 'So Gaius Gracchus became tribune for the second time'—that is, Appian himself may well have meant here to refer to the re-election and what then followed, and not to the actual inception of the second year of office several months later.[2]

Not only does that seem to me an acceptable reading of Appian's Greek, there are positive arguments which point strongly towards taking the judiciary law as a measure belonging to the first rather than to the second tribunate. To see Appian as having meant to place it in the second implies that he knew of only one significant measure worth recording, the corn law, as being carried in 123. And neither he, nor any other source, mentions any opposition to the judiciary law from Livius Drusus: Drusus is not introduced as obstructing and outmanoeuvring Gaius until some time later, on the heels of mention of the franchise bill, which certainly belongs to 122. That would be surprising if the judicary law was also a measure of 122, but not if it was proposed and carried in 123, when Drusus was not yet himself a tribune equipped with obstructive powers.

So far, this is merely to contend that Appian apparently dates his judiciary law to late summer or autumn 123. But he could, perhaps, not have meant us to read him in that way. He may be writing κατὰ γένος, singling out the most obviously popular law, the corn law, as sufficient to ensure Gaius' re-election, and then turning to note how Gaius contrived to win important support from the *equites* as well, with a mention of the law which most appealed to them: in other words, Appian was not observing, or meaning to imply, a strict chronological sequence. That is certainly possible, in my view. Indeed, it has been maintained that all Gaius' laws should be dated to the first months of 123, 'as later in his first tribunate he must have been preoccupied with administration, and in 122 Drusus was able to thwart him' (Brunt, *The Equites in the Late Republic*, 148). But I do not find the argument from 'preoccupation' compelling in itself, since, apart from any other considerations, Gaius did have collaborators who could relieve him of some of this burden; and I incline, albeit hesitantly, to date the judiciary law to autumn 123.

Here we may leave Appian, and turn to Plutarch, who treats of the legislation of Gaius in three separate groups in three different chapters:

(1) *CG* 4:   the *leges de abactis* and 'de provocatione'
(2) *CG* 5:   the *leges agraria, militaris, de civitate, frumentaria*, and *iudiciaria*
(3) *CG* 8:   a law providing for colonies at Tarentum and Capua, and another καλῶν ἐπὶ κοινωνίᾳ πολιτείας τοὺς Λατίνους.

---

[2] One may compare what Appian wrote a little earlier about the election of Gaius to his first tribunate, where he ignores the gap of several months between election and entry on office (*BC* 1.21.5): καὶ περιφανέστατα αἱρεθεὶς εὐθὺς ἐπεβούλευε τῇ βουλῇ, σιτηρέσιον ἔμμηνον ὁρίσας κτλ.

The first two groups precede Plutarch's notice of the election of Fannius to a consulship for 122 and of Gaius himself to his second tribunate (*CG* 8.1), while the third immediately follows it. But we must recall the warning about taking Plutarch's apparent chronology at its face value. In the case of the first two groups, he seems to be writing κατὰ γένος, grouping together bills which exemplify a particular facet of Gaius' activity. The two bills in *CG* 4 follow Plutarch's emphasis of the popular, demagogic character of Gaius' electoral appeal, and in particular Gaius' eloquent condemnation of the men who 'martyred' his brother: the two laws then specified fit in neatly with that theme. The second group (*CG* 5) are introduced as 'among the measures which Gaius brought forward by way of pleasing the commons and putting down the Senate'— τῶν δὲ νόμων οὓς εἰσέφερε τῷ δήμῳ χαριζόμενος καὶ καταλύων τὴν σύγκλητον: once again, a clear instance of writing κατὰ γένος and not κατὰ χρόνους. As with Appian, it is in connection with the franchise proposals (*CG* 8) that Plutarch introduces Livius Drusus and his opposition to Gaius (the apparent duplication of Plutarch's references to such proposals will be examined later). And, again as in Appian, the law establishing Junonia/ Carthage is referred to only in parenthesis, in connection with Gaius' trip to Africa in 122, as a measure which had already been passed at some time earlier—although Plutarch does specify that this law stood in the name of one of Gaius' fellow-tribunes, named Rubrius (*CG* 10.1).

The Epitomator of Livy Book 60 lists: (1) the corn law; (2) the agrarian law; (3) a garbled version of the judiciary law; then, after the words 'continuato in alterum annum tribunatu', he says (4) that 'by the agrarian laws which had been carried Gaius had several colonies founded in Italy and one at Carthage' ('legibus agrariis latis effecit ut complures coloniae in Italia deducerentur et una in solo dirutae Carthaginis'). Last (*CAH* ix. 891-2) has taken this to show that the Epitomator (and hence Livy himself, whose order the Epitomator followed) dated the *lex Rubria* which provided for the founding of Junonia/Carthage to 122, on the grounds that 'continuato in alterum annum tribunatu' must mark the beginning of the second tribunate in December 123, and that 'Plutarch definitely assigns the *lex Rubria* to a date after the counter-stroke of Drusus', who was undoubtedly tribune in 122. But, against that, Eutropius (4.21) and Orosius (5.12.1), both of whom are also dependent on Livy, date the founding of Junonia/Carthage by the consuls in office to 123; and Velleius Paterculus (1.15) independently also dates it to 123. Nor is it true that Plutarch supports the 122 dating: all that Plutarch says (*CG* 10.1) is that Gaius went out to Africa in 122 in consequence of Rubrius' having passed a law to found a colony at Carthage; which proves indeed that the *lex Rubria* had been passed before Gaius set out for Africa in 122, but not that it had itself been passed in that year—a date in 123 would obviously suit just as well. (The Epitomator, incidentally, like Plutarch, notes that Gaius went to Africa after and in consequence of the passing of the

Junonia law: 'quo ipse triumvir creatus coloniam deduxit'.) Furthermore, it is evident that the words 'continuato . . . tribunatu' can as well refer to the re-election in summer/autumn 123 as to the inception of the second tribunate in December; indeed, some such Latin phrase may lie behind Appian's οὕτως ἐδημάρχει τὸ δεύτερον. Thus we may confidently accept the firm dating of the *lex Rubria* to 123, which we find in Eutropius, Orosius, and Velleius.

Indeed, the Epitomator seems to have dated *all* his Gracchan laws to the first tribunate. After the colonies in Italy and Africa, he goes on to mention the Balearic campaign of the consul Q. Metellus, which certainly belongs to 123; then the next Book (61) opens with the foundation of Aquae Sextiae, which we know took place in 122. Hence, the break between Livy Books 60 and 61 apparently corresponded with the break between the years 123 and 122, which lends further support to the view that the bulk, if not all, of Gaius' legislation that was actually carried was carried in 123.

The continuous histories of Diodorus Siculus and Dio Cassius both fail us, for they have not survived intact. All we have are mere excerpts from their works, which cannot safely be used to establish the place of this or that measure within the overall period 123/122.

We must now come to grips with the arguments about chronology which have been based on the extant inscription of a *repetundae* law (Bruns, *FIR* 10), often known as the 'Tabula Bembina' after its sometime owner, Cardinal Bembo. But, first, it needs to be established that this fragmentary text is indeed that of the Gracchan *repetundae* law; or, to put it plainly, that Bruns 10 = Gaius Gracchus' *repetundae* law.

That equation has been doubted (e.g. by Carcopino in his *Autour des Gracques,* 205 ff., and by Mattingly in *JRS* 59 (1969), 129 ff. and 60 (1970), 154 ff; although their arguments that Bruns 10 is in fact the *lex Servilia Glauciae* have been decisively refuted by Balsdon in *PBSR* 14 (1938), 108–14, and by Sherwin-White in *JRS* 62 (1972), 83–99); but the demonstration that the equation is true can be set out quite simply, provided that particular care is taken to keep three separate propositions distinct, for otherwise an unfortunate confusion can result. These three propositions are:

(a) that Bruns 10 is the *repetundae* law of Gaius Gracchus;
(b) that Bruns 10 is the *lex Acilia* referred to in Cicero's *Verrines*;
(c) that the *lex Acilia* is the *repetundae* law of Gaius Gracchus.

Prove any two of those three, and the third must follow. But in fact only the first, luckily the most important, can be proved. The third can be shown to be quite likely to be true, and consequently ever since Mommsen it has been common to refer to Bruns 10 as the *lex Acilia*, as Bruns himself did; but it cannot be proved true, and more than one scholar has doubted that it is true. It is, therefore, of great importance that the element of uncertainty in demonstrating the truth of (c) must not be allowed to contaminate the demonstration of the truth of (a). That Bruns 10 is Gaius' law can be demonstrated far beyond any reasonable doubt; that Gaius' law in fact stood in the name of a co-operative fellow-tribune named Acilius cannot.

The demonstration of the truth of proposition (a) runs as follows. In line 74 of Bruns 10 we read: '[*Quibosquom ioudicium*] FVIT FVERITVE EX LEGE QVAM L. CALPVRNIVS L.F. TR.PL. ROGAVIT EXVE LEGE QVAM M. IVNIVS D.F. TR.PL. ROGAVIT QVEI EORVM EO [*ioudicio. . . .*]'. That shows beyond question that Bruns 10 was the direct successor of the *lex Calpurnia* and *lex Junia*, and cannot be subsequent to a *lex Sempronia* (or *lex Acilia*), since otherwise that law too would have been listed among the relevant precedent laws, the tally of which clearly closes with the mention of the *lex Junia*. Only two alternative options remain: either Bruns 10 is earlier than the Gracchan *repetundae* law, or it is itself that law. But it cannot be earlier. Bruns 10 is a law which sets up the full apparatus of a *quaestio perpetua repetundarum*; and it specifically excludes all members of the Senate ('QVEIVE IN SENATV SIET FVERITVE': lines 13 and 22) from serving as *iudices*. Given that the exclusion of senatorial *iudices* from the *repetundae* court was noted as a startling innovation of Gaius Gracchus', it would make nonsense of all our evidence to suppose that in this respect he had been anticipated by an unknown earlier legislator. It must therefore follow that Bruns 10 is the *repetundae* law of Gaius Gracchus—a conclusion of central importance, far more important than its arguable identification with the *lex Acilia* (which, in any case, itself depends on the acceptance of this conclusion).

There remains a gap in this argument, which needs to be closed. We know that the *lex Calpurnia* dates from 149; but the date and the substance of the *lex Junia* are unknown. So perhaps this *lex Junia* could be the Gracchan law, which would make Bruns 10 a later law than that. But it seems clear from line 74 of Bruns 10 that the *lex Calpurnia* and the *lex Junia* were concurrently in force up to and at the time of the passing of Bruns 10; and it is highly implausible to suggest that Gaius Gracchus' law can have been in any sense concurrent with the *lex Calpurnia*. (That same consideration undermines the force of the suggestion of A.H.M. Jones (*The Criminal Courts of the Roman Republic and Principate*, 48–50) that the *lex Junia* may have been the law which Gaius passed as a 'first shot' at reforming the *repetundae* court and which provided for mixed courts, part-senatorial and part-equestrian, while Bruns 10 was Gaius' second and lasting measure which established wholly equestrian panels of *iudices*. Cf. above, p. 143.) Further, if the *lex Junia* were the Gracchan *repetundae* law, Bruns 10 would have to be a later law concerning that court which repeated Gaius' exclusion of senatorial *iudices*. Yet the next law of which we hear which did that was the *lex Servilia Glauciae*; and that Bruns 10 cannot be identified with Glaucia's law has been proven beyond dispute by

Balsdon and Sherwin-White in the articles already cited. So Bruns 10 would have to be left to float in a sort of Limbo between Gaius' law and the laws of Caepio and Glaucia nearly twenty years later. That is a logical possibility, but only a very remote one; and Occam's razor can confidently be employed to excise it. (It might be urged that Bruns 10 must in any case be earlier than the year 111, since the agrarian law of that year is incised on its reverse face. But for several reasons that is not a secure argument: cf. Balsdon, art. cit. 114.)

So much, then, in proof of proposition (a). As for (c), viz. that the Gracchan *repetundae* law was in fact a *lex Acilia*, the argument (for which see most recently Badian *AJP* (1954), 374 ff.) may be set out and criticized thus. In all the surviving literature only two brief passages in Cicero's *Verrines* so much as mention the *lex Acilia*. At *Verrines* I. 51-2 Cicero reminded the president of the court which was hearing the case against Verres in 70, the praetor M'. Acilius Glabrio, of a law which his father Acilius had carried 'qua lege populus Romanus de pecuniis repetundis optimis iudiciis severissimisque iudicibus usus est'; and he went on to adjure the son: 'si Glabrionis patris vim et acrimoniam ceperis ad resistendum hominibus audacissimis'—which seems to show that Acilius senior's law had had a stormy and contentious passage. Later on, at *Verrines* II.i.26 ('ego tibi illam Aciliam legem restituo') we learn that the *lex Acilia* had provided for *ampliatio*, but had been superseded in this respect by the later *lex Servilia Glauciae* which substituted the process called *comperendinatio*. (For an explanation of these technical terms, see the articles of Balsdon and Sherwin-White; briefly, *comperendinatio* limited trials to two hearings of the evidence, whereas with *ampliatio* the *iudices* could occasion a succession of repeated trials simply by bringing in a succession of verdicts of not-proven: 'non liquet'.)

It has in fact been argued that the words 'si Glabrionis patris vim et acrimoniam ceperis ad resistendum hominibus audacissimis' 'clearly imply that the *lex Acilia* was an anti-radical measure (as Carcopino rightly noted)', and so cannot possibly be identified with so evidently radical a measure as that which Gaius Gracchus had carried in 123 (so Sherwin-White, *JRS* (1972), 86 n. 14). This point is, however, in my view, a good one rather than a decisive one. For while we must allow that 'homines audacissimi' sound like radical or revolutionary reformers, it is quite possible that here the reference could be to high-ranking senators of the Verres type who had been 'brazenly and forcefully' anxious to resist a bill which promised to make their selfish and scandalous despoiling of the weak and defenceless more risky. Cicero is certainly not sparing of his castigation of men of that ilk in the *Verrines*, where he has that particular sort of axe to grind.

Certainly, to judge by the first passage cited above, the *lex Acilia* seems to have had something to do with a change in the selection of *iudices* for *repetundae* trials, else Cicero could scarcely have claimed that it was 'thanks to this law that the Roman People had been served by the most stern of *iudices* in *repetundae* trials'—though we must, of course, be on the watch for venial distortion on Cicero's part here. And, in the context of the *Verrines'* all-out assault on the scandals and corruption of the senatorial *iudices* whom Sulla had ten years earlier entrusted with a monopoly of the courts (cf. Stockton, *Historia* (1973), 216-18, for citations), it is very attractive to guess that these 'most stern of *iudices*' were none other than *equites*, the class of men whom Cicero extols for their integrity as *iudices* in the past. Which suggests the conclusion that the *lex Acilia* had provided that *equites* should constitute either the whole or some part of the panels of *iudices* in *repetundae* trials. If so, the Acilian law cannot be earlier than that of Gaius Gracchus, because the latter's introduction of non-senatorial *iudices* was a novelty. It must therefore be either (i) the *repetundae* law of Gaius, or (ii) an otherwise unattested measure which dates from the period 123-106 (the latter year being the date of the *lex Servilia Caepionis*, itself superseded fairly quickly by the *lex Servilia Glauciae*), a measure rescued from oblivion and insignificance only by the courtly and exaggerated praise which Cicero flatteringly addressed to its author's son many years later. If the second of these alternatives is true—as it well could be—then we can forget about the *lex Acilia* here. If the first is accepted, the conclusion is that, just as we chance to learn from Plutarch that Gracchus' law on Junonia/Carthage was not a *lex Sempronia* but a *lex Rubria*, so too his *repetundae* law was not a *lex Sempronia* either but a *lex Acilia*. The date certainly fits, for the praetor of 70 was born about 120, so his father could so far as that goes have been a colleague of Gaius Gracchus. Not surprisingly, however, Acilius was almost forgotten, while Gaius was remembered as the true architect of the law. For all we know, several of Gaius' other laws may also have stood in the names of co-operative colleagues.

Against the identification of Acilius' law with that of Gaius has been set a passage from Tacitus (*Annals* 12.60): 'cum Semproniis rogationibus equester ordo in possessione iudiciorum locaretur, aut rursum Serviliae leges senatui iudicia redderent.' (The plurals are generic plurals, and simply mean 'a measure, or measures, like the Sempronian. . .a measure, or measures, like the Servilian'.) That language seems to carry the implication that Tacitus knew the Gracchan law as a *lex Sempronia*, not a *lex Acilia*. Tacitus may have made a slip, or he may have been writing loosely ('can hardly be taken technically': so Badian, *Historia* (1962), 205); but such suggestions are neither compelling nor self-evidently true. And even if, as is quite likely, Tacitus was here paraphrasing the words of the Emperor Claudius, we should not be in too much of a hurry to reject the prima-facie evidence of that historian-emperor any more than that of the precise and well-read Tacitus, simply because it is inconvenient for a particular (and otherwise arguable) theory. Not everybody feels the Tacitus passage to be a difficulty; but some, of whom I am one, do find it to be such. The difficulty can be met in one of two ways: we may simply conclude that the Acilian law was not Gracchan; alternatively, we can suppose that Tacitus (or Claudius) was not referring to the Gracchan *repetundae* law itself, but rather to a wider *lex Sempronia iudiciaria*, leaving it still open for the Acilian law to be the law which one of Gaius' colleagues carried in his interest and which applied the new general rules of that wider law to the *quaestio repetundarum*, as well as introducing other important changes into the whole *repetundae* process (cf. above, p. 141).

On the assumption that the *lex Acilia* was Gaius' *repetundae* law, it has been argued that we have evidence to help fix its date. A very fragmentary inscription from Astypalaea in the Aegean (*IGRR* iv. 1028), dating from the year 105, reveals the existence of a *lex Rubria et Acilia*: ὅτι [τε Πόπλιος Ῥουτίλι]ος ὕπατος τὸν ταμίαν κατὰ τὸ διάταγμα [ξενία δοῦναι αὐτῷ κε]λεύσῃ θυσίαν τε ἐν Καπετωλίῳ, ἐὰν θέλῃ, ποιή[σαι αὐτῷ ἐξῇ κατὰ] τὸν νόμον [τόν τε] Ῥόβριον καὶ τὸν Ἀκίλιον. . . . If the Rubrius in question is the author of the Junonia/Carthage law, and the Acilius the author of the Gracchan *repetundae* law, then these two pro-Gracchan tribunes are here discovered as either co-authors of a law, or Rubrius as the author of a law which was subsequently emended or amplified by Acilius.[3] Hence, if Rubrius was tribune in 122, Acilius must have been tribune either in that year (which would place the *repetundae* law also in 122), or in some later year (which would mean that the Gracchan *repetundae* law could not be his work). But, as we have seen, Rubrius was in fact tribune in 123, which means that Acilius could have been a tribune with him in that year. So this inscription cannot help us to date the *repetundae* law of Gaius to 122 as opposed to 123.

Be that as it may, we must also remember that Rubrius was not a unique name—one of Tiberius Gracchus' fellow-tribunes in 133 was named Rubrius: Appian, *BC* 1.14.5, above p. 75—and the Rubrius of the Astypalaea fragment need not necessarily therefore be the same man as the tribune of 123. In any case, the identification of the Acilian law of the *Verrines* with Gaius' *repetundae* law is at best no more than likely. The nature of the *lex Rubria et Acilia* of the Astypalaea fragment, and the date when it was passed, are both unknown, save that the date must be earlier than 105; it is not inconceivable that it was a *repetundae* law, and by that same token the Gracchan law itself could have been a *lex Rubria et Acilia* passed in 123, which could involve the easy assumption

---

[3] The contention (Tibiletti, *Athenaeum* (1953), 7 ff.) that a *lex Rubria et Acilia* could *only* be a law of the second type finds sufficient refutation in Cicero's references to a 'lex Caecilia et Didia', passed jointly by the two consuls of 98 (*Phil.* v.8), and a 'Silvani lex et Carbonis' (the *lex Plautia et Papiria*), passed jointly by two of the tribunes of 89 (*pro Archia* 7). And a law passed by the two consuls of 42 can be referred to in Greek as κατὰ ν]όμον Μουνάτιον καὶ Αἰμίλιον (Riccobono, *Leges*[2] p. 310).

that Cicero, quite understandably in the circumstances, was concerned to name only one of its co-authors, the father of the president of the court before which he was pleading in 70.

There we may leave the puzzles concerning the *lex Acilia*. Certainty is clearly unattainable. I shall merely record my own belief (above, p. 149) that the Gracchan *repetundae* law is to be distinguished from a wider *lex Sempronia iudiciaria*; that it was passed in 123; that it was more likely than not a *lex Acilia* or a *lex Rubria et Acilia*; and that the Astypalaea fragment discloses this same Acilius as co-author of a law (perhaps even this very same law) along with another tribune of 123, Rubrius. Otherwise, we must admit that we are faced with an odd collection of coincidences. But further than that it is not safe—or indeed profitable—to venture.

To come back to Bruns 10. Lines 12–14 and 21–3 of that inscription are concerned with the selection of the *iudices* who are to hear *repetundae* cases. The positive qualifications are lost, but happily some of the explicit exclusions survive; and in line 22 we read that, among those debarred from serving as *iudices*, is anyone 'QVEIVE TR.PL., Q., IIIVIR CAP., IIIVIR A.D.A., TRIBVNVS MIL. L. IIII PRIM[*is aliqu*]A EARVM SIET FVERITVE QVEIVE IN SENATV SIET FVERITVE QVEIVE L. RVBR [. . . . .]'. It has been argued that this shows that Bruns 10 must have been carried into law later than the *lex Rubria* which provided for the foundation of Junonia/Carthage; and Mommsen restored the beginning of the lacuna to read 'QVEIVE L(*ege*) RVBR [*ia IIIvir col(oniae) ded(ucendae) creatus siet fueritve* . . . .]' But, while it is obvious that we have here a reference to a *lex Rubria*, it is by no means obvious that it is that particular *lex Rubria*. For (a) the tribune of 123 could have given his name to more than the one bill we chance to hear of; (b) the Rubrius of Bruns 10 may not be the tribune of 123 but another man of the same name, for example the tribune of 133; (c) in what seems a comparable list in line 13 of Bruns 10 Mommsen preferred a different supplement ('QVEIVE IN SENATV SIET FVERITVE QVEIV [e mercede conductus depugnavit depugnaverit . . . . .]'); and (d), perhaps most importantly, we should expect *IIIviri coloniis deducendis* to be found in the list of elected officers of state which precedes the mention of senators, and not to be separated and inserted subsequently to senators, as is the case with Mommsen's restoration.

It is not, therefore, at all convincing to argue that Gaius' *repetundae* law must have been carried at some time later than the passage of the *lex Rubria* on Junonia/Carthage.

Fraccaro (*Opuscula* ii.30) produced a good argument to the effect that Bruns 10 cannot have been passed very early in any year, since the implication of lines 12 and 16 is that the praetorian provinces for the year in question had already been allocated. But his further argument from the mention of 1 September (lines 7–8) is not a cogent one, given that the very fragmentary state of the inscription at this point makes the true import and significance of the date 1 September quite obscure.

A *lex ne quis iudicio circumveniatur* attested by Cicero in various sections of his *pro Cluentio* has been held by some to have been earlier than Bruns 10, on the ground that in the *ne quis* law Gaius was still envisaging the continued presence of at least some senators as *iudices* in *repetundae* trials, and that it must therefore reflect an earlier stage in Gaius' approach to court reform than the final outright exclusion of senatorial *iudices* that we find in Bruns 10. But, though the *lex ne quis* is very probably the earlier measure, that particular argument rests on a misunderstanding of the *lex ne quis*, and so lacks any force (see above, p. 122).

It may well be that we should attribute to Gaius a law which required that the military tribunes of the first four legions should be elected directly by the People. At any rate, one plausible interpretation of a tantalizing fragment from a speech of Gaius 'in rogatione Cn. Marci Censorini' cited by the grammarian Charisius (see above, Appendix 2, p. 224) is that such elections had fallen into desuetude, that these posts had come to be filled by nomination, and that Gaius argued for a return to the old-style direct elections ('tamen necessario vobis tribuni militares veteres faciundi essent'). As we have just seen, the military tribunes of the first four legions are included in the list of elected officers of the Roman state which is found in line 22 of Bruns 10. Yet in a broadly comparable list in the *lex Latina tabulae Bantinae* (Bruns 9, line 15) they are not so included, although *IIIviri a.d.a.* are there, as in the list in Bruns 10. If the Bantia law was passed earlier than Bruns 10—as it may well have been—we could tentatively posit a law restoring election for these tribunates carried by Gaius or a co-operative colleague at some time after the passing of the Bantia law and before the passing of Bruns 10. Indeed, the Bantia law could itself be Gracchan; for it is intriguing to note that it includes a requirement to take an oath 'while facing towards the Forum' (line 17: 'in forum vorsus'); and the only other known example of such a requirement is in lines 36–7 of Bruns 10: 'IVDICES QVEI IN EAM REM ERVNT OMNES PRO ROSTREIS IN FORVM [*vorsus iouranto . . . .*]' (it is significant that this condition is not required in connection with the oath of the Delphi Piracy Law, which is almost certainly the work of Saturninus, for all that some would associate the Bantia law with Saturninus). Gaius Gracchus, so Plutarch tells us (*CG* 5.2), made a special point of always facing towards the Forum when he addressed the People, although before his time speakers had always faced towards the Senate House, his object being to emphasize that it was the People to whose interests a speaker should address himself, and not the members of the Senate: ὡς τῶν πολλῶν δέον, οὐ τῆς βουλῆς, στοχάζεσθαι.

A *lex Sempronia de provinciis consularibus* is not mentioned in the continuous accounts of Plutarch and Appian, nor by the Epitomator of

Livy, nor in the fragments of Diodorus and Dio Cassius. None the less, although we have to rely for our knowledge of it on later references to it by Cicero (*de domo* 24 etc.) and Sallust (*BJ* 27) etc., there is a possible argument for dating this law earlier than the consular elections in 123. It required the Senate to allocate the consular provinces for any given year before the consular elections had taken place, that is to say, the Senate had to name the two consular provinces for any coming year before it could be known which two candidates had been elected to be the two consuls for that year; and the law specifically prohibited the use of a tribunician veto to delay the passing of such a *senatus consultum de provinciis consularibus*—obviously because without such a prohibition a tribune could at any time be put up to delay the final allocation until after the results of the elections were known. In 125, Fulvius Flaccus had been consul, and he was posted off to the province of Gaul and thus, apparently, stopped from making further headway with his franchise proposal (above, p. 96). In 123, Gaius Fannius, a supporter of Gaius, was a candidate for a consulship of 122, and was duly elected. Although as consul he went over to the opposition and spoke against Gaius' own franchise proposal in 122, early in 123 that was in the future, and unknown; and it seems reasonable to suggest that Gaius, hoping and expecting that Fannius would be elected and prove of invaluable assistance, wanted to forestall any possibility of Fannius' being posted off out of Italy as Flaccus had been three years earlier. If there was a connection between the consular provinces law and the prospective consulship of Fannius, then the law must have been carried before the consular elections in 123 (see above, p. 129).

There remain, apart from the franchise proposal and one or two other bills which may belong to 122, a number of other laws which I should place in 123, but essentially on rather circumstantial arguments as opposed to specific evidence. The *lex de abactis* and the '*lex de provocatione*' ('ne de capite civium Romanorum iniussu populi iudicetur'), together with the corn law and perhaps the *lex militaris*, are measures which for obvious reasons fit well into the early months of 123; and with the '*lex de provocatione*' I should associate the *lex ne quis iudicio circumveniatur*, if it be a separate law. The *lex agraria*, and the possibly associated laws for road-building and colonies, could come in either the first or the second half of 123. The laws about *vectigalia* and *portoria* and *de provincia Asia* could belong to either 123 or 122: it could be urged that they should be associated with Gaius' bid for equestrian support in 123 alongside the judiciary law, or that they were measures designed to bolster Gaius' position in 122 to help secure support for his franchise proposal, measures which Livius Drusus did not seek to obstruct because he too wanted equestrian backing. But all these laws are discussed in the appropriate places in Chapter VI of this book, and there is no profit in resuming that discussion here.

It remains to deal with the franchise legislation. How early broad

proposals on this topic were publicly mooted we cannot say for sure: but
it is likely that Gaius and Fulvius Flaccus were known from the start to
have intentions in that direction. The actual bill *de sociis et nomine Latino*
seems to have been promulgated early in 122; but it must be admitted
that the accounts of both Appian and Plutarch are very unsatisfactory on
the sequence of events hereabouts and on the course of the struggle
between Gaius and Flaccus on the one side and Livius Drusus on the other.
Whether Gaius' trip to Africa (which occupied seventy days: Plutarch, *CG*
11.2) followed the failure or abandonment of the bill, or whether it preceded it, neither author makes clear. But, according to Plutarch (*CG* 12),
it was after returning from Africa that Gaius 'promulgated the rest of his
laws, as if with the intention of bringing them to the vote' (ἔπειτα τῶν
νόμων ἐξέθηκε τοὺς λοιποὺς ὡς ἐπάξων τὴν ψῆφον αὐτοῖς), whatever
exactly that may mean; and it was then that the consul Fannius responded
by ordering the expulsion from Rome of all non-citizens. On the whole,
it seems likely that Gaius first promulgated his franchise proposal in the
early months of 122, was harried and obstructed by Drusus, and finally
and unavailingly moved to bring it to the vote only after his return from
Africa, not long before the mid-year elections.

Warde Fowler (*EHR* (1905), 209 ff. and 417 ff.; followed by Last in
CAH ix. 69 ff.) argued that the evidence of Plutarch shows a development
in Gaius' approach to the question: (i) in *CG* 5.1, we have a bill from the
first tribunate in 123 making the Ἰταλιῶται ἰσόψηφοι; (ii) in *CG* 8.2, we
have another bill καλῶν ἐπὶ κοινωνίᾳ πολιτείας τοὺς Λατίνους; and (iii)
in *CG* 9.2, we are told that Drusus was upset by Gaius' offer of ἰσοψηφία
to the Latins.

There are in general serious difficulties in this argument. For example,
Warde Fowler had to invert Plutarch's order to make the 'more modest'
proposal come first, since a proposal to give *isopsephia* to all the Italians
seems scarcely 'more modest' than one to give the citizenship to Latins
alone. But all that is really by the way, because the whole discussion
(valuable though it is) is essentially misdirected, in that it fails to take
proper account of Plutarch's method of composition. The first mention
(i) of the proposal is as one of a class of proposals which Gaius εἰσέφερε τῷ
δήμῳ χαριζόμενος καὶ καταλύων τὴν σύγκλητον–a κατὰ γένος passage
where he is not giving a chronologically sequential account, but bringing
together a set of proposals which illustrate one facet or aspect or interpretation of Gaius' activity. The proposal appears to be put in its proper
place at (ii); and then crops up again at (iii), when Drusus' offer to the
Latins (immunity from flogging when on military service) is contrasted
with what Gaius was offering. I should agree with Sherwin-White (*The
Roman Citizenship*[2] , 136), against Warde Fowler and Last, that Appian's
version of Gaius' proposal was the correct one: viz. Gaius was offering
full citizenship to the Latins and the *ius Latii* to the Italians. Cicero
(*Brutus* 99) describes the speech which Fannius delivered against it as

'de sociis et nomine Latino'; and a surviving excerpt from that speech (*ORF*[2] p. 144) clinches the argument that only the Latins were being offered full citizenship: 'Si Latinis civitatem dederitis, credo, existimatis vos ita ut nunc constitistis in contione habituros locum, aut ludis et festis diebus interfuturos? Nonne illos omnia occupaturos putatis?' Fannius would have made his thrust all the more telling if he could have added the Italians to the Latins as being sure to crowd the existing citizens out of a place at public meetings and games and festivals; that he did not add them must show that the offer of full citizenship was not being made to them; and, if Gaius was offering them something less than that, it is likely that it was what Appian implies—the *ius Latii*.

If it is accepted that originally Gaius did not mean to hold a second tribunate in 122, but to leave Fulvius Flaccus to get on with the franchise proposals in that year while he occupied himself with the heavy load of work generated by his legislation in 123, that is in itself a strong argument for dating most of his legislation to 123. For a discussion of this suggestion, see above, pp. 171 ff.

I append a list of all the measures which can be attributed to Gaius Gracchus, either with certainty or with some degree of probability or possibility, and regardless of whether they stood in his own name or in that of a colleague working in his interest. They are set out here as if they were all separate measures, though some may have formed parts of others or of the same bill as others. All are referred to in Chapter VI of this book, and they are listed here simply for convenience.

(1) *de abactis*
(2) '*de provocatione*' (*de capite civis*)
(3) *ne quis iudicio circumveniatur*
(4) *frumentaria*
(5) debt-repayment
(6) *de provinciis consularibus*
(7) *agraria*
(8) colonies in Italy and abroad
(9) road-building
(10) *militaris*
(11) *de tribunis militum*
(12) *iudiciaria*
(13) *de repetundis*
(14) *de provincia Asia*
(15) *de vectigalibus et portoriis*
(16) *de civitate*
(17) electoral procedure

BIBLIOGRAPHY

The modern works listed below are those which have been cited in the footnotes and appendices to this book. There are numerous others which can be consulted with profit, and which have often furnished bases for subsequent advances; the fact that a book or an article is not included here is not to be taken as implying that I have not found it valuable or useful. In general, however, I have preferred to refer where possible to the most recent treatments of any given point or topic; these will furnish a guide to the earlier literature for anyone who desires it.

Astin, A.E. *Scipio Aemilianus* (Oxford, 1971)

Badian, E. 'Lex Acilia Repetundarum' (*AJP* 75 (1954), 374–84)

— 'L. Papirius Fregellanus' (*CR* 5 (1955), 22–3)

— 'P. Decius P. f. Subulo' (*JRS* 46 (1956), 91–6)

— *Foreign Clientelae* (Oxford, 1958)

— 'From the Gracchi to Sulla' (*Historia* 11 (1962), 197–245) (= Seager, *Crisis*, 3–51)

— 'Roman Politics and the Italians 133–91 B.C.' (*Dialoghi di archeologia* 2–3 (1970–1), 373–41)

— *Publicans and Sinners* (Oxford, 1972)

— 'Tiberius Gracchus and the Beginning of the Roman Revolution' (*Aufstieg und Niedergang der Römischen Welt* (ed. Temporini, Berlin/New York, 1972) I.i. 668–731)

Bagehot, W. *The English Constitution* (London, 1867)

Balsdon, J.P.V.D. 'The History of the Extortion Court at Rome, 123–70 B.C.' (*PBSR* 14 (1938), 98–114) (= Seager, *Crisis*, 132–50)

Bardon, H. *La Littérature latine inconnue* (Paris, 1952–6)

Beloch, K.J. *Römische Geschichte bis zum Ende der Republik* (2nd edn., Leipzig/Berlin, 1914)

Bleicken, J. *Das Volkstribunat der klassischen Republik* (*Zetemata* 13 (1955))

Boren, H.C. 'The Urban Side of the Gracchan Economic Crisis' (*AHR* 63 (1957–8), 890–902) (= Seager, *Crisis*, 54–68)

Briscoe, J. 'Supporters and Opponents of Tiberius Gracchus' (*JRS* 64 (1974), 125–35)

Broughton, T.S.R. *The Magistrates of the Roman Republic* (New York, 1951–60)

Bruns, C.G. *Fontes Iuris Romani Antiqui* (7th edn., Tübingen, 1909)

Brunt, P.A. 'The Army and the Land in the Roman Revolution' (*JRS* 52 (1962), 69–86)

– 'The Equites in the Late Republic' (*Second International Conference of Economic History*, Aix-en-Provence, 1962, i. 117–49) (= Seager, *Crisis*, 83–118)

– 'Italian Aims at the Time of the Social War' (*JRS* 55 (1965), 90–109)

– Review of Earl's *Tiberius Gracchus* (*Gnomon* 37 (1965), 189–92)

– 'The Roman Mob' (*Past and Present* 35 (1966), 3–27)

– *Social Conflicts in the Roman Republic* (London, 1971)

– *Italian Manpower 225 B.C. – A.D. 14* (Oxford, 1971)

– Review of Jones's *Criminal Courts* (*CR* 24 (1974), 265–7)

Burdese, A. *Studi sull' Ager Publicus* (Turin, 1952)

Carcopino, J. *Autour des Gracques* (Paris, 1928; reprinted with an appendix by C. Nicolet, Paris, 1967)[1]

– 'Les Lois agraires des Gracques et la Guerre Sociale' (*Bulletin de l'Association G. Budé* 22 (1929), 3–23)

– *Histoire romaine* II.i (Paris, 1929; with G. Bloch)

Cichorius, C. *Römische Studien* (Leipzig/Berlin, 1922)

Corpus Inscriptionum Latinarum (Berlin, 1863 –)

Crawford, M.H. *Roman Republican Coinage* (Cambridge, 1974)

Crook, J. 'Sponsione Provocare: Its Place in Roman Litigation' (*JRS* 66 (1976), 132–8)

Cuff, P.J. 'Prolegomena to a Critical Edition of Appian B.C. I' (*Historia* 16 (1967), 177–88)

Degrassi, A. *Inscriptiones Latinae Liberae Rei Publicae* I (Florence, 1957)

Dessau, H. *Inscriptiones Latinae Selectae* (Berlin, 1892–1914)

Douglas, A.E. *M. Tulli Ciceronis BRUTUS* (Oxford, 1966)

Dudley, D.R. 'Blossius of Cumae' (*JRS* 31 (1941), 94–9)

Earl, D.C. *Toberius Gracchus: A Study in Politics* (Brussels, 1963)

– 'Tiberius Gracchus' Last Assembly' (*Athenaeum* 43 (1965), 95–105)

Ensor, R.C.K. *England 1870–1914* (Oxford, 1936)

Ewins, U. 'Ne Quis Iudicio Circumveniatur' (*JRS* 50 (1960), 94–107)

Fraccaro, P. 'Studi nell 'età Graccana' (*Studi storici* 5 (1912), 317–448; 6 (1913), 42–136)

– *Opuscula* (Pavia, 1956–7)

Frank, T. *An Economic Survey of Ancient Rome* i (Baltimore, 1933)

Frayn, J.M. 'Wild and Cultivated Plants: A Note on the Peasant Economy of Ancient Italy' (*JRS* 65 (1975), 32–9)

---

[1] My page-references in this book are to the pagination of the 1928 edition, save when specific reference is made to Nicolet's appendix where I have specified *Gracques*[2].

Frederiksen, M.W. 'Republican Capua: A Social and Economic Study' (*PBSR* 27 (1959), 80–130)
— 'The Contribution of Archaeology to the Agrarian Problem in the Gracchan Period' (*Dialoghi di archeologia* 2–3 (1970–1), 330–67)
— 'Theory, Evidence, and the Ancient Economy' (*JRS* 65 (1975), 164–71)
Gabba, E. 'Le origini della guerra sociale e la vita politica romana dopo 1'89 a.c.' (*Athenaeum* 32 (1954), 41–114, 293–345)
— *Appiani Bellorum Civilium Liber Primus* (Florence, 1958)
— 'Studi su Dionigi d'Alicarnasso' (*Athenaeum* 42 (1964), 29–41)
— *Esercito e società nella tarda Repubblica Romana* (Florence 1973) (= *Republican Rome, the Army, and the Allies* (Oxford, 1976))
Galsterer, H. *Herrschaft und Verwaltung im republikanischen Italien* (Munich, 1976)
Gelzer, M. *Die Nobilität der römischen Republik* (Leipzig, 1912) (= *The Roman Nobility* (Oxford, 1969))
— *Kleine Schriften* i (Wiesbaden, 1962)
Göhler, J. *Rom und Italien* (Breslau, 1939)
Gomme, A.W. *A Historical Commentary on Thucydides* Vol. i (Oxford, 1945)
Greenidge, A.H.J. *The Legal Procedure of Cicero's Time* (Oxford, 1901)
— *A History of Rome* Vol. i (133–104 B.C.) (London, 1904)
Greenidge, A.H.J. and Clay, M. *Sources for Roman History 133–70 B.C.* (2nd edn. by E.W. Gray, Oxford, 1960)
Hall, U. 'Voting Procedure in Roman Assemblies' (*Historia* 13 (1964), 267–306)
— 'Appian, Plutarch, and the Tribunician Elections of 123 B.C.' (*Athenaeum* 50 (1972), 3–35)
— 'Notes on M. Fulvius Flaccus' (*Athenaeum* 55 (1977), 280–8)
Häpke, N. *C. Semproni Gracchi Oratoris Romani Fragmenta Collecta et Illustrata* (Munich, 1915)
Hardy, E.G. *Some Problems in Roman History* (Oxford, 1924)
Harris, W.V. *Rome in Etruria and Umbria* (Oxford, 1971)
Hatzfeld, J. *Les Trafiquants italiens dans l'orient hellénique* (Paris, 1919)
Haverfield, F. *The Study of Ancient History at Oxford* (Oxford, 1912)
Henderson, I. 'The Process de Repetundis' (*JRS* 41 (1951), 71–88)
— 'The Establishment of the Equester Ordo' (*JRS* 53 (1963), 61–72) (= Seager, *Crisis*, 69–82)
Hignett, C. *A History of the Athenian Constitution* (Oxford, 1952)
Hill, H. *The Roman Middle Class* (Oxford, 1952)
Hinrichs, F.T. 'Nochmals zur Inschrift von Polla' (*Historia* 18 (1969), 251–5)

Holden, H.A. *Plutarch's Lives of the Gracchi* (Cambridge, 1885)

Inscriptiones Graecae ad Res Romanas Pertinentes (Paris, 1911–27)

Johannsen, K. *Die Lex Agraria des Jahres 111 v. Chr.: Text und Kommentar* (Dissertation Munich, 1971)

Jolowicz, H.F. *Historical Introduction to the Study of Roman Law* (3rd. edn. by Nicholas, Cambridge, 1972)

Jones, A.H.M. 'De Legibus Junia et Acilia Repetundarum' (*Proceedings of the Cambridge Philological Society*, 1960, 35–8)

– *The Criminal Courts of the Roman Republic and Principate* (Oxford, 1972)

Kahrsted, U. *Die wirtschaftliche Lage Grossgriechenlands in der Kaiserzeit* (*Historia* Einzelschrift 4 (1960))

Kunkel, W. *Untersuchungen zur Entwicklung des römische Kriminalverfahrens in vorsullanischer Zeit* (Bayer. Akad. d. Wissenschaften, phil.-hist. Kl. 56, 1962)

Last, H.M. Chapters in the *Cambridge Ancient History*, Vol. ix (Cambridge, 1932)

– Review of Gohler's *Rom und Italien* (*JRS* 30 (1940), 81–4)

– Review of Haskell's *This Was Cicero* (*JRS* 33 (1943), 93–7)

– Review of Tibiletti's *Il possesso dell' Ager Publicus* (*Rivista storica italiana* 61 (1949), 432–5)

– Review of Taylor's *Party Politics* (*Gnomon* 22 (1950), 360–5)

Leo, F. *Die römische Literatur des Altertums* (Berlin, 1903)

Lintott, A.W. *Violence in Republican Rome* (Oxford, 1968)

Magie, D. *Roman Rule in Asia Minor* (Princeton, 1950)

Malcovati, E. *Oratorum Romanorum Fragmenta Liberae Rei Publicae* (2nd edn., Turin, 1955)

Marsh, F.B. *A History of the Roman World 146 – 30 B.C.* (3rd edn. by Scullard, London, 1963)

Mattingly, H.B. 'The Two Republican Laws of the Tabula Bembina' (*JRS* 59 (1969), 129–43)

– 'The Extortion Law of the Tabula Bembina' (*JRS* 60 (1970), 154–68)

Miners, N.J. 'The Lex Sempronia Ne Quis Iudicio Circumveniatur' (*CQ* 8 (1958), 241–3)

Molthagen, J. 'Die Durchführung der gracchischen Agrarreform' (*Historia* 22 (1973), 423–58)

Mommsen, T. *The History of Rome* (London, 1880)

– *Römisches Staatsrecht* (Leipzig, 1887–8)

– *Römisches Strafrecht* (Leipzig, 1899)

– *Gesammelte Schriften* (Berlin, 1905–13)

Münzer, F. *Römische Adelsparteien und Adelsfamilien* (Stuttgart, 1920)

Nagle, D.B. 'The Failure of the Roman Political Process in 133 B.C.'
    (*Athenaeum* 48 (1970), 372–94)

Nicholas, J.K.B.M. *An Introduction to Roman Law* (Oxford, 1962)

Nicolet, C. 'L'Inspiration de Tiberius Gracchus' (*Revue des études anciennes* 67 (1965), 142–58)

– *L'Ordre équestre à l'époche républicaine* i (Paris, 1966)

– 'Polybius VI, 17, 4 and the Composition of the Societates Publicanorum' (*The Irish Jurist* N. S. 6 (1971), 163–76)

Oxford Classical Dictionary (3nd edn., Oxford, 1970)

Pauly–Wissowa–Kroll *Real-Encyclopädie der Classischen Altertumswissenschaft* (Stuttgart, 1894 –)

Peter, H. *Historicorum Romanorum Reliquiae* (Leipzig, 1906–14)

Ramsay, A.M. 'A Roman Postal Service under the Republic' (*JRS* 10 (1920), 79–86)

Rawson, E. 'Caesar's Heritage: Hellenistic Kings and their Roman Equals' (*JRS* 65 (1975), 148–59)

Riccobono, S. *Fontes Iuris Romani Anteiustiniani* i. (Florence, 1941)

Salmon, E.T. *Samnium and the Samnites* (Cambridge, 1967)

– *Roman Colonization under the Republic* (London, 1969)

Schanz, M. and Hosius, C. *Geschichte der römischen Literatur* (Munich, 1927)

Schneider, H. *Writschaft und Politik: Untersuchungen zur Geschichte der späten römischen Republik* (Erlangen, 1974)

Schulz, F. *Classical Roman Law* (Oxford, 1951)

Scullard, H.H. 'Scipio Aemilianus and Roman Politics' (*JRS* 50 (1960), 59–74

– *Roman Politics 220–150 B.C.* (2nd edn., Oxford, 1973)

Seager, R. *The Crisis of the Roman Republic* (Cambridge, 1969)

Shatzman, I. 'The Roman General's Authority over Booty' (*Historia* 21 (1972), 177–205)

– *Senatorial Wealth and Roman Politics* (Brussels, 1975)

Sherwin-White, A.N. 'Poena Legis Repetundarum' (*PBSR* 17 (1949), 5–25)

– 'The Extortion Procedure Again' (*JRS* 42 (1952), 43–55)

– 'Violence in Roman Politics' (*JRS* 46 (1956), 1–9) (= Seager, *Crisis*, 151–61)

– 'The Date of the Lex Repetundarum and its Consequences' (*JRS* 62 (1972), 83–99)

– *The Roman Citizenship* (3nd edn., Oxford, 1973)

– 'Roman Involvement in Anatolia' (*JRS* 67 (1977), 62–75)

Shochat, Y. 'The Lex Agraria of 133 B.C. and the Italian Allies' (*Athenaeum* 48 (1970), 25–45)

Stampp, K.M. *The Peculiar Institution* (London, 1964)

Stockton, D.L. *Cicero: A Political Biography* (Oxford, 1971)

− Review of Badian's *Publicans and Sinners* (*CR* 25 (1975) 96–8)

Strachan-Davidson, J.L. *Appian Civil Wars Book I* (Oxford, 1902)

− *Problems of the Roman Criminal Law* (Oxford, 1912)

Taylor, L.R. *The Voting Districts of the Roman Republic* (Rome, 1960)

− 'Forerunners of the Gracchi' (*JRS* 52 (1962), 19–27)

− 'Was Tiberius Gracchus' Last Assembly Electoral or Legislative?' (*Athenaeum* 41 (1963), 51–69)

− 'Appian and Plutarch on Tiberius Gracchus' Last Assembly' (*Athenaeum* 44 (1966), 238–50)

Tibiletti, G. 'Il possesso dell' Ager Publicus e le norme De Modo Agrorum sino ai Gracchi' (*Athenaeum* 26 (1948), 173–236; 27 (1949), 3–41)

− 'La politica agraria della Guerra Annibalica ai Gracchi' (*Athenaeum* 28 (1950), 183–266)

− 'Le leggi De Iudiciis Repetundarum fino alla Guerra Sociale' (*Athenaeum* 31 (1953) 5–100)

− 'Les Tresviri a.i.a. lege Sempronia' (Hommage à la Mémoire de Jerome Carcopino (Paris, 1977), 277 ff.)

Toynbee, A.J. *Hannibal's Legacy* (Oxford/London, 1965)

Treggiari, S. *Roman Freedmen during the Late Republic* (Oxford, 1969)

Ungern-Sternberg von Pürkel, Baron J. *Untersuchungen zum spätrepublikanischen Notstandsrecht* (Munich, 1970)

Vogel, K.H. 'Zur rechtlichen Behandlung der römischen Kriegsgewinne' (*Zeitschrift Savigny Stiftung 66 Römische Abteilung* (1948), 394–423)

Walbank, F.W. *A Historical Commentary on Polybius* Vol. i (Oxford, 1957)

White, K.D. 'Latifundia' (Bulletin of the Institute of Classical Studies 14 (1967), 62–79)

Wilson, A.J.N. *Emigration from Italy in the Republican Age of Rome* (Manchester, 1966)

Wiseman, T.P. 'Viae Anniae' (*PBSR* 32 (1964), 21–37)

− 'Viae Anniae Again' (*PBSR* 37 (1969), 82–91)

− *New Men in the Roman Senate 139 B.C. − A.D. 14* (Oxford, 1971)

Yeo, C.A. 'The Development of Roman Plantation and Marketing of Farm Products' (*Finanzarchiv* 13 (1952), 321–42)

− 'The Economics of Roman and American Slavery' (ibid. 445–85)

P.S. A. H. Bernstein, 'Tiberius Gracchus: Tradition and Apostasy' (Cornell, 1978) came into my hands only after my typescript had gone to the printer.

INDEX

DATE DUE

NOV 12'84			
OCT 20 '86			
NOV 6 '86			
DEC 2 '86			
GAYLORD			PRINTED IN U.S.A.